ANTHROPOLOGICAL INTELLIGENCE

DAVID H. PRICE

ANTHROPOLOGICAL INTELLIGENCE

THE DEPLOYMENT AND NEGLECT OF AMERICAN ANTHROPOLOGY

IN THE SECOND WORLD WAR

DUKE UNIVERSITY PRESS   DURHAM AND LONDON   2008

© 2008 DUKE UNIVERSITY PRESS
All rights reserved
Printed in the United States of America
on acid-free paper ∞
Designed by Amy Ruth Buchanan
Typeset in Minion by Keystone Typesetting, Inc.
Library of Congress Cataloging-in-Publication Data
appear on the last printed page of this book.

For Jack and Fernell with love,
wonderful parents who taught me
about patience, caring, and choices.

Non-doers were the ones who chose not to fight the Nazis in the only way they could have been fought; they were the ones who drew their window blinds to shut out the shameful spectacle of Jews and political prisoners being dragged through the streets; they were the ones who privately deplored the horror of it all—and did nothing. This is the nadir of immorality. The most unethical of all means is the non-use of any means.
—SAUL ALINSKY (1971: 26)

Due to the war effort, many American anthropologists who have never before worked in the applied field are now bending all their energies in this direction. As a result, anthropologists are making rapid progress in the development of scientific methods for the application of the results to the practical problems of administration. . . . To state the matter bluntly for the sake of clarity, are practical social scientists to become technicians for hire to the highest bidder?
—LAURA THOMPSON (1944: 12)

CONTENTS

The concept of progress acts as a protective mechanism to shield us from the terrors of the future.
—FRANK HERBERT (1965: 321)

Warfare and anthropology have long intersected in two fundamental ways. This book examines the intersection that occurs when anthropologists contribute their professional knowledge and skills to further the military and intelligence endeavors of their nation at war. Another significant confluence occurs when anthropologists' fieldwork settings are shaped by wars that alter the worlds encountered by ethnographers. While frequently underacknowledged, ethnographic fieldwork has often occurred in the shadow of warfare.

In a style reminiscent of the carefully staged photography of Edward Curtis, many anthropologists have cropped out war's shadows from the ethnographic present of their writing, but some of America's finest ethnographers have placed these events in the foreground.[1] An early example of this occurred at the 1891 New Year, when the ethnologist James Mooney of the Bureau of American Ethnology arrived on the Sioux reservation just days after the U.S. Army slaughtered Sioux men, women, and children at Wounded Knee. The marching tunes of the Seventh Calvary still hung in air, but Mooney worked outside this cadence as he studied acts of cultural resistance with a purpose divorced from conquest. Instead, Mooney's studies of the Ghost Dance acknowledged the context of military conquest in ways that honored and did not make vulnerable those he studied. The care he took shows the development of an anthropology that is conscious of its responsibility to those studied. Mooney studied the Ghost Dance as a legitimate religious formation, describing it with the same honor and respect other scholars used in treatises discussing the historical developments or sacraments of Christianity. An ethnographer with different sensibilities might have studied the Ghost Dance with aims to facilitate conquest rather than to honor the beliefs as part of a great tradition. Such a proto-PSYOP ethnographer could easily have mined Ghost Dance beliefs for information of use to military strategists who wished to exploit beliefs of invulnerability. But Mooney chose to build a different anthropology, and for that choice his career suffered serious setbacks as he was subjected to congressional inquiries and administrative pressures within the bureau (Moses 1984).

Although few anthropologists have seriously examined their discipline's contributions to warfare, for over three decades anthropology's conscience has wrestled with its historical role as colonialism's handmaiden. The vital work of Kathleen Gough (1968, 1993), Talal Asad (1973), and others who have followed established historical links between the development of European and American anthropology and colonialist ventures around the globe have not only contextualized the political economy in which anthropologists have conducted fieldwork and developed theories to explain the worlds they have found. It has also examined ways that anthropological intelligence has been used to understand and subordinate other cultures.

Anthropologists are now adept at recognizing their discipline's historical ties to colonialism. And while there is an important anthropological literature that brings anthropological perspectives to the analysis of conflict and warfare (e.g., Ferguson 1995; Nordstrom 2004; Sluka 2000), there is a surprising lack of scholarly documentation and analysis of anthropology's contributions to the wars of the twentieth century.[2] It would be tempting to ascribe this silence to the relative recentness of these events, but anthropologists frequently discuss and analyze a wide range of other recent occurrences. The silence surrounding American anthropology in the Second World War is especially curious, given widely held feelings of honor and support for those American men and women who contributed to the fight against tyranny.

There is general awareness among contemporary anthropologists that many anthropologists served in wartime agencies, foremost among them the Office of Strategic Services (oss), Institute of Social Anthropology, Federal Bureau of Investigation, Office of Naval Intelligence, War Relocation Authority, Military Intelligence Division, and Office of War Information, as well as the Smithsonian Institution's Ethnogeographic Board. Some wartime contributions are widely cited, but few American anthropologists understand the range of contributions American anthropologists made to the war effort.[3]

This lack of analysis has a number of residual effects. Chief among them is the possibility of a disciplinary miscalculation—an overestimation or underestimation of the significance of anthropological contributions to the Second World War. Without examinations of the specific contributions and outcomes of World

War Two anthropologists, we are left with nothing more than lists that account for wartime deployment. These lists reveal nothing about the implementations of wartime anthropology. After a half century of hearing applied anthropologists regularly complain that their recommendations are frequently ignored when they run counter to the paradigms or goals of employers, we need to critically examine the actual outcomes of these applied anthropological contributions to World War Two.

Today, most anthropologists consider their field's contributions to the war in the context of the noble fight against fascism, totalitarianism, and racial oppression. I share these views, but my reading of this history also leaves me with concerns over some of anthropology's contributions to this war. I accept that the Axis's fascists threatened humanity and needed to be defeated militarily, but I also have a growing discomfort with the ease with which some American anthropologists contemplated and engaged in tactics that would be judged unethical by contemporary standards. I remain troubled less by what this meant during World War Two than by what such decisions meant for postwar anthropologists working for the Central Intelligence Agency (CIA) and military during the Cold War and in the present "war on terrorism." World War Two anthropology unleashed something dangerous that was not easily contained. While the fight against fascism and tyranny is perhaps the most noble and just of fights, the American wars that have followed have been far less noble and just. Now, some sixty years after the fact, the wartime applications of anthropology in the early 1940s continue to bedevil us in new and unforeseen contexts.

Because I write with the advantage of hindsight (along with the disadvantage of not having experienced the events directly), my purpose is not to criticize the choices made by anthropologists at that time. Under the rubrics of a historicist approach, it should be understood that these actors made their choices within a historical context that must be considered on its own terms. I do not question this, and if I only wanted to understand how and why these individual choices were made, that would be enough. But I also wish to examine the past from a presentist perspective, not to heap scorn and criticism on those who lived before us, but to better understand anthropology's present predicament and choices so that contemporary and future anthropologists can learn from this past.

Even George Stocking, historicism's most prolific proponent, admits "the historical utility of a strongly held present theoretical perspective" when attempting to build a present "productive synthetic interpretation" based on evaluations of past actions or interpretations (Stocking 1982: xvii).[4] If we cannot critically evaluate the actions and choices of past wartime anthropologists, then contemporary anthropology can hope for nothing more than to uncritically repeat past actions anew in similar and divergent contexts, without any hope of systemically repeating successes and avoiding failures.

Presentist concerns about anthropological contributions to warfare are informed by the activities of the Vietnam War, the Cold War, the current Iraq War, and the postwar development of ethical codes that disparage such combinations of science and warfare. It can, admittedly, be difficult not to let such concerns color interpretations of anthropologists' actions in World War Two (Price 2002c, 2003a). But such difficulties do not diminish the need to examine these past relationships and consider the past on its own terms, as well as from our own place in time, if for no other reason than to adjudicate current dilemmas and choices with a view to what can be learned from these events.

Like *Threatening Anthropology*, this book examines how political and economic forces at a particular moment in history affected the development of American anthropology. As with any ideological component of society, all scientific knowledge—including anthropological theory—is embedded within the political and economic systems of the society producing and consuming these theories and knowledge. This is not to argue that science is exactly like other ideological components of a society, such as beliefs about values, religion, mythology, patriotism, justice, or gender roles. The inherent structural demands of falsifiability of scientific ways of knowing offers the possibility that the science *could* eventually move beyond a historical moment's blind spots.

I do not argue that science—or, in the example described in this book, the social science of anthropology—is in any way free of the economic, technological, or political forces that exert their pull on knowledge systems. The formation and use of scientific knowledge is certainly determined by these forces, but this knowledge is not necessarily reducible to such formations. It is possible that science can identify truths beyond those mitigated by culture, although the weight and pull of a culture's time and place are significant.

I depart from commonplace postmodern critiques of science by not abandoning the possibility that science can provide hope for dealing with the seemingly insurmountable problems that face humankind. But I see this hope as being contingent on rigorous efforts to reveal ways that knowledge is filtered not only by the powers of political structures, but also by the very demographic, technological, economic, and resource-based features and political economy that support the development of specific social formations—social formations that include scientific systems.

I realize that such metanarratives are out of style with postmodern commitments to maintaining a stiff "incredulity towards metanarratives" (Lyotard 1984: xxiv). But the contemporary fear of the metanarrative has left anthropology incapable of explaining—much less defending itself against—recurrent encroachments of military and intelligence agencies into its research. If anthropology is going to develop a critical perspective for dealing with these unexamined ongoing relationships, it will best do so using a theoretical perspective that allows it to examine these differing recurrent formations over times.

The ways that political and economic conditions influence anthropology have been far from uniform, and even a cursory look at the theoretical formations that occurred after the war were diverse, as some anthropologists undertook work that coalesced with the dominant political economies of power while others raged against these interests. But still, these forces transformed the discipline.

The social problems with science in the present era are not distinct from those found in the past. Many of these problems are found in the prevalence of junk science, as government policies muzzle scientific findings that clash with administration policies. Religious fundamentalists' antiscientific views of the universe, for instance, lead to policies that prevent federal park rangers at the Grand Canyon from stating the known geological age of the canyon for fear of offending people (Agin 2006; PEER 2006). Other problems relate to the practice of forms of socially disengaged blind science in which the theories and products of scientific inquiry are created and implemented without consideration of their impact or ethical meaning. The failures of Nazi science, so dramatically described in the careful scholarship of Gretchen Schafft (2004), traveled down both of these damaged paths. Any hope of avoiding related catastrophic outcomes must be found in more ethically engaged scientific undertakings that disentangle political-economic blinders from findings and implementations (Nader 1996). There is no such thing as politically neutral science, and pretending otherwise will get us nowhere. The operations of science are not judged by imagined standards of apolitical neutrality; they are judged by theory-testing operations of *reliability* (ensuring that other scholars who repeat measures get similar results) and *validity* (establishing that conceptual variables are what are really being measured). What is needed is not depoliticized science but science that is ethically aware of and engaged in the political context in which it functions and is used.

Today's new wave of militarism brings pressing reasons for anthropologists to critically evaluate the full range of anthropological contributions to World War Two. As the American Anthropological Association (AAA) again publishes CIA job advertisements in its official publications (Price 2005d), and as some anthropologists argue that we must join the Pentagon, CIA, and the Office of Homeland

Security as a continuation of our discipline's World War Two service, we must not gloss over the attractive and repulsive details of anthropologists' contributions to that seminal war. Anthropologists must move beyond a cursory understanding that Ruth Benedict described Japanese personality types and Margaret Mead studied food habits. Our memory gaps have political consequences. Anthropologists' ignorance of the range of anthropological contributions to the war is now being used in CIA and Pentagon recruitment campaigns. The last decade's removal of language from the AAA's ethics code prohibiting covert research cleared the way for American anthropologists to serve the CIA and other bureaucratic descendants of the OSS.

Over the past twenty years, I have been collecting records and recollections of anthropologists' contributions to the Second World War and the Cold War. My interest in World War Two has mainly been to establish an understanding of its events to better appreciate how they shaped anthropologists' contributions to military and intelligence operations in the Cold War. This is not a book I set out to write. Failing in my efforts to collapse a mountain of notes on American anthropologists and World War Two into a manageable introductory chapter providing vital context for my larger Cold War manuscript, I expanded this overview into an extended essay that ended in the surrender of this book. As such, this book can be seen as a sort of prequel to a forthcoming book on anthropological collaborations with the CIA and military agencies during the Cold War, as well as to my book on the effects of McCarthyism on American anthropology (Price 2004a).

I regret that the generation of anthropologists who used their disciplinary skills to fight the Second World War's battles against tyranny chose to remain mostly silent about so many of the specifics, leaving it to one who was born fifteen years after the armistice to write about American anthropologists' contributions to the Second World War. If they chose to remain mute on so many of the issues and circumstances discussed here, their choices leave it to this and future ages to untangle and evaluate these events.

....

A FEW WORDS on the organizational structure of the book are in order. The book's narrative primarily follows various organizations or agencies that employed American anthropologists in the Second World War. Because Franz Boas's 1919 censure by the AAA raised fundamental questions about the propriety of using anthropology in the service of warfare, the book opens with a brief overview of anthropological contributions to World War One.

The two primary American professional anthropological associations, the AAA and the newly created Society for Applied Anthropology (SFAA), and academic programs on American college and university campuses are shown to have supported the nation's war needs. These uses of anthropology were not unique to the United States. A brief overview of some of the activities of Allied and Axis anthropologists during the war is presented to provide perspective on the ways that anthropologists contributed to the war in other nations.

The remainder of the book examines anthropological contributions to various government agencies. During the war, American anthropologists worked at dozens of such agencies under the administration of the U.S. Department of War, Department of Interior, and Department of State and the White House. Various chapters examine the duties performed by anthropologists working for the Institute of Human Relations, the Office of Naval Intelligence, the Cross-Cultural Survey Project, the Smithsonian Institution's War Background Studies, the Ethnogeographic Board, the Office of the Coordinator of Inter-American Affairs, and the Institute of Social Anthropology. The anthropologists Henry Field, Philleo Nash, and Aleš Hrdlička advised President Franklin D. Roosevelt and the White House staff during the war. Field's research with the M Project found anthropology being used to estimate various relocation schemes for the refugees that would remain in the postwar period.

More than a dozen anthropologists worked for the War Relocation Authority, the Bureau of Sociological Research, and the Japanese American Evacuation and Resettlement Study. Anthropologists at the Office of War Information's Foreign Morale Analysis Division studied Japanese social structure to help American propaganda efforts better target Japanese cultural sensitivities and to make recommendations concerning the postwar future of Japan. Ruth Benedict, Clyde Kluckhohn, John Embree, Morris Opler, and others at the OWI are shown to have supported or ignored positions recognizing that the Japanese military and civilian authorities were preparing to surrender during the final months of the war.

The FBI's Special Intelligence Service (SIS) is shown to have used anthropologists to collect intelligence throughout Central America and South America, using archaeology as their cover for spying. These methods were a return to the tactics deployed by Samuel Lothrop, one of the archaeologists criticized by Franz Boas in 1919. An examination of anthropological contributions to the OSS finds anthropologists writing reports for its Research and Analysis Branch and working as analysts and field operatives in battle theaters in Africa and Asia.

The final chapter evaluates some of the ways that American anthropology began to readjust to the world emerging at the war's end. It reconsiders the range of anthropological contributions to the war, and the ethical issues raised in the preface are reprised in light the specific details of American anthropology's contributions to the war. The importance of anthropologists' World War Two activities to anthropologists' decisions to contribute anthropology to the overt and covert battles of the Cold War is discussed.

Acknowledgments

I thank Ken Wissoker, editor-in-chief of Duke University Press, for his commitment to the development of an alternative history of anthropology and for the latitude he provides me even as some of my interpretations rankle readers who would be less abused by more standard postmodern interpretations. Alexander Cockburn's and Jeff St. Clair's friendship and their maintenance of *CounterPunch* as a safe haven for critical enquiry helped me develop my writer's voice and to explore elements of this critique. David Patton and Catharine Wilson kindly hosted me during several visits to Washington, D.C., archives. Thomas Anson provided good conversation at the Allegro and on mountain trails and helped differentiate between points important and obtuse. David Patton, Steve Niva, and Jeff Birkenstein argued analysis during conferences convened at the Eastside Club, the West Coast's answer to the Cosmos Club. Robert Lawless gave invaluable feedback. Eric Ross helped me ferret out some missing pieces and to sharpen my analysis. Bill Peace carefully read a draft of the manuscript and provided important insights and critiques. Dalia Hagan patiently read an early draft and contributed her invaluable abilities as a gentle reader to help me balance the narrative tone and trim off extraneous storylines. The supreme reference librarian Andrea Kueter helped me find countless elusive sources and add details that would have otherwise fallen to the wayside. Peter Suzuki, who for decades has been a lone scholarly voice examining anthropologists' roles at the War Relocation Authority, graciously provided invaluable feedback on an early version of chapter 7.

Over the years. many people helped me develop my analysis, shared their memories of anthropology during the war, or helped me find resources used in this book. Chief among them are David Aberle, David Altheide, Alan Beals, John Bennett, Gerry Colby, Charlotte Dennett, Sigmund Diamond, William Fenton, George Foster, Andre Gunder Frank, Charles Frantz, Nina Glick Schiller, Hugh Gusterson, Janice Harper, Jack Harris, Marvin Harris, Gustaaf Houtman, Barbara Rose Johnston, Robert Leopold, Gabe Lyon, Monty Miller, Sidney Mintz, Laura Nader, Shawn Newman, Steve Niva, Jon Noski, Tom Patterson, David

Pavelich, Harald Prins, Steve Reyna, Mike Salovesh, Gretchen Schafft, Michael Seltzer, the Sewer Snoids, George W. Stocking Jr., George Taylor, Daniel Thompkins, Dustin Wax, Kevin Yelvington, and the Network of Concerned Anthropologists. Kyung-soo Chun graciously hosted my visit to the Third East Asian Anthropology and Japanese Colonialism Forum in Seoul, where I benefited from the exceptional research presented by Professors Chun, Hibiki Momose, Katsumi Nakao, Akira Usuki, Kozo Watanabe, and Muneo Yasuda.

I wrote this book while teaching alongside exceptional scholars who bring the life of the mind into that most endangered educational environment: the non-standardized small classroom. While we mostly labor in obscurity at the edge of the known academic world, my colleagues' battles to seize, retain, and use a rare environment that fosters free inquiry and academic freedom has an impact on all I write. I am honored to be part of a scholarly community with my friends Olivia Archibald, Les Bailey, Jeff Birkenstein, Rex Casillas, Steve Fulton, Bob Harvie, David Hlavsa, Russell Hollander, Victor Kogan, Dick Langill, Father Kilian Malvey, Joe Mailhot, Gloria Martin, Kathleen McKain, Stephen Mead, Rona Rubin, Brian Schiff, Norma Shelan, Katia Shkurkin, Donna Smith, Roger Snider, and Don Stout.

I thank my lovely wife, Midge, for her encouragement, love, wisdom, and sharp wit. My son, Milo, and daughter, Nora, helped me put the manuscript down and head to local beaches and mountains.

AAA	American Anthropological Association
AAUP	American Association of University Professors
ACLS	American Council of Learned Societies
APA	American Psychological Association
ASTP	Army Special Training Program
ASTP-FAL	Army Special Training Program, Foreign Area and Language
BAE	Bureau of American Ethnology
BIA	Bureau of Indian Affairs
BSR	Bureau of Sociological Research
CAS	Community Analysis Section
CATS	Civil Affairs Training Schools
CIA	Central Intelligence Agency
CIAA	Office of the Coordinator of Inter-American Affairs
COI	Coordinator of Information
EAEIB	East-Asiatic Economics Investigation Bureau
FAAA	Fellows of the American Anthropological Association
FBI	Federal Bureau of Investigation
FMAD	Foreign Morale Analysis Division, Office of War Information
FOIA	Freedom of Information Act
G-2	Military Intelligence Division, U.S. Army
HRAF	Human Relations Area File
IAR	Institute of Andean Research
IHR	Institute of Human Relations
IIAA	Institute of Inter-American Affairs
ILP	Intensive Language Program
ISA	Institute of Social Anthropology
JACL	Japanese American Citizens League
JERS	Japanese American Evacuation and Resettlement Study
MID	Military Intelligence Division

NKL	Northern Kachin Levies
NRC	National Research Council
OFF	Office of Facts and Figures
OIA	Office of Indian Affairs
ONI	U.S. Office of Naval Intelligence
OPNAV	Office of the Chief of Naval Operations
OSS	Office of Strategic Services
OWI	Office of War Information
PEER	Public Employees for Ethical Responsibility
R&A Branch	Research and Analysis Branch, Office of Strategic Services
SFAA	Society for Applied Anthropology
SIS	Special Intelligence Service
SMRC	South Manchurian Railway Company
SOE	Special Operations Executive
SSD	Special Service Division
SSRC	Social Science Research Council
USSBS	U.S. Strategic Bombing Survey
USO	United Service Organizations
USWDSSU	U.S. War Department Strategic Services Unit
WAC	Women's Army Corps
WRA	War Relocation Authority

CHAPTER ONE

American Anthropology and
the War to End All Wars

Anthropologists lack a clear and sensible perception of their discipline. In the era of
Boas, and under his influence, one might imagine that anthropology would resemble a
secular religious order, above the rivalries and conflicts of nations and parties, and
embracing an ethos of reverence for the separate and distinct cultures of peoples lacking
literacy and power. In effect, anthropologists were to be their voice, and their protective
mediators in a world whose market economy and whose imperialisms threatened to
overrun them.
—MURRAY WAX (2002: 4)

As the First World War engulfed Europe, Americans were divided on the question of joining this foreign war. In 1916, American voters elected Woodrow
Wilson to the presidency on an antiwar platform, only to watch him reverse his
campaign promises by committing America to join the war. American opposition to the war was widespread, and new forms of political coercion were developed by the Wilson administration to silence critics of a war seen by dissenters as
fought for business interests.

The Wilson administration's efforts to mold public opinion to support the
First World War limited American political dissent. It was the First World War's
tense political climate that gave rise to America's first formal conceptualization of
principles of academic freedom. When the American Association of University
Professors (AAUP) developed its first statement championing the rights and principles of academic freedom in 1915, it also limited the exercising of these rights to
those with disciplinary expertise (see Price 2004a: 18–20). The historian James
Cattell was fired from Columbia University during the war under charges of
"disloyalty" after he publicly advocated that the war should only be fought with a
voluntary army. Cattell believed that wars in democratic societies should be
fought by those who supported the actions, not by one class pressed into action

by another. But the AAUP founder Arthur Lovejoy was uncomfortable using the newly (and weakly) delineated concept of academic freedom to allow professors to speak in opposition to the war. Instead, Lovejoy "felt professors who opposed American military actions should preserve silence during wartime" (Feuer 1979: 465).

Despite intense public pressure for academics to either support the war or remain silent, even from groups advocating for principles of academic freedom, the Columbia University anthropology professor Franz Boas openly spoke in opposition to American involvement in the war. On March 7, 1917, Boas publicly read a statement entitled "Preserving Our Ideas" expressing his disdain for the anti-intellectual campaigns supporting the war and degrading those opposed to the war.[1] Boas's statement was made partially as a reaction to Columbia's forma-tion of a committee investigating reports of individual faculty members' dis-loyalty, but it was also an expression of his feelings regarding America's involve-ment in Europe's war. Boas attacked the committee's right to examine faculty scholarship and beliefs, and he criticized the American educational system's promotion of nationalism. Boas believed that the first duties of scholars "are to humanity as a whole, and that, in a conflict of duties, our obligations to human-ity are of higher value than those toward the nation; in other words, that patriot-ism must be subordinated to humanism" (Boas 1945 [1917]: 156).

In a climate where the White House, churches, business groups, and home-grown patriots were demanding militaristic unity—or, at least, silence—Boas's proclamation that his academic obligations were "to humanity as a whole" was radical. Boas faulted the American educational system for so easily facilitating the rapid militarization of the American public, writing:

> I believe that the purely emotional basis on which, the world over, patriotic feelings are instilled into the minds of children is one of the most seri-ous faults in our educational systems, particularly when we compare these methods with the lukewarm attention that is given to the common interests of humanity. I dare say that if all nations cultivated the ideals of equal rights of all members of mankind by emotional means such as are now used to develop passionate patriotism, much of the mutual hatred, distrust, and disrespect would disappear. The kind of patriotism that we inculcate is intended to develop the notion that the members of each nation, and that the institutions of each nation, are superior to those of all others. Under this stimulus the fact that in each country, normally, people live comparatively comfortably under the conditions in which they have grown up is too often

translated by the citizens of that country into the idea that others who live under different conditions have a civilization or institutions of inferior value, and must feel unhappy until the benefits of his own mode of feeling, thinking, and living have been imposed upon them. I consider it one of the great objects worth striving for to counteract this faulty tendency. If it is not sufficient to train children to an intelligent understanding of the institutions and habits of their country, if these have to be strengthened emotionally by waving of flags and by singing of patriotic songs, then this emotional tendency should be supplemented by equally strong emotional means intended to cultivate respect for the love that foreigners have for their country, and designed to instill into the minds of the young respect for the common interests of humanity. I should prefer, however, to inculcate intelligence, love and respect for all human endeavor, wherever found, without trying to destroy the possibility of clear, intelligent thought by emphasizing the emotional side of patriotism. (Boas 1945 [1917]: 156–59)

Boas's anthropology and progressive political beliefs informed this critique, and while his critical interpretation of the cultural inculcation of patriotism can now be seen as a theoretical analysis of social superstructure, during the war such views were simply seen as subversive. When such views came from a German émigré, they could be seen as traitorous. This was a radicalized Boas who was shocked at how easily the American public had been led into a foreign war.

While Boas's words irritated Columbia's administration, they did not influence those in power, and once America entered the war, protests from academics like Boas were widely silenced. Some who spoke out found themselves unemployed. It only took a few such firings for others to learn to self-censure their criticisms if they did not want to join the ranks of the unemployed. In 1917, the Smithsonian's Bureau of American Ethnology (BAE) fired the ethnologist Leo J. Frachtenberg because of his personal opposition to America's involvement in the First World War. Charles Walcott fired Frachtenberg for "utterances derogatory to the Government of the United States" (Hyatt 1990: 128). Marshall Hyatt writes, "Shocked at the firing, Frachtenberg contacted Walcott immediately and begged for an appointment to clarify his position. He assured Walcott that he had made no statements derogatory toward the United States. He confessed only to 'grumbling against the rising cost of living and Congress' unwillingness to curb these rises,' but denied doing anything more serious" (Hyatt 1990: 128). Frachtenberg asked Walcott to reconsider his decision and not turn him out "penniless and jobless" (Hyatt 1990: 128).

Boas, James Mooney, and Elsie Parsons lobbied in support of Frachtenberg without success. He was not reinstated, despite the lack of evidence that Frachtenberg had broken any laws or specific employment policies.[2] Frachtenberg left anthropology after he was fired by the BAE; his next position was as a factory supervisor (Hyatt 1990: 129). Frachtenberg's firing, and Boas's own experiences with the limits on wartime academic freedom at Columbia, left a deep impression on Boas as he became "convinced that individual freedom no longer existed in America . . . [where] scientists and academics, blinded by patriotism, behaved irrationally" (Hyatt 1990: 129).

The war limited the speech and prospects of critics, and it brought new opportunities for anthropologists and other social scientist supporting the war. These new interactions between anthropologists and military and intelligence agencies established some new social-science applications. While the uses of anthropologists were limited in the First World War, many of these roles provided templates for the expanded role that the social sciences would contribute to the next world war.

Boas's position as a representative to the National Research Council (NRC) brought complications as the council began organizing scientists to contribute to the war effort in 1916. Given Boas's public statements in opposition to the war, "It is not surprising that when the Executive Committee of the Council decided to organize a Committee on Anthropology, they turned to William Holmes and his associate Aleš Hrdlička at the National Museum rather than to America's leading anthropologist" (Stocking 1968b: 287). This committee matched anthropologists' abilities with the needs of war.

Social Scientists and the War to End All Wars

A wide variety of social scientists contributed to the war effort. The American Psychological Association (APA) oversaw the formation of a dozen committees harnessing the findings of psychology for the war, while the American Anthropological Association (AAA) remained much less directly committed to formally supporting the war (Leahey 1991: 226). The APA coordinated the construction, administration, and interpretation of intelligence tests used on the masses of drafted citizen soldiers who were to be sorted into groups of infantrymen and officers. These psychological tests were also "welcomed by eugenicists, eager to prove their point about racial intelligence differences with the help of data from the military. They received prompt and solicitous attention from psychologists, who announced, as scientific dogma, that black solders were inferior and that there existed a mental hierarchy pegged to nationality: Anglo-Saxons were at the top while the unsavory representatives of recent immigrants groups languished far below" (Herman 1995: 65). These tests fostered the illusion that there was a scientific basis for the class-based methods of sorting military conscripts. In the postwar years, Boas and other anthropologists were still battling the peacetime domestic social damage leveled by these biased wartime tests.

The military draft also generated vast amounts of anthropometric data to be analyzed and abused by the Harvard-trained eugenicist Charles Benedict Davenport and others. Davenport's 1919 *Defects Found in Drafted Men* (Davenport 1919b) and his government report *Army Anthropology* examined anthropometric data gathered from inductees. Davenport used the physical measurements of draftees to support his theories claiming a biological basis for social class. The Carnegie Institution published Davenport's *Naval Officers, Their Heredity and Development* (1919a), which examined environmental and genetic influences in the formation of naval officers and conflated the advantages and attitudes of class with biological propensities. The Prudential Insurance Company published Frederick Hoffman's analysis of induction data in *Army Anthropometry and Medical Rejection Statistics*. Hoffman also reported his findings to the Committee on Anthropology of the NRC.[3] British anthropologists conducted similar analysis of draftee measurements (Keith 1918).[4]

American social scientists worked for a variety of governmental war agencies, but all forms of analysis were not equally welcomed. Thorstein Veblen worked as an analyst at the wartime U.S. Food Administration until he was fired for his ardent recommendations that the government end its campaigns against the Industrial Workers of the World (Chomsky 1978: 17). At the National War Labor Board and the Bureau of Labor Statistics, the sociologist William Ogburn developed new quantitative research techniques and wrote a series of publications that helped him secure a postwar academic position at Columbia University (Keen 1999:56).

European social scientists also used their professional skills to assist the war effort. In Britain, W. H. R Rivers and C. G. Seligman treated shell-shocked British soldiers (Fortes 1968: 160; Slobodin 1978). O. G. S. Crawford used his archaeological-photography skills to photograph and map battles and trenches at the front until he was eventually taken prisoner by the Germans (Crawford 1955). Some European social scientists generated wartime propaganda. L. T. Hobhouse wrote pro-war political analyses for the *Manchester Guardian*, while Émile Durkheim wrote propaganda pamphlets for the French government that were designed to convince the United States to join France in the war with Germany.

For Durkheim, the most immediate effect of the war was the death of his son and intellectual protégé, André. One of Durkheim's most promising students, Robert Hertz (later to become a significant intellectual influence on E. E. Evans-Pritchard), was killed by German machine guns while leading an attack on Marchéville as a second lieutenant in the French infantry (Needham 1979: 295). The war also killed a significant number of Durkheim's students who were part of the European lost generation that did not survive the war; Durkheim died in despair in late 1917. Most of the German sociologist Georg Simmel's students met a similar fate in the war, a fate that slowed the influence of his work in Germany, Europe, and the Americas.

The German Army Reserve Corps officer Max Weber wrote articles and position papers for the *Frankfurter Zeitung*, in which he argued that "the Great War was Germany's last chance to achieve imperial greatness and prevent 'the swamping of the entire world' by the decrees of Russian officials on the one hand and the conventions of Anglo-Saxon society on the other" (Ashley and Orenstein 1995: 266). Wilhelm Wundt and Max Scheler supported the German war effort by writing passionately anti-American and anti-British propaganda tracts (Coser 1968; Leahey 1991: 54). The specifics of some of these European social scientists' embracing of roles of public intellectuals advocating the militaristic policies of their governments suggests comparisons with contemporary intellectuals' work at the Council on Foreign Relations and other think tanks aligned with the geopolitical interests of the nation state.

German anthropologists took extensive measurements of soldiers held in prisoner of war camps. These initial studies were linguistic surveys, but soon the anthropologists Egon von Eickstedt, Paul Hambruch, Felix von Luschan, Rudolf Pöch, and Otto Reche began taking extensive anthropometric measurements of prisoners. Without consent, prisoners were subjected to various body measurements and were photographed in the nude or in seminude positions designed to identify specific national racial features. Andrew Evans argued that "practicing anthropology in the camps helped to reorient German anthropologists toward European subjects in ways that contributed significantly to the erosion of the categories at the heart of the liberal tradition" (Evans 2003: 201). That these measurements were taken among prisoners subjected to the demands of martial law, where all prisoners were categorically treated as enemy aliens, contributed to the development of a German racial analysis that "was a short step from a nationalism that coded Germany's enemies as non-European to a view of Europeans as racial others" (Evans 2003: 219).

A generation of future American anthropologists joined the war as soldiers, and these experiences profoundly shaped lives and sometimes the later adoption of specific theoretical orientations. Leslie White's postwar studies in psychology, sociology, and anthropology grew directly from his efforts to find explanations for the devastation he saw and experienced during the war (Peace 2004).[5] Ralph Linton found a deep camaraderie among the men of the Army's Forty-Second "Rainbow Division." After the war, Linton analyzed these relationships in the scholarly publication "Totemism in the A.E.F." in *American Anthropologist*, where he contrasted the "pseudo-totemic complexes" he experienced as a member of the Rainbow Division with those found among "uncivilized peoples"— noting a sense of solidarity between the division's members and the growth of in-group recognition with the development of the use of the rainbow insignia (Linton 1924: 296–98). Linton observed, "It seems probable that both the A.E.F. complexes and primitive totemism are results of the same social and supernaturalistic tendencies. The differences in the working out of these tendencies can readily be accounted for by the differences in the framework to which they have attached themselves and in the cultural patterns which have shaped their expression" (Linton 1924: 299).

The war also disrupted opportunities for anthropological fieldwork across the globe. Bronislaw Malinowski's movements as an Austrian citizen were constrained by the Australian government, though they were not as limited as those of Fritz Graebner, who spent most of the war imprisoned in Australia, where he had been attending a conference when the war broke out.[6] Ronald Ley examined the possibility that Wolfgang Köhler's years of studying chimpanzees in the Canary Islands served as a front for Köhler's management of a German spy ring during the war, though Ley's suspicions and speculations remain unproved (c.f. Ley 1990; Pastore 1990). The German ethnologist Mermann Naumann was in Australia on a research trip when war was declared, and he was interned until 1919. While imprisoned, "He produced a comparison of the myths of Indo-European, Mongolian, Polynesian, and Hamito-Semitic peoples," as well as a comparative study of calendrical systems of the New and Old Worlds (Naumann 1968: 241).

Archaeologist Spies

Anthropologists—or, more specifically, archaeologists—took on another significant role during the First World War, a role of more direct importance to battles and strategic plans, but one that Boas later argued threatened the legitimacy and trustworthiness of all anthropologists. This was the role of spy. These archaeologist-spies were drawn from the ranks of archaeologists in both the Old World and the New World.

In the winter of 1913–14, the British subjects T. E. Lawrence and Leonard Woolley were working on the Palestine Exploration Fund's project designed to map the southern Negev region known as the "Wilderness of Zin." This fieldwork project produced two separate reports and two sets of maps. One map, indicating only scant geographic details, was provided to public Palestine Exploration Fund subscribers, while the other map, indicating details of topographic features of military importance, was secretly distributed to British military personnel (Silberman 1982: 192–94). Woolley traveled through southern Turkey examining the Germans' new railroad lines connecting Europe with the Middle East. But such movements in a war theater naturally garnered suspicions. German military intelligence was aware of Woolley's plans and thwarted the efforts to gather intelligence (Woolley 1962: 88–93).

At Port Said, Woolley directed a small network of spies. Woolley later provided accounts of his hunts for enemy agents in his memoir, sneaking spies and saboteurs up the Levantine coast to broadcast clandestine reports on German and Turkish troops. In one tale, his efforts to break up a nightly Morse code lamp-base signaling out to the Mediterranean found nothing more than a baby jiggling a lamp near a window as it received its nightly bath. Woolley once used two Trappist monks as spies after Turkey expelled them from the monastery near Antioch. Because the monks had taken vows of silence, Woolley "had to get a dispensation from the Pope to get two of these monks over to Port Said to report . . . on the geography of the neighborhood of Antioch" (Woolley 1962: 108).[7]

T. E. Lawrence excavated at the Syrian site of Carchemish for four years, and during the war, British intelligence recruited him to monitor Germany's advances on a railroad line linking Berlin with Baghdad. The line had the strategic importance of connecting Germany with the Arabian Gulf (via existing lines that connected Baghdad with Basra), allowing Germany to ship oil without passing through the Suez Canal. In 1914, Lawrence wrote to his mother that these excavations were "obviously only meant as red herrings, to give an archaeological color to a political job" (Brown 2003: 44; Tabachnick 1997).

On-the-ground geographic knowledge was highly valued in wartime intelligence circles. Gertrude Bell, the British explorer, feminist, and archaeologist, traveled throughout the Near East providing invaluable geographical information to the British Arab Bureau on the eve of the war. After the war began, "She was called out to Cairo to serve in the Arab Intelligence Bureau, where her unrivaled knowledge of central Arabia proved exceedingly valuable" (Fagan 1979: 247).

The British were not the only nation using archaeologists as spies during the First World War (Dorwart 1979). The U.S. Office of Naval Intelligence (ONI) secretly trained and deployed a ring of American archaeologist-spies on missions to Central America. Over dinner and drinks at the Cosmos Club in Washington, D.C., Charles Alexander Sheldon recruited Sylvanus Griswold Morley to covertly join the ONI. Morley was a well-respected scholar of Maya archaeology, with years of field experience in Central America.[8] Sheldon arranged for Morley to use his established position as a Carnegie Institution archaeologist as cover for a series of secret missions in which he searched for German U-boats along the Gulf of Mexico coastlines of Mexico, British Honduras, and Belize. Morley was not only receptive to this proposition; he provided Sheldon with the names of several anthropologists who would also use their anthropological credentials for similar missions (Harris and Sadler 2003: xv).

Ten American anthropologists have been identified as conducting espionage in Central America during the war: Arthur Carpenter (Sullivan 1989: 132), Thomas Gann (Sullivan 1989: 132), John Held (Sullivan 1989: 132), Samuel Lothrop (Harris and Sadler 2003; Price 2000; Sullivan 1989: 132), John Alden Mason (Harris and Sadler 2003; Price 2000), William Hubbs Mechling (Harris and Sadler 2003: xvii), Sylvanus Griswold Morley (Harris and Sadler 2003), Herbert J. Spinden (Sullivan 1989: 132), W. G. Farabee (Sullivan 1989: 241), and M. H. Saville (Sullivan 1989: 241).[9]

Morley traveled thousands of miles along the coasts of the Yucatan, Mosquito Coast, Guatemala, Nicaragua, Honduras, and Belize pretending to do archaeological field surveys while hunting for secret German submarine bases. The historians Charles Harris and Louis Sadler (2003: 38) estimated that Morley was "the best secret agent the United States produced during World War I." They write, "In only ten months, Morley had become a skilled intelligence operative (he had recruited eight agents and eleven subagents, most of whom turned out to be first rate) and a first-rate analyst. . . . During his tenure as an ONI agent he wrote almost three dozen intelligence reports on a variety of topics, covering almost a thousand pages" (Harris and Sadler 2003: xxi). Morley recruited other archaeologists for similar clandestine missions. Chief among these other archaeologist-spies were Samuel J. Lothrop; John Alden Mason of the Field Museum of Natural History; Herbert J. Spinden, then working at the American Museum of Natural History; and William Hubbs Mechling (Harris and Sadler 2003: xvii).

These archaeologists primarily funded their espionage with salaries from the academic or research organizations to which they held affiliations. Thus, Spinden's American Museum of Natural History salary of $2,200 provided for both his fieldwork and spying in Nicaragua, where "he kept an eye on the local Germans and also stimulated the output of mahogany, for airplane propellers" (Harris and Sadler 2003: 109). The Carnegie Institution continued to pay Morley's salary while he spied for the government. Quetzil Castañeda's exploration of the political agendas of the Carnegie Institution clarifies that such uses of foundation funding for covert government work were in keeping with Carnegie's understanding of "how science and scientists would contribute to the US government during war time" (Castañeda 2005: 37). The Carnegie Institution president Robert Woodward's pride in his organization's contributions to the war went so far that he was recorded in the minutes of a business meeting as saying, "Amongst other men who have been called from the Institution into the Government we have one man who is serving as a spy. He is an archaeologist, and archaeology puts up a very fine camouflage for that business" (quoted in Castañeda 2005: 48).

Morley and the ONI's other archaeologist-spies fabricated a web of lies to cloak their espionage during the war. Spinden's and Lothrop's snooping and questioning of locals raised so many suspicions in Tegucigalpa that "Morley went to great pains to stress the archaeological nature of his—and, by extension, their—activities. He therefore secured an appointment with the minister of foreign relations, Doctor Mariano Vázquez, to whom he ceremoniously presented his Carnegie credentials" (Harris and Sadler 2003: 84). Morley told Vázquez a series of lies and even wrote a flattering article for the government newspaper on the archaeological ruins at Copán. Morley later met with Honduran President Francisco Bertrand and secured from him a letter of introduction, which he used to further betray the trust of his hosts (Harris and Sadler 2003: 85).

By the war's end, Morley, Lothrop, Mason, Spinden, Mechling, and the other American archaeologist-spies returned to academic positions in the United States. These men were proud of their actions, which they viewed as patriotic service to defend their country in wartime. But not all anthropologists viewed using anthropology as a cover for espionage in such a positive light. Boas saw these actions as diminishing the validity and respectability of all future scientific researchers working abroad.

Boas's Criticism: Scientists as Spies, Scientists as Prostitutes

In 1917, Franz Boas heard rumors that J. Alden Mason and William H. Mechling had abused his willingness to write letters of introduction and support to create opportunities to conduct foreign espionage. Boas then asked Berthold Laufer, curator at the Field Museum of Natural History; Alfred Tozzer, Harvard anthropologist; and Plinny Goddard, American Museum of Natural History anthropologist what they knew about these allegations, but they were not forthcoming with details. Laufer eventually told Boas that Mason and Mechling had spied in Mexico and elsewhere in Central America, but Laufer asked Boas to not tell Manuel Gamio (a friend of Boas's and the head of the Mexican Directorate of Archaeological and Ethnological Studies) about their spying (Harris and Sadler 2003: 285–87). Boas was upset that he and his scientific reputation had been used to provide false credibility for this covert operation. He wrote to Gamio, telling what he knew of Mason's and Mechling's double dealings, but Gamio had already been apprised of this by Mason and Mechling (Castañeda 2003). For whatever reason—the most publicly proclaimed being that Boas had no wish to endanger the lives of these archaeologist-spies—Boas waited until after the war's end to denounce publicly the actions of these men.

Boas learned that, in addition to Mason and Mechling, Herbert J. Spinden and Sylvanus Morley had used their anthropological credentials as a cover for wartime spying south of the border. Boas pursued whatever information he could gather on these spies, and with time he learned the names of other anthropologist–spies.[10] Once the war ended, Boas made his concerns public, though even then he did so without identifying the anthropologists by name.

On December 20, 1919, the *Nation* published a letter by Boas under the heading, "Scientists as Spies." The letter complained that four American anthropologists had abused their professional research positions by conducting espionage in Central America during the First World War. Boas wrote:

> In his war address to Congress, President Wilson dwelt at great length on the theory that only autocracies maintain spies; that these are not needed in democracies. At the time that the President made this statement, the Government of the United States had in its employ spies of an unknown number. I am not concerned here with the familiar discrepancies between the President's words and the actual facts, although we may perhaps have to accept his statement as meaning correctly that we live under an autocracy; that our democracy is a fiction. The point against which I wish to enter a

vigorous protest is that a number of men who follow science as their profession, men whom I refuse to designate any longer as scientists, have prostituted science by using it as a cover for their activities as spies.

A soldier whose business is murder as a fine art, a diplomat whose calling is based on deception and secretiveness, a politician whose very life consists in compromises with his conscience, a business man whose aim is personal profit within the limits allowed by a lenient law—such may be excused if they set patriotic devotion above common everyday decency and perform services as spies. They merely accept the code of morality to which modern society still conforms. Not so the scientist. The very essence of his life is the service of truth. We all know scientists who in private life do not come up to the standard of truth-fulness, but who, nevertheless, would not consciously falsify the results of their researches. It is bad enough if we have to put up with these, because they reveal a lack of strength of character that is liable to distort the results of their work. A person, however, who uses science as a cover for political spying, who demeans himself to pose before a foreign government as an investigator and asks for assistance in his alleged researches in order to carry on, under this cloak, his political machinations, prostitutes science in an unpardonable way and forfeits the right to be classed as a scientist.

By accident, incontrovertible proof has come into my hands that at least four men who carry on anthropological work, while employed as government agents, introduced themselves to foreign governments as representatives of scientific institutions in the United States, and as sent out for the purpose of carrying on scientific research. They have not only shaken the belief in the truthfulness of science, but they have also done the greatest possible disservice to scientific inquiry. In consequence of their acts every nation will look with distrust upon the visiting foreign investigator who wants to do honest work, suspecting sinister designs. Such action has raised a new barrier against the development of international friendly cooperation. (Boas 1919)

This radical ethical critique showed the depth of Boas's anger, as well as his conception of science's role to serve society in peace and wartime. Boas's belief in the existence of pure science independent of the corrupting influence of a militarized and politicized nation-state fueled this attack more than his disapproval of American participation in the war, but his opposition to the war must have also influenced his critique. On a very practical level, Boas's critique that "every nation will look with distrust upon the visiting foreign investigator who wants to do honest work, suspecting sinister designs" raised serious issues that still affect anthropologists conducting fieldwork in foreign settings.

Though Boas did not identify the four spies by name, ten days after its publication date his letter caused such a stir in the American anthropological community that a motion was presented at the annual meeting of the AAA to censure him. After some debate and discussion, the association's Governing Council voted by a margin of twenty to ten to censure Boas, effectively removing him from the council and pressuring him to resign from the National Research Council (Stocking 1968b: 275–76). Leslie Spier later recalled that "the resolution was passed: apart from simply stating that Boas' letter did not represent the view of the Association, passing it on to the National Research Council meant that Boas had to withdraw from the latter for the sake of peace" (Price 2001b: 11).

When the AAA's Governing Council voted to censure Boas, it did not object to the accuracy or the facts of his complaint. Instead, the body wished to distance the association from Boas's remarks and to punish him for using his professional position for political ends. However, the censure of Boas was itself a political act. George Stocking observed that the vote against Boas predominantly came from anthropologists with ties to Harvard University and Washington, D.C., outside the influence of Boas's academic stronghold at Columbia University (Stocking 1968b).[11] According to Stocking, "Outraged patriotism was simply the trigger that released a flood of pent-up personal resentment and institutional antagonism" (Stocking 1968b: 292). Other factors such as anti-German and anti-Semitic sentiments and a strong sense of postwar jingoistic patriotism contributed to Boas's censure (Hyatt 1990; Price 2001b).

Some scholars have recently questioned Boas's motives for attacking these unnamed archaeologist-spies in his letter to the *Nation*. Harris and Sadler (2003: 287) claimed that "Boas invoked high moral principals, but there was a considerable element of self-interest involved. He stated that he could not allow even the shadow of suspicion to fall upon himself, for it would ruin the work he was doing in Mexico." Likewise, David L. Browman claimed that

> there were at least ten American anthropologists engaged in the activities that Boas called "spying," two of whom were former students of Boas—not just the four noted in *The Nation*—whom were political opponents of Boas. Boas had known about these activities for three years or more, and had written many anthropologists complaining about them, to no avail, as most of the American anthropological community was actively involved in the

Allied cause. Boas had made his explicitly pro-German, anti-Allies (and many say as unpatriotic and anti-American) sentiments widely know beginning with published commentary as early as 1916. (Browman 2005)

Browman's characterization of Boas as holding "pro-German, anti-Allies" and "unpatriotic and anti-American" views misunderstood his opposition to America's entry into the war. Browman mistakenly argued that Boas's opposition to the war was based on nationalistic pro-German, anti-American, or unpatriotic views, but his complaint was much deeper than that: He viewed the European war as an unnecessary, brutal war fought for the economic gain of a minority, but his critique was also infused with his battle against the anti-German tendencies brewing in America.

The AAA's censure of Boas created a skirmish within the American anthropological community for a brief period, but the reverberations from this critical juncture continue to sound within American anthropology today. And while the censure shook Boas, it also marked the beginning of American anthropology's public debates about the propriety of mixing anthropology with military and intelligence operations. These debates have resurfaced in various forms during the American wars that have followed.

Contextualizing First World War Anthropology

The First World War established new relationships between American anthropologists and military and intelligence agencies that would remain important, if not problematic, in the wars waged throughout the twentieth century. The First World War showed anthropologists to be able assets who were familiar with regions that were to become battlefronts or of strategic importance. Whether it was Woolley and Lawrence in the Near East or Mason and Morley in Central America, archaeological fieldwork provided a natural cover for spying in theaters of interest. But Boas's complaint complicated, if not the ease, then the meaning of these relationships.

When called, American and European anthropologists easily adapted to the needs of the war. Some anthropologists wrote propaganda, others quietly contributed geographic knowledge, and still others used physical anthropology's anthropometric measurements to aid in the bureaucratization of selecting which lives would be fit to serve the nation's warfare needs. Certainly, the contributions of American anthropologists to the First World War were less significant than those made during the Second World War—and, more significant, the academic attention of focus was nowhere nearly as diverted by the questions raised during and after the First World War as it was during the Second World War, when notions of directed research peaked in ways that were not set aside at the war's end. But still, some elements of anthropology followed, and contributed to, the needs of the nation's political economy during the First World War as anthropologists contributed to the war effort.

Anthropologists' contributions to the First World War were not simply dress rehearsals for the contributions to be made in the Second World War. The limited contributions of anthropologists to World War One were mostly of a nature and scale different from those made by anthropologists in World War Two. But American anthropologists' reactions and contributions to the First World War influenced the next generation of anthropologists called on to contribute their professional skills in the subsequent world war. Perhaps the most significant outcome of anthropologists' involvements in World War One occurred *after* the war, when Boas was censured for criticizing "scientist spies." The threats presented by Nazism in the next war muted the sort of criticism of propagandistic brainwashing proffered by Boas in 1917. And beyond this silence, the Nazi threat found some American anthropologists mining their profession for propagandistic techniques to further the same sort of blind loyalty and trust degraded by Boas in his statement "Preserving Our Ideas."

Boas's criticism of scientist spies was remembered by many anthropologists serving in the Second World War, and for some these events raised residual feelings of unease as they responded to the call to join the war. As the anthropologist Jack Harris later recalled, he felt some conflict in 1942 about using his anthropological credentials as a cover to conduct espionage as an Office of Strategic Services (OSS) agent in West Africa. Harris's conflict arose "because during my days at Columbia I was told by associates of Boas that he violently opposed using our scientific reputation as a cover for intelligence activities in war. He based this on an incident in which a student of his had been involved in World War One. However, our feelings were so strong, I felt that whatever capabilities I could lend to the war effort in this war against infamy, I was pleased to do so" (quoted in Edelman 1997: 11). Harris's hesitance to use anthropology as a cover for spying or to harness anthropology for the war was shared by other anthropologists. Memories of Boas's censure had an impact on some anthropologists' responses to the Second World War, but this hesitance was short-lived. Axis atrocities soon buried most such concerns.

While Boas's criticism and his resulting censure have become well-worn features of American anthropology's political and historical self-understanding, there is perhaps more read into Boas's critique than appeared on that page of the *Nation*. It is important to recognize that Boas's criticism was limited in what it did and did not condemn. While his primary complaint was against the practice of lying to hosts about why supposed fieldworkers were present (scholars who "prostituted science by using it as a cover for their activities as spies"), Boas also felt that his personal, high modern view of pure science was violated by such duplicity. Boas implied in his *Nation* letter that he expected businessmen to "prostitute" themselves, but he considered science a more sacred undertaking. Boas believed that, for scientists, "the very essence of his life is the service of truth," though his antiwar sentiments and strong personal feelings opposing America's entry into this particular war also may have shaped the form of his criticism.

It is important to also consider what Boas's *Nation* critique did not argue. Boas did not argue that science must not be used for harm during times of warfare. He did not argue that using anthropological skills or knowledge for purposes of warfare was wrong. He did not argue that anthropologists should never work for military and intelligence agencies in any professional capacity. But Boas *did* lay the groundwork for other such criticisms to come in later wars: Laura Thompson would question the ethical propriety of anthropologists' selling their field to the highest bidder; Ralph Beals would question the propriety of anthropologists' conducting secret government research; and Eric Wolf and others would condemn those using anthropology in support of imperialist wars.

But while interpretations of Boas's denunciation of the mixing of anthropology and espionage vary, his charge and punishment have continued to stir interest in American anthropologists during the nation's wars throughout the twentieth century and twenty-first century. In 2005, the membership of the AAA overwhelmingly voted to support a referendum overturning the association's 1919 censure of Boas. Although it came more than eighty-five years after the fact, this gesture represented an ambiguous statement of contemporary anthropology's view of its past, present, and future relationships to the intelligence community. That the vote was a rout (1,245 supporting, 73 opposing) is clear, but the meaning of the vote is a mystery, and given the general reticence of the AAA's membership to forbid secret research in its official ethics code, it seems more likely to be a sentimental statement than an affirmation of the impropriety of mixing anthropology and espionage. The reasons for the association's reticence are complex, but they are partially rooted in the discipline's rarely examined contributions to the Second World War (Fluehr-Lobban 2005; Glenn 2004).

The AAA's resolution did "entirely repudiate" Boas's censure. It established that the AAA accepts that "Boas believed that it was immoral for scientists to use their professional identity as a cover for governmental spying activities" and that "other such incidents of anthropologists as spies have been repudiated by this Association."[12] But even as the AAA passed this motion, President George Bush's "war on terror" found a chorus of AAA members calling for anthropologists to covertly contribute their skills to the Central Intelligence Agency (CIA) and other intelligence agencies, and new funding opportunities secretly connected anthropology's graduate students with intelligence agencies.[13]

CHAPTER TWO

Professional Associations

and the Scope of American

Anthropology's Wartime

Applications

Before the war, very few people in this country could even give you a definition of anthropology.
—GEORGE FOSTER 2000: 195

The Second World War, like the global depression it eclipsed, left indelible marks on all Americans who lived through it. For most Americans, this was the "Good War" that galvanized American support like no other war before or since. While the First World War had significant American dissent from left-leaning labor and populist groups, after the Japanese attack on Pearl Harbor, the American war effort found broad support from most factions of the American left, middle, and right (Terkel 1984). A unique alliance developed between American capitalists and Soviet communists, and domestic labor and capital were transformed as women joined the workforce in large numbers and Roosevelt's cost-plus program limited war profiteering.

World War Two's mobilization of Americans was profound, and this mobilization transformed anthropology. After the war, individual American anthropologists came to regard their war service in different ways. Some saw their war activities as a proud adventure of service to nation (see, e.g., Coon 1980, 1981), but much more common public mentions of anthropologists' war activities are the numerous brief acknowledgments of service made without delving into details. A typical example of this is found in the passing statement made by the anthropologist-linguist Joseph Greenberg in 1986 that he was drafted during the war supposedly for a single year, but "ended up serving for about five years, including a period overseas in North Africa and Italy" (Greenberg 1986: 5). Such laconic declarations of time spent in military service without elaboration represent the predominant form of American anthropologists' professional or public descriptions of their war service. Mentions of individual anthropologists' service during World War Two in obituaries published in *American Anthropologist* or *Anthropology News* are inconsistent and most commonly make no reference to wartime activities. The meanings of such predominant silences are personal and multiple, and in the end, such silences can only be noted as a negative space that has bordered generations of American anthropologists.

American anthropologists were not silent in their opposition to the Nazi threat to humanity. Long before the United States entered the war, American anthropologists recognized that the Nazis were a danger to anthropological views of the inherent equality of all peoples. In 1938, the AAA passed a resolution at its annual meeting condemning Nazi racial "science." The association repudiated the claims that physical features were linked to cultural and psychological tendencies, asserting that "the terms 'Aryan' and 'Semitic' have no racial significance whatsoever" and declaring that "anthropology provides no scientific basis for discrimination against any people on the ground of racial inferiority, religious affiliation or linguistic heritage" (see Benedict 1950: 195–96; Lesser 2003: 22; Science 1939).

Even before the attack on Pearl Harbor, some American anthropologists had fought the rise of fascism in Spain.[1] Other anthropologists began quietly preparing for the coming war by compiling rosters listing anthropologists and their areas of expertise.[2] They realized that in a global war, the task of identifying people with needed geographical, cultural, and linguistic knowledge would take on prime importance as military and intelligence operations hinged on identifying these skills and abilities. Margaret Mead observed that the earliest efforts to link American anthropologists with the war effort "took the form of a roster of anthropologists interested very broadly in applied anthropology, as well as those particularly interested in the culture and personality approach. At an informal dinner meeting in Philadelphia at the American Anthropological Association meetings in 1940, we established this roster, which had the potentiality of becoming a Society for Culture and Personality" (Mead 1979: 148). Discussions of anthropological contributions to the war occurred in more public settings at the AAA meetings the following year.

The Japanese attack on Pearl Harbor suddenly transformed America into a nation committed to war, although some anthropologists were initially unsure how their discipline should contribute to the new war. Some of this hesitation indicated lingering memories of the controversies arising from anthropological contributions to the First World War. Like other citizens, many American anthropologists enlisted in military and intelligence work out of a sense of patriotic duty combined with a belief that military action was the only means by which the spread of Nazism, fascism, and Japanese colonial militarism in Asia could be stopped. Contributing their anthropological skills to this total war was a natural response for most anthropologists.

The AAA's 1941 annual meeting was held in Andover, Massachusetts, three weeks after the Japanese attack on Pearl Harbor—and only weeks before President Roosevelt ordered the internment of Japanese American citizens. But those attending the meeting found a somewhat ambivalent professional response to the new war. In part, the reaction was a generational one tempered by positions still guarded from the last war. As George Stocking observed, "Although the senior anthropologists who controlled the Association did not oppose the war, there was some feeling among the younger generation that the Association had dragged its feet in giving active support. At the 1941 meeting, which took place in the aftermath of Pearl Harbor, Julian Steward and Ralph Beals organized an *ad hoc* discussion on the war effort, at which Benedict and Mead gave papers" (Stocking 1976: 37).

Esther Goldfrank's account of the 1941 meeting also recalled Benedict's, Mead's, and others' support for the war, but she noted that some anthropologists' support for the American activities linked to the war was not unconditional. Goldfrank reported that Melville Jacobs

> rose to protest the U.S. government's decision to uproot Japanese residents from their homes in presumably sensitive areas—essentially in states bordering on the Pacific ocean—and relocate them in less exposed areas, where their movements were already being severely restricted. While broadening the base of Jacobs' original statement—and this may well have been done by other speakers—the minutes of the 1941 meeting . . . noted, under the heading "report of Committees," that "the suggestion of a group of anthropologists at the University of Washington for united action against the growth of racial prejudice within our borders was commended by the Council, but no agreement was reached on the desirability of centralizing our efforts along these lines." (Goldfrank 1978: 197; cf. *AA* 1942: 286–87)

Goldfrank supported Jacobs's effort, but Jacobs's call for action did not have the support of the majority of anthropologists in attendance. When Goldfrank spoke up "from the floor and asked those present to go on record for equal treatment of Whites and Negroes who were being conscripted for service in the armed forces," she met indifference from the membership at large who felt that the needs of "a desperate Britain" were greater than those of American Negroes (Goldfrank 1978: 197). Margaret Mead ruled Goldfrank's suggestion out of order.

The call of the war pushed most anthropologists to think outside of their academic specialties and training. Burt Aginsky sat aside his career-long interest in Pomo Indian culture and directed his attention to the needs of the war. Aginsky presented a paper to the association titled "Social Science and the World Situation," which was a call to arms enlisting anthropologists to join the war effort. He passionately framed participation by anthropologists in the war as being required for the survival of social science. He raised (and then dismissed) Boas's criticisms that mixing science and warfare risked the possibility of objectivity. Aginsky argued:

> Social science cannot exist under the jurisdiction of selfish ignorant leaders who rule by brutality and force, and who arbitrarily make it the tail for the kite of a dictatorial government, for the ultimate purpose of a political creed. They have imprisoned, exiled, and killed the students and professors who did not agree with them. . . . In short, this war today is a war not only of the armed forces, but a war against social science as it has been practiced during our era. We must either fight and maintain ourselves or lose and see the end of social science.
>
> The problem which confronts us is peculiar and different. Shall we lose our science by fighting? Is it possible to retain objectivity and yet participate in the war effort? Can we be Allies and remain scientists in this war of men and machines?
>
> We must not confuse objectivity with non-participation in the world-wide emergency. . . . It is up to us to impress our government with the fallacy of ethnocentrism. . . . It is of the utmost importance to understand our Allies as well as our enemies, to bring to a successful conclusion this world effort. If we expect to convince the world that we are fighting for a free and mutually considerate way of life, then we must practice that way of life ourselves.
>
> We should prepare a series of pamphlets which will contain important information about particular groups of people with whom we shall deal. These pamphlets should include information pertaining to the form of government, the family structure and customs, the economic system, the food habits, the climatic and geographical data, some basic vocabulary, and the important laws and taboos in relation to them all. We must at the same

time educate the people of the world as to the basic reasons for the conflict. To do so a knowledge of the cultures involved is prerequisite. . . . Social science must participate because this is a war of social science. If we use our tremendous accumulation and supply as intelligently as we will use our man-power, natural resources, factories, and transportation facilities, there is no question but that we shall win the social war as well as the physical war. (Aginsky 1942: 521–25)

Aginsky argued that anthropologists should use their skills in the war's prison camps and to help foster dissent among the populace of enemy nations. His call for action merged duty and "objective" science for a no-holds-barred fight in which anthropologists were to "fight back with all the weapons at our disposal." Aginsky vision of the war's new uses for anthropologists proved prescient, as the war soon found anthropologists performing most of the tasks he described. Aginsky was a student of Boas; his call at the 1941 AAA meetings for anthropologists to use their training in new ways for the war effort can be seen not quite as a dialectical transformation of the Boasian insistence on holistic anthropological training, but as a new strain of Boasian activism. Boas did not call for anthropologists to contribute their linguistic skills, field-research abilities, and cultural knowledge to the production of propaganda to the war, but his students did.

Other anthropologists spoke on anthropology and the war at these 1941 meetings: "[Julian] Steward and [Ralph] Beals promoted a discussion on anthropologists in the war effort which [Demitri] Shimkin and Beals chaired."[3] This group used their platform at the meeting to discuss "how anthropology might get more involved in the Armed Forces' specialized language and training programs."[4] George Murdock introduced a motion that was approved endorsing "the efforts of the Social Science Research Council [SSRC] to coordinate the activities of the several social sciences during the national emergency and pledged its cooperation in these efforts" (AA 1942: 287). But Fred Eggan noticed that these efforts to harness the AAA directly to the war effort were curtailed by association elders when "the council declined to set up a national committee on the use of anthropologists in World War II, which four members in Seattle had recommended, saying that centralization and government backing might lead many members to think the Association was an agent for propaganda."[5]

Although Franz Boas opposed the Nazis, his reactions to the war varied with the war's developments. Goldfrank believed that Boas's early views of the war were warped by pro-Soviet sympathies that led him to temper his criticisms of the Nazi–Soviet Pact. Boas openly opposed America's entry into the war prior to the Japanese attack on Pearl Harbor.[6] In 1940, Sidney Hook was shocked to encounter Boas "sporting a large lapel pin with the device 'Roosevelt is a warmonger,' which was being distributed by the American Peace Mobilization" (Hook 1987: 258).[7]

Boas "either joined or contributed to virtually every organization dedicated to anti-Nazi activity in the United States. His name appeared on letterheads of most of these groups, which would later have ramifications that he would have to address. Nevertheless, he forthrightly signed on as a member of the intellectual vanguard combating Nazism. Public lectures were another way of fighting this propaganda, and Boas frequently used the podium to attack anti-Semitism, pseudoscientific race theory and the suppression of free thought" (Hyatt 1990:146). He worked on a project using popular films to present anthropological views of race to Americans and others (Hyatt 1990: 150). Boas contributed to these pro-American or anti-Nazi educational and political activities, but his actions were categorically different from those of the younger generations of anthropologists who joined the war.[8]

As America entered the war, Franz Boas was in his eighties, and his students were assuming prominent academic positions in American universities. While most of these students parted ways with their mentor on some matters, during Boas's lifetime, none did so publicly regarding the concerns raised in his 1919 letter to the *Nation*. Franz Boas died on December 21, 1942, just before a large wave of American anthropologists went to work for so many military and intelligence agencies during the war.[9]

By the war's end, whatever hesitance AAA members may have felt had been forgotten as the association became a surrogate clearinghouse for multiple military and intelligence agencies. Despite the ambivalence expressed by some association elders, on December 30, 1941, the AAA passed a resolution stating: "Be it resolved that the American Anthropological Association places itself and its resources and the specialized skills of its members at the disposal of the country for the successful prosecution of the war" (AA 1942: 289). With this motion, the AAA officially joined the war effort. Goldfrank interpreted this resolution not as a show of unified support, but as a warning. To Goldfrank, "Without saying so in words, this resolution clearly warned the anthropological community not to rock the 'Ship of State' and, as already foreshadowed in the 'informal discussion' on the evening of December 27, not to continue agitating for the long overdue improvements in the condition of minorities within our borders. The Negroes got the message. They still remember, and with anger, how quickly their most ardent supporters deserted them" (Goldfrank 1978: 198). Others were more up-beat in their assessments. Ripley Bullen summarized the Saturday-night discus-sions at the 1941 AAA meeting as culminating in identifying three ways that anthropology could be of service in the "emerging world": "First, to be at the beck and call of Colonel Donovan's and similar committees or boards either as suppliers of information or personnel. Second, by continuing to disseminate anthropological information by pamphlets and teaching, possibly extending the latter into the secondary schools. Third, by maintaining and improving indus-trial morale and production" (Bullen 1942: 525).

Such eagerness was understandable, but the speed at which AAA placed itself in support of the needs of state did not provide time to consider the long-term implications of its actions, and the AAA did not discuss any limits to which the techniques and knowledge base of anthropology might be used in warfare.

The AAA Gets Its War On

As World War Two progressed, the AAA increasingly lent organizational support to the war effort. Following the request of the coordinator of transportation, the 1942 AAA annual meeting was canceled, as were the meetings for the next two years (AA 1942: 730). Although the 1942 meeting was canceled, a group of about fifty anthropologists who had already relocated to the Washington, D.C., area met there in December (see Kidder 1942). This unofficial group convened at the Cosmos Club. Without the presentation of any of the usual research papers, those assembled discussed possible anthropological contributions to the war. Holding the AAA's meetings at the Cosmos Club was convenient for some an-thropologists, such as Nelson Glueck, who later became an OSS analyst and who lived at the Cosmos Club while stationed in Washington.[10]

Given the importance of the Cosmos Club to the formation of American an-thropology, it is surprising that no substantive scholarship has been undertaken to explicate anthropologists' ongoing relationships with this institution. The Cosmos Club was founded in 1878 by John Wesley Powell and Henry Adams with the goal of establishing an intellectual salon where scientists of all backgrounds, explorers, anthropologists, bankers, industrialists, and politicians could socialize away from the pressures of Washington in a "haven for intellectual curiosity" and closed-door discussions and wheeling and dealing (Hutchinson 2000). The club has always served as a closed-door focal point for Washington, D.C., power brokers making connections and hatching schemes (see Foster 2000; Trumpbour 1989: 70). Wallace Stegner observed in *Beyond the Hundredth Meridian* that the

Cosmos Club was "the closest thing to a social headquarter for Washington's intellectual elite" (Stegner 1992 [1954]: 242). At its most innocuous, the Cosmos Club has been a snooty gentleman's club offering camaraderie and connections between a certain breed of anthropologist and American elites: at its most intrusive, it has been a stage for the recruitment of anthropologist-spies by members of the intelligence community (Harris and Sadler 2003: 109). That the AAA would hold its "unofficial" meeting in such a setting is indicative of the wartime mood of the association and of the ways that Washington's political and economic power base helped sponsor the wartime shifts of American anthropology.[11]

At the 1942 Cosmos Club AAA meeting, a motion was made by "younger members" to form a Committee on Anthropology and the War Effort.[12] The association's Executive Council decided that members serving in the armed services "who were unable to continue their dues might, upon request, be continued as members in good standing. Furthermore the Association would continue sending them publications or keep them for them if they were outside the U.S."[13]

Fred Eggan published a summary of the 1942 AAA meeting in the *American Association for the Advancement of Science Bulletin*. Eggan wrote that the war had taken over the concerns of anthropologists and their association and that

> the onset of the war found the anthropologists prepared to make a contribution on many fronts. At the December, 1941, meeting at Andover, Mass., an evening was devoted to discussing the role of anthropology and anthropologists in the world crisis. Soon anthropologists began to be called to Washington in increasing numbers until by the time for the annual meeting of 1942 almost 100 anthropologists were in government service. The request for cancellation of all meetings not directly connected with the war effort was met by holding a business meeting in Washington, D.C., for which no travel was involved.
>
> Over one-half of the professional anthropologists in this country are directly concerned in the war effort, and most of the rest are doing part-time war work. The comprehensive knowledge of the peoples and cultures of the world which anthropologists have gathered through field research has proved of great value to both the Army and the Navy, and to the various war agencies. The Association has cooperated in setting up the Ethnogeographic Board, the Committees on the Anthropology of Oceania and Africa, and the Committee for Latin American Studies. At the December, 1942, meeting a committee was appointed to make recommendations to the Army Board engaged in setting up curriculums for the Army college training program.

> Plans are underway to organize anthropological knowledge for the basic
> problems of the post-war period, particularly in areas where native peoples
> or different cultures are found. (Eggan 1943: 38)

Eggan's report did not mention that those not in government service were essentially geographically excluded from attending the AAA meeting in Washington, D.C., and thus only the views of anthropologists working with Washington-based military and intelligence agencies were represented to the exclusion of other views. Privately, Eggan observed that the "only important items which came up at the [1942 AAA] meeting centered around the importance of getting some anthropology into the new college curriculums for army officers and the appointment of a 'Franz Boas Committee' to explore the various possibilities for a suitable memorial to Professor Boas."[14]

   In March 1943, Ralph Beals, F. L. W. Richardson, Julian Steward, and Joseph Weckler wrote a logistics report for the National Research Council summarizing American anthropology's contributions to the war (Beals et al. 1943; hereafter, Beals report). While Beals's, Weckler's, and Steward's work was and would be within the boundaries of traditional academic anthropology, Richardson's perspective was firmly within the framework of industrial studies of workflow and worker management—interests that had a new importance during the war mobilization. The Beals report found that anthropologists used their skills to keep the production of key natural resources (such as rubber, petroleum, and minerals) flowing (Beals et al. 1943: 6–7). The authors observed:

> Anthropologists familiar with the needs in a given region assist in designing
> clothing and equipment in selecting types of food and preservation methods, and in teaching the utilization of indigenous food supplies and other
> resources. For military operations they provide information about the terrain; for occupying forces they provide handbooks explaining the habits
> and customs of the people and indicating how occupying forces should
> behave to ensure a friendly reception. They suggest policies to enlist the
> active cooperation of local or native populations. (Beals et al. 1943: 4)

There was some lag in finding appropriate positions for anthropologists in the war as agencies slowly began to learn how anthropology could be used. The Beals report found that, in early 1943, there were still only about forty anthropologists directly using their disciplinary skills in the war. The report estimated that

> these forty anthropologists are distributed between six government agencies
> and five private agencies.

The government agencies include the Board of Economic Warfare, the Office of the Coordinator of Inter-American Affairs, the War Labor Board, the War Relocation Authority, Office of Indian Affairs, and the Department of Agriculture. The five private organizations are the Western Electric Company, Vega Aircraft Corporation, Phillips Petroleum Company, the Harvard Business School, and the Massachusetts Institute of Technology. (Beals et al. 1943: 5–6)

The Ethnogeographic Board convened a conference to examine how anthropologists could help solve potential labor disruptions among Indian tin miners in Bolivia (Beals et al. 1943: 7). Other anthropologists were helping the Board of Economic Warfare "secure the cooperation of native peoples in increasing production" (Beals et al. 1943: 8). These anthropologists used their "regional knowledge" to help locate "supplies of needed materials, suggest better assembly points for shipment, and improved routing of marine and aerial transport," as well as to assist in disrupting Axis supply routes (Beals et al. 1943: 4).

The Beals report found that anthropologists at the Bureau of Indian Affairs were monitoring and influencing war-related opinions on Indian reservations. It observed:

> Because Indians have been handled decently and intelligently during the past 12–15 years, they are today making every possible contribution to the war. They could have been a serious fifth column, or at least a potential liability. Instead, 12,000 are in the armed forces; they have purchased two million dollars worth of bonds; they have supplied 5 per cent of all the lumber used for war purposes; their food production program has increased,—they are definitely an asset, not a liability.
>
> It will be seen, therefore, that anthropology is making one of its contributions to the war through the medium of the Indian Service. This contribution would not be materially restricted for the next year or two if every department of anthropology and every course in the subject were discontinued. However, winning the peace is going to be a much longer and drawn out affair than winning the war. Anthropology now will be effective five and ten years hence when the problem of peace will be most acute. (Beals et al. 1943: 15)

The AAA's Committee on Anthropology and the War Effort also "discussed how anthropology might get more involved in the Armed Forces' specialized language and training programs."[15] But within the association, some discomfort about anthropology's official role in the war remained. Even with the war fully under way,

> there were still hesitations among older members about just how much the profession should commit itself. When the Association met again in Washington in 1943, a letter was read from the absent president, Leslie Spier, expressing concern lest preoccupation with war work lead to the total neglect of anthropological science. Although a proposal was made at that meeting that the next should include a program devoted to problems of the war effort, the elder statesmen of the executive committee, deciding this time to find their quorum in New York, preferred simply to have a "discussion meeting" with the American Ethnological Society. (Stocking 1976: 38)

This 1943 unofficial AAA meeting again was attended almost exclusively by anthropologists living in the Washington, D.C., area. At the meeting at the Cosmos Club, it was decided "to follow the same plan as last year and hold a strictly business meeting with no papers and no addresses."[16] The meeting was poorly attended, and Father John Cooper presided over it in AAA President Leslie Spier's absence. Regina Flannery wrote to President Spier that William Duncan Strong was so consumed with the secrecy surrounding his work at the Ethnogeographic Board that he would not read aloud any portions of the unclassified report written by an AAA committee: "Strong reported for the Beals, Mead, Linton committee appointed to work with his Board to present a memo to the Army Training Personnel. The memo was sent as directed. Strong said that it had had its effect although he was not free to say just how and where. Lt. Freddie de Laguna asked him to read the report as presented to the Army. When Strong replied that it was six pages long and handed a copy to her, that was that, and the question was dropped."[17]

The unofficial 1944 AAA annual meeting was held in mid-December at the Men's Faculty Club at Columbia University. The meeting was followed by an organized session titled "Anthropology and the War," with brief papers and discussions.[18] As the Allied and Axis forces undertook unprecedented civilian aerial bombardments, the attending AAA membership passed a resolution calling for the protection of "primitives" at the end of the war. The present members declared:

> Be it resolved: That the American Anthropological Association express the hope that in the settlement of the present World War the rights of so-called primitive peoples to a way of life and possession of property be respected

and that these peoples be not enslaved under any political device whatsoever. We express the hope that principles of ethics be given preference over
doctrines of sovereignty in the future intercourse of nations to this end that
selfish wars be eliminated and just peace maintained.[19]

This optimistic motion recorded the association's awareness of the war's impact
on peoples throughout the world, but it also conveyed naïve conceptions of the
political formations that would emerge at the war's end.

The Society for Applied Anthropology's Wartime Applications

The AAA had a diverse membership, but its broad membership base, historical
commitment to academic anthropology departments in colleges, universities,
and museums, and institutional history made it a clumsy organization for addressing the needs of anthropologists interested in applying their skills to the war.
In May 1941, Eliot Chapple and Conrad Arensberg organized a small meeting of
fifty-four other like-minded anthropologists at Harvard to establish the Society
for Applied Anthropology (Partridge and Eddy 1978: 32). The meeting's participants shared an interest in establishing a practical anthropological community to
help implement social change. Some attending this first meeting thought that
designed change should work from the bottom up, while others envisioned
anthropologists implementing the designs of government administrators. As a
newly formed organization, the Society for Applied Anthropology (SFAA) used
its cadency to its advantage and it quickly aligned itself with the needs of the war.

While the SFAA provided a focal point for a wide-ranging group of anthropologists during and after the war, Chapple and Arensberg, the two anthropologists
who organized its formative meeting, shared a long-standing interest in specific
forms of social control. Chapple and Arensberg had been close friends and
graduate students of W. Lloyd Warner at Harvard, with interests in industrial
relations, community studies, and designed social change. Arensberg was one of
the first American anthropologists to conduct ethnographic field research among
what was considered a "modern," "non-primitive" culture when he undertook
ethnographic studies in Ireland during the 1930s. At Harvard he gravitated toward the sociologically and functionally influenced work of Warner, and, along
with Chapple, he helped establish studies on industrial relations that tended to
benefit the managerial sectors of Fordist American workplaces. Arensberg optimistically believed that sociological and anthropological knowledge could be
harnessed by leaders to alleviate societal problems. These views were shared by

many in the early applied anthropology community, but explanations of who would determine which sectors of society would be served were rarely forthcoming. During the war, Arensberg served in the U.S. Army's Military Intelligence Division (G-2) in various capacities, including applying anthropology in the management of interned Japanese Americans (see chapter 7).

Like Arensberg, Chapple held almost fanatical beliefs in the utopian possibilities of social engineering. As a graduate student he had "invented a machine, the *interaction chronograph*, that recorded [speech interactions] automatically" (Homans 1984: 162). Chapple's scientific faith led him to believe that his machine was measuring vital scientific social structure and that such measurements could reshape society in "beneficial" ways—but, as was representative of Harvard's intellectual climate during this period, there was little critical illumination of who would benefit from such developments. During the war, Chapple worked as a research associate at Harvard's School of Medicine, where, among other work, he studied physiological responses to human interactions in the hope that he could devise ways to evaluate individuals during job-application processes and other settings that would assist those controlling social settings (Kaempffert 1940). In 1940, Chapple told the *New York Times* that his measurements of brainwaves could be used to "'size up' applicants for jobs." Chapple believed that "the development of a technology of human relations might be comparable to the triumphs of the physical sciences in improving our material wants" (Kaempffert 1940). Chapple joined Arensberg and Carleton Coon in proposing, during the early months of World War Two, that future wars could be diverted by establishing a "United States of the World, complete with secretive, anthropologically informed philosopher kings—an idea, as I will discuss in chapter 10, that was proposed to OSS Director William Donovan by OSS Agent Carleton Coon at the war's end (Carey 1942).

From the SFAA's very conception, the anthropologists not only envisioned the society as a means whereby social change could be engineered for desirable ends; they also envisioned those for whom the ends were desirable implicitly as elites striving for more control, not the masses. The applied anthropology advocated by the SFAA's early founders did not champion increased democracy; it championed increased management of people, regardless of their free desires or intentions.

As a new institution devoted to the application of anthropology unburdened with long-standing traditions, agenda, and institutions, the SFAA soon became *the* wartime anthropological society devoted to the practicalities of applying anthropological methods and theories to the problems of the war. The SFAA's devotion to valuing designed outcomes over theoretical analysis took on a new importance once America joined the war. Like the AAA, the SFAA held its 1942 annual meeting in Washington, D.C., to be close to the core of its war-employed membership.[20] Most SFAA members contributed their anthropological skills to the war effort, and each of the three wartime SFAA presidents made active disciplinary contributions to the war.[21]

Basic distinctions between "academic" and "applied" foci on the war can be seen in the wartime issues of the AAA's *American Anthropologist* and the SFAA's *Applied Anthropology*. *American Anthropologist* continued (albeit in a reduced capacity due to wartime paper shortages) to publish a variety of book reviews and academically theoretical and descriptive articles on theoretical topics, with few articles of direct concern to anthropological applications to the war. During the war, *American Anthropologist* occasionally published "applied" articles that related to anthropologists' war work. These included works by John Gillin on "Cultural Adjustment" (1944), Clyde Kluckhohn and O. H. Mowrer on "Culture and Personality" (1944), the staging of a Sumo Tournament at the Tule Lake internment camp (Marvin Opler 1945), and community analysis studies (Embree 1944). But such articles rarely appeared in *American Anthropologist*. Far more common were conceptual pieces on topics such as American kinship systems (Parsons 1943), Tiwa kinship terminology (Trager 1943), Shawnee musical instruments (Voegelin 1943), and the anthropological sensitivities of Voltaire (Honigsheim 1945). Most of *American Anthropologist*'s articles carried on as if a world war was not raging.

In contrast, the SFAA's *Applied Anthropology* frequently published practical articles on wartime anthropology. In the first issue, Margaret Mead described how a national morale program could be implemented to coordinate local and national domestic propaganda campaigns (Mead 1941, cf. Bateson and Mead 1941). Mead worried that federal administrators would mistakenly assume that American culture would still respond to the war slogans of the last Great War, so she argued that anthropologists should design effective war-supporting propaganda campaigns rooted in understanding the specifics of 1940s culture. Later, Mead described several research methods to be used by war agencies to study domestic and foreign populations. These methods included techniques developed by Rhoda Métraux to sample what she termed "cultural character structure" data and Gregory Bateson's analytic techniques used in viewing Nazi propaganda films (Mead 1943c).

Other anthropologists published articles in *Applied Anthropology* on subjects of domestic importance to the war. Charles Loomis examined how the shortage of teachers in schools affected rural education in America (Loomis 1942). The ssrc funded Nellie and Charles Loomis's analysis of data on Mexican American laborers working in New Mexican war industries to offer suggestions on how employers could best work with this population to keep war production on-line (Loomis and Loomis 1942). Similarly, John and Ruth Useem and Gordon Magregor published their study examining problems associated with using Rose-bud Sioux Indians for war work. They found that though the Anglos and Sioux had to make crucial cultural adjustments to wartime employment needs, there were savings for governmental administrators in these new relationships (Useem et al. 1943: 8–9). Some applied anthropologists studied efforts to rehabilitate soldiers suffering from neuro-psychiatric injuries (Malamud and Stephenson 1944).[22]

In the January–March 1942 issue of *Applied Anthropology*, Bateson announced that the Council on Human Relations was working on plans for postwar recon-struction that would take into account cultural differences. Bateson sought infor-mation from others working on these problems (Bateson 1942a). Other articles on the postwar roles of anthropology discussed such topics as "governing the occupied areas of the South Pacific" (Useem 1945) and the uses of fieldwork to aid neocolonial administrators (Leighton 1942).

Some *Applied Anthropology* articles complained that wartime policymakers often ignored recommendations made by anthropologists. Morris Opler com-plained that anthropologists and other social scientists opposing the internment of Japanese Americans were ignored when they argued that these citizens should not have been interned, because "they were either long-term residents of this country or young people born on this soil and reared in its institutions, [and] the great majority would be assimilated to our ideals and loyalties" (Morris Opler 1945: 13). Opler characterized the decision to intern Japanese Americans as "Nazi-type nonsense and hysteria" (Morris Opler 1945: 14).

Loomis wrote and edited a series of articles analyzing Latin America's natural resources that advocated central roles to be played by anthropologists in "de-veloping a permanent and stable supply of needed agricultural materials" from this vital region (see Loomis 1943, 1945). Latin American sources of rubber, hemp, rotenone, and cinchona bark took on a great significance as other sources for these materials were interrupted during the war. Loomis advocated an active anthropological presence in the oversight of the human interface in the produc-tion, harvesting, and distribution of these resources.

Wartime articles in *Applied Anthropology* frequently expressed an optimistic faith in the promise of social engineering. Many articles envisioned a postwar world in which anthropologists would advise government agencies using anthropology to efficiently manage the populace. Notions of benevolent "engineers of human relations" (Chapple 1943: 32) predominated in many of these articles, with little apparent awareness that such manipulative governance might be a form of sweetened totalitarianism. In the article "Anthropological Engineering: Its Use to Administrators," Chapple wrote:

> A democratic society, in anthropological terms, is one in which the system of relations provides habitual channels for . . . compensatory movements, and thus for the maintenance or restoration of the individual's equilibrium. The administrator issues orders to and controls the activities of the administered, but the latter, though their representative or directly at hearings, conferences, and so on, are able to turn to act upon the administrator. Where this kind of balance does not obtain, serious maladjustments of personality occur and compensatory movements take a violent form. If our society is to move more completely towards a democratic system, the engineers of human relations will have to devise methods by which all our institutions are made more efficient, more adjustable to change, and more permeable to suggestions from all its members. (Chapple 1943: 32)

Several papers promoted the use of fieldwork to improve social management. In a 1942 paper envisioning the roles to be played by applied anthropologists in the postwar world, Alexander Leighton, a lieutenant in the U.S. Naval Reserve Medical Corps, recommended that anthropology students spend a period of time living among the peoples they would later "administer" as government agents (Leighton 1942: 29–30). Leighton advocated that Nazi methods of social control be studied and even emulated, though for different means:

> Many readers of German Psychological Warfare have been impressed by the Germans' terrible thoroughness and probable effectiveness, yet much of it represents no more than a systematic application of knowledge and techniques familiar to many social scientists. The all important lesson is *application* and, while deploring the end to which the Germans turned these methods, we should be illuminated concerning their employment in the service of peace and harmonious living. (Leighton 1942: 26)

It is curious that Leighton and other wartime applied anthropologists did not see the use of such propagandistic means as counter to declared goals of using the social sciences to build "a scientific democracy" (Leighton 1942: 30).

Not all of *Applied Anthropology*'s discussions of social management and social engineering were such abstract theoretical treatments. Some articles reported on anthropologists' work on wartime programs. *Applied Anthropology* published more than a half-dozen articles on anthropologists' roles in the internment of Japanese American citizens in the War Relocation Authority's (wra) detention camps. In the November–December 1942 issue, Arensberg published "Report on a Developing Community, Poston, Arizona," describing his work at Poston and evaluating the administrative structure of the camp (Arensberg 1942). John Embree (1943a) discussed Japanese American cultural traits in the article "Dealing with Japanese-Americans." After the war, *Applied Anthropology* published several papers describing wra anthropologists' war work. G. Gordon Brown's forty-nine-page report on the Gila River camp clinically recounted how anthropologist community analysts collected data on internees and used the information to manage the internees' lives (Brown 1945). After the war, Katherine Luomala published a series of postwar reports on wra anthropology, as well as the interesting analysis "The Readjustment of California to the Return of the Japanese Evacuees" (Luomala 1946, 1947).

Ethical Rumblings from within the sfaa

Although the sfaa's membership was unified by a desire to apply the methods and theories of anthropology to pressing social issues of the day, a few of the society's members questioned the ethical propriety of some anthropological contributions to the war. Some concerns were intellectually linked to Boas's critique from the last war, while others mirrored those expressed by some aaa anthropologists at the beginning of the war. Concerns were also raised about the danger that the techniques of applied anthropology would be used to manage and control populations rather than for more democratic ends.

As the war progressed and anthropologists undertook a broad assortment of tasks, ethical concerns began to emerge. In 1944, *Applied Anthropology* published "Some Perspectives in Applied Anthropology," in which Laura Thompson worried that anthropology's commitment to serving the war had irrevocably altered the course of the discipline. Thompson was concerned that some wartime anthropologists had become "social engineer[s] whose legitimate concern is not with ultimate aims or goals but with instrumentalities" (Thompson 1944: 12). She did not question the just cause for which American troops and anthropologists were fighting, but she did question whether or not

in the long run is the concept of the social engineer adequate to the nature and scope of the actual basic problems which the applied anthropologist in a country oriented toward the democratic way of life may be expected
to elucidate?

   This question is, of course, one facet of the fundamental issue which
faces all the social sciences in the United States and elsewhere, as the application of the results of research to practical social problems develops precision
in formulation and methodology. To state the matter bluntly for the sake of
clarity, are practical social scientists to become technicians for hire to the
highest bidder? Or are they to develop a code of professional ethics which
will orient their work toward the formulation and implementation of explicit, long-range goals? (Thompson 1944: 12)

Thompson's critique that the war was transforming anthropologists into "technicians for hire to the highest bidder" had links to Boas's complaint during
the First World War that anthropologists had "prostituted science," but Boas
and Thompson examined separate issues relating to anthropology and warfare.
Boas's complaint focused on how the duplicitous nature of espionage corrupted
the process of science, while Thompson argued that making anthropology subservient to the needs of war administrators was anti-democratic and needed
ethical oversight. Thompson's critique went beyond the Boasian challenge that
science was corrupted by duplicity of proclaimed purpose. Thompson asked
whether social science was corrupted by the very process of being let out for hire.
She pressed anthropologists to consider clarifying where the limits of ethical
anthropology lay. While Thompson's wartime concerns were published in *Applied Anthropology*, they were ignored by the SFAA.[23]

   Thompson was not alone in feeling concerns about the propriety of harnessing anthropology to the task of warfare. Even before Gregory Bateson joined the
OSS, he was troubled by the ethical questions raised by anthropologists using
their anthropological intelligence as a weapon in a war where anthropologists
could expect to have little say in what was done with their research. In 1941 he
wrote that the war

   is now a life-or-death struggle over the role which the social sciences shall
   play in the ordering of human relationships. It is hardly an exaggeration to
   say . . . this war is ideologically about just this—the role of the social sciences.
   Are we to reserve the techniques and the right to manipulate peoples as the
   privilege of a few planning, goal-oriented and power hungry individuals to

whom the instrumentality of science makes a natural appeal? Now that we
have techniques, are we in cold blood, going to treat people as things? Or
what are we going to do with these techniques? (quoted in Yans-McLaughlin
1986a: 209)

Bateson was conflicted about what could become of anthropology and society if
the war were to turn anthropology into a field of manipulation. Like Thompson,
Bateson set aside some of these questions and used his anthropological skills to
fight the war.

After the war, John Embree wrote of controversies that arose when anthropology was applied to the war effort. He observed,

> Within the discipline of anthropology many people feel that applied anthro-
> pology is not proper work for an anthropologist, that, in lending his services
> to a government agency administrating other peoples, he is using his knowl-
> edge to aid in their oppression, or that if the program is not one of subjuga-
> tion, he will still have to compromise himself by participating in some
> activities he knows to be mistaken.
>
> Both these objections have a certain validity. In helping a military gov-
> ernment to govern a population without bloodshed one is aiding a dictator-
> ship to avoid trouble with the masses, but—and this is the applied anthro-
> pologist's point of view—one is also helping to avoid the sorts of decisions
> that not only will lead to more trouble and expense for the administrators,
> but that will also lead to greater harshness of treatment of the people by
> their temporary governors. (Embree 1946: 494)

Concerns that some applied anthropology programs could be aiding in oppression and subjugation were infrequently publicly raised during the war. Most
anthropologists were too busy fighting fascism and totalitarianism to worry
about how the methods used in this necessary fight could in the long run be
supporting forms of the very tyranny they were fighting. It is understandable that
anthropologists in the midst of such a struggle would not stop to consider these
issues, but even at the war's end, when the SFAA formulated its first ethics code, it
chose to ignore the issues raised by Thompson during and after the war. But
during the war, the needs of total war dismissed such concerns as luxuries that
interfered with America's fight for survival.

PROFESSIONAL ASSOCIATIONS 37

American Anthropology at War

The most common estimates of American anthropologists' contributions to the war effort were that over half of American anthropologists were directly involved in war work while another quarter worked part time (Cooper 1947). This was a total war, and with time, American military and intelligence agencies recognized that anthropology could act as a useful weapon in a fight using every available resource. A few months after Japan's surrender, Father John Cooper appeared before the U.S. Senate's Committee on Military Affairs which investigated ways to improve the mobilization of national resources. Cooper testified that anthropology had played a central role in the war, but that when the United States entered the Second World War, it soon

> keenly realized that we were caught with only meager fragments of the factual knowledge we needed about so many peoples of the world. The anthropological staffs of universities and museums were hastily stripped to help provide such knowledge with which their discipline and their field studies have given them familiarity. These anthropologists were able to give invaluable assistance. But there were not enough of them to provide more than a fraction of the information needed. In many cases one or two anthropologists had to be depended upon to give the needed first-hand information on whole great cultures, tasks which to have fulfilled adequately would have required a score or more of anthropological specialists. (U.S. Senate 1946: 778–79)

By mid-1943, virtually every wartime agency had an anthropologist or two on staff. As the American war intensified, anthropologists began to play a larger role. Dozens of federal agencies used anthropologists. Some of this work drew on specific anthropological skill sets, while other positions drew on the general academic skills of scholars who happened to be anthropologists.[24] The diversity of war work undertaken by American anthropologists is staggering, but it is also surprising to find aspects of the war, such as the battlefield uses of Code Talkers, where anthropologists' talents seemed to have natural uses but were ignored or under-used.[25] While this book focuses on the activities of some anthropologists at a dozen wartime agencies, the contributions of anthropologists to the war were much broader than all of those described in detail here. To give an idea of the scope and impact of this work, a sample description of the wide range of these activities is presented later.

Many anthropologists were shuffled between branches of military and intelligence agencies. Some assignments drew directly on anthropological skills; others did not. Alexander Spoehr earned his Ph.D. just as America entered the war, and he first joined the Marine Corp Reserve, then the Army Corp of Engineers, and finally the Naval Reserve, where he was a navigator searching for pilots shot down in the Pacific. After the war, while back at the Field Museum of Natural History, Spoehr "was persuaded by the Navy to join a team working in the Pacific to convince holdout Japanese soldiers to surrender," and his war experiences in the Pacific refocused his academic specialty to focus on Oceania (Gleach 2002b: 194).

The archaeologist George Agogino began the war with "the Signal Corps where, after intensive training, he was put on detached service to New Guinea through the effort of Dr. [J. Alden] Mason, he spent the rest of the war years as an investigator for military intelligence" (Haynes 2004: 299).[26] Conrad Arensberg was in the U.S. Army's Military Intelligence Division from 1942 to 1946, but he also developed applied anthropology techniques while consulting at the Poston camp where Japanese Americans were interned (Darnell 2002c). David Aberle administered psychological tests and interviewed patients at an Army psychiatric clinic (Donald 2006: 264).[27] John Gillin worked for the Board of Economic Warfare at the U.S. Embassy in Lima, Peru (Gleach 2002c: 198). The archaeologist Paul Reiter worked as a research associate at the Massachusetts Institute of Technology's Chemical Warfare Service Development Laboratory, where he designed such new devices as an ergonomically adapted flame-thrower carrier (Kluckhohn 1954: 1085). Several anthropologists worked for secret intelligence agencies such as the oss and the Federal Bureau of Investigation's Special Intelligence Service, at times adopting false covers for covert operations in foreign countries (see chapters nine and ten).

At the Office of Economic Warfare, Clellan Ford worked under the directorship of the economist Max Millikan, future assistant director of central intelligence for the cia (see Price 1998b).[28] John Peabody Harrington's broad linguistic abilities were drafted to read and censor foreign mail written in assorted foreign languages. Wesley Bliss applied anthropology at the Army Intelligence Division; Mortimer Graves, at the Army Special Training Program; and Hallam Movius, at Air Force Intelligence. When Demitri Shimkin brought Omer Stewart to join him at the U.S. Army Military Intelligence Division Office of the Chief of Staff, he told his superiors that "French and ethnogeography could be of use in Intelligence" (Howell 1998: 127). Stewart "used to lecture to the secretary of war every morning and tell him how the war was going, then he would go inform the president. Other duties in Military Intelligence took [him] to South Africa and the Middle East as an employee of Remington Rand" (Howell 1998: 127–28). The G-2 anthropologists Weston La Barre and George Devereaux "prepared to para-chute in Indo-China behind enemy lines until the commander of the Asiatic Theatre vetoed the drop and put them on staff duty in Chungking" (Howell 1998: 174–75). At the ONI, Frederica de Laguna monitored intelligence developments at the Alaskan and German desks, and Richard Francis Starr directed the publica-tion of *Foreign Uniforms, Insignia, Comparative Rank* (Darnell 2002b: 203; Owen 1996: 5).[29]

The Strategic Bombing Survey used psychologists, anthropologists, and other social scientists to analyze the impact of Allied bombings on enemy military and civilian populations. Alexander Leighton, Alfred Métraux, Clyde Kluckhohn, Conrad Arensberg, Frederick Hulse, and Norman Tindale contributed to the survey's reports.[30] The Strategic Bomb Survey project combined quantitative and qualitative analysis to provide military strategists with specific data on the impact of various bombing strategies at the war's end. Hulse and other anthropologists working on the Strategic Bombing Survey used their anthropological skills to isolate individual attitudes toward bombings in relation to socioeconomic and family positions:

> From 1942 until 1945 [Frederick] Hulse served in the Office of Strategic Services, which used his Japanese expertise. In October 1945 he became a member of the Civilian Morale Division of the U.S. Strategic Bombing Survey. The team spent four months in Japan collecting information on morale and attitudes during and after the war by means of polling a random sample of 3,000 Japanese, interviews with selected individuals, and review of available documentary evidence. Analysis took the next five months. Hulse made the most of this opportunity to utilize and expand on his Japanese anthropology. A half dozen articles published between 1946 and 1948 were exclusively cultural anthropology, with titles like "Status and function as factors in the structure of organizations among the Japanese" and "Conven-tion and reality in Japanese culture." Quite a leap for a physical anthropolo-gist. The articles were read and used in their day, and were thoughtful and balanced, in no way marred by racism or other manifestations of wartime feelings as was some—not most—social science writing at that time. (Giles 1996:181)

The Office of War Information (OWI) used the skills of almost a dozen an-thropologists to better understand the Japanese enemy though culture and per-sonality studies (see chapter eight). This type of psycho-cultural profiling was among anthropology's best-known contributions to the war, and after the war this work flourished in various academic and government agencies. It was during the Second World War that anthropologists first considered nation-states as objects of anthropological analysis (Neiburg and Goldman 1998: 56). Sometimes these culture and personality studies were used to try to understand and control domestic populations. Margaret Mead, Ruth Benedict, Gregory Bateson, Clyde Kluckhohn, Gregory Gorer, Ralph Linton, and Rhoda Métraux served on the American Psychological Association's Society for Psychological Study of Social Issues Committee on Morale (see Neiburg and Goldman 1998: 57; Watson 1942: vi). Bateson described the work of this group as following the logic that, "since all western nations tend to think and behave in bipolar terms, we shall do well, in building American morale, to think of our various enemies as a single hostile entity. The distinctions and gradations which intellectuals might prefer are likely to be disturbing" (Bateson 1942b:89). Perhaps the most controversial instances of anthropologists' attempting to understand and control domestic populations involved the management of interned Japanese Americans in the War Relocation Authority's camps (see chapter seven).

To solve problems of the war's farm-labor shortages, the U.S. Department of Agriculture's War Board empowered the Extension Service and County Defense Council to study labor practices and to coordinate solutions to farm-labor problems. Walter Goldschmidt studied problems of coordinating farm production in California, and he evaluated the use of labor scouts and other means of keeping agricultural production under way (Goldschmidt 1943; Goldschmidt and Page 1943).[31] Over the course of three weeks, Margaret Mead wrote *And Keep Your Powder Dry*, a brief book devoted to focusing America's morale and attention on the needs of the war (Mead 1942). During the war, Mead designed curricula for the Army Specialized Training Program, and in her role as the executive director of the Committee on Food Habits of the National Research Council, she studied American food preferences (Mead 1943a). In 1943, Mead went to England to study cross-cultural misunderstandings occurring between American and British troops working together in the war.

The Bishop Museum anthropologist Kenneth Emory held classes on tropical island survival skills. Emory later taught jungle survival skills to GIs at army combat school, where "a full-scale jungle living program was established by the army, and Mr. Emory was given carte blanche to arrange the place, the staff, and the curriculum. Sites in Kaaawa and Punaluu on windward Oahu were chosen, and a training staff of six (later twelve) Army and Navy men was organized under Mr. Emory's direction" (Embree 1946:485; see also Mann 1991). Emory taught trainees how to gather and prepare wild foods and "how to get along with native peoples." In all, the program trained over 350,000 soldiers. The Bishop Museum published Emory's *South Sea Lore*, as a pocket-size, seventy-five-page book endorsed by Major-General Ralph C. Smith, as "invaluable to any man who may have to live and fight in the islands of the Pacific. This booklet shows the American soldier how to live more comfortably and keep in better physical condition than his enemy" (Emory 1943: 3). The Navy also used Ralph Linton at Columbia to teach classes on "Primitive Society" and Felix Keesing at the University of Hawaii to teach courses on colonial administration (Embree 1946:490). At Stanford University, Keesing also trained GIS preparing to battle in Indonesia. One of Keesing's young students was the future Southeast Asia scholar George Kahin, who later humorously recalled that Keesing

> had been told by Washington to get us familiar with the terrain on Sabang Island of the north-western tip of Sumatra, as that was where we would probably attack. So we went through exercises, map-reading, studying the terrain of Sabang Island as best we could. Keesing's assignment was supposed to be for a month, but no new instructions came through, so he had to continue focusing on Sabang for nine months. He implored Washington for something else to do, but they just told him to keep on attacking Sabang Island. So week after week we attacked it from every possible angle. Thirty years later, in 1971, when visiting Indonesia with my wife Audrey, I finally went there. As we landed I was still able to tell her everything about Sabang's geography, pointing out every ridge and stream and route across the island. (Kahin 2003: 12)

Anthropologists had much to offer military and intelligence agencies, but there were difficulties in locating and matching individuals and their skill sets with agencies that needed their particular talents. Five months before America's entry into the war, the Office of the Coordinator of Information was established to compile information on individuals' skills for use in the likely coming war. As the war progressed various governmental agencies compiled lists of scholars' linguistic or geographic expertise, and several anthropological consortiums devised databases listing individual anthropologists and their areas of expertise, as well as databases organizing vast amounts of cultural information that might be of use to military and intelligence agencies waging war throughout the world. The most significant of such anthropological consortiums were the Institute of Human Relations, the Office of the Chief of Naval Operations, and the Ethnogeographic Board (see chapter 5).

Anthropologists contributed to the Army Special Forces Special Service Division's Pocket Guide booklet series. Henry Field (who along with Anne Fuller produced early guides) later claimed that, while discussions of the usefulness of such regional guides were occurring, a sergeant with an important message for headquarters had become lost in a crowded street in India. In frustration,

> exasperated by a stationary white cow, apparently deaf to the strident screams of his horn, the sergeant fired his revolver. The cow fell into bovine Nirvana. The crowd, wildly incensed that one of their sacred cows was shot by a foreigner, surrounded the jeep and yelled threats at the sergeant. By a show of arms, a passing M.P. patrol rescued him in the nick of time.
>
> The cable, bearing details of this incident, turned the tide of opinion in favor of a series of G.I. Handbooks (Field 1982: 6).

These four-by-five-inch Pocket Guides presented thirty- to seventy-five page summaries of a region's geographical, historical, political, and cultural features. Pocket Guides were produced for regions including West Africa (SSD 1943a), Burma (SSD 1943b), India (SSD 1943c), New Caledonia (SSD 1943d, written by Felix Keesing; see Embree 1946: 486), the Netherlands East Indies (SSD 1943e), Egypt (SSD 1943f), and North Africa (SSD 1943g).

These Pocket Guides had a wide range of quality and coverage and were written at about a middle-school or high-school reading level. Some guides appear to have had limited or no anthropological input. At their best, these guides prepared soldiers for the culture shock they would experience as they interacted with people who might otherwise seem irrational. At their worst, the guides promulgated racial stereotypes or oversimplified cultural contexts in demeaning ways.

One of the best of these booklets was *A Pocket Guide to West Africa*, written by William Bascom and Ralph Bunche (SSD 1943a; see Crowley and Dundes 1982: 465). Bascom and Bunche drew on their anthropological training and knowledge of West Africa to provide a concise cultural overview of the region and to advise soldiers on how to act and what to expect if deployed there. Bascom and Bunche stressed that American GIS needed to leave American racial views at home, writing,

> Though darker than most people you know, and differing considerably in the way they eat, dress, and live, the West Africans are pretty much like people all over the world. In town, there are officials, clerks, artisans, laborers, and hired help; in the countryside, peasant farmers. They marry,

raise families, drink the native brews, enjoy their ceremonies and parties, react to hardship as you do. Like white folks, the West Africans have upper and lower classes and it would be a serious mistake to assume that all Africans are alike or that they all think and act alike. (SSD 1943a: 4)

Bascom and Bunche wrote that soldiers expressing racial intolerance were playing into Hitler's hand, because "race prejudice against the African or against American Negro troops in Africa would be a good way to turn the African against us. Everyone is entitled to his own prejudices but it would be only sensible for those who have them to keep them under cover when such high stakes as the war and men's lives are on the table. None of us wants to aid Hitler" (SSD 1943a: 11).

Bascom and Bunche contextualized West African work habits, pressed soldiers to respect the religious differences they encountered ("their gods are as real to them as ours is to us"), and described the practice of bridewealth and assured the soldiers that "the payment is less a purchase price than compensation to the parents for the girl's care until maturity, and then for their loss of her labor on the tribal land" (SSD 1943a: 4, 25). They also advised soldiers to adapt to the cultural worlds they found themselves in:

When you deal with Africans, it is important to understand two facts about the way their life is organized. First family ties and obligations involve much larger groups of relatives than what we mean by a "family." These ties may cause a man to turn down a good job out-of-town, even when he could take his own wives and children with him. Second, the eldest man and woman usually act as head of their group.

It is important to work through these customary and accepted channels. This means dealing with the chiefs, elders and family heads, and gaining the friendship of the priests, medicine men, and other influential people. (SSD 1943a: 26–27)

Other Pocket Guides were less nuanced, but even these gave soldiers basic useful advice about things, like not approaching Egyptian women (SSD 1943f), not concluding that East Indian men holding hands are homosexuals (SSD 1943e), and advising soldiers in India to barter in the marketplace (SSD 1943c). The worst guides had no anthropological input and contained things like overviews of the specific "races" troops might encounter. In the *Pocket Guide to the Philippines*, Lieutenant-Commander G. V. Hurley of the U.S. Army's Enemy Bases Section catalogued the various groups that soldiers might encounter. Differences in "Moro tribal organization" were presented with such categorical statements as,

"[The Lanaos] are among the fiercest of all of the Moro tribes"; the Sangils are an "unimportant tribe that has been greatly diluted with pagan blood"; and the Samals are "among the world's best small boatmen" (Hurley 1944: 8–9). As a crocodilian prophylaxis, Hurley recommended that swimmers "drop a hand grenade or two into the water before swimming" (Hurley 1944: 20).

Some guides provided word lists for soldiers. Some had guides to cultural ways of measuring time or weights and measures (ssd 1943d) or guides to dining customs (ssd 1943g). Each guide included an historical overview and ended with a list of basic things soldiers should and should not do—such as, "Don't offer Moslems pork," or "Follow your host's lead when invited out to dinner. If he eats with his fingers, follow suit" (ssd 1943c: 53).

The war changed the lives of all who survived it. Some young anthropologists and future GI Bill–educated anthropologists saw areas of the world as soldiers to which they would later return to study. Others saw their future careers as anthropologists affected by their immersion into military culture. Omer Stewart became aware of the harshness of American racial prejudice against black troops, and while on assignment at the Pentagon, he became ashamed of the levels of bigotry he observed. His time in the army convinced him that "the greatest need in the United States was to reduce this race prejudice and to popularize what I knew as an anthropologist: there was no evidence to support any notion of a superior or inferior race" (quoted in Howell 1998: 128).

Experiences in military culture produced various anthropological responses. David Schneider published articles in *Psychiatry* drawing on his experiences in army culture. His first article analyzed the culture of the army clerk (Schneider 1946); his second described the social dynamics of physical disability in army basic training (see Schneider 1947; see also Schneider 1995: 19). Schneider observed displays of aggression and power among army clerks, noting that "joking relationships are commonly observed and regarded as ideal. They imply closeness without actual involvement because of the ritual and stereotyped nature of the relationship, and frequently provide the basis for social intercourse where it might otherwise be absent" (Schneider 1946: 124). Edward T. Hall became fascinated with the ways that armies gave inductees new identities. Hall observed, "All armies have much in common, such as *a completely separate identity from the civilian population*, wastefulness, centralized hierarchies, and emphasis on discipline, yet armies are still distillates of the essential elements of the culture from which they spring" (Hall 1992: 155).

The war provided some anthropologists with fieldwork opportunities while withdrawing it from others. W. Lloyd Warner and a team of fieldworkers studied the impact of the war on a conservative Midwestern town. This fieldwork found the Midwest simultaneously frightened by the war and invigorated by the intense social solidarity, and the fieldworkers documented changes in "restless" veterans as they returned from war and tried to reestablish normal lives (Warner 1949: 266–86). The biologist Alvin Chan was stationed in the Aleutian Islands at the Dutch Harbor Naval Operating Base from 1942 to 1944, where he undertook extensive archaeological excavations of prehistoric habitation sites (originally unearthed by the excavating of foxholes)—shipping large quantities of artifacts to the Field Museum and the American Museum of Natural History (McCartney 1998). Roy Barton's 1940 ethnographic fieldwork in the Philippines ended with the Japanese army's occupation of the Luzon. Barton was interned by the Japanese army for three years first at Camp Holmes and later at Los Banos. Like that of other prisoners of war, Barton's health suffered in the camps: His weight dropped from 188 to 135 pounds, and he contracted a series of diseases that appear to have contributed to his early death in 1947 (see Price 2001a).[32] Charlotte Gower was interned by Japanese forces while studying Chinese culture in Hong Kong; after her release, Gower served in the Marine Corps' women's reserve and the OSS, and after the war she served in the CIA (Lepowsky 2000).[33]

Anthropologists with any experience living in Japan were sought by multiple military and intelligence agencies. The Harvard-trained anthropologist Gordon T. Bowles was born and raised in Japan by Quaker missionaries. Bowles's religious beliefs led him to avoid all combat-related war activities, first serving at the Board of Economic Warfare, and later in the State Department's Post-War Programs Committee's Division of Science, Education, and Art (Mayo 1982: 4, 29–30).[34] Bowles used his knowledge of Japanese society to try to influence American plans to redesign the Japanese educational system—though many of his ideas were rejected as being too accommodating to prewar Japanese cultural beliefs and practices (see, e.g., Mayo 1982: 46, 106, n. 43). Bowles lectured to the Civil Affairs Training Schools (CATS), educating military personnel about the cultural and historical forces that they would need to understand to occupy Japan successfully in the postwar period (Mayo 1982: 51).

In 1926, after living as a missionary in Japan for five years, Douglas Haring had been purged from the American Baptist Foreign Mission Society after a trial convened by the board found him guilty of "doctoral heresy." Haring held a master's degree in sociology, and his Japanese background led him to earn a doctorate in anthropology at Columbia University—where he studied under Boas, Spier, and his childhood playmate Ruth Benedict (Bowles 1964: 4–5). After the attack on Pearl Harbor, Haring, "traveled extensively in the United States to lecture about Japan in Army camps," and in 1944, Haring taught about Japanese culture in Harvard's CATS program as a visiting lecturer and was a consultant to the assistant secretary of the army (Bowles 1964: 7).

Problems linked to specific wartime needs led anthropologists to undertake a variety of research projects. Harry Shapiro used his forensic-anthropology skills to help identify the human remains of soldiers killed in battle (Marks 2002: 127). At the Peabody Museum, Alice Brues and E. A. Hooton used anthropometric measurements to improve uniforms, oxygen masks, and other equipment designed for use when flying at high altitudes (Dufour 1989: 24). Wartime global rubber shortages led Alan Holmberg to search for rubber sources in South America during the war, and he worked for the Rubber Development Corporation in Washington, D.C. (Steward 1948b: xxv).

Gitel Poznanski Steed began the war at Yale's Institute of Human Relations compiling information for George Murdock's growing Cross Cultural Survey (Berleant-Schiller 1989: 333). She remained at the Institute of Human Relations until 1943, when she began working on Frances McClernan's and Ursula Wasserman's project documenting Nazi crimes against Jews. This group published *The Black Book: The Nazi Crime against the Jewish People*, which meticulously documented Nazi atrocities while they were occurring. The activist lawyer and historian Max Radin (brother of Paul Radin) wrote the introduction to *The Black Book*, framing its detailed account during the war as preparation for charges to be brought against the Nazis at a later date. Following Radin's forceful introduction, Steed and five other contributors wrote more than five hundred pages of detailed accounts of Nazi atrocities, with chapters on conspiracy, Nazi anti-Jewish legislation, and the strategy of decimation, annihilation, resistance, and justice (Black Book Committee 1976 [1946]).

Steed's chapter on the Nazis' strategy of decimation was a 135 page account describing how Nazi laws, policies, and actions were designed to annihilate the Jews. Using newspaper accounts, correspondence, and legislative documents, she documented how the Nazis were methodically starving the Jews to death or into weakened states. That the "rations allowed to Jews and non-Jewish Poles in [occupied] Poland," Steed wrote, "were 'inadequate to maintain life' was reported by the Inter-Allied Information Committee in London, which cited official figures for 1941. Instead of the daily 2,400 calories necessary for subsistence, the food rations allowed to Poles did not contain more than 680 calories daily and those to Jews no more than 400" (Poznanski 1946: 221).

Not all anthropological contributions to the war effort were welcomed. In 1943, Ruth Benedict and Gene Weltfish were commissioned by the Public Affairs

Council to write a pamphlet presenting basic biological and anthropological arguments against racism. The pamphlet was designed to lessen the dangerous racial tensions between segregated units of the military. Benedict and Weltfish patiently argued that the differences between racial groups needed to be viewed with cultural relativism—that ethnic, racial, and religious groups were simply different, not inferior or superior to one another. The pamphlet was published as *The Races of Mankind* and was to be used in army training schools and distributed to United Service Organizations (USO) centers across the country, until it was withdrawn from circulation after Senator Andrew J. May and other Dixiecrats publicly condemned the report for offending the belief that whites were inherently intellectually superior to blacks (Benedict and Weltfish 1943; Price 2004a:113–130; cf. Weltfish 1945).[35]

As the Federal Bureau of Investigation (FBI) undertook extensive background investigations of thousands of Americans undertaking sensitive war work, hundreds of anthropologists had FBI files created during the war, and a significant number of these files continued to grow and accumulate dossiers on political activities during the McCarthy period after the war (see Price 2004a). When the FBI investigated Ruth Benedict to issue her clearance for her war work, they interviewed a half-dozen of her colleagues. The FBI's synopsis of this investigation reads in part: "Associates assert applicant is a distinguished anthropologist of international standing, with excellent reputation, both personal and professional; very liberal in her views and associated with Communistic groups; however, they believe her patriotism is unquestioned. Dies Committee records indicate applicant's name appeared in *New Masses* and *Daily Worker* as signer of open letter urging release of certain Communists and anti-Fascists and she had signed telegram to the President urging action in behalf of labor union defendant."[36]

These background checks led the FBI in various directions. Gordon Hewes's knowledge of Japanese language made him an invaluable resource in the war, but before he could be cleared for classified work, the FBI had to interview his neighbors and acquaintances to understand what he was doing as he earned "his living as a translator of Japanese shortwave broadcasts."[37] The FBI inquiries sometimes had other uses after the war. For example, Jules Henry's background-investigation for his work at the Office for Emergency Management led the FBI to interview Margaret Mead, Ruth Benedict, and other anthropologists. These files were later used by the FBI as the bureau investigated the leftist political associations of Henry's sister, Ernestine Baum, during the McCarthy period.[38] These spur investigations were common, and they frequently had dire consequences after the war.

While Oscar Lewis was driving to Mexico as a wartime field representative of the National Indian Institute, his car was searched at the Laredo border crossing. After U.S. Customs officials found Marxist literature in his car, the FBI began an extensive background investigation. Although the FBI found no evidence that Lewis was a communist, this investigation created ongoing problems for him during the war and after.[39] Elman Service's FBI background investigation raised concerns about his loyalty because he had fought fascism in the Spanish Civil War, and while Service was not granted wartime security clearances because of this, the FBI learned that his prewar battle experience had earned him the respect of all in his platoon.[40]

Paul Fejos and his wife, Inga Arvad, were investigated by the FBI during the war, as was Fejos's boss, Axel Wenner-Gren.[41] Arvad was a former Danish beauty queen who had been heralded by the Nazis as representing the Aryan ideal of beauty. She became the focus of massive FBI surveillance during and after her wartime liaisons with Joseph Kennedy's sailor son, John F. Kennedy.[42] Axel Wenner-Gren's contacts with Nazis, his ownership of Electrolux and the Swedish division of the Bofors Armament Works, and accusations that he used his yacht, the *Southern Cross*, to secretly refuel Nazi submarines at sea brought extensive FBI surveillance and investigations that blacklisted Wenner-Gren and complicated his efforts to come to the United States during and after the war (Ross 1999).[43] The FBI's investigations found no evidence that the *Southern Cross* had been used to refuel German submarines or to directly support the war in any way.

During the war, and for years afterward, Axel Wenner-Gren's past financial dealings with Nazis placed him on the State Department's blacklist of individuals prohibited from entering the United States because of his suspected dealings with Nazis (see Ross 1999). After the war, Wenner-Gren's public reputation connected him with Nazis: As *Time* magazine observed upon his death in 1961, he had "donated nearly $50 million to libraries and laboratories around the world, but never quite stilled the doubts aroused by his suspected dealings with the Nazis in World War II."[44]

The establishment of the Viking Fund, later to become the Wenner-Gren Foundation, helped Wenner-Gren curry favor with American officials as he strove to gain admission to the United States while shifting his public name from accusations of or associations with Nazi financial dealings. While the FBI's decades of investigation of Wenner-Gren found him to have profited from the Nazis' dealings with Bofors, the FBI never established that he had conducted secret transactions for the Nazis with Krupp.[45]

Applied and Theoretical Considerations of War

Anthropology was not unique; the war transformed all of American life. As the depressed American economy shifted toward a command economy producing the hardware of war, anthropological practices and theories were transformed by the needs of war. Technology transformed battlefronts. Aviation innovations, battleship production, radar, armored tank and troop transports, encryption and decryption methods, artillery- and aerial-bombardment advancements, and radio-broadcast developments all changed the face of war. Allied and Axis forces fought through captured or liberated lands, straining resources for the war effort. These changing conditions of warfare made demands on anthropologists who adapted to the needs of the war, and these adaptations transformed the field in ways that did not end with the war.

While motivations of nationalism, internationalism, racial equality, patriotism, and anti-totalitarianism naturally led a variety of American anthropologists into battle both as citizens and as citizens-as-anthropologist-soldiers, these new roles changed American anthropologists and anthropology. The war harnessed social scientists in such new roles as analysts, propagandists, foot soldiers, officers, and spies. As anthropologists directed their efforts at populations both within and outside the boundaries of their nations, and their regions of study were transformed from areas once regarded as obscure hinterlands into strategic battle regions, anthropologists' cultural and linguistic expertise came into high demand.

American anthropology's most significant scientific and political contribution during the first half of the twentieth century was the development of the Boasian critique of the concept of race. Thus, many American anthropologists found the Nazis to be an enemy of the core principles of anthropology. Some anthropologists' war service derived from their anthropological activism, when

> the anti-Nazi activism of Boasian anthropologists led them inexorably into direct involvement as the ideological struggle became a military one. In this context, there was no fundamental division among American anthropologists over United States participation in World War II. Although the younger generation of leaders of the profession came from cultural backgrounds much more central to the "old Americanism" tradition that had the earlier Boasians, both were at one in their opposition to Nazism. (Stocking 1976:35)

Few anthropologists had second thoughts about the ethics of applying anthropology to warfare; those few who did did not linger long over these concerns. The

Nazis were a fundamental threat to humankind, and they needed to be stopped by any means available.

With its Committee on Anthropology and the War Effort, the AAA advised military bodies. This consultant role brought the AAA into new territory that went beyond political advocacy to an active covert advisory role. The SFAA was more actively linked to the war effort, as it was organized by scholars who took it for granted that anthropology should be involved in social change. Though there was some division among members about the desirability of the roles that anthropology should play in pushing particular programs in a democratic society, "the progressivist impulse toward social engineering now seemed to be running very strong, and was paralleled by what was in fact a more enduring push toward a 'scientific' anthropology" (Stocking 1976: 36).[46]

The war shifted American anthropologists' attention to specific cultures and problems as it taught them to focus on questions presented to them by others. More significantly, the war birthed a new form of applied anthropology that sought not only to understand culture, but to *manipulate* it. Such developments were logical in a time of total warfare when national interests pushed combatants to find and use all means against their enemies.

The quest for anthropological intelligence that could be used as a powerful war weapon was the McGuffin that launched the formal development of applied anthropology in America.[47] The political economy of warfare created conditions that fostered the development of a particular form of applied anthropology that focused more on directing desired behavioral or attitudinal outcomes than on, say, identifying and representing the needs and wants of a studied community. Just as military strategists developed new fighting tactics, or wartime engineers designed flame throwers to incinerate other humans hiding in caves, applied anthropologists strove to design means of getting people to perform specified acts. While other forms of applied anthropology developed after the war, dominant strains of applied anthropology remained that were devoted to similar forms of social engineering or coercion. It makes sense that applied anthropology during wartime tended to develop as a means of getting individuals or groups to adopt specified beliefs or to perform specified actions, but the application of such coercive means during times of peace raises troubling questions of the proper role of manipulation in a free society.

The predominant "managers know best" strains of applied anthropology were not the only applied forms to emerge after the war. In the decades after the war, Sol Tax advocated a less externally manipulative model of activist applied anthropology under the label "action anthropology," which sought not to control and motivate cultural groups in ways desired by external groups or would-be managerial forces but, instead, to use anthropology as a means of communicating the goals of these groups themselves (see Bennett 1996; Tax 1950, 1975). Tax intentionally sought to differentiate his efforts from those of mainstream applied anthropology by stressing an activist allegiance to the desires of the communities studied and served by anthropologists. Tax envisioned action anthropologists as having "no master" and not following the questions of employers, elites, or others who sought to manage culture (Tax 1975: 515).[48] But during the war and after, ethical questions underlying who determines who is served by applied anthropology were raised and avoided with disturbing regularity.

The war was the key catalyst sparking the formation of American applied anthropology. As John van Willigen synoptically observed, during World War II, "the numbers of anthropologists involved in practical anthropology increased dramatically. Following the war the amount of applied anthropology in Britain was greatly reduced, along with the size of the empire. In the United States what emerged was an anthropology of the Cold War in which the use of anthropology in the design and evaluation of international aid programs increased dramatically" (van Willigen 1996: s44). Van Willigen's view succinctly connects the development of applied anthropology, first, with the needs of the war, then with the needs of empires, and finally with the needs of neocolonial Cold War debtors.

Even during wartime, some anthropologists raised questions about the proper use of anthropological knowledge in warfare. The dissenting voices of anthropologists like Laura Thompson and John Embree remind us that, although the war brought widespread support, there were still concerns about the impact of so closely linking anthropology to warfare. It is significant that it was primarily anthropologists embedded in the burgeoning applied movement, and not those primarily identified with more theoretically inclined organizations like the AAA, who most directly and publicly expressed concerns about the dangers and shortcomings of harnessing anthropology to total warfare. The concerns of Embree and Thompson were not spun from a disengaged ivory tower: they came from the front lines of the applied movement.

It was practice, not theory, that made ethical questions so pressing. And while these concerns were largely ignored by most American anthropologists working for the war, they permeated anthropologists' war work, and they returned with more manifest thunder during the Cold War.[49]

But the experiences of American anthropologists during the Second World War were not unique, and Americans were not the only anthropologists who used their professional skills in the war; nor were they the only anthropologists to have their discipline transformed by the needs of warfare. Though the philo-sophical principles and economic conditions of the nations waging war varied, the contributions of citizen-scholars were in some ways similar. Allied and Axis anthropologists brought their professional abilities to the war effort in ways both similar and dissimilar to American anthropologists.

CHAPTER THREE

Allied and Axis

Anthropologies

Museums and exhibitions are used in Germany for propaganda purposes. Before entering the galleries of the ethnological museum in Hanover you have to pass through several
rooms devoted to the study of race. The first room is empty except for two busts. One [is]
of an Australian aborigine labeled "the lowest race," the other of a Nordic labeled "the
highest race." In the next room are shown photographs of racial types—half of them are
Jews, Negroes, American Indians and other types carefully selected to show sullen or
stupid expressions. The other half are handsome and smiling Nordics. The observer is
supposed to infer from their happy expressions the superiority of the Nordic race.
—LAURA THOMPSON (1938)

American anthropologists were not the only social scientists to contribute their
professional skills to the waging of the Second World War. Many Allied and Axis
anthropologists, psychologists, and sociologists applied their disciplinary expertise to the needs of war. To better contextualize American anthropologists' wartime experiences, this chapter briefly considers some of the wartime experiences
of Allied and Axis anthropologists.

As the world became engulfed in a state of total warfare, motivations of
nationalism, internationalism, racial supremacy, racial equality, fear, and anti-
totalitarianism drove anthropologists to join the fight as citizens and citizens-as-
anthropologist-soldiers. Anthropologists around the world found themselves directing their efforts at populations both within and beyond their nations' boundaries. In ways similar to the American experience, some European anthropologists applied their fieldwork-honed skills in foreign lands to war needs. In some
instances, these assignments structurally and functionally overlapped with the
interests of neocolonialism as some anthropologists administered or defended
outposts of the old empire.

E. E. Evans-Pritchard mixed ethnography with military service among the

Sanusi in Libya and later joined the British army campaigns in Ethiopia and Sudan. S. F. Nadel was deployed to the Sudan with the British Defense Force and later was the Secretary for Native Affairs in Eritrea (Freilich 1968: 2; Fortes 1957: xii). Meyers Fortes monitored economic and ideological developments in West Africa, where he found:

> The ideological currents stirred up by the war in Europe, which reach West Africa very quickly now through the British propaganda machinery have also stimulated [a] move to the Left. Ten years ago, for instance, many educated West Africans looked on Japan as a worthy model for imitation by a backward territory. Today Japan is in disrepute and the ideal is the U.S.S.R. The Atlantic Charter, the Philadelphia Charter, all our anti-Nazi Propaganda and our war-time slogans, as well as the solid social and economic achievements of Great Britain, from aircraft production to school meals, have been publicized and widely discussed among the African elite. (Fortes 1945: 209)

Expatriate fieldworkers living in the bush who knew the backcountry were invaluable resources. Louis Leakey smuggled arms for British intelligence to "anti-Italian guerrillas" along the Ethiopian border (McIntyre 1989: 224).

The war curtailed most opportunities for international fieldwork, but it occasionally brought unusual chances for research. When America entered the war, Bronislaw Malinowski was in the United States, where he was based at Yale and conducted fieldwork in Mexico (Kuper 1996: 18). The Nazi bombings of London brought new archaeological discoveries to light as the destruction cleared buildings and other structures, and "for the first time in hundreds of years great areas of the city [were] literally cleaned of all surface structures" (Phillips 1945: 476).[1]

Paper shortages in Britain and throughout Europe led to disruptions in the publication of anthropology books and journals not directly linked to the interests of warfare (Stocking 1985: 7). Much of the British university system was dislocated, and anthropologists compiled cultural and historical information to serve the war effort. As Britain came under attack, the London School of Economics,

> was evacuated to Cambridge, where [Raymond] Firth was also posted in a subcenter of the Naval Intelligence Division of the British Admiralty, which was run by the geographer H. C. Darby and which was responsible for the production of a series of geographical handbooks designed as tools for the contingency planning of naval operations throughout the world. Firth was the principal compiler and editor of the four volumes of this series which

relate to the Pacific islands. Originally issued as internal Admiralty documents in 1943, 1944 and 1945, they became more generally available ten years
later. Much of the information which they contain would still be hard to
obtain from any other source. (Leach 1979: 188)

Raymond Firth, a native New Zealander, was later appointed to be the first
secretary of the Colonial Social Science Research Council. The British Naval
Intelligence Division's Admiralty Handbooks were similar to those produced for
the Smithsonian's War Background Studies (see chapter 5), but their analysis was
notably more ethnographically, historically, and geographically sophisticated.[2]
These volumes provided British and Allied forces with invaluable information on
the natural resources and ethnohistory of the Pacific, as information was presented in a format that could be easily used by military administrators and
strategists coping with rapidly changing Pacific battle settings.

In some instances, the British military used anthropologists with ethnographic field experience to arm and train native peoples for guerrilla warfare.
At the war's onset, the British anthropologist Tom Harrisson was examining
working-class attitudes in Bolton as part of his study "Mass-Observation," studying what he jokingly called his "cannibals of Lancashire." After declining government requests to use his mass-observation data for domestic propaganda, Harrisson was recruited into the British forces' clandestine "Z Special Unit," where he
trained in the skills of guerrilla warfare and spycraft. Harrisson had already
participated in expeditions to the Artic and Melanesia, including a formative trip
to Borneo. The Z Special Unit was impressed with Harrisson's experience in
Borneo, and he was drafted to head a secret operation drawing on his anthropological and field linguistic skills (Harrisson 1959).

While preparing for the mission, Harrisson pored over articles from the
Sarawak Museum Journal describing explorations of Borneo's interior region of
the early 1900s and 1930s. With the Japanese occupation of Borneo, these peacetime writings by ethnographers, geographers, and biologists took on a military
significance. Harrisson was surprised to find records of agriculturally complex,
multi-cropping, irrigation-based, self-sufficient cultures in the remote regions of
central Borneo. The articles revealed important details about a poorly understood interior cultural system. His Australian colleagues had never "suspected an
upland plain, let alone irrigated rice fields and independent people living in para-
troop country, right inside Borneo" (Harrisson 1959: 182). Many of the articles
were by the Welsh anthropologist Edward Banks, curator of the Sarawak Museum.[3] The obscure *Sarawak Museum Journal* articles persuaded the Z Special

Unit to parachute to the interior for their operations rather than attempt a submarine operation that held high risks of Japanese capture or landing failure, as submarine-launched rafts in Borneo's cross tidal areas could easily pull landing parties out to sea.

In 1944, Harrisson and three other Z Special Unit members parachuted into Sarawak's interior to train a Kelabit guerrilla army to fight Japanese forces occupying coastal regions (Harrisson 1959). Harrisson and his comrades' airborne arrival produced an awed respect, as the Kelabits making first contact wanted to know if the Z Unit members were humans or supernatural beings (Harrisson 1959: 196). Harrisson identified his commando team to the Kelabits as "relatives" of the known explorers Edward Banks and R. O. Douglas. The Kelabits soon pledged their allegiance to Harrisson and the British forces.

The Z Special Unit set up their operations in a grand longhouse, and their radio station established encoded contact with forces in Darwin. Harrisson oversaw the distribution of British preciosities dropped from planes; the Kelabit women received shares of white parachute cloth, and the men were given explosives and small arms. The weapons brought a sense of elation among the Kelabits, as "the idea that white men might actually sanction a return to arms for murderous purposes seemed almost as marvelous as the para-facts of our appearance" (Harrisson 1959: 207). This sanctioning of violence against the Japanese created problems in the postwar period—a common problem in many of the lands touched by the war.

As more arms fell from the sky, one of Harrisson's chief duties involved reining in the use of the new weapons to settle old scores between neighboring groups. Harrisson and his Kelabit troops constructed a secret inland landing strip and undertook training exercises. The Kelabits proved loyal allies, with not a single person of an estimated one hundred thousand Kelabits betraying Harrisson's presence or his military operation to the Japanese, although in early 1945 a group of Tagals did betray some downed American airmen to the Japanese (Harrisson 1959: 230).[4]

The Kelabits supplied Harrisson and the Allied forces with detailed intelligence on the number of Japanese and positions they held throughout Sarawak. The Kelabits helped Harrisson's troops learn to negotiate their difficult native terrain. The interior jungles were treacherous, and the Z Special Unit's members and the Allied soldiers who arrived later had difficulty traversing the terrain. Harrisson observed, "There are few things simpler than getting lost anywhere in the interior of Borneo. Step two paces off the track, turn around, not notice a mark—and that may well be the last anyone hears of you" (Harrisson 1959: 200).

On June 10, 1945, more than twenty-five thousand Australian and seven thousand British and American troops landed at Brunei Bay. Harrisson coordinated attacks from the inland against Japanese strongholds. Some Kelabit fighters used poisoned blowpipes; others risked using rusted shotguns and small-caliber rifles. The fighting was fierce, and the operation was successful.[5] The Kelabits were adept fighters, and while Japanese forces moved nosily through the jungles in heavy boots, the Kelabits moved with barefoot stealth (Harrisson 1959: 215). Harrisson later reflected on the Kelabits and their neighbors' skills as great soldiers:

> The Kelabits made the best soldiers on the whole in these ambush and other guerrilla affairs. But then it came easily to them . . . by the fact that they were almost the last people in Borneo to come under any sort of outside control towards pacification and a quiet life. Indeed, they were one of the last such people in the world. Secondly, I would put the closely related Muruts, of the Trusan River and the interrelated Potoks, Milaus and other Kelabit-Murut groups who occupy a great section of the mountainous land and upland valleys in the northwest corner of what was then Dutch Borneo. It is often said, by the unthinking, that when such people become Christians they lose a great deal. They do. But one of the things that the small proportion who by that time were already Christian definitely had not lost was the martial quality and the aggressive trait. If anything, I would say that the Christian Muruts were just an edge better than the pagan ones in fighting. (Harrisson 1959: 250)

Armistice came to Sarawak with news of the American bombs being dropped on Hiroshima and Nagasaki. After the war, Harrisson continued his explorations of Borneo as the curator of the Sarawak Museum.

Edmund Leach also used his ethnographic expertise and linguistic skills to organize guerrilla fighters against Japanese forces. Leach began conducting ethnographic research in the Kachin highlands of Burma in August 1939, before the war brought the Japanese occupation of Burma and Germany began its European war. Like most anthropologists who engaged native populations during the war, Leach seldom wrote about the experiences after the war, yet this militarized fieldwork setting was the backdrop for his classic *Political Systems of Highland Burma*.

After England entered the war, Leach "signed up with the Burma Rifles and went into the field to Hpalang to conduct his research" (Tambiah 2002: 40). As a British army captain, Leach trained and led a ragtag band of Burmese resistance fighters of a unit known as the Northern Kachin Levies (NKL). Captain Leach and Australian Lieutenant-Colonel Gamble, who had spent some years in northern Burma, crash-landed in Kachin country in the summer of 1942 (Fellowes-Gordon 1957: 12).[6] Leach later reflected, "As far as the Burma army was concerned, I was odd man out, but I was potentially useful because I spoke the Kachin language and the Kachins were, in effect, the Gurkhas of the Burma army" (quoted in Kuper 1986: 377). Leach and Gamble organized the Kachins into efficient guerrilla bands, and by late 1942 they had been "joined by other officers and the unit reorganized itself in six companies. Recruiting gathered speed and soon the companies consisted of 125 levies each. A separate force of 'Home Guard' was formed, whose duty it was to stay in its villages growing rice as fast as it could, meanwhile reporting all Jap movements to Sumprabum. Like its English equivalent, it was expected to rally to the defense of its areas if the enemy launched a major attack" (Fellowes-Gordon 1957: 15).

According to Shizuo Maruyama, a Japanese war correspondent who traveled with the Japanese army in Burma as Leach was directing his Kachin irregulars, the Japanese military faced the same strategic problems as Leach. Maruyama wrote that, while trying to break the British army's intelligence network, the Japanese army faced many obstacles and

> could not carry out any activities without the help and cooperation of the ethnic minorities in the target area. We could expect of the local peoples not only information but also works such as constructing roads, guiding, and supply of foods for the task forces. To serve these purposes, we tried to placate local peoples through persuasion, provision of gifts (textiles, medicines, hatchets, kitchen knives and other types of knives, pans, kettles) . . . and helping people to deal with personal problems.
>
> One cannot carry out the placation of the local peoples without any preparations. As the first step, one needs to investigate the lifestyle of the target people. Specifically, one has to observe the shapes of their heads and faces, hair and skin colors, the size and figure of their bodies, clothes, foods, ways of cooking, language, religion, funeral and festivals, customs, houses, and the way of farming, and finally one has to grasp their ethnic character and their geographical distribution. It is also important to recognize the members of [major] families, kinship relations among them and the allocation of power in each community. By tracing these relationships, one can see the operation channels reveal themselves. (quoted in Nakao 2003: 241)

Leach's familiarity with Kachin culture gave the British army's counterinsurgency program an upper hand against the Japanese. As Maruyama observed, "The basic research for placation of local people was quite similar to anthropological research" (quoted in Nakao 2003: 242).

Leach's irregulars fought the Japanese with cunning and brutal guerrilla tactics. They set panji-stick booby traps (fire-hardened bamboo stakes coated in festering human excrement that inflicted lethal infections on the enemy) in brush along trails, then fired on approaching forces, causing them to dive for cover onto the hidden panji sticks (Webster 2003: 50). After Leach and Gamble acquired more arms for their NKL forces, "the NKL began refining their guerrilla tactics. While the panji-pointed ambushes continued, the Kachins also grew adept at making booby traps of trip wires attached to hollowed-out bamboo cups, beneath which they placed instantaneously fused hand grenades that had been pegged tightly to the earth. When the trip wire was pulled and the cup yanked free by an enemy footfall, the grenade's spring-loaded firing lever would pop upward, setting off the explosive and taking more casualties" (Webster 2003: 53).

When word of the high Japanese casualties reached U.S. Army General Joseph Stilwell, he did not believe that so few forces could have killed thousands of trained Japanese soldiers. Stilwell had one of the Kachin irregulars brought to him. When the NKL soldier was asked how he was so sure of the number of Japanese soldiers he and his fellow fighters had killed, "without missing a beat, the Kachin unhooked a bamboo tube that had been hanging on his belt. Then he pulled a stopper from the tube's top, and—turning the tube upside down—he dumped a pile of small blackish lumps onto the tabletop between himself and the general. The blackened lumps resembled bits of dried fruit: apricots perhaps or peaches" (Webster 2003: 55). When Stilwell asked what the objects were, he was told they were Japanese ears. "Divide all of these by two," he was told, "and you know exactly how many Japs I've killed" (Webster 2003: 55). Stilwell ordered the end of this practice.

Other Allied nations tapped anthropologists for domestic and foreign contributions to the war. In Australia, the anthropologist Norman Tindale joined the Royal Australian Air Force, where he advised the American military on strategic bombing, worked on decrypting Japanese codes, and used remarkable detective skills to examine the remains of wrecked Japanese aircraft to deduce which alloys were in short supply (Jones 1995).[7] Camilla Wedgwood supplied the military with information on the cultures of New Guinea, and Lieutenant-Colonel Ian Hogbin of the British Solomon Islands Defense Force became the Australian army's adviser on native problems (Gacs 1989: 368; Herskovits 1950: 82; Wise 1985: 151). A. P. Elkin designed Australian public-opinion surveys to measure war attitudes. His survey data were used to design propaganda tailored to the particular needs

and appetites of the Australian public (Gray 2005; Wise 1985: 149–50).[8] Donald
Thompson and W. E. H. Stanner advised the Australian army on how to best deal
with aboriginal peoples in the Northern Territory (Gray 2006: 157). The primary
use of Australian anthropologists during the war was "concerned with the employment of Aboriginal peoples as labourers, the formation of segregated united,
policy formulation, propaganda and the effects of the war on indigenous peoples" (Gray 2006: 178).

F. E. Williams and W. C. Groves helped write the booklet *You and the Native*
(Allied Geographical Section 1943; Gray 2006: 163), which was distributed by the
Allied Geographical Section, Southwest Pacific Area, to U.S. and Allied troops
deployed throughout the South Pacific. The booklet portrayed these "natives" as
primitives in awe of the white man's magic, claiming, "The native has always
looked up to the white man. He admires him because of the marvelous things
that white men at large can do—make electric torches, fly in aeroplanes, etc. . . .
He is also rather afraid of the white men, with all the power of their civilization
behind them. Therefore he is afraid of you. It is not too much to say that he
stands in awe of us. He thinks we are superior beings" (Brown 2004: 132).

After receiving a copy of *You and the Native*, Florence Murray, a reporter for
the *People's Voice* (the Chicago paper that proclaimed itself "America's greatest
Negro newspaper") sent a telegram to the War Department, inquiring whether
the pamphlet's instructions to white troops to " 'always maintain [their] position
or pose of superiority' in dealing with New Guinea" represented the "official
policy of the War Department" (Murray 1945: 3). Adjunct General J. A. Ulio
replied, "Since theatre commanders are in positions of greatest familiarity with
local conditions, the War Department leaves with them the determination of
policies which are most advisable in dealing with native populations. It is pre-
sumed that in this case the commander attempted to announce a policy which
would lead to the most efficient handling of a local situation" (Murray 1945: 3). As
I will discuss in chapter 5, American anthropologists contributed to similar
pamphlets designed to help troops better interact with the "native" peoples they
encountered.

Some anthropologists and other social scientists were arrested and imprisoned as the Nazi forces occupied Europe.[9] Anthropologists were among those
social scientists identified on Nazi lists of those to be apprehended and executed
(Peace 2005). The French sociologist Maurice Halbwachs died at Buchenwald
(Friedmann 1968: 304). Paul Ricoeur served in the French army, was captured by
German forces, and, during his five years in a German prison camp, translated a
work by Husserl into French. The prison camp was reportedly "a place of such

intellectual ferment—the many French scholars there organized lectures, classes and even examinations—that the Vichy government eventually accredited it as a degree-granting institution" (Fox 2005). Fernand Braudel spent most of the war as a prisoner of the Nazis in Lübeck prison, "where he wrote, more or less from memory, his work on the Mediterranean, ferreting out chapter after chapter to [Lucien] Febvre" (Wallerstein 1979: 70). V. Gordon Childe organized air-raid drills in Edinburgh and was listed on Nazi apprehension manifests because of his communist links and his explicit denunciations of Nazi Aryan racial myths (Peace 2005).[10]

In Belgium, the anthropologist Th. E. de Jonge was arrested by the Nazis, and at the war's end, C. Fraipont and J. Maes were convicted as Nazi collaborators. In the Netherlands, the anthropologists J. P. B. Josselin de Jong and B. J. O. Schrieke were imprisoned (Herskovits 1946: 301–303). After refusing to sign the Nazi loyalty oath as a student of social geography at the University of Utrecht, the future anthropologist Herbert Prins "joined the resistance movement, becoming Chief of Intelligence in the VIth Brigade (Veluwe). Following the 1944 Battle of Arnhem, he was secretly incorporated into the Second British Army as First Lieutenant in a Special Force Detachment and helped liberate his homeland" (Prins and Prins 2005: 22).

But the Nazi war machine did not just seek to imprison or kill anthropologists; it also relied on anthropologists to collect and provide vital information and to help rationalize the Nazis' worldview.

Axis Anthropology: German Wartime Anthropology

Most German anthropologists who survived the war later claimed that they had done as much as they could to resist the implementation of Nazi policies. Today, some discomfort remains among German anthropologists when discussing the roles played by German anthropology during the war. In 1946, Franz Termer maintained that, during the war, many German anthropologists recognized that anthropology "was in danger of becoming a servant of colonial propaganda. The wisest among us saw the danger and protected themselves against it. They did their best to have museums and research overlooked as otherwise might not have been the case" (quoted in Métraux 1948). Such claims whitewash the extent to which German wartime anthropology coalesced with the pseudo-scientific racial philosophy of the Nazi regime and the Holocaust.

Robert Proctor found that "anthropology as a profession fared rather well under the Nazis," and that few German anthropologists opposed the officially sanctioned views of racial science (Proctor 1988: 166). With the exception of a few anthropologists such as Karl Saller and Julius Ernest Lips, German anthropologists fell in line with Nazi racial views, and Proctor identified "disturbingly little evidence that anthropologists resisted the expulsion of Jews from Germany" (Proctor 1988: 164; Pützstück 1991: 416). Michael Burleigh found evidence of anthropologists willingly contributing to the needs of the Nazi state. He argues, "No one asked these scholars to put their knowledge at the service of the government: they did so willingly and enthusiastically. . . . Deportations, resettlements, repatriations and mass murder were not sudden visitations on high, requiring the adoption of some commensurate inscrutable, quasi-religious, meta-language, but the result of the exact, modern, 'scientific' encompassing of persons with card indexes, card-sorting machines, charts, graphs, maps and diagrams" (Burleigh 1988: 8).

Gretchen Schafft's groundbreaking *From Racism to Genocide: Anthropology in the Third Reich* documented how anthropometric research was adapted and used to justify Nazi policies and established that many German anthropologists performed their scientific tasks without meaningfully questioning the uses of the work. Schafft shows that, while many German scientists worked for the Nazis before and during the war, there was something fundamentally different about the Nazi anthropologists that distinguished them from the thousands of chemists, engineers, physicists, and other scientists who worked for the Nazis. While these other scientists contributed their science to the Nazi cause in very direct ways, they did not falsify research or propagate false science for these goals. The research measurements by Nazi medical doctors and chemists were at times unethical, but they were reliable—that is to say, they could withstand the scrutiny of repeated independent measurements to find similar results. The measurements and resulting analyses undertaken by Nazi anthropologists, by contrast, were not scientific in that their subjectivity and outright falsification could not withstand such scrutiny. The most notorious Nazi formally trained in anthropology was Josef Mengele (Schafft 2004: 183).

As the Nazis gained power, they narrowed the range of accepted academic scholarship by intimidating and removing anthropologists whose views diverged from party doctrine. Days after the Nazis came to power, Eugen Fischer was summoned before the Schutzstaffel (ss) Office of Population and Genetic Health, where he was interrogated and told he would be forced into early retirement if he did not recant earlier statements and research that indicated, among other things, that "racial mixing" could have positive outcomes (Schafft 2004: 71).

Fischer complied and became an active leader in the new Nazi academic world, although, as Schafft points out, many of his views (on such topics as "*Volk*," and "race"—or cultural and biological elements of identity) were already aligned with Hitler's visions of a socially engineered "pure state." This alignment of anthropological science with the desires of the state helped pave the way for Nazi racial laws, and Fischer later maneuvered to capitalize on his disciplinary "expertise" by selling his services to produce the racial certificates needed under the 1935 Nuremberg Race Laws (Schafft 2004: 73). Through such means, some anthropologists became pseudo-scientific legitimizers of Nazi ideology, lending their professional names to justify sterilization policies and laws promoting racial purity. Anthropologists at the Anthropological Institute of Vienna lent their skills and reputations to validating the racial-heredity certificates required by the Nazi regime (Schafft 2004: 17–27).

Nazi racial "science" was established with funding from German and American anticommunist philanthropists. American philanthropic institutions such as the Rockefeller Foundation funded Nazi racial scientists even after it became clear what the research was being used to rationalize. When she examined reports by the Nazis' Kaiser Wilhelm Institute for Anthropology, Human Genetics, and Eugenics from 1933, 1935, and 1940, for instance, Schafft found Rockefeller Foundation support had been used to fund aspects of Nazi racial "science." She criticized the foundation for not alerting the world "to the nature of German science and the racist folly" that German anthropology promulgated and that the foundation was funding (Schafft 2004: 251). Schafft further wondered what benefits were accruing to Rockefeller (and, I would add, his class interests) "by disregarding the early elimination of Jews and liberals from the [Kaiser Wilhelm Institute for Anthropology], as if it had no particular meaning" (Schafft 2004: 251). She quoted the anthropologist Eugen Fischer as reporting that the institute,

> on the basis of families, [was studying] instances of anomalies and illnesses as well as instances of special cognitive or other talents. They were studying twins to determine the biological influences of the life of the Volk. The staff members were giving lectures on race, genetic pathology, and eugenics as well as on conducting examinations. They were giving continuing education courses to doctors, teachers, and social workers. They were doing genetic counseling and determination of fatherhood. They were watching over the racial and genetic tendencies of the Volk, making the necessary suggestions for racial "measures" to the state and influencing lawmaking. (Schafft 2004: 77)

But even as awareness grew of the uses to which the Nazi administration was putting the research, the Rockefeller Foundation's funding continued for years, even after the passage of the 1935 Nuremberg Race Laws. Schafft cited correspondence between Rockefeller Foundation staff and researchers at the institute noting concern about how the racial "science" that was emerging was being used, but the funding continued until Germany's 1939 invasion of Poland (Schafft 2004: 79–80). The foundation refrained from criticizing the Nazi-linked research and "made no reference to the fate of the Jews in Germany, which was becoming more critical each year that the Hitler reign continued" (Schafft 2004: 80).[11] Through such avoidance and denial, the Rockefeller Foundation supported research aligned with the interests of the Nazis and the class interests represented by the foundation.

German archaeological excavations and interpretations were also shaped by the war needs of the Nazi regime. Some of these influences derived from the Nazi state's needs to justify territorial claims to Poland and Czechoslovakia as prehistoric homelands, and the Nazis funded the creation of eight new university chairs in German prehistory in the mid-1930s (Arnold 1990: 467–68). Nationalism and archaeological interpretations were fused as Nazi archaeologists searched for relics from an imagined, glorious Aryan past that could be used for irredentist ends. Bettina Arnold examined how Hans Reinerth's *The Prehistory of the German Tribes* (1940) picked through real and imagined archaeological records to demonstrate Germanic superiority and prehistoric claims to most of central Europe. As Arnold observed, while such pseudo-scientific interpretations of German prehistory were popularly displayed to the German masses, "the majority of German archaeologists were *Mitläufer*, or passive fellow-travelers, to translate an untranslatable German term. These were the unnamed thousands who taught what they were told to teach in schools and universities, and accepted state funding with little question or comment" (Arnold 1990: 472). A few archaeologists produced critiques of these propagandistic fantasies, but they were mostly ignored, as few Germans wished to be identified as opposing the Nazi regime.

Japan Wartime Anthropology

As occurred in postwar Germany, most postwar Japanese anthropologists chose not to cite or quote from their wartime research. Jan van Bremen has noted that "the evasion of war anthropology lasted for nearly fifty years in the post-war academic discussions and publications. Up to the end of the Cold War it remained common to avoid direct references to war anthropology, or make it a subject of discussion or research" (van Bremen 2003: 27). Most Japanese anthropologists continue to avoid examinations of wartime anthropology.[12]

As was the case in Germany and the United States, the needs of war gave anthropology and ethnology a new prominence and respectability in Japan. In the prewar period, few Japanese universities had anthropology appointments, but the war brought increased interest in the uses of the discipline (Shimizu 2003: 86–87). During the war, the Institute of Ethnology (*Minzoku Kenky*) coordinated the efforts of Japanese anthropologists to "assist the ethnic and national policies of the Japanese civil or military administration" (van Bremen 2003: 29). Anthropologists, historians, sociologists, folklorists, a linguist, and a religious studies scholar conducted ethnographic research in areas such as Manchuria, Sumatra, Java, Thailand, and Mongolia (van Bremen 2003: 29). The Institute of Ethnology was directed by a combination of Japanese government and corporate bodies, the most prominent of which was the South Manchurian Railway Company, which funded and directed ethnographic research on traditional customs and land tenure in southern Manchuria (Nie 2003: 211).

Japanese anthropologists provided military commanders in occupied China with information that facilitated subjugation, as well as information of use in specific military actions (Shimizu 2003: 56–57).[13] As the Japanese military moved into New Guinea, Java, Borneo, Singapore, Sumatra, and the Philippines, anthropologists studied and managed the native peoples of these areas. Most of this anthropological work was directed through academic research institutions and funded by corporate entities such as the Mitsubishi Economic Institute (Shimizu 2003: 58). To better meet the changing needs of the war, the Imperial University of Tokyo reconfigured its Institute of Anthropology into its faculty of science (Shimizu 2003: 66).

Japanese and U.S. military and intelligence agencies faced many of the same deficiencies in knowledge about the Pacific cultures they encountered during the war. The vast cultural diversity found in the battlegrounds of the Pacific created a pressing demand for the sorted, itemized, and readily accessible cultural information that anthropologists could provide. In the United States, this information was compiled and made accessible by the Ethnogeographic Board, the Pacific Survey, and the Institute of Human Relations (see chapter 5); in Japan, the Imperial Academy established the Research Committee on East Asian Peoples (Tōa Shominzoku Chōsa Iinkai), which was staffed with anthropologists, cultural geographers, and other scholars. The committee's mission was "to conduct research and compile encyclopedic data on the Asian *minzoku* (ethnos, peoples and/or nations) in the geographical extension from Siberia southward to Indonesia and from Micronesia westward to Xingjiang and Tibet. The committee published a gazetteer of peoples' proper names. The committee sent out Eiichirō Ishida to Sakhalin to conduct research on the peoples living there" (Shimizu 2003: 66). The committee planned to rapidly publish a series of Handbooks of the Peoples of Eastern Asia by commissioning "more than twenty specialists, each to write an ethnography of a given ethnic group in two years," but only four volumes were ever produced (Sasaki 2003: 157). The Japanese government also established the Ethnic Research Institute in 1943 to contribute ethnographic information for use in the establishment of ethnic policies. The institute employed anthropologists, economists, historians, archaeologists, folklorists, and linguists (Shimizu 2003: 67).

Japanese ethnographers gathered a wide range of information throughout the war. Eiichirō Ishida collected ethnographic data in South Sakhalin on the Uilta (then known as the Orokko; Shimizu 2003: 88). Seiichi Izumi worked for the 1943 Japanese Naval Expedition to New Guinea collecting ethnological data. His classified expedition report contained demographic data on the peoples of the Geelvink Bay area of western New Guinea, as well as "action plans to be taken for the effective suppression of the millennial cult then rapidly expanding in the investigated area; and the urgent necessity of anthropological research to be conducted on the local peoples under the military administration and the necessity to establish a system of training administrative officers on the entirely different cultures, customs and temperaments of the peoples under the Japanese rule" (Shimizu 2003: 88–89). The anthropologist Tadao Kano disappeared in Borneo at the end of the war (Shimizu 2003: 58).

The anthropologist Yoshitar Hirano's actions before, during, and after the war demonstrated how even in a society that demanded high levels of conformity and contribution to the war effort, individual deviants still emerged—though such deviants shaped their rebellion within the confines allowed by the strictures of wartime. In the 1920s, Hirano "made a brilliant debut as a promising scholar with his Marxist interpretation of civil and labour laws" (Shimizu 2003: 69–70). But Marxist critiques were as unwelcome in Japan as they were in the United States, and in 1930, after a clash with the Special High Police, he was removed from his professorship at the Imperial University of Tokyo. Outside the academy, Hirano sharpened his Marxist critique, publishing works that analyzed the class structure of Japanese society. After he was arrested along with other prominent Japanese Marxists in 1936, Hirano underwent a remarkable transformation into a vehement Asianist ideologue. In 1939, he joined the Institute of the Pacific as the head of the Planning Department (later as the head of the Research Department) and lead [*sic*] a large part of the research projects and publications of the institute until the institute ceased to function in 1946. Under his leadership, the institute was extremely productive in disseminating practical information on Southeast Asia and the South Pacific. In the early years when he worked for the institute, he also participated in the research on rural customs in North China, a project of the Sixth Research Committee at the East Asia Institute. Besides those contributions to the projects of the two institutes, he published numerous articles and books and presented his own Asianist philosophy on the one hand and his ideas on the colonial and military administration of the South on the other. (Shimizu 2003: 70)

Hirano understood that cultural theory and an anthropological understanding of cultural nuance were vital components of successful military conquest and occupations. In 1942, he wrote:

> The peoples [in the regions of conquest] are extremely various and complicated in their race, culture and polity, so that we shall adopt the policies that are fully customized to the actual situations of those peoples. . . . Ethnology and sociology, which shall be in charge of observing those people's contemporary situations, investigating their unique cultures, and recognizing their history, traditions, folk customs and social organizations, shall now inspire themselves and, in collaboration with each other and with human geography, provide pertinent data for constructing our ethnic policies. Moreover, those disciplines should positively propose a guideline for the construction of our ethnic policies. (quoted in Shimizu 2003: 76)

Shimizu noted that Hirano modeled his approach of domination on the Dutch successes in indirect rule in Indonesia (Shimizu 2003: 77–78).

At the war's end, Hirano underwent another transformation and resumed his prewar Marxist analysis without publicly disassociating himself from his wartime work. Akitoshi Shimizu wrote that Hirano "lived the rest of his life as a prominent figure in numerous organizations, both international and domestic, that worked for democracy-promoting, anti-imperialist and peace-seeking movements, all closely associated with the Japanese Communist Party" (Shimizu 2003: 70). Not only did Hirano avoid explicating his own ideological shifts and his wartime complicity, but Japanese academe felt no need to publicly acknowledge or analyze these actions. Hirano rose to a highly respectable position of authority in Japanese anthropology, and, when he died in 1980, "quite a few journals of law dedicated special issues to his memory, but none of them frankly mentioned his works in the early 1940s" (Shimizu 2003: 71). Shimizu observed that Hirano "was not alone" in making such shifts during this period (Shimizu 2003: 71).

The war provided new opportunities for Japanese ethnographers to study indigenous cultures. On Sakhalin Island, the cultures of the Ainu, Uilta, and Nivkhi were studied by Japanese anthropologists to legitimatize folk history–based ethnic claims to this island. After the Japanese negotiated the 1875 Sakhalin Island Treaty with Russia, they relinquished claims to the islands and moved large populations of Ainu peoples to Hokkaido Island. This resulted in devastating poverty for the Ainu, as well for as the Uilta and Nivkhi cultures left on Sakhalin Island (Sasaki 2003). In 1905, the Japanese–Russian War ended with Japan regaining rights to the southern half of Sakhalin Island, with a further encroachment of Japanese claims following the power vacuum in the East during the Russian Revolution. Disputes intensified on Sakhalin Island during the Second World War, and the Soviet and Japanese armies both "trained native peoples, who were familiar with the geographical conditions of the area, and sent them to the other side [of Sakhalin] as spies" (Sasaki 2003: 154). Japanese anthropologists worked as colonial administrators among the native peoples of Sakhalin with the primary mission of enforcing cultural assimilation with government schools.

Japanese anthropologists used their understanding of Sakhalin cultures to facilitate the subjugation and co-optation of the island's cultures during the war. In the summer of 1941, Eiichirō Ishida conducted fieldwork on Sakhalin, studying and describing "the clan system of the Uilta people, which he assumed to be their fundamental social system. . . . He insisted that any Japanese policy to control them would be unsuccessful without a precise understanding of their clan system. It was useless to implant the Japanese family system among them. He no doubt conducted the research with the purpose of providing policy makers with useful data about the native society" (Sasaki 2003: 158). Ishida's research was incomplete, and his fieldwork provided only partial data to be used for such managerial outcomes.

Kōji Miyazaki's research into links between Dutch colonial anthropology and Japanese wartime anthropological models found that Mabuchi Tōichi, "the first and only student who majored in anthropology in pre-war Japan," had drawn on the Dutch anthropological theory of the Leiden School (Miyazaki 2003: 231). Mabuchi's attraction to Dutch ethnography derived from the shared

Japanese and Dutch goals of establishing and maintaining colonial outposts. During the war, Mabuchi worked for the East-Asiatic Economics Investigation Bureau (EAEIB) division of the South Manchurian Railway Company (SMRC), where he wrote ethnographic reports on various cultures, customs, and laws within the theater of war (Nakao 2003: 246–47). A remarkably independent and free academic environment prevailed at the SMRC during the war because of a recognition that the company

> needed first-rate staff members to serve Japan's overall military aims. To get researchers of distinction, the Company hired key people who often disagreed with government policies, and some of whom by the end of the 1930's were Marxists. These researchers were safe as long as they served the needs of the military and the Japanese Empire and as long as they concerned themselves only with China and the areas where [SMRC] facilities were located. Once they began to analyze the basic social structure of Japan, however, they encountered trouble. (Young 1966: 26)

The racial studies of Japanese wartime physical anthropologists had parallels with Nazi wartime racial theories. Atsushi Nobayashi (2003: 146) observed that as the Japanese military dominated new colonial lands there were new uses for a physical anthropology that supported a specific "model of the formation of the Japanese race, which physical anthropology had formulated, supported the formation of colonial ideology for governing colonial areas." Physical anthropologists who presented data that demonstrated the heterogeneous nature of the "Japanese race" found themselves in increasingly dangerous disagreements with government-aligned intellectuals, as well as military and political leaders, who were arguing for homogeneity (see Nobayashi 2003: 146–47). Most Japanese wartime physical anthropology focused on Japanese and Asian racial research, but the anthropologist Gorō Uchida also measured the physical variations of British and Australian prisoners of war, seizing the opportunity to study these rare body types under confined conditions (Nobayashi 2003: 148). Japanese physical anthropologists helped monitor and control Manchurian populations by devising fingerprint-cataloguing schemes used by the Ministry of Justice's Fingerprint Control System, which required all Manchurians to be fingerprinted from 1940 onward (see Watanabe 2004).

In occupied Xinjing, Japanese forces established Kenkoku University, where the Japanese ethnologists Tokuzo Omachi and Hikoichi Oyama taught courses designed to facilitate Japanese "military strategies and colonial controlling policies" (Yin 2004: 33). Omachi and Oyama contributed to Kenkoku University programs designed to build "ethnic group harmony" among students drawn from occupied Han, Man, Mongolian, Hui, and Korean populations (Yin 2004).

At least one wartime Japanese ethnographer plied his native informants not with more traditional gifts of textiles, tobacco, or food, but with opium. The anthropologist Izumi Seiichi, who established his career in the postwar years at Tokyo University, was given opium by the members of the Japanese army intelligence to gain cooperation from informants in occupied Manchuria. Kyung-soo Chun found that "opium delivered by a young fieldworker for the Orochon could be containing the unidentified military strategic intentions of the Japanese military intelligence purpose at that time" (Chun 2004: 55).

In 1938, Takashi Akiba broadcast propaganda over the Korean Broadcasting Corporation's radio station, instructing occupied Koreans on "the social form during emergency." He argued that occupied Koreans should be united through their shared cultural features in opposition to the Allied threats (not the Japanese occupiers). Akiba instructed that such unity during crisis gives

> true focus to a society. Some present examples of well-focused social forms include Nazi Germany and Fascist Italy, which have clear-cut social centers in Hitler and Mussolini, and are well-defined and to the point. But if the focus is adjusted to an absurd point, disaster results, as in China, which, under the leadership of Chian Kai-shek, mobilizes resistance against Japan. It is not necessary to point out that thoroughgoing preparation, intelligence, judgment and a lot of effort [is] required to adjust focus. Fortunately, only Japan in the world has a great constant centre around which all the people can wholeheartedly gather. In this sense, I can say that, unchanged from ancient times till today, Japanese society is a well-focused society with a crystal-clear centre unparalleled among contemporary social groups. We were not born Japanese because we calculated that being Japanese is advantageous. The cord that joins the Japanese is never something thin and feeble that can be arbitrarily tied or untied like a telephone connection or a change of clothing. Rather, we are tightly bound with an unbreakable cord that has united us ceaselessly since the time of our most distant ancestors. We are united by the bond of a strong, deep affection and pride in feeling that we are Japanese in our bodies. In this sense, I believe that Japan has traditionally had the social form to meet emergencies. (Kilsūng 2003: 179)

Akiba used his knowledge of Korean culture to strike familiar chords of agreement shared between Korean and Japanese society, although the contradictions of an invading power speaking about unity to those who have been conquered limited the success of such pleas.

Connecting Wartime Anthropologies

In the years following the war, a silence engulfed Japanese and German anthropologists' considerations of their nations' uses of anthropology during the war. Such silences are common in the writings of nations that have lost wars, but this silence was remarkably similar to that which emerged in the writings of the postwar Allied anthropologist victors.

The ethnographic works that resulted from wartime and postwar field experiences generally ignored the ways in which the war affected fieldwork and the studied cultures. Nothing was hidden per se—after all, everyone knew that a bloody world war had just raged. It was almost as if anthropologists agreed that they should anachronistically conjure and depict representations of villages from a pre-nuclear age. In ways reminiscent of 1940s treatments for post-traumatic stress disorder, postwar ethnographies worked around touchy topics, thrusting anthropologists and the villages they studied back into their "normal life" so that everything would be "just fine." The postwar milieu looked past the war as theory ascended.

Sir Edmund Leach's biographer, Stanley Tambiah, wrote that "Leach did not consider it relevant to discuss in detail how his extensive recruiting of 'frontier tribesmen,' and his later involvement with the Kachin Levies, which was 'a network of guerrillas and spies,' actually enabled him to collect information and to gain panoramic insights about the distribution and interrelations between the hill communities" (Tambiah 2002: 417). Tom Harrisson's ethnographic account, *World Within: A Borneo Story*, stands in stark contrast to Leach's *Political Systems of Highland Burma*: Harrisson blends a traditional ethnographic presentation with his own role in organizing guerrilla warfare against the Japanese, while Leach crops out the war's impact on the Kachin. Leach's ingenious focus on political systems was so intensely cerebral that readers could almost forget the skeletons impaled with feces-encrusted panji sticks tucked away in the bushes.

But the war had an impact on all who had contact with it. During the war, anthropologists occasionally expressed concerns about how the war might affect the remote cultures they had studied before it began. In 1943, Gregory Bateson replied to a letter from Ian Hogbin containing information on the war's impact on Solomon Island communities that Hobin had studied before the war. Bateson wrote that he and Margaret Mead "get not a word from Bali or the Sepik River and are becoming increasingly interested to know what is happening there. Have you considered all the problems which head-hunting is going to present? My Iatmul had unwillingly but finally given up the native sport, but now, with the Pax Britannica removed, they are surely going at it hammer and tongs, and it's going to be just four times as difficult after the war to persuade them to stop it. They know now that that way boredom lies."[14]

Some scholars may be interested in examining differences in what could be termed "defensive" and "offensive" uses of anthropology in warfare. Such distinctions may add an interesting depth to considerations of wartime uses of anthropology—although the act of selecting a particular historical slice complicates distinguishing between "defensive" and "offensive" engagements. Such distinctions have their own internal complications, but there do appear to be fundamental differences between using anthropological knowledge and techniques to facilitate the occupation (as some Japanese anthropologists did in Manchuria and elsewhere) and the liberation (as Harrisson did in Sarawak) of nations or peoples. However, "liberation" arguments can be complicated to maintain, as liberators easily become occupiers, and occupiers can make impressive historical arguments that frame occupations as acts of overdue liberation. But differences in motivations for fighting and in employing anthropology in warfare do matter.

Despite differences in national motivations for fighting the Second World War, there were many similarities between the contributions of American, German, British, Japanese, and Australian anthropologists. Allied and Axis nations faced similar needs derived from the management of foreign populations in occupied lands. But Axis anthropologists were not alone in disregarding the ethical issues that underlay using their profession in warfare. As Geoffrey Gray observed, "The ethical problems of using anthropological knowledge to assist in the best use of colonised peoples in the Australian war effort was not considered. There was no problem with using colonised peoples, who had no citizenship and no political or civil rights, in pursuit of the war aims of the nation. Only [Kenneth] Read and [Ian] Hogbin raised the matter of loyalty, and that was after the war. The use of colonised people in the war effort was unproblematic, other than suggesting a more humane way of recruiting and using native labour" (Gray 2006: 178).

Axis and Allied forces needed domestic and foreign propaganda. They also needed to educate troops. Both Allied and Axis anthropologists researched cultures in occupied and colonial areas (see Sekimoto 2003: 136). Takashi Akiba used his anthropological skills to broadcast radio propaganda to Koreans, but as we will see in chapter 8, teams of anthropologists at the Office of War Information were designing radio broadcasts and leaflets directed at Japanese citizens and soldiers, while other anthropologists helped with domestic propaganda broadcasts designed to boost wartime morale.

German, British, American, and Japanese anthropologists compiled handbooks that provided cultural or linguistic information on the peoples who inhabited occupied—or anticipated occupied—areas within the war arena. Anthropologists made significant contributions to the British Admiralty Handbooks; to Germany's ethnographic mapping programs; and to Japan's Research Committee on East Asian Peoples, Ethnic Research Institute, and South Manchurian Railway Company—each of which was designed to facilitate the management of peoples in occupied territories. These projects were similar to the efforts of the American anthropologists working on the Cross Cultural Survey at the Institute for Human Relations, the Ethnogeographic Board, and the Smithsonian Institution's War Background Studies, as will be discussed in chapter 5. Japanese wartime anthropologists were funded by corporations such as Misubishi and the SMRC in ways similar to the Rockefeller Foundation's funding of war projects in the United States.

The problem with Nazi anthropology was not that Nazi anthropologists necessarily employed bad methods. Some of their field methods for recording Roma and other minority cultures may indeed have been "methodologically sound" (as judged by criteria of validity, reliability, and so on). But because both means and ends matter, Nazi anthropology was tainted by the end goals of the Nazi program—goals that included genocide and implementing a political economy based on racial hierarchies and eradicating non-Germanic cultural systems. Nazi anthropology listed toward twisted ends as anthropologists compartmentally divorced themselves from ethical concerns about the uses of their contributions. This was accomplished because "both a carrot and a stick were held out to anthropologists in the Third Reich" in order to produce specific anthropological forms of use in wartime (Schafft 2004: 71).

As the following chapters describing American anthropologists' contributions to the war illustrate, though they did so to an extreme, Nazi anthropologists were not the only anthropologists to ignore fundamental ethical concerns. Their ability to so significantly divorce their concern from their participation in the larger processes of war marked them as an extreme cautionary reference point. Somewhere near the core of all that was wrong with Nazi anthropology were the answers to Laura Thompson's question of what would become of anthropology if practical social scientists were simply to become technicians for hire to the highest bidder.

CHAPTER FOUR

The War on Campus

Suddenly in 1942 Americans had to confront "the others" on an unprecedented scale, and the concept of culture was drafted to help the war effort. The enemy had to be understood, and for the first time anthropological concepts were applied to nation-states. Exotic languages had to be analyzed so that they could be rapidly taught to those who were to be governors and analysts of hitherto unknown places in the world. Millions of Americans found themselves face to face with the "others" in the Pacific, in India, the Middle East, North Africa and Europe. Populations at home and abroad had to be controlled and made to participate in the all-out effort. For the first time anthropology was seen to be a relevant social science in that anthropologists knew about the "exotics," and appeared to have methods to study them.
—BERNARD S. COHN (1987: 26–27)

As American anthropologists joined the war effort, they suddenly undertook a dizzying array of new tasks and roles. Because the first months of the war were hampered by an administrative lag as old and new government agencies struggled to locate and sort the many Americans who were drafted or volunteered to serve, few anthropologists took on new wartime roles until late 1942. Even then, most military and intelligence agencies failed to understand how anthropology could advance the war effort. American college and university campuses were among the first places that anthropologists took on new wartime roles. Campuses were already a central part of anthropologists' natural habitat; thus, it was an easy conversion for those who adapted existing teaching techniques or subject areas to instruct a new cohort of military students.

The Boasian commitment to field-based linguistic anthropology provided the military with a small army of linguistically savvy anthropologists capable of quickly learning and teaching the languages of the new theaters of warfare. As the Beals report observed, "Many anthropologists, because of their familiarity with the numerous little-known and unwritten languages, have proved extremely useful. Moreover, through their study of American Indian languages, anthropological linguists in the United States have developed their techniques to a higher point than anywhere else in the world. These techniques are now being applied to Asiatic, Oceanic, and African languages in order to facilitate their teaching, regarded as essential by the armed forces" (Beals et al. 1943: 5).

At the Intensive Language Program (ILP), developed by the American Council of Learned Societies (ACLS), anthropologists and linguists produced spoken-language guides and language courses for more than two dozen languages. After Pearl Harbor, the ILP's first reaction was "to corral the practicing linguists," then to establish important liaison relationships between the civilian and military bodies that could fund and organize such a large undertaking (Cowan 1975: 30). The anthropologist Milton Cowan explained the goals and methods of ILP in a 1942 pamphlet designed to plug American campuses directly into war preparedness. Cowan wrote:

> Totalitarian war on a world-wide scope is a new experience. No government, Axis or Allied, was prepared for it, though probably not so badly as was the United States. A war in which prisoners would have to be interrogated in Japanese, communications carried on in Chinese, propaganda spread in Hindustani, scouts interviewed in Arabic, correspondence censored in Malay, broadcasts monitored in Siamese, and military and naval operations conducted in Swahili, Russian, Turkish, Pidgin English, and a school or college was a phenomenon which our responsible leaders could hardly have been expected to foresee clearly enough to be ready for it.
>
> The Intensive Language Program of the American Council of Learned Societies is a belated attempt to make up some of the deficiencies of our preparation. Under it, universities and colleges throughout the country, particularly those with special facilities in collections and personnel for language training, have been encouraged to offer intensive full-time courses in a considerable number of languages unusual in the American educational pattern, with a view to preparing as many people as possible in those languages for which it is likely that the armed forces and governmental and civil agencies will have call.
>
> The sponsors of the program believe that valuable results can be secured within a reasonable period only on the basis of the intensive course. The standard intensive course is designed to absorb the full time and energy of the student during the period of study. With minor variations it will consist of fifteen hours of formal presentation of the structure of the language,

fifteen hours of supervised drill with native speakers of that language and twenty hours of outside preparation per week. The period necessary to acquire a useful knowledge of any language will depend, naturally, on its difficulty to an American.[1]

Language-study materials were developed by the anthropological linguists Charles Hockett (spoken Chinese), Leonard Bloomfield (spoken Dutch and Russian), Morris Swadesh (spoken Spanish), and Thomas A. Sebeok (spoken Finnish and Hungarian; Cowan 1979: 164). Leonard Bloomfield set aside pressing research on mathematical approaches to linguistic analysis to work for the American Council of Learned Societies' wartime language program, where he supervised younger linguists and produced wartime language manuals for soldiers in Dutch and Russian. Charles Hockett (1968: 98) estimated that Bloomfield's devotion to this "grueling work undermined his health" and hastened his death.

ILP phrase books and pocket language guides were written and produced under conditions of great secrecy, because "the Language Guides were issued to soldiers on board ship so they could have language instruction on the way to their destinations. An enemy spy would have had a pretty good notion early in 1942 that we were going into North Africa had he known we were giving priority to seven North African dialects of Arabic. And when our men invaded Algeria and Morocco on November 8 they had had our Language Guides for quite some time before" (Cowan 1975: 32).

The formation of the ILP indicated the preparatory steps some scholars made in the late 1930s for what appeared to be an inevitable American entry into the global war. In 1939, Mortimer Graves, executive secretary of the ACLS, used Rockefeller Foundation funds to organize the ILP. Graves reasoned that, "if these linguists he had been giving grants [to] analyze unwritten American Indian languages, they could certainly do the same for other languages, why not some likely to be of strategic importance in the worldwide conflict he was convinced was inevitable? He set up a committee to explore the founding of a National School of Modern Oriental Languages and Civilizations . . . and one of Intensive Language Instruction" (Cowan 1979: 159).

The programs were staffed with some of America's most gifted linguists. The speed with which the anthropologists and linguists had to develop language materials frequently demanded ingenuity and improvisational skills.[2] Cowan recounted how the ILP linguist William S. Cornyn developed language materials for Burmese—a language that would have obvious wartime applications as the war progressed. The ILP had failed to locate any Burmese speakers in the State

Department's Alien Registration Act files, and the Immigration and Naturalization Service had no records identifying any Burmese Americans. Finally, with the assistance of Dean Rusk at the Pentagon, a single native Burmese speaker, Tung Alamon, was located in New York City (Cowan 1975: 30). Secretive arrangements were made to move him and his dog, Spotty, to a dormitory on the campus of Yale University. There, "things went well for about a month; then one day, Franklin Edgerton turned up in our office looking very embarrassed. He said that [Jung Alamon] had not been entirely frank about his sources of income, and although he rather enjoyed the atmosphere of Yale and Spotty was happy and well adjusted, he was losing money on the deal. It seems he had been running a little numbers racket in lower Manhattan. Our work was so far along and the problem of getting a replacement so great that we finally settled for doubling his salary" (Cowan 1979: 162).

Charles Hockett and Morris Swadesh were assigned the task of producing condensed language-training materials, and Swadesh (who taught Russian and Mandarin Chinese) produced a series of succinct phrase books that later became the foundation of the popular Berlitz foreign-language series.[3] Like a number of gifted anthropologists during the war, Swadesh found himself working for several government agencies. Swadesh prepared language materials for the Signal Corps; wrote pamphlets for the oss on topics such as "How to Pick Up a Foreign Language" and "The Words You Need in Burmese"; "edited dictionaries, and worked in the New York City office of the Linguistics Section of the War Department, known as '165 Broadway' " (Newman 1967: 948). The army assigned Private First Class Charles Hockett, who had previously been "raking leaves at Vint Hill Farms in Virginia just waiting for such an assignment," to design a crash program in Mandarin Chinese (Cowan 1975: 31). Hockett knew no Mandarin, but he worked intensely with six native Mandarin speakers and developed an efficient teaching program. Because there was no time for classroom instruction, "the instruction was conducted on board ship on a full-time intensive basis and without regard to military rank. It would otherwise have been too embarrassing to have a noncom ordering lieutenants, majors and colonels around. The group went halfway around the world by slow boat taking 35 days and then over the hump to China with Hockett managing their Chinese instruction all the way. When they finally arrived, the officers were using a respectable amount of colloquial Mandarin and were able to carry out their training assignment" (Cowan 1979: 162).

Hockett's Chinese-language work led to the publication of the military's *Spoken Chinese*, and his classes made a tremendous difference for the soldiers he taught. General Clayton L. Bissell gave an account of how Hockett's language training saved the day when his troops fighting in remote China were caught in "disorganized fighting between the Japanese and Chinese guerrilla detachments. [Bissell] described how one day his reconnaissance group came up over a small rise in the ground to find themselves looking down the muzzles of a long line of nasty looking rifles. They didn't know whether they were up against Japanese or Chinese guerrillas. Realizing that [if] they were Japanese they wouldn't understand anyway, one of the boys called: wò-men shà-mey-gwo-bīng, whereupon the rifles were lowered and the Chinese came out for a happy and relieved exchange of greetings" (Cowan 1975: 31).

In 1942, the ILP began teaching sixteen languages on fifteen university campuses. Students could intensively study Amharic at the Iranian Institute; Arabic at Columbia, the Iranian Institute, Johns Hopkins, the University of Minnesota, and the University of Pennsylvania; Chinese at Berkeley and Harvard; Hausa at the University of Pennsylvania; Hindustani at the Iranian Institute and the University of Pennsylvania; Hungarian at Harvard; Japanese at Brown, Berkeley, Columbia, Harvard, the University of Michigan, the University of Washington, and Yale; Kurdish at the Iranian Institute; Malay at Yale; Mongolian at Berkeley; Punjabi at Berkeley; Persian at the Iranian Institute and Columbia; Russian at the University of Chicago, Columbia, Cornell, Harvard, the University of Iowa, the Iranian Institute, the University of Minnesota, and Yale; Swahili at the University of Pennsylvania; Thai at the University of Michigan; and Turkish at Indiana University and the Iranian Institute.[4]

The ILP planted seeds that would later grow into powerful and well-funded Area Study centers that would continue to transform anthropology and language acquisition across the country during the Cold War. Army Specialized Training Programs (ASTPs) were established on 227 college and university campuses and were designed to quickly teach basic cultural and historical background information on regions of military significance. ASTP–Foreign Area and Language programs (ASTP-FALS) were established on fifty-five campuses and added language study to the basic ASTP curriculum. On ten campuses, the Civil Affairs Training Schools (CATS) installed elite programs for commissioned officers who needed to acquire linguistic and cultural information quickly for use in battlefield assignments (Embree 1949: 210–12; Fenton 1947b: v–vii). Stanley Newman and Henry Lee Smith developed curricula for teaching English as a second language (Bock 1991: 505). Anthropologists were key components of these programs. Some, like Douglas Haring, who taught courses on Japanese language and culture in Harvard's CATS program, taught languages they had learned while living abroad (Bowles 1991: 270). ASTP anthropologists were seen as particularly useful instructors in the ACTP, ACTP-FAL, and CATS classes, and "several archaeologists discovered that geography had been a continuing background theme in their studies, and they carried to the classroom a feeling for time and space that few others can impact to the teaching of civilization" (Fenton 1947b: 11). Typical of many ASTP anthropologists' experience was that of Hortense Powdermaker at Queens College, who "taught exotic languages and wrote handbooks for servicemen headed for the Pacific Islands and Southeast Asia" (Rossiter 1995: 9–10).[5] Other anthropologists took on similar tasks. At Berkeley, Alfred Kroeber directed campus ASTP operations until a heart attack required him to delegate these responsibilities to others (Peri and Wharton 1965: 22). Robert Spencer was an ASTP instructor at Berkeley, and Samuel Alfred Barrett was the associate director of the ASTP-FAL Far East program. Barrett's classroom sessions featured linguistic field training sessions in which native language speakers were interviewed by students, after which "the informant would rate the researcher as to his ability to derive factual knowledge through interviews" (Peri and Wharton 1965: 23). At the University of Pennsylvania, John Witthoft taught a variety of languages for ASTP (Herskovits 1950). Anthropologists teaching under ASTP protocols met with mixed results. Some excelled under these demanding conditions, while others discovered that teaching military personnel about the subtleties of culture could be difficult.

The war brought interdisciplinary innovations to these classrooms as war needs supplanted disciplinary territoriality. In some cases, this meant that non-anthropologists were teaching anthropology; in other cases, it meant that anthropologists taught outside their discipline (Fenton 1947b: 26). In 1943, Margaret Mead wrote "Proposal for Allotment of Soldiers to Become Regional Ethnogeographic Specialists under the Army Specialized Training Program."[6] Mead recommended that between one hundred and three hundred soldiers be trained each year for a two-year regiment as "regional ethnogeographic specialists" to be used in military and intelligence operations. Mead argued that such a training program was needed because, she estimated, about 75 percent of anthropologists were either doing or applying for war work and, thus, "the small supply of available anthropologists is virtually exhausted."[7] Mead outlined a curriculum of basic anthropology, geography, linguistics, English composition, language training (in a language of a specific geographic area), economics, history of exploration, native cultures, and colonial history.

The Council on Intercultural Relations used anthropologists working with military educational programs to produce a number of culture and personality studies relating to war regions, an activity that increased in the postwar period, when the council became the Institute for Intercultural Studies.[8] Under the auspices of the Council on Intercultural Relations, Mead wrote letters to anthropologists and other scholars soliciting their help in designing course materials for ASTP curriculum. Mead asked Gordon Hamilton at the New York School of Social Work for materials on intercultural conflicts. She asked Arthur Parker and Carl Guthe for suggestions of how ASTP classes could best use museum materials to teach soldiers about other cultures. George Herzog was asked to write a memo on "using music to teach culture, perhaps with separate comments for Europe and for Asia." She asked Geoffrey Gorer to generate a curriculum on using cartons and drawings, and Clyde Kluckhohn produced a memo outlining curricula on types of culture contact. Solon Kimbal was asked to organize informational materials on relocation centers. Gregory Bateson wrote a curriculum on using movies and photographs to study other cultures. Mead, Ruth Benedict, and Dorothy Lee were assigned to write curricular materials on how instructors could use informants from other cultures in the classroom.[9]

Clyde Kluckhohn produced a report for the ASTP and the Council on Intercultural Relations titled, "The Use of Culture Contact Situations in Regional Training" (Kluckhohn 1943; cf. Fenton 1946: 704). Kluckhohn outlined basic definitions of culture and explained how the forces of ethnocentrism and cultural expectations shaded intercultural contact. Kluckhohn wrote curriculum for a limited audience at ASTP, and we are left to wonder what these military administrators made of provocative statements such as, "Had the 'civilized' nations, who so brashly pried open the door of Japan during the middle of the last century, truly understood and given due regard to the significance of these then 'backward' peoples, there might today be no 'Pearl Harbor' to remember" (Kluckhohn 1943: 3). Kluckhohn passionately argued that an anthropological perspective of culture change could help American and Allied forces avoid the sort of colonial blunders that characterized the previous century's culture contacts. To illustrate this point, Kluckhohn described traditional functions of "prestige" in Fiji:

> Prestige used to depend on how big a feast and how much goods a man could give away to his clan. A man was not refused that for which he asked, but was expected to give if he could, and social approbation went to the giver. Thus a strong competitive motive, both for production and for an

equitable distribution of food, was ordinarily answered. Seeking to replace this custom by encouraging thrift and by other well-meaning gestures, British officials and missionaries succeeded only in undermining the whole economic system. With great proportions of the population dying in epidemics introduced from Europe, and the pauperized survivors barely existing on hand-outs of rice, it seemed for a time that the Fijians were doomed to extinction. This was because Europeans had unthinkingly assumed that the incentives which worked well among their own people necessarily were also the underlying motivations for the economically productive efforts of the Fijians. (Kluckhohn 1943: 4)

Kluckhohn moved from this historical example to wartime applications of these same dynamics, arguing that such "tragedies" could be avoided in the present context. He then considered the situation of the Trobriand Islands: "Presumably these islands are now in Japanese hands, but it is quite possible that we may occupy them. Provided we are enlightened enough in our policy to consider the matter at all, will we know how to treat the inhabitants to their own as well as to our advantage?" (Kluckhohn 1943: 4–5). Kluckhohn summarized Malinowski's analysis of *kula* trading patterns and stressed the magical, economic, and symbolic elements embedded in the elaborate regulated transfer of shells and other goods. While Kluckhohn did not elaborate on the meanings of kula in the Trobriands, he stressed that its meanings were culturally embedded in ways that could evade occupying forces. He asked students to

> suppose, then, in administering these Trobriand Islands, we persuasively demonstrate to the natives the futility of these hazardous voyages [between islands to deliver kula goods]. Should we rejoice in having rooted out their pagan practice of magic thereby? Perhaps not, for we can see how, despite the apparent lack of major economic significance in the trade, the whole present structure of their society is dependent upon it. The art of boatmaking might deteriorate; the standards for social grading would break down; and the agricultural life, the political organization, yes, even the sexual and reproductive capacity of the race—would become disorganized and anarchic. (Kluckhohn 1943: 5–6)

To avoid such blunders, Kluckhohn advised the ASTP to teach students anthropological theories of culture, principles of culture contact and culture change, and specific information on the cultures with which they would engage.

Mead wrote a paper for the ASTP administration, "On the Use of Living

Sources in Regional Studies, General Considerations." She encouraged ASTP instructors to bring living cultural informants into the classroom so students could undertake brief intercultural fieldwork sessions to help them break through to a level of psychological comprehension of these alien cultures. She argued:

> By contact, observation, interchange and controlled observation of an individual member of the foreign culture, the students will learn to think in terms of the people of the country, not in terms of the country as an entity— of Bulgarians instead of Bulgaria, of Chinese instead of China. This is essential if they are to act efficiently inside a region, operating through contacts with the local population. . . . By observing the behavior of living members of the culture, all of the various aspects of that culture which have been analyzed out as the economic, political, social, etc. aspects, will again be seen as a whole, and the student can see at first hand that the way in which a people handle their finances, their habits of political factionalism, the type of discipline used in their army, and the type of guerrilla warfare in which they engage are all systematically related to each other. The living informant, whether he be a wine merchant, a colonial administrator, a newspaperman, a diplomat, an army officer, a labor leader, a priest, a refugee or a naturalized American citizen, and whether the students encounter him alone or among a group of his nationals, will provide a synthesis of all that the student learns in the more analytical courses dealing with the history of banking and taxation, the development of agriculture, or the growth of political parties within that country.
>
> The student needs to know how to judge the people of the regions to which he is going, how to tell whether a man is to be trusted, how to recognize whether his own people trust or distrust him. He must be able to spot a leader in the terms in which the foreign culture recognizes leadership, must be able to distinguish shilly-shallying from courtesy, lying from etiquette, anger from drama, trust from mere submissiveness, responsibility from dominance. He needs to know the characteristic tones and gestures, manners and customs which distinguish members of different regions, the rural from the urban, the proletarian from the shopkeeper, the professional politician from the landed gentry, those with definite ideological positions from those who act in terms of their status, religious group, and occupation in their society. He needs to be able to tell whether a group of six people are working together or actually engaging in a quiet sort of mutual sabotage, whether there are factions and antagonisms within the group or not,

whether raised voices mean interest or anger. He cannot learn these things from books and lectures, or even from moving pictures, radio recordings of speeches, still pictures, although all of these will provide valuable supplementary materials. He must actually see and hear and when possible also participate in scenes in which living representative members of the region which he is studying are acting. (Mead 1943b: 1–2)

Mead knew the value of participant-observation-based fieldwork to understanding culture. She recommended that army students be required to observe cultural behavioral regularities and to gather nuanced differences between various social segments. She advocated that students gain experience in observing and interacting with groups from these foreign cultures so that they could generalize beyond the idiosyncrasies of individual native informants (Mead 1943b: 3–4).

Mead developed five classroom exercises to be incorporated into the curriculum. The first of these required students to make a series of sophisticated observations on appropriate cultural behaviors and expressions in the target culture. This was accomplished through viewing films, pictures, and, if possible, observing public interactions. Students were to consciously identify nuanced cultural differences between American culture and the foreign culture. The second exercise used a linguistic informant to gather information on daily life and interactions in their culture, with the army students each sharing specific views on topics. As students from across the United States and from various class backgrounds expressed their cultural differences, these differences would be used to teach students the non-monolithic complexities of foreign cultures. The third assignment sent students to "foreign communities in adjacent cities" to conduct interviews. This allowed them to gain firsthand experience in interviewing and negotiating the difficulties of working in other cultures. The fourth assignment placed army students in group activities organized by foreign groups or in homes of foreign groups. The final assignment stressed the importance of having the army students gain cross-cultural experiences in groups and then have them debrief on these experiences so that "individual student reactions [could] be systematized and made available to the entire group" (Mead 1943b: 6).[10]

America's top anthropology departments assisted or developed campus-based military training programs. Harvard and the University of Chicago hosted army programs, while Stanford's School of Naval Administration drew heavily on the experiences of "anthropologists as advisers in preparing navy personnel for work in Micronesia" (Partridge and Eddy 1978: 31).

When Schuyler Wallace established the U.S. School of Military Government and Administration at Columbia to train naval officers for duty primarily in the Pacific theater, Ralph Linton and other anthropologists lent their skills. The Beals report said that, in 1943, the School for Naval Administrators at Columbia was "teaching naval administrative officers to deal with the native groups in Southeastern Asia and Oceania. One anthropologist gives a detailed regional description of the environment and the people, etc., while a second gives a background in the understanding of alien cultures and various types of social situations and institutions, enabling the administrator to discover why specific alien peoples behave and think as they do and to perceive the interrelations of various aspects of culture" (Beals et al. 1943: 8). At Columbia, Linton taught survey courses on the cultures of the South Pacific, while the naval officers George P. Murdock and John Whiting taught linguistics (Linton and Wagley 1971: 60–61).[11]

The University of Chicago Anthropology Department's contributions to the war were less unified than those of other campuses, but "within a week after Pearl Harbor, Dean [Robert] Redfield circulated to all social science departments a memo asking for reports on the 'national defense activities' of their staff retroactive to the summer of 1940" (Stocking 1979a: 31). The chief anthropological contribution was assisting in the establishment of an army officer-training school at Chicago, and Captain Fred Eggan directed Chicago's Civil Affairs Training Program, in which "Fay-Cooper Cole, John Embree, and Abraham and Mary Fujii Halpern also served" (Stocking 1979a: 31). Cole drew on his experiences in Southeast Asia in the CATS courses he taught to army and naval officers (Gleach 2002d: 67). Eggan's contributions to the army school were limited, but during the course of the war he held jobs that ranged from serving as a Board of Economic Warfare consultant, teaching at the School for Military Government, and working for the Philippine government in exile to undertaking diverse tasks at the U.S. State Department (Darnell 2002a: 147–48; Fogelson 1979: 164).

As an undergraduate, Murray Wax studied mathematics at the University of Chicago. In December 1942, Wax began working as a mathematician at the Naval Research Laboratory "on projects involving underwater sound, such as counter measures to acoustically directed torpedoes" (Wax 1997: 6). While attending a meeting of the Zionist socialist organization, Avukah, Wax met the linguist Zellig Harris, who was working with Japanese materials for the ASTP at the University of Pennsylvania. Wax later recounted:

> Harris was in charge of the academic side of this program, which relied upon native speakers of Japanese (Issei), but also required linguists, who under the circumstances were non-Japanese. To make it possible for me to

work on his political project—as a Research Assistant, so to speak—Harris offered me a position working as a linguist, and I left the Naval Research Laboratory for this position. Harris was contemptuous of traditional linguists (philologists) and claimed that anyone who understood higher mathematics could easily master linguistics. With my background I easily fitted his qualifications, and I took graduate courses with him, but because of the political assignments with which he tasked me, I had but little time for systematic study of either linguistics or Japanese. . . . Trying to cope with this weight of intellectual labor—linguistics, Japanese, Marxism, anthropology— I presume that I was less helpful to Zellig than he had hoped. . . . Meanwhile, he tried to kick me upstairs and sideways, and I was offered a position in Washington, D.C. in a hush-hush program (under anthropological linguist Martin Joos) that, as I later came to realize, was the U.S. counterpart to the cryptographic effort on "Enigma." (Wax 1997: 7–8)

Wax declined the invitation to join Joos's code-cracking team, a decision that apparently led intelligence officers to question Harris about Wax (Wax 1997: 8). When the ASTP disbanded at the war's end, Wax went on to graduate school with funds supplied by the GI Bill of Rights.

Other Impacts on Campuses and Students

John Cooper estimated that in 1940, 61 percent of American colleges and universities had anthropology departments (Cooper 1947: 2). Student enrollments in anthropology departments across the country declined as students volunteered or were drafted into military service, but the absence of male students on campuses provided room for increases in female undergraduates and graduate-student enrollments.

Ernestine Bingham, secretary for the University of Chicago Anthropology Department, observed that during the war the campus had "lots of new people around. Most of them young and of the female sex with simply ferocious IQ's. They devour reading lists, lectures, labs and term papers in a fashion comparable to nothing I've ever seen in my entire life."[12] In the years immediately after the war, these women were "eclipsed by the returning veterans, who, aided by the famed GI Bill, itself a measure to guard against another depression, overwhelmed the nation's better colleges and universities. Aided by quotas and other enrollment restrictions, male veterans soon displaced female applicants and, before long, female staff and faculty" (Rossiter 1995: 27). Returning male vets evicted

women from classrooms in ways similar to the workplace gender purges occurring in American factories after V-J Day, and the GI Bill's educational benefits
were used by white men at rates much higher than those for minorities.

Anthropology departments tried to stay in contact with students and faculty
enlisted in military service. At the University of Chicago, some of the correspondence of student soldiers and occasional faculty members was published in
Euphoria, a newsletter produced by Ernestine Bingham during the war. In the
early months of the war, issues of *Euphoria* were filled with excited chatter and
brief updates from Chicago students who sent in information on where they had
been stationed and their hopes for future assignments. Some students reported
on being trained as soldiers; others, on conducting surveys, language training, or
taking anthropometric measurements.[13]

Many of the dozens of names that appeared in the war issues of *Euphoria*
remain unknown to the anthropology discipline—in some cases because they fell
in battle; in others, because they pursued other careers after the war. Some,
however, would become important figures in anthropology. *Euphoria* reported
on Tom Sebeok's work at Chapel Hill with Harry Hoijer and other linguists, on
Fred Eggan's work on the Philippines, and on Marshall Newman's exploits at sea.
Hilgard Pannes reported on being an American Field Service driver for the
British army division stationed in Cairo,[14] and Bernard Siegal reported that he
was 4-F.[15] Scotty MacNeish gave an account of spending several days in an oxygen
tent and weeks in the hospital recovering from Landry's disease, which, readers
were assured, "is quite a phenomenon in medical circles because nobody ever
recovers but that is what Scotty did."[16]

Bingham sometimes wrote reports of what was happening on campus for
those fighting on distant fronts. In 1943, she wrote that there were a dozen
"registered graduate students this quarter, over a hundred in Anthropology 201,
and both Warner's classes are too big for the study room; Redfield's Folk Society
has about 20 and Krogman's classes are as big as usual, also Braidwood's. Besides
there are the usual members of the department working on either exams or
theses."[17]

Euphoria published Lieutenant Dave E. Thompson's gory account of his U.S.
Marine Corps Third Battalion, Ninth Division's storming of the beaches on
Pacific islands and fighting entrenched Japanese forces with machine guns, hand
grenades, and flamethrowers. Thompson wrote graphically of bloody battles
where friends took mortar shells in the head or were "blown to bits." After
describing an intense battle following the seizing a beach, Thompson wrote:

At an intermediate objective on a little ridge we started digging in. We could look back and see Nip mortar raising hell on the beach and in the water. Planes were bombing and strafing the hills ahead—there was plenty of noise, but it seemed very quiet where we were. It was a hot, bright morning. Below us was a little valley with a grass shack among some banana trees and on the other side a steep grassy hillside. A Jap came ambling down the hillside without a weapon. We held our fire in case he was trying to surrender or was a native. He looked up, saw us and started to run. I sang out "Kill him!" and the boys cut him down. Watching through the binoculars I saw a big crimson patch appear on his thigh almost before he hit the deck. It shocked me a bit and I thought briefly "life is brief at best. Insecure. And here it's dirt cheap." Somehow that cliché "dirt cheap" went against the grain, for it's never cheap to anyone—it's cheap to the taker, not the giver. Then we spotted a squad of Nips working up a wooded draw to our right rear and got into a little fire fight with them and I had a near enough miss to teach me to keep my head down.[18]

Contemporary readers are left to wonder about the stateside sensibilities of those reading Thompson's Mailer-esque combat narrative as well as the ways that post-traumatic stress entered the field during the postwar years. *Euphoria* was such an eclectic mixture of wartime reports that four pages of Thompson's hardboiled account were nestled between Women's Army Corps (WAC) Treva Thomas's chipper description of a New Guinea feast and Jim and Virginia Watson's dry report on their project translating American social-science works into Portuguese.

Some contributors to *Euphoria* bought their anthropological eye with them to the war. Bert Kraus of the School of Military Government observed how the war had altered the way of life on remote islands of Melanesia and Polynesia. Natives of South Pacific islands now paddle up to ships, he wrote, holding out "hastily fashioned wooden war club or cross and say 'fifteen dollars.' " Kraus assured his readers that these trinkets could be bargained down to five dollars and a carton of cigarettes.[19] From North Africa, after the battle of El Alamein, Corporal Hilgard Pannes wrote, "This is lousy country for an anthropologist when one listens to the talk that goes on about the native population. Everybody is a 'Wog'— whatever that means—that isn't European or somewhat according to home standards. Most of the lads here would just as soon run over them as not. Attitudes here are a good sight worse than they are towards Negroes at home—generally speaking. But what in hell would one expect from the best families in Boston?"[20]

Lieutenant Walter L. Tichenor of the Eleventh Infantry Division wrote after

Christmas 1942 that his friends from Chicago "needn't worry about me getting thru this show. Only the good die young, and I'm certainly not included in that category. . . . [L]ooks as if Jerry should be reaching his last stage pretty soon. Before long I'll be back at school looking for a vacant spot in the lab."[21] Two years later, the cover of the January 22, 1943, issue of *Euphoria* announced, in memoriam, the death of Walter Tichenor, who was killed in action.[22]

The Impacts of Transformed Campuses

The war's most enduring impact for anthropologists and campuses came after the war, as the GI Bill funded college educations for a generation of veterans. Many of those who became GI Bill anthropologists came from working-class backgrounds that otherwise would have precluded attending college, much less studying at the prestigious universities whose doors were opened to them. This postwar generation of veteran anthropologists would transform the field.

And while the impacts of the war were not always obvious on the surface, they were deep and profound. Robert Murphy observed that this generation, "more than any other in this century and perhaps since the Civil War, had undergone a collective experience of such magnitude and force that it had transformed us. We post-war Columbia students were children of the lower and lower-middle classes who had been brought up in the full rigors of the Great Depression, and when we came of age we went to war. We had gone through a 15-year puberty ordeal, and some even had real scars to show for it. And amazingly, we never talked to each other about the war until we were much older" (Murphy 1991: 72–73).

During the war, universities found themselves quickly adapting to its needs, and American campuses proved capable of harnessing academics' brainpower to meet those needs. The speed with which military language and regional specialty programs were implemented on American campuses was as impressive as the efficiency with which they trained legions of soldiers and analysts. But such quick decisions often have unanticipated enduring consequences. For instance, while most of the Quonset huts and other temporary structures quickly built to house these new wartime programs have been removed from American university campuses, the language-based Area Study Centers that were so quickly birthed in these buildings have long since moved to grander structures of more central importance.

Anthropologists' roles in these centers were vital to America's efforts in the Second World War, and these interactions established the viability of anthropology in the postwar period. War-era language and culture programs demonstrated to federal officials and university administrators that anthropology was more than a curiosity—that it had tangible uses in a world where America was the emerging superpower. The transition from wartime centers to Cold War area-study centers was smooth and rapid. During the Cold War, upgraded versions of the language and area-study programs became financiers and directors of anthropological projects large and small, and while a few anthropologists occasionally remarked on the ways these centers linked the needs of state and of the academy, few saw direct lines to the openly militarized setting that had given birth to the centers (Price 2003b; Rauch 1955). As George Steinmetz observed, "The funding and direction of social research by corporations and, especially after 1940, the U.S. state played a crucial role in [all disciplines], but it was more pronounced in some than others, and perhaps nowhere more than in area studies" (Steinmetz 2005: 20).

The war realigned the posture of American universities. Wartime funding trends on campuses continued after the war ended in ways that transformed anthropological teaching methods and courses taught. The national culture of total war naturally led universities to reposition themselves to best acquiesce to the desires of warfare, but at the war's end they remained bent to the dictates of area-study centers, and few major universities resumed their prewar postures. The transformations of American universities during the coming Cold War illustrate how funding trends begun during World War Two left proverbial kinks in university backs that complicated later efforts by some to straighten up and stand intellectually, independent of the needs of the nation-state.

Wartime campus programs not only passed along geographically useful knowledge of specific cultures; they also confirmed that anthropology's conception of the culture concept was both important and useful. This was useful, as Kluckhohn observed, if Americans were to "know how to treat the inhabitants to their own as well as to our advantage" (Kluckhohn 1943: 5). The war's needs shone so brightly that they seemed to blind anthropologists to the possibility that America's interests and those of the cultures they were studying might diverge.

For more than seventy years, anthropology had recognized that the complex whole of culture shaped human interactions and reactions. The Second World War brought the importance of this understanding to the attention of the military and intelligence community. The culturally sensitive military curriculum devised by Margaret Mead, Clyde Kluckhohn, and others elucidated how the culture concept could be weaponized by anthropologists linked to military outcomes. Mead's and Kluckhohn's militarized ASTP curricular adventures implemented a view that anthropological methods, data, and theories should be relinquished to the military during the war. Kluckhohn's curriculum taught the military how to draw on past colonial successes and how to avoid repeating past pitfalls. Mead's curriculum gave the military anthropology's distinct contribution to twentieth-century social science: the basics of participant observation. Mead knew that interactions with individuals and groups from other cultures could behaviorally teach these student-soldiers subtle and obvious truths that would be difficult to learn from the best books or lectures. The pressing needs of war obscured considerations of what it meant to the discipline to turn over the methods of participant-observation fieldwork skills, anthropology's crown jewels, to the military.

The ease with which these techniques were made available to those waging war is surprising. Given the disciplinary precedents established by James Mooney during the nineteenth century, it is surprising that Mead, Kluckhohn, and others do not appear to have seriously pondered the implications of using participant-observation techniques as a tool of warfare; nor do they appear conflicted about teaching these techniques to military personnel. Mead's and Kluckhohn's correspondence does not show them as concerned that the military might be a hungry master with needs that stretched beyond the conflict at hand.

As wartime anthropology moved off American campuses and into the world of military and intelligence agencies, anthropologists found themselves increasingly working among non-anthropologist military personnel and civilians. The war's urgency pressed anthropologists to quickly commit their skills to defeat these enemies, and these conditions influenced the sort of anthropology that emerged during and after the war.

CHAPTER FIVE

American Anthropologists
Join the Wartime Brain Trust

Mr. Emory, until 1942, had made a career of museum ethnology. He spent part of his time visiting strange peoples in remote Pacific islands, learning how they made baskets, cooked food, what language they spoke, their economics of gift exchange; the rest of his working time was spent in an old, somewhat musty museum "writing up" what he had learned in the field. In other words, he was a typical ethnographer. In World War I no one had any use for such a person, but in World War II there were not enough to go around.
—JOHN EMBREE (1946: 486)

In 1929, the Institute of Human Relations (IHR) was established at Yale University as an interdisciplinary research center combining the findings of anthropology, sociology, and psychology to understand "the basic problems of human nature and the social order" (May 1971: 142). Between 1929 and 1939, the Rockefeller Foundation and the Laura Spelman Memorial established the research directions of the IHR by making grants totaling two and a half million dollars (May 1971: 146–47). The early years of the IHR pursued more of a psychological research focus than an anthropological research focus, with a heavy emphasis on "mental hygiene" studies. In 1937, George Peter Murdock began work on his Cross Cultural Survey, a project that tried systematically to create a representative sample of data from hundreds of societies that could be used to test various cross-cultural theories.[1] Of all of the research programs undertaken by the IHR, Murdock's Cross Cultural Survey would become the most historically significant, and as the IHR became the Human Relations Area File (HRAF) in the postwar years, Murdock's database of cross-cultural information became a resource used by academic anthropologists and the intelligence community.[2] The survey was a "project which had been conceived to be purely scientific in nature, providing organized information for basic research in the behavioral and social sciences, was seen to have potentially great practical value" (Ford 1970: 7). It was the Second World War that transformed the Cross Cultural Survey from a theoretical enterprise to an applied one.

Once America joined the war, anthropologists at Yale quickly recognized the need for anthropological knowledge in the coming fight:

> Less than a week after Pearl Harbor, [Mark] May announced that the Institute [of Human Relations] would accept contract work from any government agency, and he launched an immediate crash program to study the "cultural and racial characteristics" of the Japanese. George P. Murdock, one of the leading cultural anthropologists at Yale, shifted the Cross-Cultural Survey to the collecting and classification of materials on the people of the Pacific, and he began a fresh study of Micronesia, and especially the Japanese Mandate Islands. The Institute drew up a list of anthropologists throughout the nation who had firsthand knowledge of the islands and sent it to the Army and Navy departments. (Winks 1987: 43)

The Rockefeller Foundation provided the IHR with more than four and a half million dollars between 1941 and 1951, with additional wartime funds coming from the Carnegie Foundation (Morawski 1986: 219; Murdock 1971: xiii). Nelson Rockefeller also steered more than eighty thousand dollars from his Office of the Coordinator of Inter-American Affairs (CIAA) budget to the IHR "for the preparation of a Strategic index of Latin America" (May 1971: 148). Because the American military advance through the Pacific suddenly thrust American soldiers into contact with so many unfamiliar cultures, the Office of Naval Intelligence (ONI) drew on anthropologists to produce a series of reports (see Farish 2005: 669–70). Even before the war ended, the U.S. Navy had begun planning for the postwar administration of Micronesia. In 1943, the ONI directed George Murdock, Clellan Ford, and John Whiting to establish a research unit operating under the Office of the Chief of Naval Operations (OPNAV) "to process data on all the islands of the Pacific held by Japan—from the Marshalls to the Ryukyus and Formosa—in accordance with the [IHR's] Cross-Cultural Survey system" (Ford 1970: 7; Howell 1998: 175). Clellan Ford later identified twenty reports published during the war by OPNAV that were based on information from Murdock's Cross Cultural Survey. This report series covered the Marshall Islands (OPNAV 50E-1, E-1S), the Kuril Islands (OPNAV 50E-2), the Japanese Mandate Islands (OPNAV 50E-4), the Eastern and Western Caroline Islands (OPNAV 50E-5, 50E-7), the Mandated Marianas Islands (OPNAV 50E-8), the Izu and Bonin islands (OPNAV 50E-9), Taiwan (OPNAV 50E-12–14, 13–21–22, 13–24–29), and the Ryukyu Islands (OPNAV 13–31;

see Ford 1970: 27). Some of these handbooks were issued as unclassified publications; others were classified "restricted" (e.g., OPNAV 1944e, 1944f).

The Civil Affairs Handbooks organized geographical, resource, historical, cultural, economic, and administrative data under a uniform format resembling the standardized classification systems developed by the IHR and later used by HRAF. This bureaucratization of anthropological intelligence allowed administrators to quickly find and contrast data from different island cultures. This reductionist view of cultures proved managerially efficient, but meaningful cultural distinctions were easily damaged through the processes of compression, where standardization of data presentation shaped the data themselves.

All of the cultures were described using a standardized organizational framework. For example, each handbook organized information on Section 15, "Customs," under the subheadings:

151. Clothing and Ornamentation
152. Life Routine
153. Sex and Marriage Customs
154. Funeral Practices and Religion
155. Art and Recreation
156. Native Warfare
157. Attitudes and Values
158. Etiquette
159. Conduct Considered Especially Offensive
(OPNAV 1944b: viii–ix)

Some information on sexual practices included in the handbooks bordered on the prurient—though it may well have helped avoid some hostilities between natives and military personnel. Many of the handbooks' discussions of sexual mores salaciously focused on sexual practices believed to have been practiced prior to contact with Western or Eastern cultures, when "premarital chastity was esteemed nowhere" (OPNAV 1944b: 46). Reports focused on menstruation huts and the coordinated sexual activities that occurred within men's clubhouses—which were frequently discussed under the handbook subheading "Prostitution."[3] Such entries apparently generated interest as quasi-pornographic material; these sections of the copies of the reports I consulted consistently had well-worn, dog-eared pages with highlighted and notated passages.

Handbook discussions of etiquette covered general protocols of respect and greeting, indicating the acceptability of such familiar practices as handshakes and uncommon ones such as "nose rubbing." They included specific island expectations for modesty, wherein readers learned that on the Marshall Islands, chiefs "carefully avoid being seen urinating or defecating in public" (OPNAV 1943: 31). Sections on "Conduct Considered Especially Offensive" (Section 159) described practices to avoid on specific islands, advising, for example, that "to embarrass another person without providing a means of 'saving face' is considered extremely rude conduct" on the Ryukyu Islands (OPNAV 1944e: 69), and that in the East Carolines it is "considered irreverent to mention the name of a dead person or to trespass on the property of a person recently deceased" (OPNAV 1944a: 50).

While large amounts of data in such categories as "racial characteristics," "language," "clothing," and "sexual relations" were oversimplified and recycled between reports (cf. OPNAV 1944a: 26–41, 1944b: 32–48, 1944c: 33–42), the handbooks were in fact mostly accurate and useful for purposes of conquest and basic administration. For example, the following representation of Yap's political organization presented a Eurocentric schematic of power relations to be harnessed and supplanted as needed by Western administrators:

There are about 100 villages on the island. Some are inhabited by landless serfs, who work on lands owned by persons of superior social status. They owe feudal labor to their lords and can be driven from the land at the will of the latter. Other villages are occupied by freemen of intermediate or higher rank. Each village is governed by an assembly of headmen, the hereditary representatives of its constituent wards or families. Presiding over the assembly is a village chief, who usually holds his position by virtue of his ownership of a particular plot of land. . . . Each district is ruled by a paramount chief, who is the highest ranking village chief of the district. The position is dependent upon the ownership and inheritance of particular houses and lands, to which the title attaches. The eight districts and their chiefs are arranged in a fixed order of rank, as follow: Tomil, Rull, Gagil, Gillifitz, Nif, Kanif, Gorror, and Okau. . . . All the lesser islands and atolls of the Yap district are politically dependent, and from time immemorial their chiefs have annually sent tribute in mats, turmeric, and spondylus shells to Yap. (OPNAV 1944b: 67)

Such Western representations of islanders as "landless serfs" owing "feudal labor" to "lords" and other erroneous analogies to European historical experiences distorted perceptions of the particulars of West Caroline culture. Even with such serious distortions, though, these distillations of anthropological data served useful ends, as they presented administrators with some cultural context beyond that of the Albuquerque, Bronx, or Pismo Beach neighborhoods of their upbringing in which to contextualize these cultures they encountered. For the most part, the ethnographic usefulness of these reports appears to be minimal. If the importance of these representations was measured in their managerial useful-ness, not in their epistemological robustness, then they appear to have served their basic purposes.

Sections of the handbooks became "boilerplate" that were cut and pasted from one regional handbook to another. Thus, statements such as, "Although unmarried girls were formerly very lax in their sexual behavior, they are consid-erably more strict today in consequence of the influence of Christianity," ap-peared in the handbooks for various island groups (cf. OPNAV 1944b: 56, 1944c: 52). Some of the handbooks' cultural data were outdated or selected to exoticize island cultures, but the presentation of the data was designed to facilitate the smooth co-option and management of the described culture. Most of the peoples managed by these military and civilian forces initially welcomed the Americans as liberators, although the processes of such occupations necessarily created conditions of subservience and inequality.

Reports of such military uses of anthropology were circulated in the popular press. In the *American Mercury*, the reporter Charles Walker popularized anthro-pology's contributions to the war in the article "Anthropology as a War Weapon." Walker reported an apocryphal tale in which some Seabees wanted to build an airport on an inhabited island in the Marshall Islands. Supposedly, a GI who had been "taught by Murdock how to deal and how not to deal with a Polynesian" undertook "a two-hour conference with the king of the atoll," after which "the natives migrated peaceably to a neighboring island, and the building of the airport was started" (Walker 1945: 89). In another vignette, Walker credited anthropologists with teaching a U. S. pilot how to negotiate land needed for a New Guinea airfield. Supposedly, the pilot "talked to the chief of the tribe and put into his hand a small bag of sea coral—money in that part of New Guinea. Next day every man, woman and child on the plateau was our ally against the Japs. By sunset they had cleared the ground for a landing strip. Now it is a modern air field, serving as a base for bombing the Japs ever since" (Walker 1945: 85).

Walker referred to "Lt.-Commander Murdock's" Cross Cultural Survey proj-ect as a "bank," conjuring up images of anthropologist bank tellers or loan officers who withdrew chunks of knowledge for War Department customers.[4] Walker reported, "One day a newspaper had called [the IHR's Cross Cultural Survey] 'the Culture Bank,' and the name stuck. Till Pearl Harbor, the 'Bank' made 'loans' to scholars only, but after that the Navy swallowed Pete, his col-leagues and the Bank. Ever since, Lt-Cmdr. George Peter Murdock has been backing the attack in the Pacific. Helping save the lives of American soldiers and sailors is one of the most dramatic dividends of Pete's Bank. This operation is carried on through what might be called the 'Robinson Crusoe' or 'survival' department of the Bank" (Walker 1945: 86). Walker portrayed the "super-chiefs" of the Marshall Islands as exotic lords who, upon receiving the gift of guns, demonstrated their new powers by shooting dead one of their subjects. This same "paramount chief has access (the anthropologists have a word for it) to all women in his kingdom at all times" (Walker 1945: 87). Walker assured his readers that Murdock and the IHR provided a roadmap through this dangerous and exotic world. This map was needed, he said, because

> the average GI from Brooklyn or Arkansas who lands on a coral atoll is either scared stiff or humorously unimpressed by the natives. They seem to him quite unlike Dorothy Lamour—stupid, uncouth, probably dangerous, and certainly unpredictable. Even a little anthropology will make his stay in the islands a happier one. For instance, however outlandish native behavior appears when measured by American standards, it does follow definite rules; and if you know those rules, Professor Murdock insists, you will also know what to expect—and avoid. (Walker 1945: 87–88)

Walker reported that Murdock had determined that from "New Guinea to Fiji" GIs should not flirt with native girls or touch natives' heads (the "seat of the soul"); they should divert their eyes from natives eating meals, avoid standing up in the presence of superiors, and never enter the back doors of people's houses (Walker 1945: 88).

Smithsonian Institution War Background Studies

Between 1942 and 1945, the Smithsonian Institution published twenty-one volumes of a War Background Studies series. The ethnographic reports in the series featured brief synopses of culture areas that were of importance during the war, written for a general, educated audience.

The reports covered Egypt (Roberts 1943), the Indies (Kennedy 1943), Siam (Deignan 1943a), the Far East (Bishop 1942), India (Gilbert 1944), China (Wenley and Pope 1944), Indochina (Janse 1944), the Soviet Union (Hrdlička 1942), Japan (Embree 1943c), Polynesia (Weckler 1943), Burma (Deignan 1943b), New Guinea (Stirling 1943), Micronesia (Krieger 1943), Melanesia (Krieger 1943), and the Philippines (Krieger 1942). There were significant variations in approach and depth from one ethnological tract to another, but most of the reports presented data in ways that offered only limited useful information in a military or intelligence context. This should be expected in non-classified public publications.

The Smithsonian's War Background Studies series was mostly a mixture of geographical and cultural information with no unifying organization of direct military application. For example, the New World archaeologist Frank Roberts's monograph on Egypt avoided discussing the Suez Canal's strategic value as a military choke point. Instead, Roberts discussed various Suez shipping schemes stretching from the nineteenth century B.C. to the present, with only the briefest discussion of the strategic importance of the canal in the war. Some of these publications also circulated in other forms or were even classified as restricted or secret for use by military and intelligence agencies—for example, see Embree's OSS/Coordinator of Information (COI) report discussed in chapter 10 (COI 1942; Embree 1943c).

Herbert Krieger's volume *Peoples of the Philippines* and Aleš Hrdlička's *Peoples of the Soviet Union* are well-written and useful summaries of these culture areas that served well as basic briefing aids for individuals who knew nothing about the Philippines or the USSR. Although they are far from comprehensive, they filled gaps of knowledge for general readers. Other books in the series had little to contribute to the war effort. Carl Bishop's archaeological overview of the ancient civilizations of Central Asia and Eastern Asia, *Origin of the Far Eastern Civilizations* (1942), and John Swanton's *The Evolution of Nations* (1942) seem better designed to clear off the desks of contributors than to vanquish Axis foes.[5]

Herbert Friedmann, ornithology curator at the Smithsonian, published an essay in the series examining principles of camouflage as revealed in nature (Friedmann 1942). Friedmann's approach to the principles of camouflage was based on his work as a naturalist, but his concern with these principles was political. He wrote, "It is probably no exaggeration to say that military camouflage has a greater and more vital importance now than it did in previous wars" (Friedmann 1942: 2–3). The military applications of Doris Cochran's *Poisonous Reptiles of the World: A Wartime Handbook* (1943) were likewise apparent as the battles in the jungles of Asia and the Pacific exposed troops to unfamiliar, dangerous reptiles.[6]

The Ethnogeographic Board

The Ethnogeographic Board was established in June 1942 as a Smithsonian-based wartime think tank that used anthropologists, linguists, and cultural geographers to generate information relevant to anticipated theaters of war. The Smithsonian provided office space for the Ethnogeographic Board, funded the director's salary, and made institution personnel available for needed tasks. More funds were later provided by the Carnegie Corporation and the Rockefeller Foundation (Guthe 1943: 189; Lagemann 1989: 174).[7] As the board's first director, William Duncan Strong collected the talents of diverse anthropologists, including Elizabeth Bacon, Homer Barnett, Ralph Beals, Wendell Bennett, Henry Collins, J. M. Cowan, William Fenton, Robert Hall, John Peabody Harrington, Melville Herskovits, Raymond Kennedy, George Murdock, Frank Roberts, and Douglas Whitaker. Strong directed the board from 1942 to 1944, when he returned to Columbia University, and Henry Collins succeeded as director. The full Ethnogeographic Board met twice a year, and the day-to-day practices of the board were largely determined by the requests it received from government and private agencies. These were wide-ranging requests for help. For example, when the Army Tactical Center was searching for "information on insect repellents as used by primitive peoples," the AAA referred it to the Ethnogeographic Board.[8] The Ethnogeographic Board had six subcommittees: African Anthropology; Anthropology of Oceania; Asiatic Geography; Investigative Language Program; Latin American Studies; and Smithsonian War Committee.

Most of the Ethnogeographic Board's anthropologists also served other wartime military and intelligence agencies. For example, in 1942–43 Elizabeth Bacon worked for the army's area-studies program and the Smithsonian's Ethnogeographic Board, and in 1944–46 she was a senior analyst for Iran and Afghanistan at the U.S. State Department's Office of Research and Intelligence (Herskovits 1950: 8). Because the Ethnogeographic Board was not linked to any specific military or intelligence agency, "it was outside most of the competition and suspicion. Its services were open to all agencies. Since it had no fixed place in the Government hierarchy, it could receive a general or a private, the chief of an agency or a junior research assistant" (Bennett 1947: 2).

The Ethnogeographic Board's primary task was to connect knowledgeable individuals with specific requests made by military and intelligence organizations. The army asked the board to compile a roster listing individuals' geographic and linguistic expertise so the information could be shared with the Selective Service. But as Bennett wryly observed, "This request produced intense activity among the Staff but, fortunately for the peace of the Board, the Army completely forgot about this plan 3 weeks after it had first suggested it" (Bennett 1947: 30). During the first years of the war, there were many uncoordinated and duplicated tasks such as this, but despite the lack of coordination with Selective

Service and other agencies, the Ethnogeographic Board compiled an impressive index of anthropologists. Known as the Ethnogeographic Area Roster, it listed the geographical and linguistic knowledge base of more than five thousand Americans (see table 1).[9] William Fenton directed the construction and analysis of the Ethnogeographic Area Roster, which was compiled by focusing first on regions of pressing military importance—for example, the Mediterranean, North Africa, and Japanese-occupied regions in the Pacific. To begin compiling the information, Fenton

> appealed to professional societies and institutions, such as the American Political Science Association, the Rockefeller Foundation, and the Library of Congress, whose members might have special knowledge of these regions. Others, like members of the American Association of Petroleum Geologists, and the American Malacologists Union, could be expected to have special knowledge of terrain and beaches. The offices of both Army and Navy Intelligence gave their assistance. Government agencies with foreign service divisions were not overlooked. The Department of Agriculture and the Board of Economic Warfare agreed to send the roster questionnaire to their International Labour Office, the Explorers Club, and the International Committee of the YMCA furnished names of nonprofessionals with area knowledge. Names of missionaries were obtained form the American Friends Service Committee, the Baptist Foreign Mission, the International Missionary Council, and others. The National Roster of Scientific and Specialized Personnel supplied basic lists of specialists with foreign travel or residence. (Bennett 1947: 26)

Most of the societies turned over their lists to Fenton, and as the Ethnogeographic Area Roster organized sub-lists of "specialized area personnel," some of the lists were classified as "confidential," with restricted distribution (Bennett 1947: 33).[10] The board also compiled a directory of anthropologists living in the Washington, D.C., area who could be contacted quickly as specific needs arose.[11]

The construction and maintenance of the roster was a large undertaking. Military and intelligence agencies regularly sent requests for specific regional-cultural information.[12] Upon receipt of these requests, personnel consulted the roster and other directories, then recommended individuals who were likely to have the needed knowledge.[13] This was one of the board's most significant contributions to the war. Bennett reported that the roster "was consulted at some point

Table 1. Summary of Ethnogeographic Area Roster Cards, December 1943

REGION	NUMBER OF IDENTIFIED REGIONAL SPECIALISTS
Africa	2,450
Asia	1,300
(e.g., Japan, 200)[a]	
(e.g., Burma, 75)	
Europe	2,550
(e.g., Germany proper, 200)	
Latin America	1,600
North America	300
Oceania	2,450
(e.g., Sumatra, 175)	
(e.g., Philippines, 500)	
TOTAL	10,650

Source: Bennett 1947: 30. These rosters compiled information on more than 5,000 individuals.

by every war agency and by most of the prominent civilian agencies" (Bennett 1947: 32). He explained:

> Most requests were for the names of individuals who had lived or traveled in some area. Some were turned over to the cooperating committees for answers. For example, the Africa committee handled an Office of Strategic Services request for a short list of businessmen, government employees, and native leaders resident in Liberia; and an Army request for individuals with experience in Africa who had served in any branch of the Armed Forces previous to 1935. A reply to a simple request such as a list of people who had lived or traveled in Gambia included the name, address, business or profession, and months and years residence in the area. (Bennett 1947: 33)

The Ethnogeographic Board fielded a wide range of questions—or, as Bennett put it, "The anthropological range of questions have the range and world coverage of a preliminary Ph.D. examination" (Bennett 1947: 52). Anthropologists answered questions, for example, about the details of Arctic coastlines, Arctic fishing techniques, sod houses, blowgun construction, languages of Angola, and the distribution of wild hemp. The Ethnogeographic Board's roster identified more than five thousand individuals with cultural and linguistic knowledge of more than ten thousand cultural groups (see table 1).

The Ethnogeographic Board organized several conferences that drew together communities of regional specialists. The first of these was a conference of African specialists held on September 21, 1942, at the Cosmos Club. The small meeting gathered members of the Ethnogeographic Board and specialists from the Board of Economic Warfare, OSS, Military Intelligence, ACLS, State Department, and Department of Commerce for a "confidential meeting" (Bennett 1947: 68). Other meetings assessed the specific geographical intelligence needs of war-related institutions (Henson 2000: 32).[14]

Survival on Land and Sea

The most visible and widely distributed product of the Ethnogeographic Board's efforts was the card-deck-size, 187 page, waterproof book *Survival on Land and Sea*, which was printed and distributed by the ONI (Ethnogeographic Board 1944 [1943]). By the end of 1944, 970,000 copies of the survival guide had been printed and distributed to soldiers and sailors serving in the Pacific. The guide was created after George Murdock wrote to William Duncan Strong about his frustration in reading reports of downed U.S. soldiers dying of starvation in Pacific jungles because they knew nothing about edible foods or basic survival. The ONI charged the Ethnogeographic Board with producing a survival manual. The anthropologist Frank Roberts oversaw its production; Henry Collins wrote a chapter on Arctic survival; M. W. Stirling gave an overview of native peoples and tropical forest subsistence; and Strong contributed a section on sea survival skills (Bennett 1947: 74, 135). *Survival on Land and Sea* was organized around a series of specific geographical and topical situations that a downed airman or otherwise marooned serviceman might encounter. To give a sense of the tone and range of information conveyed in *Survival on Land and Sea*, the chapter titled "Natives" is presented here in its entirety:

> **Chapter IV**
> **Natives**
> If you are in a region inhabited by native peoples make every effort to get in touch with them and ask them for help. You run little danger if you approach them in a friendly manner. Never show fear, or threaten, or flourish a gun. As a rule it is fear on the part of natives that makes them attack strangers and if you do nothing to cause concern you will be perfectly safe.

Go up to them as you would to individuals of your own race and color, smile, offer a cigarette if you have one, and make your wants known. You may need to use signs to show them what you want—food, water, or directions—but natives are accustomed to such procedure, as they often communicate in that fashion themselves and will understand. The important thing is to treat them with dignity. Most of them have a strong sense of self-respect and do not regard themselves as "natives" or primitive. They will appreciate being treated as human beings just like yourself, neither as inferiors nor as superiors.

Should the natives be inclined to be shy or unapproachable do not rush matters by going right up to them. Stop where you are. Sit down and light up a smoke. If you know any tricks with string, take out a piece and proceed to do things with it. Most natives have and are fond of an elaborate variety of string figures, such as the familiar cat's cradle, which they make for their own amusement and on some occasions for ceremonial purposes. They also are very curious and in a short time some of them may not be able to hold back any longer and will come to see what you are doing. When they do, hand them the string and they will probably show you a few tricks. If you don't have string take some trinket and show interest in it. They will want to see, too. Once the ice is broken, you can go ahead and ask for what you need. This method of approach has been used many times in many parts of the world by those going to study native peoples and rarely has it failed to produce the desired results.

Most native houses are small and crowded and more often than not are infested with fleas, lice, bedbugs, and other disease carrying creatures. It is strongly advised that you do not stay in them unless compelled by extreme circumstances. If it is apparent that you are to be there for some time they can and probably will be willing to build you a shelter in short order. Of course, one should never enter a native house without being invited. They don't like to have strangers come barging into their homes any more than you would. Without making it seem that you are doing so, it is advisable to avoid as much as possible all physical contacts with the natives. They often suffer from serious skin diseases, syphilis, tuberculosis, and other communicable ailments. If it can be done without giving offense, one should prepare his own food and drink in such surroundings.

Should it be necessary for you to remain with a native group for any length of time you must be very observant and learn from experience what you can and cannot do. Respect their customs and manners. They have an entirely different form of etiquette from ours, but one that they believe in as strongly as we do in ours. In general you will find that the less civilized the natives are, the stronger the local taboos or restraints will be and the more you will be expected to conform to them. Respect for personal property, as well as for privacy, is very important. Never pick fruits, kill pigs, or take other food without first ascertaining their ownership, gaining permission and paying for them. Remember that in isolated regions money has little value; paper money is actually worthless and coins only are a medium of exchange insofar as they have trinket or jewelry value. Oftentimes matches, cigarettes, empty containers, or other odds and ends that you may have in your pockets are worth more to the native than any form of money. An exception, of course, would be a group that is living close to the outposts of civilization and white man's stores. Under such conditions money may be the preferred medium of exchange, but unless it is, don't try to force it on them. Be sure, however, that you make some form of payment. Also, if you make a promise of any kind, keep it loyally. You can't pull a fast one on a native and get away with it.

One thing above all to bear in mind is to leave the native women alone. More white men have been killed by natives for trying to make some dusky dame than for any other reason. Even if the circumstances are favorable, which they may be under certain conditions with a father, brother, or husband offering a woman to you, it is better to skip the opportunity, as a case of venereal disease usually can be expected as a follow-up, this being one of the "benefits" of civilization bestowed by the white man where he has gone. If you must play with fire regardless of all considerations, do your dickering with the men and pay them first. Native women are often considered as chattels and do not have free say in such matters. Permission in such cases must come from some male relative as well as the woman herself. Also remember that among native peoples there is frequently little secrecy about such affairs. They usually become a matter of common village gossip.

When staying with natives there are certain things you can do that will help you to become accepted as a member of the group more quickly than if you hold aloof. Entertain them with match tricks, games, feats of skill, dances and songs. Unless you are unusually strong and proficient along that line, don't try to impress them with plain bull strength, as the natives probably are better equipped than you are in that respect and might show you a thing or two. They like to entertain too, so be a good audience and let them perform for you and be duly appreciative of their efforts. Show admiration for products of native handicraft, but don't be too profuse in your praise or they may feel they should give the object to you. Most "primitive" peoples are rather fond of playing practical jokes and probably will do so at your expense. If you find yourself the victim of some native form of "hot-foot," join them in their laughter; don't lose your temper and show anger even though they have hurt you. Another thing that is of great help in winning favor is to learn as many words of the native language as you can pick up. They will take delight in teaching you if you show a willingness and desire to learn. Whatever you do, leave a good impression because other white men may come along later and need help. If you have abused your privileges or taken advantage of the people those who follow will suffer for it.

Should you be stationed where you have time ashore and there are natives, make friends with some of them and have them show you many useful tricks they know—how to fish, how they make snares and traps to catch birds and small animals, what plants are good for food, and how they cook their various dishes. This not only will help you pass the time, but it may give you a fund of knowledge that will some day save you. (Ethno-geographic Board 1944: 53–57)

Despite a heavy dose of ethnocentrism and gross ethnographic oversimplifica-tion, there is still a good degree of useful general advice in this chapter, consider-ing that *Survival on Land and Sea* was designed to be used by eighteen-year-olds whose sum total of cross-cultural experience usually consisted of that acquired at boot camp. Such an audience benefited from reading that, "whatever you do, leave a good impression because other white men may come along later and need help," and from being reminded to act kindly and relatively nonjudgmentally toward those they encountered and to whom they entrusted their survival, to reserve their admiration of objects lest they be offered, and not to enter houses without invitations. While this information was presented as simplistic exaggera-tions, it did impart basic reminders of relativistic tolerance, courtesy, and under-standing to a wide audience.

It is understandable that much of the cultural information in *Survival on Land and Sea* would be imprecise, considering that it was broadly written as a generic guide to help stranded sailors, airmen, and soldiers survive in desert, tropical, and Arctic environments. Given the wide variations in cultural practices that might be encountered, telling downed troops to befriend, learn from, and respect the "natives" they encountered was not bad survival advice. But recommendations to "dicker" with "native" men before having sex with "native" women (who are represented as "often considered as chattels") was not only ethnographically questionable advice, but it could create life-threatening conditions for those who took it.

Despite obvious shortcomings, *Survival on Land and Sea* packed an extraordinary amount of information and contingency plans into a small, waterproof book. The chapter on survival in tropical environments guided readers through various scenarios and offered survival strategies, each one unlikely to be encountered in the exact described form, but the residual strategies for how to cope and survive were useful to those reading the book under dire conditions. Consider the likelihood of engaging in each of the activities in just one paragraph on following jungle water sources:

> If you follow a stream you will not only be provided with water, but with such edible creatures as crabs, shrimps, mollusks, and fish. If it is a large stream build a raft and float it down. Use soft woods, the lighter the better, for the raft. Lash the pieces together with vines or fibrous strips of bark. Sections of bamboo, because of their hollow air-filled segments, make the best rafts if that type of growth is available. Fibrous woods such as the palms do not float well and will soon sink. While drifting downstream on a raft keep your ears open for the roar of rapids or falls so that you don't get caught and swept over them. You may have to abandon several rafts in the course of your journey and build new ones, but that is better than trying to ride out a bad stretch of water. (Ethnogeographic Board 1944 [1943]: 61–62)

This advice sounds like a contemporary computer-game walk through, but it provided a useful paradigm to be applied to the obstacles encountered when surviving any particular jungle stream. When negotiating a jungle path in a tropical forest and encountering a fork in the trail, *Survival on Land and Sea* recommended, one should "take the path that seems to have had the most travel. Never follow one that is closed by a string, rope, grass mat, or some other obvious barrier. It may lead to the scene of native religious rites that are forbidden to strangers, or you may fall into a pit or other dangerous trap set for large game" (Ethnogeographic Board 1944 [1943]: 62–63).

Survival on Land and Sea advised military personnel stranded in Arctic environments to mimic the hunting habits of the Eskimo hunter, who

> crawls forward cautiously while the seal is sleeping, being careful to keep downwind of it. When the seal moves the hunter stops and imitates its

movements, lying flat on the ice, raising his head up and down and wriggling his body slightly. In order to look as much like a seal as possible the hunter approaches the seal sideways instead of head on and keeps his arms close to his body. Since the seal is lying on smooth ice and usually at an incline near the edge of the breathing hole, it must be killed instantly by a shot through the brain, for with the least movement of its body it will slide into the water. (Ethnogeographic Board 1944 [1943]: 147–48)

Would-be survivors were also encouraged to learn which foods were edible by studying the environment carefully, stating that, "One rule that can be relied upon is that whatever the monkeys eat is safe for human beings" (Ethnogeographic Board 1944 [1943]: 83).[15] The book even provided a guide to abandoning ship in an ocean of burning oil:

Should you have to jump from the ship into burning oil, you may, if you are a good swimmer, avoid being burned by the following procedure. It has been tested and proved successful. Jump feet first through the flames. Swim as long as you can under water, then spring above the flames and breathe, taking a breast stroke to push the flames away; then sink and swim under the water again. Men have been able to get through 200 yards of burning oil in this way. To do it, however, you will have to remove your life belt and other cumbersome clothing. (Ethnogeographic Board 1944 [1943]: 5)[16]

The utility of *Survival on Land and Sea* was not found in the specific recitations of steps to be taken to survive a particular pitfall; it resided in the strategic mind set it tried to impart to readers. While the specific tips were about as high in quality as could be generically issued, the residual tactical approach helped stranded sailors and soldiers keep a cool head and survive until a rescue presented itself.

Beyond the mind set of improvisational adaptations, *Survival on Land and Sea* imparted the particular beliefs of the anthropologists and military personnel who oversaw its construction. The book was not a neutral collection of survival facts; it bore traces of anthropology's mid-century conception of "primitive" cultures, as well as universalist presumptions about the best ways to deal with the "others" that soldiers encountered throughout the world. The text's view of these "others" was consistent with a range of nascent anthropological frameworks, including the neo-evolutionary views of White, the cross-cultural computations of Murdock, and the cultural determinism of Boasians such as Mead and Benedict.

Anthropologists, Rockefeller, and the New War in the New World

Anthropologists were also recruited to support various government agencies concerned with the strategic importance of Latin America in the war. The principal agencies engaged in this work were the Institute of Social Anthropology, the Inter-Departmental Committee on Cooperation, the CIAA, and the Division of Cultural Relations.[17] The U.S. State Department consumed and directed anthropological research at these agencies. As Charles Wagley observed, through such wartime programs "many U.S. scholars served in one way or another in Latin America, and their later studies benefited from this experience. Many young men got their first taste of Latin American culture while they were stationed at U.S. military or naval bases in the region. Scholars became cultural or economic attachés in U.S. embassies. Others served in strategic wartime programs such as those to increase wild-rubber production in the Amazon Valley or in one of the bilateral health or agricultural programs of the Institute of Inter-American Affairs" (Wagley 1964: 10). These programs gathered strategic fieldwork and library data that shaped American policy directives. They also sent anthropologists into regions that would become their fieldwork "homes" after the war.[18] Some programs implemented State Department policies—policies that frequently were beneficial to the financial interests of American business elites. Such a confluence of interests was strengthened with the appointment of Nelson Rockefeller as director of the CIAA.

President Franklin D. Roosevelt established the CIAA in August 1940. With Nelson Rockefeller as director, the CIAA strengthened U.S. wartime relations with Central America and South America. The primary qualification Rockefeller held to oversee aspects of American wartime policy in South America was having been born the son of one of the wealthiest men in America; with this inherited position came certain managerial skills and an eye focused on protecting or cultivating foreign political and financial interests that sometimes coalesced with America's national interests. The CIAA's concerns were both economic and cultural, and Rockefeller's agency monitored everything from supplies of vital natural resources to the censoring of Hollywood movies distributed in Latin America to maintain positive relations. The CIAA was charged with the goals of overseeing propaganda campaigns directed at Central Americans and South Americans using U.S. and foreign press outlets such as shortwave and regional local radio stations; collecting Latin American economic data of use to U.S. policymakers; supporting public education in Central America and Latin America; and promoting improved public-health policies in Latin America (CIAA 1947).[19]

In 1942, Rockefeller established the Institute of Inter-American Affairs (IIAA), which operated under the purview of his CIAA (Halle 1948). The IIAA was, as George Foster observed, "the first technical aid foreign program that our government ever had, as far as I know, in the modern period" (Foster 2000: 118). Like many of the aid programs that followed, the IIAA used promises of beneficial outcomes to entrench American interests and to create relationships of obligation that could be used to influence domestic policies in recipient nations.

In ways similar to J. Edgar Hoover's guarded management of the FBI's Special Intelligence Service (described in chapter 9), Rockefeller resisted efforts to share his oversight of operations with other American agencies operating in South America. Within months of assuming the directorship of the CIAA, Rockefeller successfully fended off efforts by William Donovan, Coordinator of Information, to encroach on his Latin American domain. Rockefeller enlisted the help of his friend Adolf Berle to contain Donovan's power. Berle was concerned that Donovan's rise would diminish the power of his own State Department Bureau of Intelligence, and Berle formed a coalition with Hoover,

> who threw his formidable weight behind Nelson [Rockefeller]. At Berle's suggestion, Roosevelt had given Hoover power to establish a 'Special Intelligence Service' that would extend FBI activities throughout Latin America.
>
> Donovan never really had a chance. Roosevelt acceded to the demands of vested interests, including [Rockefeller's] domain over psychological warfare. "I continue to believe that the requirements of our program in the [Western] Hemisphere are quite different from those of our programs to Europe and the Far East," the president wrote Donovan. "In order that information, news and inspirational matter going to other American republics . . . may be carefully adapted to the demands of the Hemisphere, it should be handled exclusively by the Coordinator of Inter-American Affairs in cooperation with the Department of State. (Colby and Dennett 1995: 113)

Under this arrangement, Rockefeller retained his concession to gather and control vital South American economic information, but his inquiries were to be subservient to Hoover's Special Intelligence Service (SIS). Donovan was so angry that he "did not talk to Rockefeller for two years" (Colby and Dennett 1995: 113).

Prior to America's entry into the war, the Rockefeller Foundation had funded a broad range of anthropological research aligned with Rockefeller's economic interests and America's political interests in Latin America. For example, in 1940 the Rockefeller Foundation funded the anthropologist Mary Doherty's investigation of Latin American government programs for Indians for the U.S. Bureau of

Indian Affairs (BIA). "This survey was a key component of a broader intelligence operation by Washington. The Indians of the Americas had been decreed honorary Aryans by the Nazis as part of Hitler's propaganda drive among the major labor force of the Andes and Central Americas" (Colby and Dennett 1995: 96). The United States' prewar economic policies concerning American Indians generated enough ill will in some regions of Central America and South America to cause American policymakers to worry that the Nazi pronouncements might attract some Indians as Nazi allies. But even as Rockefeller kept one protective eye guarding the wartime mineral- and natural-resource needs of the United States, his other eye focused on the postwar horizon, with visions of personal profits to be gained though investments south of the U.S. border. His wartime work as the CIAA's director served both of these interests. Rockefeller's priorities were clear: "After he accepted the job as head of the Office of Inter-American Affairs, Rockefeller told his staff, in essence, that their job was to use the war to take over Latin American markets. While Britain and France fought a bloody struggle against the Third Reich, Rockefeller's primary concern was to monopolize Latin America's raw materials and exclude the Europeans" (Loftus and Aarons 1994: 165).

The CIAA inventoried and catalogued Latin American cultural and natural resources as if they were commodities. Gerard Colby characterized Rockefeller's primary concern as CIAA chief as "with extracting the minerals and natural resources from Latin America needed by the U.S. war machines" (Colby and Dennett 1995: 108). Cultural knowledge was of importance to Rockefeller's CIAA projects if it expedited these extractions. Disruptions of the world economy meant reduction of profits and the creation of new opportunities. America's national interests focused on securing and protecting access to Central America's and South America's rich petroleum, rubber, tin, aluminum, pharmacological-plant, and other resources that were in limited supply during the war.

Raw natural resources were not the only commodities that Rockefeller and American policymakers wanted from Latin America. They also desired access to cheap labor with which to extract and process these resources, and Indian populations in many of these settings were the cheapest labor sources available. Anthropologists analyzed these vital labor relations, and their reports helped secure Rockefeller's status in Washington. As Colby observed, "Latin America's Indians were one of [Nelson Rockefeller's] major instruments in proving his worth to President Roosevelt in a time of cabinet shake-ups and resignations in Washington between 1943 and 1944. In his drive to extract the most strategic resources from Latin America with the least expense he spared no means" (Colby and Dennett 1995: 150).

The anthropologists working at the IIAA tended not to focus on the larger interagency power struggles nor did they spend much time dwelling on the possible postwar political-economic uses of their work. George Foster later contextualized anthropologists' contributions to the IIAA as being part of

> "the Good Neighbor policy," which is a term that nobody uses anymore, but it described our attitude toward Latin America. We wanted to be good neighbors. We wanted to help our neighbors in Latin America.
>
> There were three different branches of the Institute. One was agriculture, where it was argued that food supplies would be disrupted and the supply of rubber would also be disrupted, so it was essential to maximize agricultural knowledge and get rubber growing back in the Amazon—tapping the rubber trees in the Amazon had been largely abandoned after the success of the first rubber trees in Malaysia. Synthetic rubber was not yet very far along. So that was one branch of the IIAA. The second branch was education, and the third branch was public health. (Foster 2000: 122)

The Good Neighbor policies fostered good relationships and brought benefits to those giving and receiving aid (Gellman 1979).

As an administrator, Rockefeller oversaw his budget with the lack of concern befitting one of the world's richest men. He was originally allotted an annual budget of three and a half million dollars, but by 1944 he had spent one hundred forty million. But Rockefeller "could never have gotten approval for such expenditures if his activities were only the cultural events most people saw. Underpinning these activities was a hidden economic agenda: drawing Latin America into the economic matrix of the war-supplies programs being run by corporate leaders" (Colby and Dennett 1995: 115). Rockefeller accomplished this with the assistance of anthropologists and others at the CIAA.

Willard Park was one of the first anthropologists hired at the IIAA. He was soon joined by George Foster, Alexander Lesser, and Ruth Landes (Cole 2003: 228). Kalervo Oberg conducted economic and ethnological surveys in Ecuador and Peru.[20] Foster and Lesser wrote background reports on Haiti and the Dominican Republic by consulting "all the standard sources and [putting] together kind of a synthetic statement, from public sources, and it came out stamped 'Classified. Not for General Distribution'—it made me wonder about all sorts of classification. That's the only thing I remember we did—we worked the whole summer on it" (Foster 2000: 119). Foster found that even articles that had been published in journals such as *American Anthropologist* were sometimes later classified as secret (Foster 2000: 119).[21]

At the CIAA's Political Analysis Division, Morris Siegel undertook

> daily analysis of press and radio news of Latin America, with special em-
> phasis on political, economic and social events as they affect the general
> political scene. After culling and digesting the news, I summarize the most
> important items for a confidential bulletin which is mimeographed and
> distributed daily among various war agencies. In addition, I write special
> reports on current political situations in Latin American countries; on re-
> actions in Latin America to important world events . . . and provide political
> information to other Government agencies in response to special requests.
> State Department, Navy and Army Intelligence, FBI and material from the
> Office of Censorship is regularly routed to me.[22]

Anthropologists compiled ethnographic maps that could facilitate the acquisition of cheap native labor (see Embree 1946: 488). One CIAA map of the
Brazilian Amazon pieced together data from reports by American and Brazilian
anthropologists published in *Strategic Index of the Americas* that included "population counts and the possible number of Indians who could be recruited from
each area to tap rubber. The total was close to 10,000, or 10 percent of a grossly
conservative estimate of 100,000 Indians in prewar Brazil. Nelson [Rockefeller]
recruited some well-known anthropologists into the rubber effort, including
Charles Wagley, who was on close terms with the Service for the Protection of the
Indian's leaders, and former BIA tribal arts official René d'Harnoncourt, both of
Columbia University" (Colby and Dennett 1995: 147).

The Institute of Social Anthropology

In 1943, the State Department created the Institute of Social Anthropology (ISA)
within the Smithsonian's Bureau of American Ethnology. The ISA was charged
with coordinating the collection of wartime ethnographic information on Latin
America and to foster good relationships with anthropologists and others in these
countries (Foster 1967a). The institute's 1943 budget was funded by the Department of State at a modest level of sixty thousand dollars.[23] As the ISA's first director, Julian Steward oversaw anthropologists and other scholars working in Washington, D.C., conducting library research, and doing fieldwork throughout Latin
America. His assistant director Alfred Métraux helped oversee various projects.

Even before the establishment of the ISA, Steward had searched for funding
for American anthropologists to train Central Americans and South Americans
to conduct field research in their own countries.[24] George Foster saw Steward's

work at the ISA as driven by a realization that the postwar period would bring modernization to new regions of the world. Anticipating these changes, Steward "thought it would be highly desirable to have social scientists, especially anthropologists and cultural geographers, trained to do research on a whole series of developmental problems" (Foster 2000: 123). Foster traced the roots of Steward's vision for the ISA to the work of the sociologist Donald Pierson, who developed an aggressive social-engineering program at the Escola Livre de Sociología e Politía in São Paolo in the 1930s (see Foster 2000: 123). Following Pierson's model, the ISA sent U.S. anthropologists to academic institutions in Mexico, Peru, Brazil, and Colombia. The exchange programs "were organized by means of formal *convenios*, or small treaties, between the Smithsonian Institution and the ministry of education of the countries concerned, so that when we went, we were not just going as regular exchange professors, we were going as representatives of the U.S. government, and we were dealing with their governments" (Foster 2000: 123). The ISA stationed Ralph Beals, Lois C. Northcott, Ethelwyn C. Pecora, and George Foster in Washington, D.C.; Allan Holmberg in Lima; Isabel Kelly and Stanley Newman in Mexico City; Oberg and Donald Pierson in São Paulo; and John H. Rowe in Popayan, Colombia.[25]

Foster spent his first year in Mexico City at the Escuela Nacional de Anthropología. Later, he and his family moved to Michoacan, where they undertook a village study in Tzintzuntzan. When Tzintzuntzan villagers became suspicious of Foster, he explained his presence by saying, "In the United States a lot is known about how city Mexicans live, about the upper classes and how politics work, but nobody knows anything about the village people like you. And we want to be able in our classes to tell students, there's another Mexico, and you are that Mexico" (Foster 2000: 135). The ongoing postwar efforts to control such peasants would indicate that the villagers were wise to be suspicious of any American interest in them. There was nothing remarkable about the peasants' suspicions. With hindsight, it seems remarkable that Foster and other ISA anthropologists were not more suspicions of their own government's interest in the peasants they were being paid to study.

ISA staff not only were interested in Latin American ethnology; they also collected and tracked information on regional ethnologists. One undated anonymous report titled "Paraguay" summarized the political inclinations of various Paraguayan anthropologists in a rambling format:

> The key-man for scientific studies is Andres Barbero, who, though not a scientist himself, finances the Socieded Cientifica del Paraguay with his own

fortune. Max Schmidt, German, the only true anthropologist of Paraguay, is his intellectual guide. Their activities center in the natural history museum, for which Barbero is building with his own funds a new six story building in Asuncion. Ivan Belaieff has ethnographic interest in the Chaco Indians, but is mainly concerned with their welfare, especially their fate as a result of the Chaco war. His essays on ethnography for the journal of Barbero's society are rejected (and rightly!) leading Belaieff to believe that Barbero opposes him for political (mainly pro-Nazi) reasons. . . . Politics enter the Paraguay situation in two ways: 1) local politics bring continual change in offices held, but do not affect Barbero, who uses his private fortune. 2) Schmidt is a German, though not vocally pro-Nazi (was paid a pension by Berlin Museum until recently), and Barbero is said to be pro-fascist and to dislike Americans. Both, however, will cooperate in science.[26]

Such dossiers allowed the ISA to vet the political allegiances of foreign scholars with whom they might enter into partnerships.

Other projects advised the Lima Geographical Society, funded small local research efforts, or helped establish anthropology departments at the University of Cuzco and the University of San Marcos.[27] Steward proposed that Frederick Johnson work with Gregorio Hernández de Alba at the Institute of Archaeology.[28] Ongoing passport problems plagued some ISA social scientists. Henry Bruman was denied a passport needed for an ISA assignment in Mexico, so he left to work for another agency. Similar problems prevented Donald D. Brand from conducting ISA work in Peru, and those problems led John Gillin to complete this project.[29] Before his appointment to the ISA, Steward directed the production of *The Handbook of South American Indians*, a monumental work of South American anthropology and archaeology. Steward viewed his work on the *Handbook* as contributing to the American war effort (see Kerns 2003: 225).

The ISA's publication series began during the war and included a village study by Ralph Beals, Pedro Carrasco, and Thomas McCorkle (Beals et al. 1944), and some of the fieldwork used in the ISA's postwar publications was conducted during the war (e.g., Beals 1946; Gillin 1947). The ISA continued to carry on research after the war, focusing on concerns of the Cold War, until it was disbanded in late 1952 (see Foster 1979: 205). Although the wartime fieldwork of ISA anthropologists had no significant impact on war planning or policies, the establishment of wartime goodwill relationships and postwar studies by these anthropologists were important contributions to the new literature on underdevelopment, poverty, and traditional culture that emerged after the war.

Evaluating Enduring Wartime Formations

As the war progressed, anthropologists were increasingly relied on as some sort of cultural librarians, possessing access to obscure but vital data needed by military and civilian authorities. In government agencies and privately funded institutions, American anthropologists rapidly joined the wartime brain trust, where they threw their expertise into the war's furnace. Vast amounts of private and public money fueled the brain trust as it directed an extraordinarily wide range of anthropological research projects, and while this research headed off in very different directions, it was unified in the drive to gather and analyze cultural information to help the Allies defeat the Axis.

Working in both the private and the public sector, Murdock met the rapid pace and changing battlefronts of the Pacific war with his own clerical approach to the sorting of cultures and traits. The procedures used by Murdock and his staff in turning passages of ethnography into standardized units for his "culture bank" were an important milepost in cultural anthropology's efforts to emulate the scientific procedures deployed by their colleagues in physical anthropology as they struggled to study features of physical variation that they believed were indicative of race. Some of the operations and quick readings reduced entire cultures to numerical representations similar to the numerical misrepresentations of individuals on military-induction IQ tests. Murdock's operationalizations would later launch a new era of comparative anthropological analysis and theoretical developments in the decades after the war as HRAF enabled scholars to sample and make quantitative statements about the prevalence or geographical distribution of neo-locality or the co-variance of matrilineality with pastoralism. Some of this work provided interesting analysis of specific or recurrent social formations (Murdock 1949); other aspects of this work became lost in the data, as anthropologists seemingly mindlessly looked for correlations between often unrelated cultural features (Textor 1967).

Anthropologists at the Ethnogeographic Board answered streams of theater-specific questions, and anthropologists' contributions to *Survival on Land and Sea* and military survival schools helped save uncounted lives. Anthropologists producing Civil Affairs Handbooks created a series of readily usable resources that helped reduce culture clashes and prevented unintentional conflicts between island inhabitants and soldiers and civilians undertaking military occupation. Rockefeller's CIAA staff of anthropologists collected and digested data on the natural resources and labor resources and restraints of Central America and South America. These tasks tended to reduce anthropological analytical inputs to those of collector functionaries, disarticulating anthropologists from decisions on the interpretation or uses of the information. Anthropologists easily became part of this large, segmentary delivery system.

Anthropologists had long collected and analyzed the sorts of data that these agencies hungered for, but the war transformed the contextual meaning of the data in ways similar to colonial experiences. This transformation occurred as the war created new uses for anthropological knowledge. The uses of anthropologists' contributions to these projects were multiple. The Civil Affairs Handbooks were designed to decrease potentially deadly clashes between military forces and members of native cultures, but they were also designed to enable more efficient military occupations.

Nelson Rockefeller acknowledged anthropology's usefulness during the war, and the war's demands reduced anthropologists' need to consider what it meant to the field, or to those they studied, that one of the world's richest men was managing pools of tactical anthropological knowledge. The Rockefeller Foundation was already a growing supporter of anthropological research, although anthropologists had not asked why they drew sponsorship from such deep pockets with financial interests in the resource-laden underdeveloped worlds ethnographers described. During the war, anthropologists' knowledge was tapped to inform those protecting American interests in South America and elsewhere; after the war, such knowledge was again tapped to inform those protecting American interests, as understood by sponsors at the Rockefeller, Ford, Carnegie, and other robber baron trusts.

After the war, Rockefeller and those who had served as staff anthropologists built on the work they accomplished at the CIAA. Rockefeller expanded his personal economic sphere of influence in South America, and most anthropologists who had served as CIAA staff built careers at least in part based on their ethnographic experiences during the war.

Anthropologists' war experiences at agencies like the CIAA helped establish the practice of foundations such as the SSRC and Rockefeller Foundation using their private funds to support government policies with which they aligned. During the war, alignment of anthropology and government policy meant fighting fascists and militarism, but later, during the Cold War, the policies and research supported by the SSRC and the Rockefeller, Carnegie, and Ford foundations increasingly focused on specific ways to view peasants and land reform (Price 2003b; Ross 1998, 2003, 2005), counterinsurgency (Horowitz 1967), and the Green Revolution (Ross 1999). While these later programs were beyond the more modest wartime aims of the IIAA and the ISA, they did follow models of coordinated and directed anthropology birthed during the war. These wartime agencies also shaped the nature of anthropological research in ways that changed the face of postwar anthropology. Most significantly, these war experiences helped regularize and make acceptable the notion of directed research.

During the Cold War, some of the wartime drives of directed team-research projects were drawn on and redirected into research projects sponsored by military and private foundations that found anthropologists continuing on research trajectories established during the war. Some directed-funding patterns developed during the war also transferred seamlessly into the postwar period. For example, the Ethnogeographic Board's reliance on public and private funding for directed research was indicative of the Cold War's dominant funding paradigm, which increasingly directed the questions anthropologists asked and answered.

Some of these anthropological contributions to the war raise questions about the frequent, but seldom examined, claims of contemporary anthropologists aligned with military and intelligence agencies that Second World War anthropology necessarily contributed cultural knowledge in wise and useful ways. The Ethnogeographic Board, Institute of Human Relations, and Civil Affairs Handbooks' summaries of cultures as lists of traits created distortions, some of which were sizable enough to raise questions about how useful their anthropological contributions really were. Glossing cultural mores is always a risky proposition, and it is difficult to disentangle the successes of these culture-broker operations from the inherent efficiency of short-term military occupations. When culture contact is accompanied by machine guns, the differences in cultural customs appear less significant than when such contact occurs by fieldworkers trying to understand the world with only word lists, mosquito netting, a notebook, and a copy of *Notes and Queries*.

CHAPTER SIX

Anthropologists and White

House War Projects

In wartime you do all kinds of things that you hope will work, and very often they don't.
And very often, things are very well worth doing are overruled for reasons which you
don't know anything about.
—JOHN FRANKLIN CARTER (in Morrissey 1966: 24)

During times of war and peace, anthropologists have periodically served as White
House advisers or confidants. Sometimes these roles have been formal in nature:
working on the White House staff or on specific roles on projects overseen by the
White House. At other times, anthropologists have served in less formal advisory
roles to presidents or first ladies.

Throughout her years as America's preeminent public anthropologist, Margaret Mead met and corresponded with a number of presidents, first ladies and
White House advisers. During the Second World War, Mead carried on an interesting correspondence with First Lady Eleanor Roosevelt, in which she freely
waxed on about the issues of freedom, democracy, and progressive views on race
and equality—which were at the heart of many anthropologists' commitment to
fighting the Axis forces. In 1943, Mead wrote Mrs. Roosevelt, advising her on how
she might respond to an inquiry she had recently received on topics relating to
issues of freedom and racial equality:

> There will be no democracy and no free world society until no human being
> is judged—or allowed to be proud—of any single thing which he (or she) did
> not do himself. This has, of course, even wider ramifications than that of
> race. Not only must race, sex, nationality, religious affiliation (which it is a
> matter of birth), residence in any given spot in the earth's surface (when one
> lives there merely because one's parent's did) be given up, but also even the

very fact that one's ancestors fought for freedom and tolerance and the breakdown of just such barriers as these—that, too, must be given up. The grandchild of an abolitionist and the grandchild of a slaver must be able to stand side by side and expect to be taken on their own terms, just as well as white and yellow and black men must be able to stand side by side and be taken for what they are, themselves. This is not a statement of a religious belief; it is merely a statement of the logic of democracy, from a scientific analysis of the necessary conditions of democracy. As long as any single person's pride and position depend upon his possession—by inheritance and through no effort of his own—of something that another, because of inheritance, is debarred from obtaining—we will all live in a prison, but it is a prison made by man, a social prison, not a prison which reflects any biological reality.[1]

Mead's letter expresses some of the drive that motivated many anthropologists' contributions to the war, but it also shows how anthropologists regularly tried to influence the views of powerful Washington elites throughout the war.

The anthropologist who exerted the most significant influence on President Roosevelt was Aleš Hrdlička, America's most prominent physical anthropologist of the early twentieth century. Born in Bohemia in 1869 and trained in Paris in the 1890s, Hrdlička had pioneered the study of physical anthropology in the United States, first at the American Museum of National History, then at the National Museum of Natural History from 1903 onward, where he established his career as a curator and oversaw the world's largest collection of human skeletal remains. President Roosevelt consulted with Hrdlička on a regular basis before and during the war. His influence on the president was great enough that, after his death, a World War Two naval Liberty ship, the ss *Ales Hrdlicka*, was named in his honor.[2]

Hrdlička's role as an adviser was informal, and his letters to President Roosevelt reveal more about his particular prejudices than they do about scientific knowledge from this period. For over a decade, Hrdlička and Roosevelt corresponded on topics that ranged from the morale of American youth to the Smithsonian's funding difficulties. Prior to America's entry into the war, Hrdlička shared his opinions on the untrustworthiness of the Japanese, who he described in a 1937 letter as "insular pirates, who have but a veneer of civilization and whose late history is full of perfidy, usurpation and brutality, respect but one factor in us, which is that of greater than theirs intellectual and material power. Woe to us if we should ever become weakened in these respects. A powerful open gesture of ours towards England and—above all—Russia in the present humiliating state of affairs, would best reach through the thick hides of their vicious egotism."[3] Hrdlička's racial views of the Japanese were aligned with President Roosevelt's, and these anti-Japanese views influenced American military policy once America entered, and later contemplated ending, the war.[4]

After the Japanese attack on Pearl Harbor, Hrdlička began advising President Roosevelt on issues relating to international refugees. In September 1942, he encouraged the president to consider planning for the resettlement of the war's millions of refugees in remote locations around the globe. Back in 1938, President Roosevelt and geographer Isaiah Bowman had discussed the possibility of relocating Jewish refugees to the jungles of Venezuela or Colombia, and America's entry into the war awakened Roosevelt's interest in exploring resettlement plans for war refugees of various ethnicities and nationalities (Smith 2003: 295). Hrdlička's managerial views coincided with Roosevelt's vision of the rights and duties that would be afforded by an American war victory. He wrote:

Dear Mr. President:

In accordance with your wishes as expressed to me at our conference and later through Mr. [John Franklin] Carter, I have looked as carefully as was possible into the problems of the chances of post-war immigration into northern South America and British East Africa; and into the suitability as emigrants of the Italian people. The results are given in the three accompanying Memoranda. I do not know how far they may meet your expectations, but the subjects are beset with great difficulties. Aside from personal knowledge in these matters I have consulted the works of our and other best geographers, besides various governmental documents, and have asked for and been given valued personal advice of Professors [Isaiah] Bowman and Preston E. James. The results, regrettably, are not all that could be wished for, but may nevertheless, I trust, be of some use.

So far as the Italians are concerned, there will be plenty of them who will need and want to migrate once the war is over, and they constitute a good stock for the warmer and especially the South American countries; but there will be many obstacles to overcome in placing them, political, economical, as to land, and from labor.

Concerning the Orinoco basin, colonization in the higher lands would theoretically be possible, but practically as yet is almost unfeasible. Much better chances, if due and effective cooperation of the involved governments could be secured, would be the lands of the extensive Paraná watershed, in southern Brazil, Paraguay, Argentina, and the eastern sub-Andean regions. All over these parts, however, if their colonization was to meet with success, would necessitate thorough expert surveys of conditions.

To British East Africa, more particularly in Kenya and Tanganyika, there are parts that apparently would be fit for white man's occupation. But they are in the elevated hinterlands, communication with which is both very costly and difficult, there is the great check of the numerous native Negro population with whom the white farmer or stock raiser would have to compete, and the political obstacles are particularly serious.

The important problem of migration must after the war be faced, if troubles for the future are to be checked. The matter must be made one of the major concerns of the future "League" of Nations. Meanwhile much could be done in advancing the matter on this continent. There is needed a great amount to direct expert study of conditions. Such studies must be properly organized and sustained. They call for the establishment of a "Pan-American Institute of Population" (of "Immigration"). I have mentioned this in my initial letter to you, Mr. President, and am now more convinced of the need of such an establishment than ever.

Hoping you will have some further items in which I may be of use, I am, Mr. President,

Sincerely Yours,

Dr. Aleš Hrdlička[5]

Hrdlička's letter optimistically drew on the history of colonial management, and his remarks that refugees of Italian "stock" were well suited for the warmth of South American countries, or that the Orinoco basin was an empty environment awaiting the arrival of civilized people, finds elements of racial essentialism (traces of which may also be found in some of Hrdlička's scholarly publications) and a colonial-managerial ethos informing these considerations. As Gabrielle Lyon observed, Hrdlička believed "not only was it possible to solve problems of immigration and refugees, it was also possible precisely because the science existed to make it possible" (Lyon 1994: 104).

The following month, Hrdlička further advised the president on how the United States should respond to the inevitable postwar refugee crisis. In that memorandum to President Roosevelt, he repeated his wish that a population institute be established to consider postwar relocation plans, and he outlined how European refugees could be resettled in South America. He wrote to the president that it would be most desirable if there could be formed from a small body of our own foremost students of the conditions, and appointed representatives of the Latin republics, an "Institute of Population Studies," to which could be relegated the tasks in question. Unless direct systematic and comprehensive studies of this nature are organized there can be little hope of any effective accomplishments. It would be greatly to the honor of this country, and of you as its enlightened leader, if such a step were taken. As to expenses, with due thrift they would not need to be excessive, and if found necessary or preferable, a call by you on one or more of our great research supporting Trusts, especially the Rockefeller Foundation which is already interested in this field, would I feel confident bring the needed support.[6]

Roosevelt replied that Hrdlička and others might produce estimates of the costs involved in resettling Europeans to various regions of South America or Africa.[7] Two months later, Hrdlička produced a memorandum estimating the costs associated with such mass movements.[8] Hrdlička's memorandum also described how policymakers might determine where such vast numbers of war refugees should be settled:

1. *The most promising regions for substantial post-war immigration:*
It is the general opinion of our geographers and other students that such regions are located especially in South America: and that they are, in order of their importance:

    a) The interior of Southern Brazil, and particularly the Gran Chaco;

    b) Portions of the pampas region of Argentina;

    c) Portions of the eastern parts of Peru, Bolivia and possibly Ecuador;

    d) Parts of the upper Orinoco basin in Venezuela and Columbia.

2. All the above regions suffer from lack of communications; . . . great distance of markets, of schools; difficult natural conditions (forest, swamps, land conformations, climate); insect and microbe pests, of both man and domestic animals.

3. Wherever in these parts there are favorable plots of land and conditions, the land is preempted, even if not actually occupied, and would have to be purchased, and the price would doubtless rise as soon as knowledge . . . spread that it was wanted for supported colonization.

4. No large colonization could be attempted without the full cooperation of the governments of the countries in question and this would call on one hand or modification of the present strict laws for immigration, and on the

other hand for safeguards lest there be established colonies that in the future would cause internal political trouble.

5. Any larger assisted colonization in any of the regions mentioned will indispensably necessitate preliminary surveys, terrestrial, sanitary, agricultural, and economical; and such surveys, necessitating time, should now be organized as soon as possible.

6. With everything arranged, the cost of bringing in the immigrant and his necessities into any of the above regions could hardly be expected to be less than $200–300 per adult and one-half of that per child to adolescent (excepting infants).

7. To assure success of the project it will be necessary to assist the newcomers with the building of dwellings, with some cattle and poultry, with machinery for clearing and tilling the land, with doctors, dentists, and medicines, and for one to three years with more or less of sustenance clothing and furniture. Such assistance could hardly fall, in all, below $2,000 for an average farming family. It would be less for industrial workers, provided these could secure employment.

8. Even if all the above needs were met, there is no rational hope than any really large annual surplus of the European population could be placed in any or all of the above regions.

9. The whole subject will need greatly some special body or Institute that could devote to it all needed attention.[9]

This was an impressive list of serious political, agricultural, epidemiological, financial, and legal obstacles that could prevent the likely implementation of any conceivable large-scale relocation project. But even Hrdlička's pessimistic view of the costs and problems associated with such an undertaking did not deter President Roosevelt from pursuing the development of a systematic consideration of such a global refugee planning system.

Henry Field and the M Project

In the spring of 1940, two and a half years before Hrdlička's cautionary memo to President Roosevelt describing the difficulties to be encountered with massive refugee relocation, Henry Field, assistant curator of anthropology at the Field Museum, was contacted by a representative of President Roosevelt and asked to estimate the maximum population that Iraq could support in the postwar period. Specifically, he was asked to evaluate the reliability of a recent Italian estimate that Iraq could support between ten million and seventeen million people. Field estimated a figure closer to eight million, and he found that "to accomplish the Italian estimate of 17,000,000 would still require another generation and vast expenditures, probably even beyond the hopes of an oil-rich land" (Field 1962: 2).

Field did not identify the presidential envoy who contacted him in Chicago, but in a 1966 oral-history interview, Roosevelt's adviser John Franklin Carter recounted his role in contacting Henry Field. Carter claimed that Field later exaggerated President Roosevelt's involvement in this work, stating that he had contacted Field on his own, without Roosevelt's knowledge. Carter had decided to approach Field for several reasons. Primary among them was that he was looking for someone who had good relations with the British and who could help him in his dealings with the interned German citizen Putzi Hanfstaengl. Field later assisted Carter's work with Hanfstaengl, and Carter used Field to leak information about Hanfstaengl to the British Embassy (Morrissey 1966: 9–20).[10] Carter also knew that Field would likely be willing to leave Chicago and come to Washington to escape an uncomfortable work climate resulting from the Field Museum's decision not to publish his manuscript on Southwest Asian folklore. Carter believed that Field's uncle had discovered that the manuscript had been plagiarized, but the reasons were instead related to editorial decisions regarding the manuscript's lack of theoretical analysis (Lyon 1994: 89–93, 99–100; Morrissey 1966: 9).

Carter outlined the basic mission of the M (for Migration) Project for presidential approval. The plans specified that Carter would be an intermediary overseeing elements of the program with Field, and the input of Hrdlička would be kept at a minimum (Lyon 1994: 107).

On November 1, 1942, President Roosevelt appointed the geographer Isaiah Bowman to direct the M Project, which was charged with studying migration issues related to the war by searching for regions where vast numbers of war refugees could be resettled. Field became the M Project's administrator, though there are conflicting versions of how this occurred. Field later claimed that President Roosevelt invited him to a small dinner at his presidential retreat in the fall of 1943, and that after dinner, the president took him aside to discuss a proposal for his postwar refugee-resettlement program. Field wrote that Roosevelt "began by saying that he was counting upon our studies to assist him to make some of the most significant political decisions of the postwar world. The resettlement of millions of Refugees was not only desirable from an humanitarian standpoint, but essential from a military point of view, 'for the discontented can and will cause trouble, serious trouble' " (Field 1962: 327).

Field claimed that he and the president discussed the fate of Assyrians in Iraq and problems of morale among Allies after the eventual victory. Field claimed that Roosevelt envisioned aggressive resettlement campaigns involving the movement of tens of millions of people displaced by the war to arid regions in North Africa and to Australia's Nullarbor Plain. Roosevelt believed that the agricultural limits of these arid environs were only temporary inconveniences to be overcome with the application of American engineering and scientific know-how. Roosevelt described grand plans for massive desalinization programs to increase agricultural production in semi-desert areas around the world. Field's account portrayed the president talking at length about the world he would rebuild after the war, including his plans to make

> North Africa the granary of Europe, just as it was in Roman days. We can pump desalinated water from the Mediterranean for irrigation and build air-conditioned cities in the desert. Technicians will be recruited from among the displaced persons. Steel pipe and housing materials can be manufactured as each European country converts from wartime production to peaceful economy. We will transport the men and equipment in an international fleet. We will pay high wages, probably with a withholding tax to force savings. This will encourage the technicians to bring their families. That will be one practical way to take up the slack and encourage migration and settlement. Although this will be expensive, it will be far better than the dole—just handing out billions for doing nothing. The North African project will have a counterpart to help Southeast Asia and the Pacific area. We may have others along the Khabur in Syria, the Jordan, and the Tigris-Euphrates Valley. (Field 1962: 328)

Field's Roosevelt was planning America's postwar role as a global master presenting the world with the privileges he would earn as the emerging leader of the free world. This was a high-modern imperial fantasy fully trusting that larger scientific solutions would prevail where political forces had failed.[11] Field does not inform us of how Roosevelt envisioned the political-economic relations of these relocated populations. While a glorious world of productive farmers, cattlemen, and industrialized workers was envisioned, we are not told whether these populations would be hourly workers, slaves, indentured servants, unionized federal employees, or itinerant workers producing export products or products for their own consumption.

Carter later claimed that Field wholly invented this dramatic interaction with Roosevelt. Carter had "approached him without the President's knowledge. . . . He's a glory grabber in a pleasant academic way" (Morrissey 1966: 21–22).[12] Carter's statements undermine Field's credibility and make it difficult to evaluate which elements of Field's account were fact or fiction.

Field was given a navy commission, made a lieutenant, and assigned to administer the M Project under Librarian of Congress Archibald MacLeish in a secret intelligence detail, funded by one hundred eighty thousand dollars of unvouchered funds administered by Carter (Morrissey 1966; Smith 2003: 302). The M Project hired Robert Bowman, Wellington Jones, Owen Lattimore, Karl Pelzer, Robert Pendleton, Robert Strausz-Hupé, Glenn T. Trewaartha, Warren S. Thompson, Griffith Taylor, Leo Waibel, and Alan Wolman as consultants or staff members (Smith 2003: 302). The mission of the M Project was "first, to investigate the complex problem [of migration] in its most minute details without regard for national or international prejudices, sensibilities and jealousies; and second, to suggest ways and means whereby the problem could be solved once and for all— even if it takes from 20 to 50 years to solve it. It was top-secret because of the manifold political implications inherent in the investigations, but chiefly because a premature revelation of its findings would have alerted the perennial opponents of all migration studies against the Project" (Field 1962: 374).

Field oversaw the compilation of basic data on refugees. His group collected information on regions around the world that appeared to be relatively empty or underpopulated and that were capable of serving as new homelands for displaced peoples of various ethnicities. The project estimated that there would be an estimated twenty million war refugees—a figure that, by the war's end, was actually fifty million (Field 1962: 3). Field followed policy directives issued by Bowman. But while Bowman's directives led to some interesting geographical research, Bowman did not develop any plans to assist the millions of refugees while the war raged. Instead, all of Bowman's projects were designed to begin after the coming peace (Smith 2003: 303–15). Following Bowman's instructions, Field directed his staff "to compile from all available sources a series of studies on world-wide settlement possibilities as well as population problems"; they were also instructed to keep all matters relating to this work secret, as they were dealing with "political dynamite" (Field 1962: 3; cf. Field 1967: 248).

Given the international political problems that would result from the disclosure of such planning, it is understandable that the government kept the program's existence secret. But as almost all of the provisional plans developed by the M Project were never implemented (in part for exactly the reasons that would have been the focus of public criticism had the program been subjected to public scrutiny) these wasted efforts might have been redirected to more practical ways of assisting refugees if these conditions of secrecy had not been imposed. If free criticism of these outlandish plans had occurred, Field and others could have worked on projects of greater importance to the war effort, or on more realistic refugee assistance programs. With time, some staff members grew impatient as the reports they generated did not lead to any action and "eventually frustrated by their inability to accomplish anything useful, many M Project staff drifted away for sterner challenges" (Smith 2003: 302).

Over the years of the M Project's existence, Bowman thwarted efforts to undertake refugee-rescue operations during the war. Even after knowledge of Nazi atrocities was established, Bowman was still "stalling, trying to block any significant action aimed at emergency refugee resettlement that might circumscribe his scientific 'experiment'" that was designed to run after the war's end, not during the war (Smith 2003: 304).

Field's research team worked out of Study Room 115 at the Library of Congress, up the hall from a series of OSS library-based research projects.[13] For almost three years, Field and his staff read scholarly literature, news, and intelligence reports and churned out a steady stream of classified, confidential, and secret reports on refugee-resettlement plans. Thirty copies of each report were printed and circulated to the president, the OWI, the OSS, and other agencies (Field 1962; Smith 2003: 302). Field wrote that the M Project "studied and appraised dozens of previous resettlement attempts and the immigration laws of many countries and, wherever possible, their practical application. By the latter part of 1945 we had prepared world-wide studies on areas with surplus population, their racial and religious composition, and their nationals' potential skill and adaptability as emigrants. As a result, we found on paper many potential areas of settlement with an appraisal from economic, social geographic, ecological, demographic and geopolitical angles" (Field 1962: 4).

The M Project drew on other anthropologists and other scholars for the compilation of its reports. The Canadian anthropologists Diamond Jenness and William Mackintosh worked on early reports analyzing Canadian data, but the political sensitivity of the project required that they be lied to and told that they were collecting data for a nongovernmental program (Lyon 1994: 114).

Declassified M Project reports found library-bound bureaucrats designing contingency plans to move tens of millions of people thousands of miles away from their native lands. Field and his staff appear comfortable planning to move inventoried people about the globe like fungible commodities. That a president was comfortable with such global brinksmanship is not surprising, but an anthropologist's comfort with such paternalistic relocation schemes is disquieting. Field and his staff generated hundreds of reports without focusing much on the likely harm to come from such plans—potential harm for those moved and for those living in or adjoining regions of relocation.

The M Project focused primarily on European refugees and almost entirely ignored the millions displaced in Africa and Asia. Instead, European displaced people would be moved to regions of Africa, South America, North America, and Asia that were imagined to be "vacant" or "underutilized." Field and his staff constructed a substantial database supporting a geographical representation of a world where indigenous peoples and others either were not there or were not using land as wisely as the new settlers would.

Between 1943 and late 1945, Field and his staff wrote 666 M Project reports.[14] Most of the reports were declassified in 1960, and at the urging of Clyde Kluckhohn and Arthur Schlesinger Jr., Field published a book of M Project report summaries (Field 1962). Most M Project reports provided summaries of economic, geographic, cultural, and historical information about regions around the world. The majority were dry compilations of data. Many reports betrayed naïve assumptions about history, culture, and the politics of geography. In some reports, Field and his staff appear as giddy social engineers collecting cultural and geographical data and calculating outcomes of speculative relocation schemes for specific cultures in distant lands and unfamiliar environments. In almost every case, the peoples identified for relocation were victims of the aggression of others (e.g., the Roma, Jews, etc.), as if the reward of being victimized was being moved so that the aggressor could live in peace. These plans were often devoid of historical contexts and power relations. People, cultures, and land became objects disarticulated from the past, present, and future. Many reports betrayed misguided —and, more important, already scientifically discredited—assumptions about racial and ethnic proclivities suiting them to live in specific environments.

The M Project produced four series of documents: reports, translations, memoranda, and lectures.[15] The biases underlying the M Project's global expropriation approach to refugees was shown in the absence of proposals to relocate displaced persons in the vast expanses of "unused" lands of the western United States. Refugee populations were problems to be relocated elsewhere, in other imagined regions of terra nullis. While the population densities of wartime eastern Oregon, Idaho, or Montana were comparable to those of regions in Central America and South America, considered by the M Project as prime relocation centers for displaced persons, there are no declassified projects proposing such relocation schemes. In practice, postwar displaced persons most frequently settled not in the "underdeveloped" western U.S. states, but in mid-Atlantic and east-north central states, a fact that reveals some important agrarian biases in the relocation schemes pursued by Bowman and Field (Daniels 2004: 111; Smith 2003: 315).

The United States was not considered a primary resettlement area by the M Project largely because of Bowman's racial biases. Bowman believed that "a people having staked out a territory as we have done in America certainly has the right to look at itself from the eugenic standpoint" (quoted in Smith 2003: 308). Bowman did not want to allow refugees to "weaken" America; instead, he advocated relocating them to strategic locations in other regions, where their labor could contribute to the growth of markets in ways that would benefit the American economy (see Smith 2003: 314–16).

The M Project searched outside the United States and throughout the past and present for information indicating how and where refugees could be reestablished. One report analyzed how the Japanese had successfully resettled populations to Hokkaido during the nineteenth century; another evaluated the Belgian Congo's capacity to relocate "white agricultural settlers" due to its "vast stretches of productive land but also immense supplies of mineral wealth."[16] Another report evaluated an orphanage program developed by a Quaker organization in eastern Poland following the First World War.[17] A whole series of reports summarized economic and demographic conditions in various regions of Asia, Africa, and South America. The prospects of resettling European refugees in the Kimberley region of western Australia were described in reports M-4 and M-43. Report M-45, "Settlement Possibilities in the Virgin Islands," concluded that about four thousand refugees could be relocated there for a cost less than one million dollars.

Some report summaries read like real-estate prospectuses in which entire countries or vast regions were hyped for occupation, as if inhabitants would welcome invaders moved from another continent at the behest of an American president. Report R-160, "Settlement Possibilities in Nicaragua," pitched that country as "the largest but relatively least densely peopled and the least known of all the Central American Republics," and demographic data presented population-density figures for different regions of Nicaragua (Field 1962: 102). But it was the racial judgment of the M Project staff that "it is more than doubtful whether white small farmers of European descent can endure the climate of these hot lowlands and do heavy manual work" (Field 1962: 103).

Racial essentialist attitudes permeated the M Project. Some of the racism is implicit within larger arguments, but explicitly racist statements are also present. In report R-143, "Population and Planning in the Pacific," the empirical statement, "Mankind has now fallen short of cultivated area to the extent of at least 20 percent" is followed by the claim that "the unoccupied arable lands of the earth lie mostly in the hot climates, *where only the Asiatic groups can toil in the fields.* Freedom of Asiatic emigration may not only remedy the present severe global food shortage, but also improve the purchasing power of a thousand million Asiatics so as to prevent an industrial slump in the postwar world" (in Field 1962: 95–96; emphasis added). While this entry later criticized the threats that colonialism presented to peace and advocated for a dismantling of "economic imperialism in the colonies," there were still the racial assumptions that "Asiatic groups" possessed a predisposition to toil in the equatorial fields of the world. Thus, Asians, and not European displaced persons, were to be selected for such work.

Other reports pressed race-based analysis even further. The report "Demographic Consequences of European Contact with Primitive Peoples" (M-230) examined S. F. Cook's (1945) argument that World War Two had disrupted a state of equilibrium in which "primitive peoples" had been thrust into contact with the modern world and his claims that the destructive forces of miscegenation would accelerate. Cook believed that this mixing of "the White and Yellow races" would lead to a state "in the not too far distant years to come [that] must inevitably be the leveling off of the human race, with the extinction by hybridization of all existing primitive and semi-primitive peoples" (in Field 1962: 259).

In "Report on South American Indian Social Resistance to Western Civilization" (R-61), Alexander Stern examined the obstructionist strategies that Indian peoples might enact as their lands were occupied by foreign refugees. The Mayan views of production, political economy, and settlement were presented so that American policymakers could subvert whatever forms of resistance would be offered by indigenous peoples attempting to defend their lands. The report's summary stated:

> The contemporary Maya Indian can support his family by sixty days of labor out of the entire year. It is certainly presumptive for a race which aspires to a forty hour week to give advice to a race that has already achieved a twelve hour one.
>
> The state of war between Indian culture and European civilization has existed in South America for three centuries. . . . This Report is a brief historical and cultural survey of the evidence to show that the native Indian populations of the Western Hemisphere have established a definite tech-

nique of resistance to Western civilization as represented by political authority and commercial practices current since 1492. The purpose of including
this study is as a caution to the assumption that the South American Indians
are susceptible to the same economic and social motives which are applica-
ble to the peoples of European stock. This consideration is considered pertinent to any inter-governmental planning for migration and settlement.
(Field 1962: 46)

Thus, an anthropological understanding of what George Foster later called the
"Image of Limited Good" was identified with the purpose of cautioning would-
be interlopers that different cultural motivations might require different incentives (cf. Foster 1967b: 123–24).

The M Project and Jewish Refugees

The M Project considered various proposals to move displaced European Jews to
scattered "homelands" in locations ranging from Palestine to Australia, Nigeria,
or Brazil after the war. Most of these proposals were of a small scale—designed to
break up and move small segments of Jewish refugee populations rather than to
establish anything like a Jewish Homeland of the scale and scope of what eventually became the State of Israel. There are suggestions that this diasporatic
approach was influenced by Bowman. In 1943, Henry Wallace observed that
"Bowman's plan essentially is to spread the Jews thin all over the world," a plan
that combined Bowman's anti-Semitism with his desires to establish scattered
rural settlements (in Smith 2003: 313). Some proposals were as surreal as Michael
Chabon's fictional postwar Jewish state located on Sitka Island (Chabon 2007).
Report R-26 explored establishing Jewish colonies in Saskatchewan, and reports
R-30–34 and R-40 considered settlements in various African locations. Report
M-44, "Settlement Possibilities in Nigeria," proposed moving two thousand Jewish refugees from Poland and Czechoslovakia to Nigeria on the conditions that
these refugees be from a professional class and "pledge their intention to spend
their life in Nigeria" (Field 1962: 168). Report M-49 described plans to build
Jewish settlements in northwestern Australia.

Some studies were more evaluative than prescriptive; others combined both
of these elements. For example, Report R-19, "Settlement Possibilities in Southern Brazil," first examined the recent migration of German Jews to southern
Brazil, then proposed a large-scale settlement venture based on a recent irriga-
tion plan. In the 1930s, the Jüdische Landarbeit Company had financed the

purchase of large parcels of property in southern Brazil and arranged for the transport of German Jewish refugees. Under this program, the company

> concluded an agreement with Paraná Plantations, Ltd., subject to the currency regulations imposed by the German Government, for the purchase of settlers' plots against payment in Reichsmarks. Paraná Plantations, Ltd., utilized the credit balance so created for the purchase of machinery of German make, having agreed to complete the construction of a railway line linking the town to Londrina with a point on the Paraná River and thus with the frontier of Paraguay. It is this clearing agreement involving the purchase of German equipment against blocked German currency ("emigrant" or "refugee" marks) which made possible the land purchases of Jüdische Landarbeit. Unfortunately, the outbreak of World War II put an end to these activities. Few immigrants were able to settle on the plots purchased from Paraná Plantations, Ltd. (Field 1962: 16)

The M Project considered reviving this unfinished jungle Ashkenazi relocation fantasy, although nothing occurred beyond the planning stage. The project's summary of report M-27's "Plan for Jewish Settlement in Northwestern Australia" demonstrated both the managerial and racial-determinist assumptions that directed the work:

> For many years Australians have wondered how they could settle Northern Australia. The difficulties in the way of settling men of the White race are many. The climate is subtropical, with a long dry season. The good soils are in scattered areas and the competition of the more fertile south and east made this area unattractive for Australians. But Australians were always conscious that the empty North was both a menace and a reproach. Even though a great deal of money had been spent in experimental settlement, there was no outstanding success anywhere.
>
> In 1939 Dr. I Steinberg, Secretary of the Free Land League, submitted a Memorandum to the Government of Western Australia setting out the principles upon which the proposed settlement was to be formed. These were the four main points:
>
>> 1. The settlers should not become a political island, but would become Australian Citizens and be welded into the political structure of the Commonwealth.
>> 2. Control of the local Government would be entrusted to the settlers and they would have complete religious and spiritual liberty.

3. The Free Land League would provide all the capital required, would be responsible in cooperation with representatives of the Australian Government for collecting the settlers, and would be responsible for developing the settlement so that there would be no incentive to leave the area.

4. The settlement would be scientifically planned on a cooperative basis so that it would become self-supporting at the earliest possible moment.

The consent of the Western Australian Government was given in August, 1939. However, certain leaders expressed the opinion that no association, Jewish or otherwise, would be likely to throw millions of pounds into an experiment foredoomed to failure. If any people in the world could make a success of this settlement it would be the exile refugees of Europe, because they had the greatest incentive known to man to ensure it—the desire for a home and freedom. Moreover, the settlers were not to come in great number, but in small groups, as engineers and experts could make ready for them. Despite the postponement of this plan because of World War II, the Memorandum concluded with the words: "Australia will find a home for all those who have suffered with us for a democratic way of life." (Field 1962:169)

The discussion of "settling men of the White race" and the report's diminished concern for the Aborigines' rights clarifies biases against native populations and a privileging of European displaced peoples. Report 48 summarized the Soviet resettlement of Jews in Birobidzhan, examining the impact of the "negative psychological attitude of the settlers" on this effort to establish an ethnic autonomous region of the USSR (Field 1962: 37).[18]

The R-49 report recommended the resettlement of two hundred fifty thousand European Jews each year in eastern Peru. This was advised because the land was "fertile, rich in natural resources, climatically magnificent and suitable for Europeans. The population is so sparse that the region is almost empty. There are no endemic diseases except malaria which occurs only in a few marshy places" (Field 1962:38). It is remarkable that a project directed by an anthropologist and geographer envisioned eastern Peru as an "almost empty" region devoid of indigenous peoples and descendents of Europeans who had already conquered the land. To even theoretically ponder such ideas, Field had to ignore basic anthropological knowledge about land use, imperial history, and the struggles of indigenous peoples.

Another series of reports considered establishing a permanent "Jewish national home in Palestine" (M-240, in Field 1962: 263). They described developments in Palestine during the war (M-305), the fate of Jews in Europe (M-248), and the establishment of "Communal Settlements in Palestine" (M-327). One report, "Absorptive Capacity of Palestine" (M-60), estimated that the wartime population of Palestine was about one and a half million people, yet it was about the same size as Sicily (with a population of four million), Holland, or Belgium (both with populations of about eight million). Archaeological reports estimating Palestine's population levels as high as four million people during the Greco-Roman occupation were cited to justify radically increasing the population, arguing, "It is reasonable to suppose that with the aid of modern technology that figure will not only be reached once more, but considerably exceeded" (Field 1962: 177).

Like Australia, South America, and central Africa, Palestine was constructed as an underused and empty land awaiting the arrival of industrious newcomers. The M Project drew on erroneous claims that the Muslims, Jews, and Christians of Palestine had wastefully left vast tracts of arable land unfarmed. These distortions led the M Project's recommendations to coincide with Zionist recommendations for the settlement of Palestine. The M Project's historical analysis "Jewish Settlements in Palestine, 1935–1945" (M-270) accepted these biased accounts of land-use history:

> It is basic to the Palestine program that agricultural settlement should be fostered. The agricultural expansion stimulated and financed by the Jewish Agency during the War period has been striking. One-third of all funds spent by the Jewish Agency from 1936–43 was devoted to that activity. After a description of new and older settlements, a list of all settlements since 1939 is given, together with the name of the colonizing Agency, the area and population, as well as the information on Jewish settlements in Palestine since 1939, and the source of information. The money given for settlement provides for a house, a stable, poultry, a horse, cattle, machinery, seeds, irrigation or water supply, and maintenance for a few months. The Colonization Department of the Jewish Agency estimates that to settle one family on the land an investment of LP [Palestinian Pounds] 500–600 is required excluding the cost of the land. When the latter is included, this would be about LP 900. For comparative purpose, it may be noted that the cost of settling a family in Australia is figured at about LP 2000. (M-270)

This skewed analysis and these findings pertaining to the planned resettlement of Jewish refugees in Palestine was no worse than the M Project's overall misreading of the world as an unclaimed or underused resource waiting for American management—but this misreading was taken seriously. These assumptions about underdeveloped lands in the postwar, post-Holocaust world contributed to American policies favoring the establishment of Israel in Palestine (Farago 1947). Such claims about Palestine had political uses, as Steve Niva observed:

> The claim that Palestine was largely empty and underutilized has a long pedigree in the Western encounter with Palestine. This attempt to erase and deny the presence of Palestinians on the grounds of their alleged backwardness can be found in any eighteenth or nineteenth century travel accounts, from Chateaubriand, Mark Twain, Lamartine, Nerval and Disraeli to its contemporary exponents like Joan Peters, Benjamin Netanyahu and Alan Dershowitz. It is precisely this kind of thinking that informed the Zionist slogan: a land without people, for a people without the land. But no matter how relatively less industrialized the Palestinian Arabs were, they not only constituted the majority population on the land for the past 500 years, but by the 1940's they outnumbered recent Jewish immigrants three to one and were in the process of building a national society under foreign military occupation.[19]

In the end, the M Project was but one policy piece that informed postwar American approaches to questions regarding the establishment of the State of Israel. But this piece contained all of the political, economic, and logistical problems inherent in each of the M Project's proposals.

M Project Results

The M Project's global postwar refugee-relocation schemes proved to be expensive and impractical. The project was such a misguided effort that, having estimated that only one million families would require relocation at a cost of twenty-five billion 1945 dollars spread out over a twenty-five period (see Smith 2003: 303), it did not even come close to estimating how many refugees were affected by the war. When President Harry S Truman canceled the M Project on November 30, 1945, "Its legacy was a truckload of documents and two thousand pages of unpublished reports, which were by one account, 'filed and forgotten.' The scientific will to study refugee resettlement was severed from the will to do anything about it" (Smith 2003: 303; cf. Field 1982: 99–102).

While President Roosevelt's grand plans for postwar relocations and high-tech reclamations of land for refugees were not implemented, they reveal important elements of America's dreams for the postwar world. But Henry Field's reports of the postwar dreams he shared with President Roosevelt reveal an intriguing postwar anthropological vision. Field claimed he told President Roosevelt that, after the war, he hoped the president would call for

> the creation in Washington of an Anthropogeographical Research Center, where a file of data (excluding all military, political and economic information), continent by continent, country by country, would be concentrated. This would necessitate a large team of experts going through and making copies of all recent data in the Government files, especially the Research and Analysis Branch of the Office of Strategic Services, ONI, G-2 [a subdivision of MID], A-2 [gathered air intelligence] and the Department of State. All U.S. representatives abroad would be ordered to send information to this Center to keep the files up-to-date. Of especial importance would be all world population figures and projected estimates; these would be furnished to the Department of Commerce for correlation with their figures on world-wide natural resources. While this Center would duplicate existing, but scattered, data, it would prove of the greatest value for political planning and incidentally to the military. (Field 1962: 329)

Field claimed that Roosevelt approved the plan and that he had been instructed to prepare a memorandum to formally present the ideas "after the Victory was won" (Field 1962: 329–30). Roosevelt died before Field could present a detailed proposal to be enacted after America proved victorious in Europe and the Pacific, but similar programs were pursued by others proceeding along these wartime trajectories during the Cold War.

At the war's end, President Truman addressed issues of reconstruction and relocation without paying much attention to the M Project's work, although resettlement of Jews in Palestine did follow the logic of some recommendations made by the M Project. Without Roosevelt's patronage, all the work ended without specific applications. The Truman administration focused on other issues, and there were increasing realizations of the serious political problems that would have been unleashed by the orchestrated relocation of such vast numbers of refugees across the globe. Under the Displaced Persons Act of 1948, America took in more than two hundred thousand war refugees and orphans. Later, Congress, President Truman, and Cold War intelligence agencies devised postwar immigration policies to regulate the influx of refugees.[20] John Carter believed that, "if Roosevelt had lived, maybe something could have been done along these lines. Roosevelt did not live. This was all waste[d] effort. The postwar [displaced persons] problem became almost exclusively a Jewish problem except for those wretched bastards who were sent back to Russia because Stalin said they were ethnic Russians or whatnot" (Morrissey 1966: 24).

Presidential Adviser Philleo Nash

Henry Field and Aleš Hrdlička were not the only wartime anthropologists advising Roosevelt's staff. Philleo Nash began the war studying domestic racial dynamics at the Office of Facts and Figures (OFF) on the recommendation of his former professor Harold Lasswell. Nash also worked on the problem of racial discrimination in the armed forces. Late in the war, when the army agreed to let one "Negro platoon" fight along with "white platoons" in Europe, Nash reedited the army manual's discussion of race relations, a policy change that became a significant step toward integrating the armed services (Hess 1973: 70–72).

Nash's primary duties were to compile public and secret reports on domestic wartime racial clashes for Roosevelt's administrative assistant Jonathan Daniels. The White House was concerned that racial unrest threatened the American war effort. Nash viewed these riots as social phenomena that applied anthropologists could study and control. Nash later recalled, "In those days it was common theory that race riots were both unpredictable and uncontrollable. This is like supposing that a tornado or a hurricane is unpredictable merely because you can't control it after it gets started, but if you have good information, good incoming intelligence, you can anticipate the developments, you can anticipate the course of the hurricane and even of tornadoes and you can take evasive action: Communities can be warned; people can get out of the way. This is the very least that modern science ought to be able to do" (Nash quoted in Hess 1973: 53). In August 1943, Nash monitored racial hostilities in Detroit as high unemployment and rationing increased animosity between blacks and whites until acts of mob violence erupted in the streets. During the war, racial tensions and discrimination were generally interpreted as state rather than federal problems, so the White House was cautious about allowing federal agencies to intervene. As the fighting in Detroit escalated into racial warfare, and "carloads of Blacks, on their way to the war production plants, were attacked by gangs of angry Whites," Nash and others in Washington, D.C., became increasingly concerned about the effects of using federal forces in these tense situations (Nash 1986: 191). Nash later wrote:

> The police asked for help, and some state guards attempted to restore order, but were inadequate. A battalion of military police was situated in Detroit, camped in a race track unused because of the war. They had practiced drills,

being aware—from their own sources—of Detroit tensions, but their drills had been to deploy their forces around City Hall, which was in no danger. An officer from the Fifth Service Command flew from Chicago to Detroit, reading en route, we were later told, the Constitution and laws regarding the use of Federal troops in domestic emergencies. Thirty lives were lost and property was damaged to the amount of five million dollars before the proper procedures could be sorted out, the necessary Presidential proclamation be issued, and the full force of Federal troops be used to restore order.

Throughout the day Mr. Daniels, acting for the President of the United States, found that the fastest information on the rapidly changing situation came from the teleprinters of the Office of War Information (OWI), which I was watching for him. . . . As a courtesy to the OWI, all the major news networks provided us with news printers which were arranged in a bank in the OWI press room. Jonathan Daniels was a newsman, and having reporters keep him up to date appealed to him. Their information proved to be accurate as well as fast. It was a matter of pride to me, of course, to be ahead of the numerous intelligence agencies, both military and civilian, that were also called on by the White House. (Nash 1986: 191)

Nash's tracking and analysis of the rumors surrounding these events allowed the government to identify specific locations where violence was likely to occur. Nash found, "Among the prime tension centers were Washington, D.C., and Detroit, Michigan. Numerous memoranda went out from OFF to all the War Agencies naming these and other cities where sporadic violence was occurring and where it seemed likely to grow" (Nash 1986: 191).

Nash believed that using the military or police forces to quell outbreaks of racial violence or other riots were useless because such interventions led to interruptions of work at war-production factories. Nash used his White House credentials to establish a communications network to track rumors, news stories, and other sources of information relating to possible domestic race riots. The OWI tickers and memos from the army's domestic counter-intelligence unit and other agencies provided basic information. Nash wrote that his

method of operation was simplicity itself. I scanned the tickers each day for news of tension-revealing incidents in a city, a military camp, or a war production plant. If it was of a scale that seemed threatening, I attempted to get all the information possible over the telephone. These calls were made from the Office of War Information. . . . The so-called Black press, the Negro Weeklies, were helpful. Their Washington representatives all knew what I was doing and why. . . . If no mention had been made in the weekly report from Counterintelligence, I called my opposition number there and asked for details. Usually that took too long, for our theory required that we cope with small incidents while they were still small. Coping was, of course, more difficult than finding out about them. Once we had pinpointed a problem . . . Daniels could call the agency representative if he wished to ask for action. (Nash 1986: 192)

Nash maintained close contact with members of the black press corps. During the war, the FBI suspected that Nash might be the identity behind the pseudonym Charley Cherokee, the *Chicago Defender*'s "National Grapevine" columnist.[21] (The journalist Alfred E. Smith wrote these columns, though Nash used his contacts to get important information to Smith and other black journalists during the war (see Price 2004a: 264–66, 377, n. 1). Nash occasionally helped introduce domestic propaganda stories stressing racial harmony or other unifying racial themes in the American press and other forms of media. In 1943, he tried to get the Censor Board, the War Relocation Authority, and the OWI to pressure those syndicating the "Superman" newspaper comic strip to remove or alter a racist storyline depicting interned Japanese Americans as saboteurs and spies (Chang 1993).

Nash studied various domestic racial problems. The specific issues varied but included workplace pay inequities and disputes over parking-space availability between whites and blacks. When Nash identified specific potential problems, he contacted local officials and helped them take proactive measures to prevent nascent seeds of conflict from sprouting into violent or disruptive action (see Nash 1986: 192). While Nash could not solve every problem, he found that having someone connected to the White House who appeared concerned about these issues made a profound difference, because "the fact that they were being worked on was often enough to reduce tensions" (Nash 1986: 192). As his wife, Edith Nash, observed, support from the White House expedited action because "the War Powers Act gave the White House the ability to radically address grievances of black workers and prevent interruptions. Several incidents were prevented from escalating into major work stoppages. Thurgood Marshall once told Nash that if he'd 'been at Lincoln's side there never would have been a Civil War . . . (and we'd all still be slaves')" (E. Nash 1989: 34).

Nash's work for the Truman White House continued after the war's end, and during the final months of the war he worried that race riots, similar to those that followed the First World War, could break out as troops returned home.[22]

Appraising White House Social Engineers

Henry Field's and Philleo Nash's contributions to presidential projects developed strains of applied anthropology that shared desires to control relatively powerless groups of peoples. Field's vision was global, while Nash focused domestically, but both Field and Nash used ethnographic data to study and understand the populations they wished to manipulate. But most significantly, neither Nash nor Field used ethnographic data to generate input from these populations on how to improve the fundamental problems that affected them. Rather, they used the data to manipulate these populations in ways that were convenient to the national interests determined by the White House.

Nash helped the nation's war production by using applied anthropological-research methods to influence the actions of justifiably disgruntled domestic minority populations. Although these acts of social engineering occurred for commonly accepted goals, they also raised questions about the role of social scientists in the manipulation of members of a democratic society. Nash's mentor, Harold Lasswell, felt at ease with a high degree of social manipulations, but he also thought that democracy was too dangerous a tool to be left to the populace. As early as 1933, Lasswell had argued that "successful social and political management often depends on proper coordination of propaganda with coercion, violent or non-violent; economic inducement (including bribery); diplomatic negotiation; and other techniques" (quoted in Simpson 1994: 18). The war made such arguments palatable to many in Washington, and Nash found himself using anthropology to manage social unrest in the interest of keeping war production online. In such instances, the root problems of racial inequality were set aside for the needs of war.

War necessitates such choices, and given the conditions that racial minorities and all Americans would have faced after a Nazi victory, it was a wise choice to finish the struggle against the Axis before undertaking a domestic civil-rights struggle. But this necessity should not camouflage the reality that these techniques were developed to serve the interests of a powerful social sector moving against and manipulating the immediate desires of less powerful individuals. Yet even as scholars routinely trace the roots of American applied anthropology to the war, there has been a reticence to examine how applied anthropology's beginnings simultaneously served a noble cause while honing contra-democratic skill sets designed to undermine the will of people. In the instance of Field's research, these outcomes were engineered in a democratic society at war, but a hesitance remains to openly examine applied anthropology's lineage of manipulation in the name of freedom.

Field's efforts to engineer resettlement also strove to design and manipulate social outcomes, but they had no definitive results. If the enactment of plans is used as a measure, the absolute failure of the M Project is obvious. The failure of the project can be declared tragic, given its inattention to aiding Nazi victims.[23] But such outcomes were apparently never a real driving force for the project. As the historian Neil Smith argues, Isaiah Bowman's true intentions for the M Project were

> not at all about rescuing the victims of Nazism but about marshaling refugees for the economic development of underdeveloped areas. Refugee resettlement was a means to that end. It sought to fill in the economic interstices of an already occupied world and take advantage of the gross geographic unevenness of capitalist development to engage all corners of the planet in the web of the world market.
>
> This precisely described Bowman's experiment. The interstices of developed space were simultaneously a laboratory for science and for capital. Land, labor, and capital were the crucial ingredients: the M Project was about identifying the location and condition of "underdeveloped" land and about galvanizing government capital subsidies for their development. Refugees—"excess population"—were the motive force, the labor in the form of yeoman entrepreneurs. (Smith 2003: 315)

Since the 1930s, Bowman had nurtured visions of expanding American economic interests on a more global scale, and these interests were the guiding force that determined how the M Project would proceed in planning massive refugee-relocation schemes. Smith argued that Bowman's larger vision of globalism was the guiding force behind the M Project's relocation plans, because

> the resettlement of different populations in different places around the world could become an economic weapon in a trade scramble after the war. . . . While it cynically cashed in on popular concern for the victims of Nazi terror, especially after 1942, the entire rationale for the M Project and its Hopkins predecessor was a direct and practical application of Bowman's 1930s pioneering and settlement research on a world scale and in U.S. interests. The United States would confront less a frontier line after the war than an accumulation of pockets that could still be colonized, developed, and brought into trade relations with the country: the "possibility of increas-

ing the development of underdeveloped land" became crucial. "The whole earth is occupied and there is no such thing as unused land," only under- developed land, uneconomic use, inefficient distribution of populations, unrealized resources of human strength, aptitude and skill. (Smith 2003: 313)

Anthropology had been easily led into assisting plans that would have used survivors of the Nazis' horrific genocidal campaigns as pawns in a global drive to expand American capitalism's developing global markets. Field later gave no indication that he considered the M Project to have been anything but a grand idea that was foolishly terminated by a new president who did not understand its potential.

Smith's analysis that Bowman's interest in relocating refugees had more to do with spreading international capitalism than offering humanitarian aid compli- cates our understanding of Field's anthropological contributions to the M Proj- ect. The war easily created such blind spots. That Field and his staff could labor on the project for three years and not consider the uses of such a program has parallels in numerous postwar development projects that similarly used anthro- pologists as foot soldiers to advance undeclared economic agendas (Hancock 1989; Mosse 2005; Price 1998c).

One of the side effects of secret programs like the M Project was that, as secrecy disengaged the normative, potentially self-correcting features of the open academic scientific process, members of research groups who became mired in fallacious thinking labored unchecked under increasingly questionable assump- tions and flawed logic. Because the M Project was not open to scrutiny by outside members of an academic community, internal reified pressures reinforced beliefs that the United States could somehow move tens of millions of people across the world without creating serious problems. The dynamics of "groupthink" com- bined with institutional secrecy to keep critical eyes and minds from focusing on the flaws embedded in the inner workings of this project.

Lyon's assessment of the M Project's contributions to the war found only a single instance in which the project's data resulted in action—although this action had nothing to do with the relocation of refugees. "During 1943 Field and his staff, while looking for islands in the Pacific that would be of strategic impor- tance to Japan, realized that one island in particular, Nauru, was the coun- try's largest source of phosphate," Lyon found. "Field passed the information to [William] Donovan, who in turn passed it on to the Navy. The island was bombed and raided" (Lyon 1994: 133).

While the M Project envisioned moving foreign, rather than domestic, populations into new lands for economic and political ends, its vision did share basic conceptual elements with German and Japanese wartime expansion schemes. As Michael Bess has observed, Germany and Japan envisioned relocating their populations into the newly occupied lands of Europe and Asia under new colonization schemes that (in the Japanese case) "would offer an outlet to surplus population at home, and simultaneously consolidate Japanese power around the western Pacific. Asia was weak and internally divided; it seemed natural to the Japanese that a vigorous and dynamic people like themselves should take over the region and run it properly" (Bess 2006: 30). Japanese, German, and American plans all viewed such relocation schemes as properly facilitating the improved use of resources over those of former occupants. The United States did not invade sovereign nations claiming historical rights to impose relocations, but the White House's dreams of relocating tens of millions of refugees shared visions of grand economic advantages to be accrued by the United States upon its victory at the war's end.

While the M Project's grand schemes were rejected in favor of more modest plans, the establishment of the State of Israel in Palestine followed some of the project's general recommendations and, more important, the Israeli state used the same claims of "empty lands" to justify its occupation of land. Just as the usurpations necessitated by the creation of Israel spawned violent conflicts, one can imagine similar conflicts following the implementation of many of the M Project's relocation scenarios. It is possible that the implementation of the hundreds of relocation plans in the M Project would have created an equal number of conflicts as land disputes and sovereignty issues followed the occupation of lands so carelessly construed by anthropologists as empty.

Some might argue that these secondary problems were not the concern of the M Project. Such an argument disarticulates actions from consequences, but it does highlight a larger problem faced by applied anthropologists in times of war and peace: When presented with limited designated outcomes, anthropologists often find themselves doing "piecework" on large projects that have grand designs beyond their control or comprehension. Operating on narrow charges diminishes the holistic perspective of an anthropological view and relinquishes all control of the coming implementations.

Constraints on what would be done with anthropologists' work were even more pronounced at other war agencies, where some anthropologists struggled to diminish the horrible effects of harsh wartime policies on populations they were assigned to study.

CHAPTER SEVEN

Internment Fieldwork:

Anthropologists and the War

Relocation Authority

> Inevitably, anthropologists in such a bureaucratic situation are constrained to assimilate
> the language, perspectives, categories of thought, organizational codes, concerns, and
> values of the encompassing bureaucracy in order to be successful. The anthropology
> which results deviates markedly from the issues, methods, and concerns of traditional
> anthropology.
> —PETER T. SUZUKI (1981: 42)

On February 19, 1942, just over two months after Japan attacked the American
fleet in occupied Hawaii, President Roosevelt issued Executive Order 9066 authorizing the Secretary of War to exclude all Japanese Americans and Japanese
foreign nationals from all "prescribed military areas." On March 2, Public Proclamation 1 designated the regions of western California, western Washington, and
western Oregon and a small portion of southern Arizona "Military Area Number
1"—a region off limits to all Japanese Americans. "Military Area Number 2"
consisted of only a few areas specifically designated as off limits to Japanese
Americans in the remaining areas of eastern Arizona, California, Oregon, and
Washington. While some of the issued legal proclamations could have led to the
removal of Americans with German or Italian ancestry, no such internments
occurred.[1] Executive Order 9066's authority to incarcerate and move such a
diverse group of people en masse without any further legal process was legally
problematic and was challenged on several fronts in the courts. As legal battles
slowly moved through the courts, the army oversaw the internment of 110,000
citizens who were guilty only of having Japanese ancestry, although the U.S.
Supreme Court found the internment to be legal in the *Korematsu v. United States*
decision issued on December 18, 1944.

FBI Director J. Edgar Hoover opposed the indiscriminate internment of Japanese Americans, preferring more discriminating forms of internment. In a 1943 FBI report, he argued that it was "extremely unfortunate that the Government, the War Relocation Authority, and the public, did, in the past, seize upon what they first believed to be a simple determining factor of loyalty. There actually can be only one efficient method of processing the Japanese for loyalty, which consists of individual, not mass, consideration" (quoted in Powers 1987: 250). While Hoover publicly opposed the detention of Japanese Americans, his reasons appear to have been derived in part from discontent at surrendering the authority for such a massive domestic campaign to the army rather than concern about the injustice of accusing individuals of mass guilt by association. In the first months after Pearl Harbor, 2,192 Japanese Americans were arrested as the FBI conducted West Coast raids (Thomas and Nishimoto 1946: 5). Henry Field's M Project staff used data they had secretly, possibly illegally, acquired from the U.S. Census Bureau to provide the FBI with the names and addresses of "suspicious" Japanese Americans (Field 1982: 11; Hayashi 2004: 37–38).

The army directed the evacuation of all Japanese Americans living in Military Area Number 1. With little warning, residents in individual communities were told to dispose of property and report to specified areas. Almost two-thirds of those interned were American citizens. The speed of these evacuations violently disrupted and scarred the lives of those who were so quickly moved and then interned. Edward Spicer observed that, across western California, Oregon, and Washington, the public watched "boys and girls, young men and women, and older people of Japanese descent stand by piles of baggage waiting for Greyhound buses to take them to camps on former fairgrounds and race tracks. The public was not as passive as it appeared. It merely felt worn but relieved. A scapegoat was carrying off the baggage of their fears, anxieties, doubts and frustrations" (Spicer et al. 1969: 38).

In March 1942, soldiers suddenly arrived on Bainbridge Island, Washington, and posted fliers in public places announcing that all Japanese Americans had six days to pack up their possessions and report for relocation at a designated assembly area. Similar scenes were rapidly repeated in towns throughout western Oregon, Washington, and California from February through July as the army suddenly evacuated Japanese American communities.

The army's Wartime Civil Control Administration managed the temporary regional centers (fifteen "assembly centers" and two "reception centers") where evacuees were initially taken. They were makeshift detention centers with inadequate sanitation or basic living facilities. Families were forced to live in dirty horse stalls or crammed into tents and left to eat spoiled food and live among raw sewage. These centers were located on racetracks and fairgrounds in communities in relative proximity to the evacuated communities in Arizona (Parker), California (Fresno, Manzanar, Marysville, Merced, Sacramento, Stockton, Tanforan, Turlock, Pinedale, Salinas, Tulare, Santa Anita), Oregon (Portland), and Washington (Puyallup).

The War Relocation Authority (WRA) was established by presidential decree on March 18, 1942. It was charged with establishing and managing ten "relocation facilities" where Japanese Americans were to be detained. The ten "relocation centers" were located in Arizona (Gila, Jerome, Poston, Rohwer), California (Manzanar, Tule Lake), Colorado (Granada), Idaho (Minidoka), Utah (Topaz), and Wyoming (Heart Mountain). Despite the presence of armed guards, the WRA's official policy was that the camps were not internment camps or prisons.[2] Instead, the WRA claimed that the camps were to meet two temporary needs: first, "to provide communities where evacuees might live and contribute, through their work, to their own support pending their gradual reabsorption into private employment and normal American life"; and second, "to serve as wartime homes for those evacuees who might be unable or unfit to relocate in ordinary American communities" (WRA 1943).

After September 1942, the WRA's official policy was that all "loyal" Japanese Americans could leave the camps to "reenter private employment in agriculture or industry" to work in areas located in the interior of the United States (WRA 1943). In practice, most Japanese Americans remained at the "relocation centers," which functionally became prison camps. The management of the interned people was accomplished with the assistance of about two dozen anthropologists who studied, managed, or acted as advocates for the 110,000 Japanese Americans.[3]

Edward Spicer later observed that the internment of Japanese Americans was not only "the greatest mass migration of American residents in history," it was "far greater than any movement of American Indians from tribal lands to reservations. America had learned something about human engineering since the Indians were moved. The engineering exhibited in the evacuation of the Japanese from the West Coast was a magnificent tour de force, as different and superior in technique and administrative management from the transfer of Indians as the oxcart differs from the latest bomber" (Spicer et. al 1969: 43).

Remarkably few people protested Executive Order 9066 (Cockburn 2005). As Alexander Cockburn observed, "The overall collapse of progressive America's moral leaders was breathtaking. The political left, swept away on the currents of 'the good war' and the fight against the Axis did nothing. Only a few brave souls piped up, some of them very gallantly. It was the usual sprinkle of Unitarians, Quakers, cranky libertarians and that thin line of decent exceptionalists who have the moral, historical and spiritual resources to say 'No!' when the chips are down and the Gadarene swine are stampeding over the cliff" (Cockburn n.d.).

The Communist Party supported the removal of Japanese American citizens into camps, as did other left-leaning organizations such as the Young Democrats and the Nisei Democratic Club.[4] Leaders of the Japanese American Citizens League (JACL) encouraged other Japanese Americans to cooperate with the military and civilian forces that would soon be incarcerating them (Robinson 2001: 117). Some members of the JACL argued that Japanese Americans were interned for their own safety, and while white mobs did attack and threaten some Japanese Americans, the internment was not a protective measure. The evacuated Nisei and Issei were told by the JACL: "You are not being accused of any crime. You are being removed only to protect you and because there might be one of you who might be dangerous to the United States. It is your contribution to the war effort. You should be glad to make the sacrifice to prove your loyalty" (Spicer et. al 1969: 60).

Few white Americans spoke out in opposition to the internment. Most of those who spoke in opposition did so in ways that opposed only some of the government's decision. For example, Tacoma's Mayor Harry P. Cain opposed the government's internment of all Japanese Americans because he "did not think eye slant or skin color had anything to do with loyalty." Instead of racial tests, Mayor Cain advocated for cultural or religious tests, arguing, "If born in this country; if a Christian; if employed side-by-side with others who fill that same classification . . . ; if educated in our schools; if a producer now and in the past; if maintained in a position of production—I should think that person could be construed to be a loyal American citizen" (Spicer et al. 1969: 45).

A few anthropologists spoke out against internment and other forms of discrimination directed against Japanese Americans, although their voices were largely ignored. Morris Opler's opposition to the internment of Japanese Americans led him to write a legal brief supporting the plaintiff's position in *Korematsu v. United States*, arguing that internment was an unconstitutional act (Starn 1986: 710).[5] When Melville Jacobs prepared to organize anthropologists at the December 1941 AAA meeting to protect Japanese Americans from an increasingly dangerous racist climate, he wrote to Margaret Mead asking for her support: "I know Benedict feels . . . as we do." He added, "If you feel the way we do . . . we would all be grateful for your support" (Mabee 1987: 6). But Mead did not publicly support Jacobs. At the 1941 AAA meeting, Jacobs proposed that the association unite in opposition to acts of racial prejudice against Japanese Americans. His proposal met mostly with silence and received little support voiced beyond that of Esther Goldfrank (see *AA* 1942: 286; Goldfrank 1978: 197). Mead later claimed she had worked behind the scenes preparing for congressional hearings held in March 1942, presumably opposing the internment. Mead took no public stance in opposition to the relocation. Carleton Mabee wrote that, while Mead remained publicly silent on the issue of internment, she

> seemed uncomfortable with treating the American-born Japanese as if they were not Americans, yet she avoided natural opportunities to protest the evacuation directly. In the summer of 1942, writing about what skills Americans have learned to help build a better postwar world, she mentioned incidentally, "we have learned . . . to take the children of Japanese parents and make them Americans without a gesture or a thought to show their cultural origin," but she did not add a word to say how tragic evacuation could be for such Americanized children. Available evidence does not indicate that Mead, Benedict, or any of their close associates, or anthropologists collectively, or the Committee for National Morale took any clear leadership to prevent the evacuation while it was being considered, or to protest it while it was being considered, or to protest it while it was occurring. (Mabee 1987: 6)

In the years after the war, a number of anthropologists stated opposition to the internment, but many such voices were silent when voices of protest might have mattered.[6]

BSR, JERS, and CAS Anthropologists

Three different organizations used anthropologists and other social scientists to study interned Japanese Americans. The Office of Indian Affairs (OIA) employed social scientists at its Bureau of Sociological Research (BSR) at the Colorado River Relocation Center in Poston, Arizona; the University of California, Berkeley, conducted aggressive studies of internees through the Japanese American Evacuation and Resettlement Study (JERS); and the War Relocation Authority employed dozens of social scientists in its Community Analysis Section (CAS).

While newly envisioned conceptions of applied anthropology were implemented in a wide variety of war agencies, it was perhaps these groups of anthropologists studying the captive populations of Japanese American who most clearly envisioned themselves as implementing a new form that could both manage and serve the populations they studied. Various strains of applied anthropology emerged in the camps, as most anthropologists studied populations to better manage them during their internment, while some anthropologists used their positions to try to better represent the needs of the interned to those in power to ameliorate a horrible situation.

Each of the agencies employing anthropologists in the camps operated under different directives and constraints. The social scientists at the BSR studied the "evacuated" populations at Poston under the directorship of John Collier of the OIA. Collier appointed Alexander Leighton and Edward Spicer to direct the research operations of the BSR. The sociologist Dorothy Swaine Thomas, director of JERS, employed anthropologists and sociologists to track the ethos of internee culture. Thomas attempted to maintain extremely strict control over the work of her employees and strove to have her workers operate outside of the influence of WRA administrators. CAS anthropologists worked directly for the WRA and they used anthropological field methods to study interned populations.

All fieldworkers faced obstacles in the camps. Under conditions of forced confinement, all outsiders were viewed with great suspicion. Internees who cooperated with researchers risked being labeled "*Inu*" (literally, "dog") or "informer," and such identifications carried very serious consequences. Most field researchers focused great attention on the nature of Japanese American loyalty to the United States (Kurashige 2001: 393). WRA and JERS analysts examined the influence of the prewar social matrix and assimilation on the life and reactions of those interned in WRA camps: "In a statistical analysis of Manzanar protesters, Opler found that they came disproportionately from rural communities and specific types of occupations, such as gardening, farming, fishing, and small business. Thomas, on the other hand, observed that pro-WRA internees tended [to] be college educated, Christian or secular in their religious convictions, and from urban, nonagricultural backgrounds. What distinguished them, she concluded, was that they were the 'most highly assimilated segments of the Japanese American minority'" (Kurashige 2001: 401).

The most significant difference between WRA and JERS researchers was that the WRA overtly used its research to effect changes in the camps, although, as with all applied research in wartime, opinions as to what constituted an "improvement" were highly subjective. All WRA anthropologists did not strive to be objective recorders or observers of the internment of Japanese Americans. Instead, some strove to help interned populations adapt to internment; still others collected data on internees that could be used by government agents to increase control over them.

The OIA and Poston's BSR

At Poston, Arizona's Colorado River center, Alexander Leighton established the BSR under the OIA to systematically study interned Japanese Americans.[7] Leighton was a medical doctor, and although his advanced degrees were not in anthropology, he approached his work at the BSR, and later at the OWI, with anthropological sensitivities. Before the war Leighton, had conducted psychological and ethnographic fieldwork among the Navaho and Inuit; he was a fellow of the AAA; and he became a professor of anthropology and sociology at Cornell University after the war.

Poston was the single camp managed by the OIA. In 1945, Leighton published *The Governing of Men* to promote his vision of an emerging applied social science that could facilitate designed social change, as the book jacket proclaimed, "to problems of race and labor relations, civil liberties, relief and rehabilitation" in a brave new world where anthropologists and other social scientists would manipulate policy and the public (Leighton 1945). These were strains of an applied anthropology seeking to serve populations through engineered manipulations. The BSR employed the anthropologists Conrad Arensberg, Elizabeth Colson, David French, Edward Spicer, and Tamie Tsuchiyama (Arensberg 1942). Among other duties Leighton, Spicer, and Colson "gave lectures on an ongoing basis that were intended to instruct the Japanese American personnel in the art of fieldwork," and Tsuchiyama and Spicer taught introduction to anthropology courses to interested internees, with University of Chicago credit awarded under arrangements made by Robert Redfield (Hirabayashi 1999: 45, 53–54).

Leighton observed the culture of Poston internees as well as the culture of those managing the camp. *The Governing of Men* adopted the narrative tone of a dispassionate, outside "scientific" observer recording data. Using the neutral voice of a textbook's prose, he assured readers that "there has been no intention to marshal data to show whether or not the evacuation was justified, or to analyze the way it was carried out. These questions involve matters concerning which data for forming an opinion are not available at present and they are not taken up in this study" (Leighton 1945: 44). The moral responsibility for these acts was systematically relegated to others. From his imagined perch as a distant observer, Leighton recorded both the justifications of administrators and internees' claims that the American government had unconstitutionally aided the theft of property (Leighton 1945: 46). But Leighton did not even look like a neutral observer. At Poston, he regularly wore his naval uniform, which, Tsuchiyama observed, helped "increase the distrust of the Japanese people" and created the appearance that Leighton was fulfilling a military role at the camp (Hirabayashi 1999: 53; Suzuki 1981: 57, n. 179).

Leighton characterized Poston staff members who developed personal relationships with evacuees and tried to treat them with respect and dignity as "people-minded." He described staff who thought that Poston "ought to be a concentration camp" as "stereotype-minded" (Leighton 1945: 85). He observed:

> To the stereotype-minded staff members the evacuees were Japanese first and people secondarily. Inherent in this was a feeling that they were all alike with motivations and behavior different from that of "white men" and therefore requiring different treatment. This conception of the evacuees varied a little from one staff member to another, some leaning more to hostility and suspicion than others, but for each individual it remained pretty constant no matter what kind of evacuee he was dealing with. It constituted a caste line between the staff members who felt this way and the residents of the camp, but it did not embody any accurate knowledge of Japanese culture and custom. (Leighton 1945: 84)

Leighton recorded that Poston evacuees were given limited democratic frameworks for self-governance, noting that administrators cautiously viewed even these limited measures "like Frankenstein, [as they] wondered uneasily what its creation would do" (Leighton 1945: 111), but he also recorded internees' view that this self-governance was only "a 'puppet government,' a creature of the Administration" (Leighton 1945: 123).

The "democracy" that the camps offered was not designed to bring freedom; it was designed to bring control. Camp administrators predetermined the range of electoral outcomes by limiting not who could vote, but who could run for elected positions. The WRA imposed specific "democratic" outcomes by only allowing Nisei to hold elected offices, thereby disempowering the Issei's otherwise natural leadership roles. The illusion of "self-government" in the camps was not convincing.

Leighton's allegiances to the camp managers were apparent in his writing. This bias was shown in his conceptual division of different social behaviors into oppositional categories of "social organization" (e.g., the camp advisory board, the evacuee police department, religious organizations) and "social disorganization" (e.g., resistance activities, including complaints about low wages, complaints upon learning that other camps had better living conditions, collapse of the agricultural efforts, violence against camp informers). Leighton described social behaviors that enabled a smooth captivity as "social organization," while those that complicated or resisted captivity were designated "social disorganiza-tion." Lane Hirabayashi argued that such biased conceptualizations not only left Leighton ignorant of the ways in which the camp's management was encouraging Issei "to reintroduce elements of their pre–World War II political organization," but they contributed to Leighton's misunderstanding that certain defiant be-haviors indicated "community disorganization" (Hirabayashi 1999: 109–10).

Nevertheless, Leighton's critical views of WRA staff biases illuminated details of staff reactions to the November 1942 Poston strike. The strike occurred after two community members were detained as suspects in the severe beating of an internee believed to be an informer. Leighton observed that protestors were correct in their legal interpretation that, under the Arizona State Constitution, suspects needed to be either arrested or released. They could not legally be held without charges. Leighton chronicled the reactionary views of many WRA staff members who seemed intent on using the strike as an excuse to unleash violence on internees (Leighton 1945: 172–82). He observed that both sides displayed emotional postures before and during the strike: "It has been suggested that among the evacuees one of the motivating forces of the Poston strike was the accumulation of many repressed feelings of anger and indignation from a great many different frustrations. The same reaction could be noted in the staff, and from some of them there rushed a white heat of hostility to meet the antipathy of the residents" (Leighton 1945: 176). Some staff members relished the prospect of being able to unleash "legitimate" violence on internees as they "expressed the desire for an opportunity to shoot them" (Leighton 1945: 179). Despite such passions, the prisoners were released, and the strike came to an end without violence. Leighton studied these events as if the camp were a wonderful labora-tory full of opportunities to study and learn to control social movements.

In the fall of 1943, the OIA relinquished administration of Poston to the WRA. The BSR was disbanded, and Alexander Leighton began working at the OWI's Foreign Morale Analysis Division (see chapter 8). Edward Spicer moved to Wash-ington, D.C., where he used what he had learned at Poston to direct the WRA's Community Analysis Section.[8]

Anthropologists at the WRA's Community Analysis Division

John Provinse was among the first anthropologists hired by the WRA after the agency was created in March 1942. He helped establish many of the policies that governed the camps. In 1943, Provinse helped the FBI establish a system for tracking interned Japanese Americans within the camps that would also record which internees were "a persistent and serious source of trouble in a relocation center [and] should be returned to an internment camp or transferred to an isolation camp" (Suzuki 1986b: 5). In Washington, D.C., Robert Redfield and John Embree advised Provinse on developing guiding policies for agency records management (Spicer 1946: 17). Redfield was the architect of the camps' stilted democratic system that allowed only American-born Japanese Americans the right to hold elective office (Hayashi 2004: 112). He justified these limits using Straussian logic that argued it was necessary to limit democracy in the camps because, "if the Authority had allowed the older people to hold the elective offices, the communities might have been controlled by the smaller Japanese element. These communities must be democracies, we have said, but they may not be pro-Japanese democracies" (Redfield 1943: 157–58). Redfield described the camps as keeping prisoners occupied and distracted, rather than empowered, by democracy. Observing that "people seem to be meeting constantly to discuss some measure or to vote on some issue or simply to divert themselves" (Redfield 1943: 154), he noted how councils selected beauty queens, fire departments, block representatives, and shopping opportunities. But none of the recognized committees was organized to confront the real problem facing these confined people: confinement itself. Redfield also worried that this was "a strikingly un-American thing we have done: to confine tens of thousands of our fellow-citizens against whom, individually, no charge is made. . . . Very well, it is a strikingly un-American thing we have done. It may be added that we have done it in a strikingly American way. For within certain broad limits the evacuees are to make their own government, institutions, and social life as they want to make them" (Redfield 1943: 153). Thus, anthropologists were sent out not only to study the social formations emerging in these un-American controlled communities but also to churn out reports that became policy fodder for those managing the camps.

By October 1942, Embree had reported that conditions at Manzanar were fostering discontent that seemed to be leading toward a breakdown of authority. In the months that followed, tension escalated at the Manzanar and Poston camps, with a riot at Manzanar following the December 6, 1942, arrest of several internees after the beating of a JACL representative (see Thomas and Nishimoto 1946: 49–52). Embree was soon transferred to the Community Management Division, and a month later he was appointed director of Community Analysis, a new division that would study the attitudes and culture of internees. In that capacity, he hired twenty-two community analysts—fourteen anthropologists and eight sociologists—who were sent to the ten WRA camps. Peter Suzuki established that Embree envisioned using community analysts not only to study internees, but also as FBI informers. Suzuki found that Embree "recommended to the FBI in a [March 1943] confidential memorandum that [community analysts] be used as a channel of information to the FBI" (Suzuki 1986b: 3–4).

The WRA hired fourteen anthropologists to work as community analysts in the camps. They conducted fieldwork with the explicit intent of studying factors leading to protests and riots and designing means of imposing social pacification that would encourage the smooth operation of concentration camps. The analysts examined the social stability of internee communities; how and why internees were resisting resettlement in their imposed communities; and factors influencing internees' loyalty. Anthropologists worked in WRA camps at Gila River, Arizona (G. Gordon Brown, Robert F. Spencer, Rosalie Hankey); Granada, Colorado (E. Adamson Hoebel); Heart Mountain, Wyoming (Asael T. Hansen); Jerome, Arkansas (Rachel R. Sady); Manzanar, California (John de Young, Morris Opler, John Provinse); Minidoka, Idaho (Gordon Armbruster, John de Young, Elmer R. Smith, Edward Spicer); Poston, Arizona (Conrad Arensberg, Elizabeth Colson, David French, Edward Spicer, Tami Tsuchiyama, Laura Thompson); Rohwer, Arkansas (Margaret Lantis); Topaz, Utah (Weston La Barre); Tule Lake, California (Marvin Opler, Rosalie Hankey) and in administrative roles in Washington, D.C. (John Embree, Sol Kimball, Rachel R. Sady, Edward Spicer).[9]

Most anthropologists working as WRA community analysts employed some form of participant-observation research. Some lived among internees for extended periods of time, but most lived in separate quarters. G. Gordon Brown observed that internees who cooperated with WRA staff could have problems with fellow internees because "some will brand as *inu* [dogs] all of their fellows who have more than necessary contacts with Administrative personnel" (Brown 1945: 6).

In February 1943, WRA staff developed and distributed a four-page registration questionnaire to all WRA detainees. Questions 27 and 28 asked detainees to declare their loyalty to the United States. Question 27 asked interned male citizens over the age of seventeen, "Are you willing to serve in the armed forces of the United States on combat duty, wherever ordered?" Question 28 asked, "Will you swear unqualified allegiance to the United States of America and faithfully defend the United States from any or all attack by foreign or domestic forces, and forswear any form of allegiance or obedience to the Japanese emperor, or any other foreign government, power, or organization?" (Thomas and Nishimoto 1946: 57).[10]

As Richard Drinnon observed, question 28 "asked the Issei to become stateless persons by renouncing the only citizenship they had and by affirming their unswerving fealty to a government that had made their race the legal basis for denying them U.S. citizenship" (Drinnon 1987: 78). While the language of this question was later modified to a slightly less objectionable form, question 28 continued to ask Issei and Nesei to proclaim their loyalty to the system imprisoning them. The Manzanar community analyst Morris Opler complained that it was improper to ask for such loyalty declarations, because

> the matter of questionnaires and the persistent inquiries about "loyalty" was becoming galling to the Nisei. At the beginning of the war their "loyalty" was questioned. They pointed to their good record and to the lack of sabotage—but to no avail. They met and pledged their loyalty in statements, resolutions, and letters to government officials. They volunteered for the armed services, they bought bonds, they became blood donors, they did everything and more than other American citizens were doing to demonstrate their loyalty. They were told that the evacuation and their attitude toward it would be considered a test of their loyalty. After evacuations they were expected to take an oath of loyalty before becoming members of the WRA Work Corps. Those who had been inducted into the armed forces and later dismissed had taken the soldier's oath. Even all this fanfare about "loyalty" was paralleled by a chain of events which clearly indicated that their protestations of loyalty were viewed with [suspicion], that they were not trusted and that their citizenship rights were being disregarded. Now from behind barbed wire, after all that had gone before, they were being asked for another affirmation of loyalty. (Quoted in Drinnon 1987: 79–80)

Two-thirds of the detainees affirmed their loyalty to the United States even as they were forced to "relocate" without due process. Of those who refused to declare their loyalty, most appear to have been reacting to the conditions of imprisonment. Many Issei subjected to the camps' segregation and discrimination became embittered. Dorothy Thomas convincingly argued that so-called disloyals were created more by the conditions of confinement than by any true prewar loyalties to Japan. Detainees' "loyalty" soon became an important subject of study by camp anthropologists (Weglyn 1976). In July 1943, the WRA designated the Tule Lake camp as the facility where all so-called disloyals (those who refused to answer question 28 affirmatively) were transferred. The choice of Tule Lake for use as the WRA's high-security center had dark historical undertones, given the area's tragic role in suppressing the Modoc uprisings of 1872–73 and the killing of the Modoc independence leader Captain Jack (a.k.a. Kintpuash).

Morris Opler's extensive interviews with Manzanar internees who answered "no" to question 28 found that those who chose segregation did so for many reasons, few of which seemed to have anything to do with being disloyal to the United States (Morris Opler 1945; Thomas and Nishimoto 1946: 91–98). Many of those interviewed by Opler believed they would be safer in the camps; others expressed disillusionment with the American system of due process; while others still refused to affirm loyalty to a system so entrenched in racial hatred. Policymakers were not interested in the details of the segregation system they had created. Opler's detailed reports on the deleterious effects of segregation at Tule Lake seem to have been ignored, as "no one at the Washington Office, and indeed in WRA, seems to have read closely nor took seriously Marvin K. Opler's insightful reports on Tule Lake, particularly on the effects of segregation if that Camp were to be turned into a special place of segregation" (Suzuki 1981: 33).

Brian Hayashi's examination of field reports found indications that pressures from the WRA may have led community analysts to overstress the fundamental loyalty of some detainees, who were assuming that the Japanese would either emerge victorious or would negotiate an advantageous peace agreement to end the hostilities. Hayashi found that, "under pressure from the House Committee on Un-American Activities hearings, Authority officials took the offensive, asserting that the Nisei were 'loyal' and deserving of acceptance into American society based on their stellar performance on the field of combat, while the Issei had turned their backs on Japan and its militaristic aims" (Hayashi 2004: 160).

Varieties of Anthropologist Community Analysts

Weston La Barre used his position as community analyst at Topaz to gather ethnographic data, which he analyzed with his own psychoanalytic interpretations. La Barre knew very little about Japanese culture, and his hostility against the Japanese permeated his writings, in which he freely characterized Japanese culture as neurotic (La Barre 1945; Suzuki 1980). La Barre confidently proclaimed, "The Japanese are probably the most compulsive people in the world ethnological museum" (La Barre 1945: 326). He even found proof of aggression in Japanese politeness:

> That stereotype of the Japanese, who is "so sorry, please" at any discovered aggression, has an adequate basis in fact. Psychoanalysis has shown that extreme politeness is a reaction-formation against repressed hostile aggressiveness, and everyone can recognize the spuriousness and the overtone of hostility in extreme politeness. Japanese ceremoniousness is even expressed

in the varying grades of honorific language, which differ not only in vocabu-
lary but also in the grammar itself. The basic function of Japanese politeness
is to use the conventional to mask the real, in emotional matters. (La Barre
1945: 327)

La Barre believed that the Japanese suppression brought explosive tantrums and
that "the Japanese needed Pearl Harbor, an ultimately suicidal attack upon the
powerful, disapproving authority, America. But like all compulsives, they have
chosen the wrong object for aggression, they have not recognized the real internal enemy" (La Barre 1945: 337). La Barre's analysis went beyond the psychological profiling of interned Japanese Americans. He also drew up detailed maps for
individual blocks of the Topez camp indicating suspected "trouble makers."
These maps were turned over to camp administrators, who were then in con-
sultation with the FBI. Suzuki wrote that on La Barre's maps, colored legends
identified

> key groups among the interned. For example, "SS" designated the "FBI
> Sabotage statement" (perhaps in reference to a group which had written a
> statement about sabotaging FBI efforts in the camp?); "AK" stood for the
> "FBI articulate-Kibei" (A group of [Japanese-educated Americans] who
> were articulate in English?; "9 SC" stood for the "Committee of 9" (A group
> which had protested conditions about the camp to the Spanish Consul,
> Japan's representative in the U.S. to look after Japanese citizens (hence the
> "SC"); the red dots for "Bachelor citizens-Kibei"; blue dots for "non-citzens"
> and so on. (Suzuki 1986b: 5)

Many community analysts were deeply affected by their work in the camps.
Robert Redfield's student Asael Hansen went to work for the WRA because he
wanted to help the detainees:

> [He] thought he could help explain the needs of the detainees to the army
> and the WRA. But those were the same people that built the barbed wire
> enclosures surrounding the detainees, and patrolled those fences armed
> with rifles, machine guns, and live ammunition. When Hansen got to Heart
> Mountain where he was one of those in charge, he found out that nobody in
> the army gave two hoots in hell what "those Nips" needed or wanted. The
> army was there to keep them inside the camps, and how or whether they
> survived inside was of no concern to the army. . . . Hanson told of turning in
> despair to the next guy up the chain, a prominent anthropologist—and
> being told to shut up and do his job, which was to keep the army happy.[11]

Hansen tried to resign but found that this was impossible, despite his civilian status. Instead, he was "frozen" in his position—putting him in an untenable situation where he was forced to administer question 28 to internees.[12]

As Tule Lake became the WRA's "segregation camp," Marvin Opler gathered ethnographic data on camp life as the character of the camp changed. Opler accomplished this with respect for those he studied. Suzuki characterized Marvin Opler's work at Tule Lake as "unswayed by the madness which was going on around him and [he] continued to write sympathetic, compassionate reports on, among other things, the effects of the inane policies which were imposed upon their victims" (Suzuki 1981: 41).

In March 1943, Marvin's brother Morris Opler moved to Manzanar. Riots in early December 1942 left two internees dead after military policed fired machine guns into crowds of protestors. Other internees were severely beaten. WRA community analysts and JERS researchers analyzed the forces behind the riots (see Kurashige 2001). One of the aftereffects of the Manazanar riot was to push WRA administrators to try to relocate "loyal" internees into American communities in the U.S. interior.

Even with the tensions at the camp, Opler conducted his fieldwork with an open patience. Some in the WRA criticized him because he wrote his community-analysis reports too much "like an old-fashioned ethnologist,"[13] (and efforts were made to remove him from his position for his impartial analyses of WRA communities (Hansen 1995: 626). Morris Opler's CAS reports were anchored in a commitment to participant observation, not in a commitment to WRA administrative policies. Unlike other CAS ethnographers, Morris Opler lived in the barracks among internees, socialized with them, and came to appreciate and represent their views of internment. But this commitment to an anthropological understanding of internee culture did not endear him to his WRA superiors, who "was castigated for not having done enough policy analysis studies to suit the Washington Office" (Suzuki 1981: 33).

Opler's reports warned that the horrible conditions in the camps would lead to deepening problems, and he urged his WRA superiors to "not allow segregation, least of all the motivation behind it, to become transformed at Tule Lake into a comic opera of the disloyalty myth. More important, we must guard against the promotion of disloyalty where none actually existed in fact" (quoted in Suzuki 1981: 33). Opler studied the specific reasons that individuals at Manzanar refused to sign loyalty statements. He "attended several hundred hearings for [individuals refusing to sign loyalty statements] and took down verbatim much of the proceedings, noting the setting and the attitudes and reactions of board members and internees" (Hansen 1995: 627). After interviewing hundreds of prisoners at Tule Lake, he concluded that decisions to declare loyalty were complex ones, most often having more to do with specific social generational dynamics, expressions of social conservatism, or conditions of internment than they did with actual feelings of loyalty to either the American or Japanese governments. His analysis of the testimony of 155 Nisei appearing before the WRA's segregation hearing board in August 1943 found that many of those who wished to renounce their American citizenship were not doing so out of disloyalty, but were availing themselves of the only way to protest the innumerable indignities to which they had been subjected (see Kurashige 2001: 398).

But WRA administrators had little use for Morris Opler's analyses, and like those of so many other wartime analysts reporting findings that were at odds with fundamental institutional preconceptions, his meticulous findings were easily ignored.

The Japanese American Evacuation and Resettlement Study

The Sociologist Dorothy Swaine Thomas directed JERS for the University of California, Berkeley. Unlike the BSR and CAS fieldworkers, JERS fieldworkers operated outside the supervision of the WRA. JERS was established with funds from the University of California and the Giannini, Rockefeller, and Columbia foundations to conduct an interdisciplinary anthropological study of "forced mass migration" (Thomas and Nishimoto 1946: v). Thomas's fieldworkers collected hundreds of internees' life histories, which documented individuals' experiences before and during their internment. JERS hired anthropology and sociology graduate students as fieldworkers; they lived among internees at WRA detention camps. The anthropologists Robert Spencer, Rosalie Hankey, and Tamie Tsuchiyama conducted fieldwork for Thomas at Gila, Tule Lake, and Poston. Each of these young anthropologists had serious clashes and disagreements with Thomas because of her exploitive management style and unrealistically demanding standards for fieldwork reporting.[14]

Thomas paid minimal wages and later harvested her fieldworkers' data for use as she saw fit (see Hirabayashi 1999: 170–173; Murray 1991). Fieldworkers' reports were frequently rejected, and Thomas harshly criticized the research methods and writings of her staff. She tried to enact unusual methodological measures designed to reduce the biases of individual field researchers and increase the validity and reliability of the research, and she demanded that employees maintain high levels of secrecy (Thomas and Nishimoto 1946: vii).[15]

Thomas hired at least twenty-five Japanese Americans for her staff.[16] Because the Berkeley campus was off limits to Japanese Americans, meetings to discuss research findings were held elsewhere. Meetings were "arranged every few months in Denver, Phoenix, Salt Lake City, or Chicago, and extended over a period of a week or more, during which each observer and staff member presented his problems and findings for the detailed criticism and appraisal of his colleagues" (Thomas and Nishimoto 1946: xi). In fact, the entire JERS program itself was secret.[17]

In the spring of 1943, the Berkeley anthropology graduate student Rosalie Hankey (later, Rosalie Hankey Wax) began fieldwork for Thomas and JERS after Alfred Kroeber encouraged her to apply for a research position at Gila (Wax 1971: 65). She later wrote that her arrival at Gila more than half a year after the internees had arrived had provided her with a research advantage because the internees had already been exposed to countless humiliations (most notably, the degrading "registration") under conditions not associated with her (Wax 1971: 61).

Thomas instructed Hankey that she was "on no account to give any information or 'data' to the WRA. . . . Some of the Japanese fieldworkers employed by the study had been accused by their fellow evacuees of being informers or 'spies for the administration.' Some were made so uncomfortable that they left the centers soon after the registration crisis" (Wax 1971: 65). Hankey received little support from WRA administrators and was viewed with trepidation by Nisei and Issei. Her presence naturally drew the suspicions of internees, and despite her commitment to not sharing her works with the WRA or other federal agencies, interned Japanese Americans had no reason to trust her. These suspicions and the severe heat and deprivations of the camp weighed heavily on Hankey.[18]

Hankey described internees' lives in the camps as filled with "petty discomforts, broken at intervals by a humiliating experience with a Caucasian supervisor or social worker, or by some new bureaucratic foul-up" (Wax 1971: 60). Hankey's initial report brought objections from Thomas, who complained about the lack of specific details without acknowledging the obvious problems involved in having Hankey interview internees about their views of "loyalty" and "disloyalty." Thomas did not acknowledge the extent to which the context of incarceration framed all interrogatives. Hankey continued asking questions on topics of interest to Thomas, but she also worried about her ability to produce accurate representations of camp views.

We are left to imagine what these imprisoned people, deprived of their inalienable civil rights, their homes, their land, and their livelihood, thought of this young woman who introduced herself as an anthropology graduate student "working for a group of professors who had no connection with the [WRA] administration. [She] explained that the object of [her] employers was to obtain and publish a true picture of the evacuation and of life within the centers. [She] emphasized the confidential nature of 'our data' and added a description of some phase of the study which was likely to meet with the approval of [her] listeners, for example, that a study of Japanese financial losses due to evacuations was under consideration" (Wax 1971: 70).

Thomas pressed Hankey to ask politically dangerous questions concerning individuals' feelings about loyalty to Japan and to America. She urged Hankey to gather detailed information on why internees had answered question 28 in the ways they had. Surprisingly, some internees—fewer than half of those approached—who were being removed to Tule Lake as "disloyals" discussed their reasons for these actions with Hankey:

> Some talked for hours, telling me again and again that they were not disloyal but they had lost faith in America and felt that they had no future in this country. Some became so distressed they could barely hold back their tears. Other put on a bold front, saying: "heck—I'm going to Tule Lake anyway, so why shouldn't I say what I think?" Some denounced the American government for its treatment of the Nisei and its abrogation of democratic principles. Some urged me to come and see them again before the "entrainment," and one young man even wrote a long essay for me, describing how he had once felt toward the United States and how he felt toward it now. (Quoted in Wax 1971: 73)

Despite the drawbacks of Hankey's identity, she gathered some answers to Thomas's questions about loyalty.

Thomas disapproved of Hankey's commitment to an anthropological participant-observation approach to studying the Gila community and of her efforts to study Japanese language and culture. The only WRA official at Gila who was supportive of Hankey was the community analyst and anthropologist Gordon Brown. Thomas ordered Hankey to steer clear of Brown to send clear messages to the community that she was not with the WRA or any other federal agency. Thomas's insistence left Hankey isolated, but with time her liminal identity as neither an outsider nor an insider seemed to make her approachable. Hankey later reflected on her ability to use her position as an outsider to her advantage:

> I would not have been able to do fieldwork in Gila and Tule Lake if my respondents and I had not been able, jointly, to invent and maintain many

of these relationships. Some Japanese Americans felt more comfortable if they could treat me like a sympathetic newspaper reporter. I knew very little about how a reporter behaved (indeed, I had never seen or spoken with one), but I responded and we were able to converse more easily. In Tule Lake the super-patriots and agitators found it easier to talk to me once they had convinced themselves that I was a German "Nisei," "full of the courageous German spirit." I found this fantasy personally embarrassing, but I did not make a point of denying my German ancestry. Finally, I was not a geisha, even though a shrewd Issei once suggested that it was because I functioned as one that I was able to find out so much of what happened at Tule Lake. His explanation was that Japanese men—and especially Japanese politicians —do not discuss their plans or achievements with other men or with their wives, but they are culturally conditioned to speak of such matters with intelligent and witty women. Though vanity has tempted me to accept the Issei's hypothesis, I think it would be more accurate to say that the Japanese agitators and I developed a new role which fitted their temperaments and mine. This role had no precise place in either the Japanese or the American culture, but in Tule Lake it permitted us to converse with considerable mutual satisfaction and enlightenment. (Wax 1971: 53)

In February 1944, Thomas asked Hankey to visit Tule Lake to observe what was happening with the "disloyals." At Tule Lake, Opler helped Hankey make arrangements to interview eleven "segregants," who told her how they had come to be interned there. Hankey returned to Gila with forty pages of notes and wrote a detailed report. Thomas repeatedly sent Hankey back to Tule Lake for observations and interviews, and in May 1944, Hankey finally moved to Tule Lake.

As she interviewed members of Tule Lake's Nisei underground, she began to develop extremely sympathetic identifications with the internees, producing an effect like an inverse Stockholm syndrome. While reviewing her field notes more than two decades later, Hankey reflected on her own mental instability during the stressful period of her fieldwork at Tule Lake in September 1944. In a section titled, "I Become a Fanatic," she wrote that she "went a little crazy. I came to believe that observing and recording what went on at Tule Lake was my transcendental task, and I went about this task with an unflagging energy and relish that today seems rather frightening. I did not think or have fantasies about being killed. But I knew I might be killed, and this knowledge made me feel happy and well" (Wax 1971: 139). But beyond this apparent rush of mental instability, Hankey worried that the WRA "might find out how much I was learning and order me off the project" (Wax 1971: 139). While empathetic responses are common effects of fieldwork, Hankey crossed over into a state of hyper-identification with the internees. She reported feeling "shocked and somewhat repelled" when one interviewee told her that he had only come to Tule Lake "to escape the draft," and she developed sympathies for those who terrorized camp members believed to be *inu* (Wax 1971: 139–40). She later wrote that, during the time, she "had constructed an ideal model of 'true Japanese' behavior—for the Japanese and for myself—and I proceeded (in my own mind) to criticize and despise anyone who deviated from this model. That my model was melodramatic and unreal I did not then perceive. Nor did it occur to me that as a social scientist I had no business sitting in judgment on myself or on the people I was supposed to be studying and understanding" (quoted in Wax 1971: 140).

Hankey's alliances took on deeper meanings when some Tule Lake internees murdered and beat others believed to be *inu*. After she became convinced that an internee she identified as "Mr. Kira" was involved in a camp terror campaign, she secretly provided information to the FBI. Suzuki later determined that "Kira" was Kinzo Ernest Wakayama, who was eventually forced to renounce his American citizenship under duress (Suzuki 1986a: 194–99). While Hankey discussed some of the events that led her to report Wakayama to the FBI, she avoided addressing the ethical meaning of an anthropologist becoming an FBI informer against a member of the community she was studying. Suzuki concluded, "Not only was a certain family (the Wakayamas) victimized by [Hankey's] enculturated values, infelicitously actuated at Tule Lake, but the entire Tule Lake population and the scientific community [was victimized] as well" (Suzuki 1986a: 205).

In May 1945, Thomas ordered Hankey to leave Tule Lake immediately, without telling anyone. When she returned to Berkeley, Hankey learned that a WRA official had called Thomas and demanded that Hankey be removed from the camp. Hankey was told that the WRA official claimed that she "had consorted with pro-Japanese agitators and attended ceremonies devoted to the worship of the Japanese emperor. I had had immoral (sex) relations with a number of Japanese Americans. I had made disrespectful remarks about the project director. I had been a general troublemaker and had tried to subvert WRA policies. I was by temperament an anarchist, and since my mother had been abused by members of the Los Angeles police force, I had no respect for the law. I had communicated with the Department of Justice" (quoted in Wax 1971: 169).

Thomas advised Hankey that it would be best not to respond to the allegations and that she should just resign and move on. Thomas seemed to realize that Hankey had produced all the useful data she could. Hankey left the JERS project with mixed emotions and began graduate work at the University of Chicago. After some decades, she came to view her fieldwork on the project as resembling that of "a fighter in a resistance movement" (Wax 1971: 174).

Another Berkeley graduate student in anthropology hired by Thomas to conduct fieldwork for the JERS was Tamie Tsuchiyama, a Hawaiian-born Nisei whose Japanese heritage and advanced studies in anthropolgy gave her unique preparation for the work—although the FBI undertook extra precautions in investigating her background (Hirabayashi 1999: 25–31).

Tsuchiyama's initial JERS fieldwork was at the Arcadia, Santa Anita, "reception center," where Japanese Americans were processed and held before being sent to one of the ten WRA camps. Under the supervision of Robert Lowie and Thomas, Tsuchiyama moved into the center, where she observed numerous degrading adjustments to life in a total institution. She used her Nisei identity to facilitate her research at the Santa Anita center; as Hirabayashi has observed, she "did not ask permission of the residents of Santa Anita to do ethnographic research on her compatriots" (Hirabayashi 1999: 29). At Santa Anita, she reported on a work strike (for better wages and working conditions while making camouflaged nets for military use) and a riot. The riot broke out in July 1942, after police had seized not only forbidden materials such as knives and alcohol but also knitting needles, money, and diaries. The specific incident that set off the riot, however, involved the police grabbing a boy who was stopped crossing the compound. Tsuchiyama observed that some internees used the riot as an opportunity to settle scores with others. Martial law was imposed at the camp; two hundred soldiers restored order; and all non-forbidden confiscated items were eventually returned (Hirabayashi 1999: 40).

In August 1942, Tsuchiyama was sent to Poston, where she found her cultural, (limited) linguistic, and fieldwork skills to be in great demand. Initially, she worked for JERS and Leighton's BSR, but after a few months she severed her official connections with the BSR and worked exclusively for JERS. At Poston, Tsuchiyama moved into the camp, where she directed the research of several Japanese American research assistants.

Tsuchiyama came to rely increasingly on Richard Nishimoto (referred to as "X" in her reports to Thomas) as her primary ethnographic informant. Nishimoto had originally suspected that Tsuchiyama was an FBI agent, but he came to trust her and provide her with a detailed inside view of camp political life (Hirabayashi 1999: 86).

Tsuchiyama's connections to the BSR and JERS and the time she spent writing reports garnered suspicions that she was some sort of spy, but with time the suspicions subsided as internees came to know her and her sympathies. In November 1942, Tsuchiyama wrote to Thomas, "The fact that our files are confidential and inaccessible to any group including the administration has aroused the curiosity of some of the people of Poston and many of us have been branded Inu, or F.B.I. informers and individually notified of the public's dislike for such behavior" (Hirabayashi 1999: 53). But there were good reasons for such paranoia, and despite the fact that police officers at Poston confiscated her Santa Anita field notes (Hirabayashi 1999: 50), Tsuchiyama mailed copies of her reports to Thomas using the U.S. mail.

Hirabayashi's publication of Tsuchiyama's correspondence with Thomas finds Tsuchiyama continually worrying that her confidential reports could be intercepted and read by the FBI as they passed through the mail, or that her records could be subpoenaed by the Dies Committee. Tsuchiyama sent numerous letters fretting about the FBI's possible interception of mailed reports, but she seems to have assumed naïvely that such an interception of documents would be detectable by the non-receipt or the noticeable delay in the receipt of a report. These incessant worries about FBI monitoring during January 1943 were initially viewed by Thomas as paranoia, but Thomas eventually admitted that such concerns were not as "crazy" as they first appeared (Hirabayashi 1999: 84).[19] It seems remarkable that Thomas, Tsuchiyama, Hankey, and others working for JERS did not assume that the FBI or army were intercepting and reading the correspondence and reports sent from camps.

Throughout the Second World War, the FBI monitored phone calls and opened the mail of groups believed to hold foreign loyalties. William Sullivan, onetime FBI assistant director in charge of domestic intelligence, has written that, during the war, he and other FBI agents were told that the one million German, Italian, and Japanese Americans living in the United States were " 'dangerous to the peace and safety of the United States.'. . . . [W]e went after them with everything we had, including hidden microphones, telephone taps, and physical surveillance. . . . Every one of us believed that tapping phones and opening mail was official government policy, necessary to national security" (Sullivan 1979: 22–23). It is still unknown whether the FBI and other wartime agencies intercepted and read Tsuchiyama's reports to Thomas. Freedom of Information Act (FOIA) requests have not led to the complete release of FBI records on Tsuchiyama, so it is premature to declare that such invasive mail intercepts did not occur, and given what is known about the FBI's mail-interception and -reading practices during the Second World War, this remains a distinct possibility.[20]

Tsuchiyama collected rumors of Japanese victories and a coming liberation.

She reported that Tojo's promise, on December 9, 1941, to "amply compensate" interned Japanese Americans after the coming Japanese victory gave some Californian Japanese Americans "a renewed determination to carry on," despite hardships in the camps. She reported on the widespread distrust of American newspapers' claims of U.S. battle victories and that some internees had hidden shortwave radios that occasionally received Japanese propaganda broadcasts disseminated from surfaced submarines (Hirabayashi 1999: 99–101). In a March 27, 1943, letter to Thomas describing the prevalence and power of these rumors, she noted that there was "little doubt that there are several short wave radios in existence in Poston" (Hirabayashi 1999: 99). FBI agents suddenly appeared in late May and removed two internees for secretly having shortwave radios. It is not clear whether Tsuchiyama considered the possibility that her reports played a role in the FBI's actions (Hirabayashi 1999: 120).

Tsuchiyama ended her work for Thomas's project after the wife of her primary informant, Richard Nishimoto, became jealous of the time he was spending with her—including several lengthy trips away from Poston. Tsuchiyama cited Thomas's lack of trust and "constant surveillance" and maintenance of abusive working conditions as contributing to her decision to quit (Hirabayashi 1999: 150). Thomas coldly dropped Tsuchiyama, demanding final reports and otherwise severing ties with her in ways reminiscent of Hankey's termination.

When Dorothy Thomas and Richard Nishimoto published their detailed account of life in the WRA camps in *The Spoilage*, they drew heavily from Tsuchiyama's JERS reports and correspondence. Hirabayashi argued convincingly that Thomas's "cannibalization" of Tsuchiyama's writings was inappropriate, given Tsuchiyama's difficulties in finding academic employment after the war and the level of her contributions to the JERS project (Hirabayashi 1999: 149).[21] While Thomas extensively published the findings of JERS researchers, there are reasons to wonder whether any government agencies had access to JERS researchers' field reports or notes during the war.

Evaluating Detention Anthropology

In the decades after the war, anthropologists' activities at WRA camps became one of the most publicly visible and volatile topics relating to anthropology's wartime contributions. The developing discomfort with anthropology's contributions to this internment had more to do with shifts in interpretive perspective than it had to do with the discovery of new documents or facts relating to the internment. WRA anthropologists published numerous articles and reports describing their activities during the war or soon after the war's end (see, e.g., Brown 1945; Embree 1944; Leighton 1945; Provinse and Kimball 1946; Spicer 1946). Beginning in the 1980s, articles by the anthropologists Peter Suzuki (1980, 1981, 1986b) and Orin Starn (1986) critically evaluated the actions of WRA anthropologists. These evaluations generated waves of defensive responses from anthropologists who had worked in the camps (Opler 1987; Sady 1987, 1988; Wax 2003).

Suzuki examined a wealth of WRA reports, correspondence, and other primary documents to delineate the nature of anthropologists' interactions with the WRA. His analysis included important critiques of anthropology's duplicity and co-optation of mission for that of the state. Suzuki concluded, "For all those within CAS the analysis of and preoccupation with WRA policies took precedence over doing the kind of work they were most qualified to undertake, namely, ethno-graphic and ethnological studies. This in turn, led to a commensurate lack of respect for the dignity of the people and their culture" (Suzuki 1986b: 2). Orin Starn's analysis sought a middle path in the controversy, maneuvering between the polarized interpretations in which one side represented these events as "as-serting that anthropologists eased the relocation process for both Japanese Amer-icans and War administrators," and the other side saw ethnographers as "accom-plices of the government in relocation" (Starn 1986: 702). But Starn's measured critique still generated rebuttals from camp ethnographers who felt that their wartime efforts to make the best of a horrid situation were unappreciated.

The sort of applied-anthropology theories and methods employed in the WRA's camps suggest the degree to which various forms of anthropology were useful to the WRA, JERS, and the BSR. Many of the anthropologists who had come from the University of Chicago soon after Radcliffe-Brown's residency brought strands of structural functionalism linked to colonist settings. Elizabeth Colson recalled that, at the Poston camp, "Spicer encouraged me to read materials that linked to the Radcliffe-Brown school including Lloyd Warner" (quoted in Mac-Farlane 2006). As Starn observed, there were also clear links between WRA an-thropologists' efforts to manipulate interned populations in ways the camps keepers desired and classic industrial applications of applied anthropology by Lloyd Warner in 1931 at the Western Electric Company's Hawthorne plant in Cicero, Illinois. Starn noted that the WRA anthropologists Conrad Arensberg and Sol Kimball had been students of Warner at Harvard. But more significantly, Starn recognized what Warner's Hawthorn plant study and the WRA's anthropo-logical work shared: "Anthropologists were employed by management to study the managed; in both, anthropologists did predictions, evaluations, and research on causes of conflict with the ultimate goal of keeping the system running smoothly. Just as Warner 'demonstrated that fatigue could be reduced through manipulation of interactional variables,' WRA fieldworkers researched ways to 'control stress' through 'proper attention to the dissemination of the right facts to the right people at the right time'" (Starn 1986: 705–706). Many of these anthropologists not only incorporated theoretical assumptions that promoted assimilation (see Luomala 1947; Redfield 1943), but, on the basis of minimal knowledge of Japanese culture, they treated the culture of the camps as if they were "self-contained systems" that were "decontextualized not only in time but also in space" (Starn 1986: 713).

As a result, La Barre's culture and personality analysis today reads like a caricature of the worst sort of non-falsifiable racial-ethnic stereotyping. But such junk science fit the views of WRA managers. Morris Opler also produced work deeply influenced by the culture and personality school, but his writings were far more descriptive and not marred by the sort of heavy-handed psychoanalytic judgments found in La Barre.

It was anthropology's methods, not its theories, that most significantly marked the anthropologists' presence in the camps. They all brought with them some version of participant-observation skills to the job. Some (like the uniform-wearing Leighton) were so clearly identified with the camps' keepers that their most significant observations focused on camp staff rather than the internees. Others (such as Hankey, Tsuchiyama, and the Opler brothers) relied on some participant-observation methods that framed their perspectives in ways aligned with internees.

The overall uses, impacts, or meanings of all this anthropological participant observation is unclear. Starn critically observed that using Boasian field methods in this context transformed this work to the extent that "WRA anthropologists reformulated the classic Boasian axiom: instead of confronting power with truth, anthropology was to supply information to power" (Starn 1986: 705). That some of the anthropologists viewed their work as a means to improve the disgraceful conditions in the camps, not as camp informers, does not belie the fact that there were few measurable outcomes that supported such self-perceptions.

"Replaying the history of anthropologists and the WRA from 1941," Starn has argued, "one can at least imagine the development of an ethnography that seriously challenged the relocation decision. This would have required a broad paradigm shift—a theory locating the camps in the wider context of war hysteria, economic interest, and racism; a practice advocating for the dispossessed instead of advising the authorities" (Starn 1986: 710). Starn's point is a vital one, but it seems unrealistic to expect such a change to come from individuals working within a government agency—especially one that was under military control in wartime. If such an anthropological advocacy were to arise during wartime, it would almost have to come from outside the captive thinking of a government bureaucracy. Anthropologists could only be expected to undertake limited analysis under the sort of conditions mandating that WRA analysts view disruptive behaviors in racial prison camps as unnatural or negative—instead of as healthy reactions to demented national policies.

In 1945, Morris Opler argued that after Pearl Harbor American policymakers had faced a choice between two "philosophies." The first was that of "modern social science," which held that Japanese Americans had been enculturated to the American way of life and presented no unified threat to America. The second view was "the racist doctrine" that held that the Japanese " 'blood' would impel these people to help the enemy" (Morris Opler 1945: 13–14). Opler lashed out in criticism of the policymakers who had made such a racist choice:

> The manner in which the American public and its leaders turned their backs on social science in choosing between these two philosophies was disgraceful enough, but the whole anti-intellectual, anti-scientific tenor of the decision can be comprehended from the fact that a myth was invented out of whole cloth and sent over the entire nation to justify the evil that was brewing. This is the Pearl Harbor sabotage myth, a tissue of false and fantastic tales which purport to describe how the Japanese and Japanese-Americans of Hawaii aided the enemy and were responsible for the great damage suffered by our forces at Pearl Harbor on December 7, 1941. (Morris Opler 1945: 14)

But Opler's concluding paragraphs went even further in their reproach of what America had done. He wrote that Americans were "pre-scientific" and still "passing through the infantile stage of democracy." He saved some of his scorn for his own profession: "Most men still accept what they want to believe rather than what they know to be true. And what men want to believe is often shallow and sordid. But that does not absolve us from the obligation to teach the best of social science where we may to apply it where we can, and to exemplify it in our own thinking and conduct" (Morris Opler 1945: 14).

Three decades after the war, Walter Goldschmidt argued that the internment "was a case of rape, but the anthropologists who went into the War Relocation Authority felt that they could serve to ameliorate this situation even if they could not stop it, and this they did" (Goldschmidt 1977: 298). Suzuki has argued against this, stating that "neither anthropology, the anthropologists involved nor the administered were measurably aided and advanced by field work in the wartime camps for Japanese Americans. What the anthropologists accomplished could have been readily achieved by run-of-the-mill bureaucrats, whose roles as Community Analysts or social researchers would not have left the sense of disappointment that now exists because professional anthropologists did, in fact, work in these camps" (Suzuki 1981: 45). Jan van Bremen echoed such sentiments, writing that "the most discouraging finding" in his reading of the work produced by WRA anthropologists "is how little ethnography of camp life was produced. In every camp priority was given to policy analysis studies" (van Bremen 2003: 32).

Suzuki's search of WRA records found almost no anthropological studies of linguistics and kinship in the relocation centers. The absence of such basic anthropological records led him to ask whether "anthropology's traditional strengths—linguistics and kinship studies—were not energetically pursued by WRA social scientists, could others not trained in anthropology or sociology have performed as well in the same situation? The answer to this question must be in the affirmative" (Suzuki 1981: 35).

The limited value of anthropological insight was ultimately underscored by the fact that even the anthropologists who served as administrators at the WRA made little use of reports from their own colleagues who worked as community analysts if those reports ran counter to the primary bureaucratic assumptions of the agency. Looking further ahead, anthropologists such as John Embree, Morris and Marvin Opler, Katharine Luomala, and Tamie Tsuchiyama even wrote reports that recommended ways to help detainees make smooth transitions back into lives outside the centers, but these reports were also generally ignored (e.g., Luomala 1947).

Far from drawing on their discipline's strengths, some anthropologists drew on its historical ethical weaknesses. As Hirabayashi argued,

> The social conditions of production pertaining to the Poston phase of JERS fieldwork had many features that parallel a colonial arrangement. And for whatever conscious or unconscious reasons, the pertinent details that might have suggested this conclusion were conveniently omitted from the official JERS publications. This point seems especially critical given the totally self-serving way that Thomas characterized JERS methodology in research articles, four years and then eight years, respectively, after she had used and discarded both Tsuchiyama and Nishimoto. (Hirabayashi 1999: 170)

The power relations of the camps naturally pulled anthropology toward such a colonialist arrangement, and research under such conditions inevitably precluded dissenting scientific or humanistic views from having a significant impact on policies governing citizens who were so easily converted into racial prisoners.

The act of studying prisoners, particularly war prisoners, has particular ethical problems, given the structural impossibilities of gaining meaningful consent from the detained, who are stripped of such freedoms when they enter total institutions. This lack of consent forcing war prisoners to become unwilling subjects connects the prisoner studies conducted by Egon von Eickstedt, Rudolf Pöch, and Otto Reche during the First World War with those by Thomas, Leighton, Mengele, and Tsuchiyama during the Second World War. While the outcomes of these projects had very significant differences, the objectification of prisoners and the lack of ethical safeguards or informed consent separates such studies from normal anthropological research practices.

Ethnographic studies of interned Japanese Americans placed anthropologists in the potentially compromising position of advising agencies functioning as prison wardens. These ethnographic roles shared similarities with the roles of some ethnographers working on Indian reservations or with Indian groups under attack by the American government. The range of approaches to reports in these settings demonstrates different commitments to serving those studied and to serving government agencies. James Mooney's efforts to record the culture and hardships of the Cherokee as they were under siege had parallels in the Opler brothers' detailed ethnographic records of detained Japanese Americans. The reports of most other WRA community analysts never approached such standards and strove instead to increase the legibility of detainees to managers.

While many of the individual anthropologists working in the camps treated the individuals they encountered with kindness and compassion, it remains unclear whether the detained Japanese Americans would have been worse off if anthropologists had refused to work for the WRA or JERS. But such questions are perhaps overridden by the importance of the ethical issues raised by studying prisoners unable to give any meaningful voluntary consent as research subjects.

As the next chapter clarifies, anthropologists' influence during wartime was also constrained by basic questions of whether or not administrative superiors (or even entire agencies) chose to listen to their analyses and recommendations. Anthropologists at war often found themselves confronting the same situation that applied anthropologists face in the present: frustration when the policymakers who have hired them do not listen to the advice they have been hired to give.

CHAPTER EIGHT

Anthropology and
Nihonjinron at the Office
of War Information

Ideological warfare is an important phase in modern conflict. Destroy propaganda and
fabrications of the enemy, by your unshakable faith in the cause for which the Empire
stands, and endeavor to spread Kodo.
—CODE OF THE JAPANESE ARMY, Chapter II, Entry IV, 1941

The Office of War Information (OWI) was established under Presidential Executive Order 9182 on June 13, 1942. It inherited the institutional duties and personnel of the Office of Facts and Figures, the Division of Information of the Office of Emergency Management, the Office of Government Reports, and the Foreign Information Service, but it also took on the new tasks of analyzing foreign news reports and generating domestic and foreign propaganda. Elmer Davis of CBS News was appointed director of the OWI, and he used this position to fill the agency with some of America's top scholars (Davis 1943; Doob 1947; Winkler 1978). After the War Relocation Authority took over the Bureau of Sociological Research's research roles at Poston, Alexander Leighton became the Director of the OWI's Foreign Morale Analysis Division (FMAD) in Washington, D.C.

The OWI collected an extremely diverse group of scholars. Davis hired Paul Linebarger, a political scientist trained at Johns Hopkins who specialized in psychological warfare. Linebarger was the OWI's first chief of the Far Eastern Section, Psychological Warfare Branch, Operations Group, Military Intelligence Service. In the postwar era, Linebarger drew on his OWI experiences and in 1948 published the classic text *Psychological Warfare*, in which he described his wartime strategy of first understanding a culture before trying to manipulate it.[1] Linebarger recruited George Taylor to be the deputy director of the OWI's the Far East Division.

Anthropologists at the OWI's FMAD developed theories accounting for Japanese national character, or *nihonjinron*, as they theorized the likely impacts of various American military attacks and produced propaganda. Taylor's superiors at OWI wanted to know: "Who are the Japanese? How do they think? What makes them tick? Should the U.S. attack the Japanese homeland?" (Price 1996). Because Taylor recognized that these were fundamentally cultural, not psychological, questions, he and Leighton recruited anthropologists to work at OWI to study and manipulate the morale of Japanese soldiers and civilians.[2]

Leighton and Taylor hired about thirty social scientists, including the anthropologists Ruth Benedict, Ruth Bunzel, John Embree, Royal Hassrick, Fred Hulse, Clyde and Florence Kluckhohn, Dorothea C. Leighton, Alexander Lesser, William Lipkind, Morris Opler, and Kathrine Spencer (see Leighton 1949: 223–25; Price 1996). While they shared a basic research background in individualistic or psychological approaches to culture, the members of this OWI team combined individuals from diverse anthropological schools.

OWI anthropologists at FMAD immersed themselves in books, articles, and films that revealed Japanese culture, history, literature, and popular culture. They read intelligence data on the shifting morale of Japanese soldiers that included a cache of five thousand translated Japanese war diaries seized after Pacific battles (Boswell 1996: 7). They also had access to analysts, translators, and clerical staff from Poston's BSR division. Many of the methods used would later be associated with the Study of Culture at a Distance movement after the war. While the OWI reports using this approach contextualized the cultural roots of an American enemy, many of them now read as one-dimensional, stereotypical summaries of a complex cultural system. The reports tended to minimize the economic and political reasons for the war as they overemphasized possible psychological reasons.

FMAD analysts produced memos characterizing Japanese personality types governed by strict self-discipline, shame, group conformity, and a strong sense of duty to the state as represented by the emperor. Clyde Kluckhohn observed:

> Anthropologists were asked [these sorts] of questions by policy makers; in reporting the early events of the war, ought we to minimize the disasters? Will this course give greater confidence? Will greater confidence give greater efficiency? In anthropological terms, the policy makers were asking: which types of motivation are preponderantly standardized in American culture? The greatest services of the anthropologist were in preventing his colleagues from casting both enemies and allies in the American image and in forever reminding intellectuals of the significance of the nonrational. Certain pro-

fessors and literary men wanted to use [OWI shortwave] broadcasts to discuss democracy with the Japanese on a high intellectual plane. But you can't reason men out of irrationality. (Kluckhohn 1949: 152)

OWI anthropologists designed propaganda campaigns directed at Japanese cultural sensitivities rather than Western cultural principles. Clyde and Florence Kluckhohn were among the first anthropologists hired at OWI. Leighton and Taylor knew Clyde Kluckhohn and held his work among the Navajo in high regard. Because only a few anthropologists had conducted any fieldwork in Japan, Taylor decided that the most valuable contribution anthropologists could make to the work of OWI would be found in their ability to identify meaningful cultural patterns regardless of a lack of such experience.[3] Clyde Kluckhohn assisted Taylor in selecting other top social scientists who came to work at OWI (Price 1996).

Although many OWI anthropologists brought culture and personality approaches to the study of Japanese culture, Taylor distrusted heavily Freudian cultural analyses. When Geoffrey Gorer approached him about working on one of Taylor's projects at OWI, Taylor asked him what made the Japanese soldiers such determined fighters. Gorer confirmed that the answer to these questions could be found in their toilet-training techniques. When Taylor asked Gorer whether Japanese men and women had been subjected to identical toilet-training methods, Gorer replied that this was the case. When Taylor pressed Gorer to account why identical toilet-training techniques had led to such gender-specific differences, Gorer had no answers, and Taylor "quietly let Gorer go off on his own way" (Price 1996). Gorer worked on other OWI projects and later worked for the British Embassy (Yans-McLaughlin 1986b: 197; see Harris 1968: 443–44).[4] But Taylor did not consider Ruth Benedict's application of culture and personality theories to be as psychologically reductionistic as Gorer's applications (Price 1996). Although Margaret Mead's postwar work on Culture at a Distance studies at the Institute for Intercultural Studies carried on the sort of research undertaken at the OWI, Taylor never asked Mead to join his OWI team because he thought she was a "victim of a psychological movement which believed [the Japanese] couldn't change from their culturally determined ways" (Price 1996).

John Embree and Ruth Benedict at the OWI

In 1935–36, John Embree had conducted ethnographic fieldwork in rural Japan, where he studied relationships between villages and the larger Japanese state in the village of Suye Mura. His ethnography *Suye Mura: A Japanese Village* examined the stratification of a village's economic systems and the impact of religious beliefs and social customs on village members, but it also provided a detailed view of Japanese culture (Embree 1939). Because Embree's firsthand Japanese expertise was in high demand during the war, he worked for several American military-intelligence agencies.[5] In early 1942, he worked as a technician for the Coordinator of Information (before it was transformed into the oss); in late 1942 and 1943, he was a "principal community analyst" for the wra; and from 1943 to 1945, he was an associate professor and director of the Civilian Affairs Training School (cats) area-studies program at the University of Chicago. In 1945, he became a supervisor in the Psychological Warfare program at the owi in Washington, D.C., where he worked with Benedict and Kluckhohn.[6]

Embree recognized that because so many of the military and intelligence studies of Japanese society were based on secondary scholarship, they repeated unexamined anti-Japanese stereotypes. During the war, he complained that "the writings of the national character-structure groups have been largely in the form of 'confidential' mimeographed pamphlets and so not subject to scientific criticism; nonetheless their conclusions are presented to government agencies as the findings and methods of 'anthropology'" (Embree 1945a: 636, n. 3). Embree worried that anthropologists applying their research to the war would "fall into the fallacy of regarding his culture as the only one that can provide a yardstick of values" (Embree 1945a: 636–37). His assessment of the low quality of these anthropological war reports made Embree worry "whether or not applied social anthropology is real anthropology" (Embree 1945a: 635).

Where the more psychologically oriented Gorer, La Barre, and Benedict tended to look for psychological or value-driven roots of wartime behavior, Embree examined economic, demographic and geopolitical factors. Embree saw the roots of Japan's militarism in the constraints of tariffs and the limits of natural resources on a circumscribed island environment, not in hypothesized internal psychological defects (see Embree 1943b: 16; Janssens 1995: 216).

Within military and intelligence agencies there was widespread interest in the sort of one-dimensional psychological studies that Embree had critiqued. Perhaps it was because these studies reinforced rather than challenged prevalent views of the enemy that most military and civilian analysts preferred the sort of racially essentialized, psychologically deterministic views produced by wartime culture and personality anthropologists. John Dower found that such views were widespread "from the beginning of the war to its end, for instance primitivism and its cognates (savagery, barbarism, tribalism) were not only central to everyday Allied commentary on the Japanese enemy, but also usually offered as if they were genuinely historical or anthropological observations" (Dower 1986: 140). When knowledgeable analysts like Embree tried to complicate these one-dimensional caricatures of the Japanese, their informed analysis were often ignored in favor of analyses that reinforced commonly held prejudices.

Embree's account of life in Suye Mura provided useful details on rural Japanese cultural values and political enculturation. His analysis embedded cultural beliefs and behaviors within the village's economic, political, and ecological system. Embree's descriptions of how Japanese children came to revere the emperor in all aspects of life showed how villagers routinely showed reverence not as a sign of emotional weakness, but as a unifying feature of social solidarity. He viewed nationalism and adoration of the emperor as a functional manifestation of hegemonic control:

> The outstanding element in Japan's response to Western civilization is the controlled form in which the government has allowed it to reach the countryside. The substitution of central governmental control for feudal control has resulted in a great emphasis on nationalism. Whereas, formerly neither the farmer nor the government was ever much worried about such an abstraction as patriotism so long as the farmer produced his rice, today, as a powerful tool of social control, nationalism is stressed in education, in conscription, in public talks in the school auditorium, and in the encouragement of societies such as the Women's Patriotic Society. The Emperor is used as the symbol of the nation and represented as the father of his people in all such propaganda. (Embree 1939: 301)

Embree's political sophistication added an important layer to his OWI analysis, but Benedict, Embree, and other analysts at OWI found it increasingly difficult to find receptive audiences for views that did not align with the common prejudices about Japanese culture.[7]

Before she joined the OWI, Ruth Benedict had no research interest or training in Japanese culture. All of her studies of Japanese literature, history, and culture were conducted in translation, often with the assistance of Japanese Americans working with OWI staff (Price 1996). The war caused Benedict to draw on her past culture and personality research in new ways as she moved from simply analyzing culture to making policy recommendations. As Benedict's biographer Judith Modell observed, the Second World War "justified anthropology for Ruth" (Modell 1983: 295).

In 1943, Leonard Doob assigned Benedict to write culture and personality profiles for Thailand, Burma, and Romania (see Modell 1983: 268–70). Margaret

Caffrey observed that this work was "multi-thematic, reflecting her acceptance of the use of a multiplicity of patterns in Culture and Personality studies" (Caffrey 1989: 319). In June 1944, Benedict began working under Leighton on Japanese culture and personality studies. The most significant focus of this work examined the role of the emperor in Japanese culture.

In an effort to isolate core Japanese social-psychology themes, Benedict read large volumes of analytical reports, Japanese novels, ethnographies, and historical works; interviewed Japanese Americans; and watched Japanese movies. Benedict and Herman Spitzer compiled a ninety-one page "Bibliography of Articles and Books Relating to Japanese Psychology" that was classified restricted (Spitzer and Benedict 1945).

The two works that most significantly shaped Benedict's culture and personality research were the ethnographic writings of Embree and the philosophical writings of Inazō Nitobe. Benedict's reading of Embree's ethnographic writings provided an understanding of contemporary ethnographic details and a feeling for daily life and culture. In Nitobe's book *Bushido: The Soul of Japan*, Benedict identified themes of Japanese nationalistic character that archetypically connected Japan's traditional past with the current war. As Emiko Ohnuki-Tierney has argued, Nitobe's *Bushido* led Benedict "to her famous, or infamous, thesis distinguishing the cultures of guilt and of shame" (Ohnuki-Tierney 2002: 119). She used reports of food shortages, translations of monitored broadcasts, and the writings of Embree and Nitobe to frame an understanding of ongoing Japanese efforts to cope with wartime hardships by building social solidarity and generating hope.

Benedict wrote a series of owi reports profiling the psychological makeup of Japanese culture, many of which later appeared in consolidated form in the classified owi report "Japanese Behavior Patterns" (Benedict 1945).[8] In it she argued, "It is even more necessary than in the case of most alien cultures to understand Japanese categorical imperatives in their own terms" (Benedict 1945: 2). Benedict examined Japanese psychological themes that included questions of "Japanese fatalism," "Japanese systems of obligations" (e.g., *On, Gimu, Giri,* etc.), the role of shame in Japanese society, Japanese self-discipline, and "Japanese attitudes toward primary pleasures."[9] Some of Benedict's psychological interpretations followed arguments first developed by Gorer in the 1941 memo "Japanese Character Structure and Propaganda" (Gorer 1942, 1943a, 1943c).

Benedict warned that the American military and civilian leadership should not subject the Japanese leaders or public to forms of public humiliation at the war's end:

The totally destructive technique which Occidentals will run the risk of using with Japan is that of humiliation. According to Western ethics, it is desirable to humiliate a wrongdoer because he will thereby learn to admit his sin and being defeated in a war is itself humiliation. The Japanese have a different ethic, and the famous story of the surrender of the Russian commander at Port Arthur in 1905 shows how they applied their ethic in international warfare. When General Stoessel, the Russian commander, signified his willingness to receive Japanese propositions of surrender, a Japanese Captain and interpreter went to his headquarters bearing gifts. . . . Defeat in war, in other words, was simply what it said—a defeat in battle. It was not complicated by humiliation, which, to the Japanese, is ridicule and belittling, and insistence on symbols of dishonor. (Benedict 1945: 58)

Benedict incorporated key elements from an earlier memo, "What Shall Be Done about the Emperor?" into "Japanese Behavior Patterns," as she argued that symbols of aggression in wartime could be usefully transformed into symbols of harmony in peacetime. Benedict observed:

The symbolic power of the Emperor has been, in the last decade, the chief device for promoting aggression; it is, however, a power that can operate in any direction. It is not in itself synonymous with conquest and concentration camps as the regime of Hitler was in Germany. The *chu* [deep loyalty] of Japanese subjects for their Emperor could be just as consistent with their world, at least with a war-torn world, or it could be sloughed off in time as Japan's social objectives change. It would be desirable if Westerners differentiated between Emperor veneration as such and the immediate militaristic uses to which it has been currently put. (Benedict 1945: 33–34)

Themes and passages in "Japanese Behavior Patterns" were later reproduced unaltered in Benedict's book *The Chrysanthemum and the Sword* (1946). With the postwar publication of *Chrysanthemum*, Benedict's work at OWI became the most famous American social-science contribution to the Second World War—although this fame contributed some misunderstanding of how her work (and that of others at OWI) was used and ignored by military and civilian agencies during the war.[10]

OWI Propaganda Aimed at Japanese Soldier and Civilians

After the war's end, Ellis Zacharias, deputy director of the ONI, publicly criticized the White House and the War Department for believing propagandistic claims generated by the Japanese that the Japanese national character was immutable and incapable of betraying the emperor through acts of surrender. In his book *Secret Missions*, Zacharias wrote:

> For reasons which I still cannot understand but which must be similar in background to those which caused Pearl Harbor, Admiral Nimitz was persistently advised against the use of psychological warfare against the Japanese. This advice was based upon a shallow conception which took as a fact an imaginary situation actually created by Japanese propaganda itself: the delusion that the Japanese would never surrender and that any attempt to interfere with their mental processes would be doomed to failure. This concept was never tested, it was just accepted. And for two years of war the Japanese benefited from it. (Zacharias 1946: 291)

Zacharias complained that the rigid hierarchy of military procedures and institutional suspicions delayed the OWI's ability to undertake aggressive propaganda campaigns directed at Japanese soldiers and civilians. He observed, "The Office of War Information experienced great difficulty when it tried to join the offensive against Japan. According to [presidential directive], the theater commander had complete control of everything in his zone; and psychological warfare could be conducted, if at all, only with the approval and under the supervision of the local commander in chief" (Zacharias 1946: 291). Kluckhohn and other anthropologists at OWI faced military commanders who resisted their propaganda proposals. These military commanders argued, "We know that the Nazis are fanatics, but the Japanese have proved themselves still more fanatical. How can leaflets and broadcasts possibly affect soldiers who will go readily into a Banzai charge or fight under hopeless conditions in a cave, finally blowing themselves to pieces with a hand grenade? Why should the lives of our men be risked in attempting to secure more prisoners when it is obvious that Japanese prisoners will not provide us with intelligence information?" (Kluckhohn 1949: 153–54).

The low surrender rates of Japanese soldiers during the early years of the war suggested that, while the United States would win the key battles of the Pacific war, total victory would be a long, bloody fight. Most military leaders saw OWI social scientists as wasting time and resources as they attempted to engineer increased surrenders. Japanese troops were trained to fight to the death, and, in some cases, to commit suicide before submitting to capture. As Ohnuki-Tierney has described:

> The first lesson student soldiers . . . were taught was how to use their own rifles to kill themselves, rather than to be captured alive. This included the practice of using a toe to pull the trigger and to point the gun precisely at a certain point under the chin so that the bullet would kill them instantly. They were supposed to use this technique if they were trapped in a cave or in a trench surrounded by the enemy. If they did not kill themselves but tried to escape, others would shoot them from behind anyway, since their superiors and even some comrades believed in the state dictum not to be captured by the enemy. In other words, once you are drafted, you had reached a point of no return. (Ohnuki-Tierney 2002: 167–68)

This training and dedication hardened the resolve of Japanese soldiers, and news of such commitment hardened the resolve of American military commanders to fight as if the Japanese could never surrender.

In August 1943, Paul H. Clyde wrote the OWI report "A Brief Analysis of the Japanese Attitude toward Death with Emphasis on Its Implications." In it, he argued that, as the Japanese defeat became increasing inevitable, Japanese soldiers would be less prone to die in combat and more prone to surrender (see Janssens 1995: 188). In the spring of 1944, the OWI was granted permission to begin broadcasting shortwave transmissions from San Francisco to Japan and the war theaters of the Japanese military (OWI Leaflet News Letter 1945: 3). These broadcasts were first scripted in English by OWI social scientists. Scripts were then reviewed by native speakers of the target language, who helped assure that the messages were culturally appropriate. The messages were then translated into the target language and usually broadcast by native speakers (Price 1996).

OWI propaganda campaigns were not only aimed at the Japanese. Some campaigns were directed at indigenous populations in theaters of battle. Gustav Sword reported in April 1945 that the OWI's Burmese leaflet campaigns directed at the Kachin had been very well received:

> I was very pleased to meet a large number of Kachins and to listen to their reactions to our leaflets and gifts. Our leaflets were more effective than I had dared to believe. Hundreds of people repeatedly told me that the leaflets and newspapers dropped by us had saved their lives.
>
> [News] leaflets about the Maingkwan and Walawbum victories brought the people of Myitkyina and the Mogaung Valley the first word of the Al-

lied advance. Refugees from Myitkyina reported that pro-Allied groups were given new hope and that persons willingly collaborating with the Japanese became uneasy and fearful. The Japanese issued orders prohibiting the reading of Allied leaflets. Despite Japanese repression, American news spread. Natives not under the direct eye of the Japanese read the papers thoroughly and spread the news via the "jungle wireless." (OWI Leaflet News Letter 1945: 5)

The OWI organized "Railway Bombing Warning" campaigns in India, "designed to reduce the enemy labor supply and to protect the native workers from Allied bombs." The result of these campaigns was that "trackmen, switchmen, and laborers 'went off to visit relatives' or 'took sick' at an unprecedented rate" (OWI Leaflet News Letter 1945: 7). But initial efforts to encourage Japanese troops to surrender had little impact. In the early battles in Burma, so few Japanese soldiers surrendered to American forces that the "capture" to "dead" ratios was as low as 1:120 (142 prisoners ; 17,166 dead) (Benedict 1946: 38).

FMAD produced leaflets to be dropped over China designed to build morale among Chinese soldiers fighting the Japanese. Other leaflets told Japanese soldiers of the increasing futility of their fight and that Allied victory was only a matter of time (OWI Leaflet News Letter 1945: 9). FMAD undertook massive leafleting campaigns in the Philippines directed at Japanese occupiers and potential Filipino resistance fighters. Between October 20, 1944, and May 12, 1945, the OWI produced more than fifty-three million leaflets that were dropped on the Philippines. They included

> texts of official proclamations, news leaflets, messages to the guerrillas, and instructions for helping in the liberation. Later, there were warnings of American landings, instructing Filipinos how to avoid death or injury by our bombings and shelling of beaches and military installations, and finally, the red, white and blue leaflets proclaiming that "MacArthur has returned."
>
> For the Japanese, leaflets of two general types were produced: news leaflets designed to give troops the facts about the progress of the war, and leaflets devoted to a single theme appeal, designed directly to reduce the morale of the enemy troops and induce their surrender. The "surrender pass" gave instructions on how to surrender and bore in English on one side instructions to American troops on how to accept the surrender and turn the prisoner over for questioning
>
> These included the threat of terrific pounding by artillery, promise of good treatment for prisoners, news of the new American landings, explana-

tion of the superiority of U.S. weapons, explanations of the fact that U.S. forces had cut off supply lines, the truth about Japanese leaders, the lack of support for ground troops from the Japanese navy and air forces, and "surrender passes." (OWI Leaflet News Letter 1945: 10–11)

As the war progressed and Japanese losses grew, the OWI was able to measure dramatically increased surrender rates among Japanese soldiers in the Philippines. But while Taylor and his OWI staff were impressed with the increased surrender rates, military commanders remained skeptical of the significance of the surrenders. OWI reports stressed:

> Careful study and detailed statistical analysis of battle data from the Philippines showed that this spring for the first time there was important evidence of weakening of Japanese military morale, not, as previously, in small, isolated units at the end of a protracted defensive campaign fought under impossibly difficult conditions, but in the relatively fresh and still integrated main body of the Japanese force in the field. The decline in Japanese troop morale was demonstrated by the number of deserters, the prisoners' descriptions of morale conditions in their own units, and a marked lack of prisoner faith in victory.
>
> Of 251 Japanese prisoners captured in the Philippines between January 15 and March 15, 1945, only 18 resisted capture with every means at their disposal or attempted suicide as an alternative to capture. Thirty-eight deserted outright and came over to our lines voluntarily. One Japanese officer formally surrendered with six men. Such formal surrender by an officer with troops under his command was specially noteworthy at that time because no previous occurrence had been authentically reported to OWI. Interrogation of a sample group of the POW's revealed for each man who expressed faith in final, over-all Japanese victory, that there were for others who conceded Japanese defeat. In no previous group studied by OWI's Foreign Morale Analysis Division had more than 50% conceded lack of faith in ultimate Japanese success.
>
> A report from the XXIV Corps stated that the majority of 278 POW's taken by that organization as of January 11, 1945, either surrendered with leaflet in hand or proved to have been directly influenced by our propaganda.
>
> Between January 25 and February 15, 1945, there was a 750% increase in the distribution of leaflets on Luzon, as contrasted with the average distribution during the first 115 days of the campaign there. During this period of intensified psychological warfare, the average number of prisoners taken on

the island was noticeably higher than it had been previously. (OWI Leaflet
News Letter 1945: 10–11)

Along with the growing American military victories came an increased tonnage
of leaflets encouraging Japanese troops in hopeless situations to surrender—as
well as advising them on how to safely go about surrendering. Gone were the
terrifying 1:120 "capture-to-death ratio" campaigns of earlier in the war. Reports
of the increased surrender rates linked to leafleting campaigns were circulated in
military circles, but they had no visible impact on the military's view of the
possibility of the Japanese surrender.

One 1945 report on the impact of OWI propaganda campaigns on Japanese
soldiers and civilians noted:

> Japanese reactions, which have come back to us variously, through captured
> documents, the reports of Intelligence Agents and radio intercepts indicate
> that the leaflet campaign was effective. [Japanese] radio broadcasts warned
> against reading leaflets and threatened severe punishment for keeping them.
> An intercepted message, referring to leaflets dropped, pointed out the neces-
> sity of avoiding falling into the trap set by the enemy (i.e., the Americans),
> and said that whenever leaflets were discovered, they should be forwarded to
> the Police Bureau. "Punishment will be severely meted out as for a traitor or
> spy to anyone retaining these leaflets and not giving them to the Police
> Station." A captured document issued by a high Japanese military [head-
> quarters] expressed acute concern over the influence of Chinese propaganda
> on their troops. (OWI Leaflet News Letter 1945: 9–10)

In one Japanese broadcast monitored in China, the OWI found "evidence of a
kind of desperation." This broadcast expressed fears that Japanese civilians would
be especially susceptible to American propaganda campaigns because of their
lack of experience in adjudicating such messages from the outside world. The
intercepted message worried, "Whereas [we Japanese] have been given training
in putting out incendiary bombs, how to cope with 'paper bombs' has never been
taught us. Counter measures must be devised by government authorities as
effective as those devised against bombs. It must be anticipated that propaganda
leaflets will be dropped among the people during air raids which will be confus-
ing to mind and will. . . . The people of Japan are like hothouse flowers and truly
it can be stated that our ears have been given very little training as regards enemy
propaganda" (OWI Leaflet News Letter 1945: 10). As Americans intensified the
bombing of Japanese civilians, using jellied gasoline bombs and undertaking the

widespread bombing of civilian populations, Japanese civilians on the home front became increasingly aware that they were losing the war. This knowledge opened possibilities for OWI propaganda—and, as Clyde Kluckhohn later observed, anthropologists trained in distinguishing between ideational and behavioral realms of culture helped break through claims by the Japanese that soldiers were never taken alive and that anthropologists were instrumental in

> challenging the assumption that the morale of any people was or could be absolutely impregnable. Morale might be relatively high under certain conditions, but it could not be a constant under all conditions. The problem was to find the right means for widening the cracks and fissures that would inevitably open up with local and general defeats, the pressures of starvation and of isolation. The official Japanese line was that no Japanese was taken prisoner unless he were unconscious or so badly wounded he could not move. We swallowed this for a long time. Days or weeks after capture an interrogator behind the lines would ask a prisoner how he happened to be taken. He would give the standard reply, "I was unconscious." This would be entered in the tabulations. Eventually, however, skeptics began to check the reports made at the time of the incident. It was found that Private Watanabe who had been listed as taken while unconscious was actually captured while swimming. The difference between behavior and cultural stereotype is important. (Kluckhohn 1949: 154–55)

But the OWI's detection and interpretation of these increasing surrender rates meant little, as the military and civilian leadership remained unpersuaded that the shifts were meaningful. Those directing the war still believed that the Japanese could not surrender without massive military and civilian casualties.

Aiming OWI Propaganda at the White House and Pentagon

Even as the OWI was engineering propaganda campaigns to convince Japanese citizens, soldiers, and leaders to surrender, George Taylor and others within the OWI focused increasing efforts toward convincing American civilian and military decision makers that the Japanese could surrender.

When I interviewed Taylor in 1996, he insisted that, at the beginning of the war, he viewed his psychological-warfare programs as a means of ending the war by helping the Japanese overcome cultural obstacles that prevented surrender, but as the war advanced and the American advantage became clear, he increasingly focused OWI efforts on educating U.S. civilian and military leaders that they

did not have to annihilate the Japanese home front to end the war. Racial stereotypes of maniacal Japanese soldiers and civilians fighting to the death dominated
the War Department and the White House, and Taylor and his staff increasingly
saw these domestic views as significant deterrents to peace (Price 1996).[11]

President Roosevelt believed that the end of the war would not come until
large numbers of casualties had been amassed on the Japanese home front. John
Dower wrote,

> Elliott Roosevelt, the president's son and confidant, told Henry Wallace in
> 1945 that the United States should continue bombing Japan "until we have
> destroyed about half the Japanese civilian population." While the president's
> son was expressing such personal views in private, the chairman of the War
> Manpower Commission, Paul V. McNutt, told a public audience in April
> 1945 that he favored "the extermination of the Japanese in toto." When asked
> if he meant the Japanese military or the people as a whole, he confirmed he
> meant the latter, "for I know the Japanese people." A week later, McNutt, a
> former U.S. high commissioner in the Philippines, called a press conference
> to make clear that his comments reflected his personal views rather than
> official policy. Several days before the atomic bomb was dropped on Hiro-
> shima, Vice Admiral Arthur Radford was quoted as saying that "the Japs are
> asking for an invasion, and they are going to get it. Japan will eventually be a
> nation without cities—a nomadic people." (Dower 1986: 55)

Such views were common among policymakers who received and largely ignored
the intelligence reports produced by the OWI. In one speech made to military
strategists (in late 1944 or early 1945), Taylor argued:

> If we accept, as we must, the view that Japanese soldiers, in spite of their
> indoctrination, are as human as other troops, we shall be the less surprised
> at the mounting evidence of their very human reactions to defeat. We are
> taking more and more prisoners. Two years ago it would have been very
> unusual for sixty men to allow themselves to be picked up out of the water
> when their transport had been sunk. In New Guinea and Burma stragglers
> are coming in out of the jungles to surrender without a struggle. We have
> known for a long time that many Japanese officers have been evacuated
> from indefensible positions and that their reaction on places such as Attu,
> where escape was impossible, was not to fight to the last man. They often
> slaughtered themselves and their men long before they had spent the last
> cartridge. Once separated from his officer the main fear in the mind of the

Japanese soldier is that of being tortured by his captors. Many of the Japanese atrocities have been committed as a demonstration to peasants in uniform of what would happen to them in case of capture.[12]

But this sort of analysis, arguing against a campaign to inflict devastating damage on a "race" believed incapable of surrender, was ignored by the War Department and White House as they undertook increasingly devastating bombing campaigns against Japanese civilians.

The OWI had little success in convincing President Roosevelt of the importance of not including the demise of the Japanese emperor in America's demands for unconditional surrender. According to Taylor, when Truman became president, he accepted the OWI's position regarding the importance of exempting the emperor from postwar punishment (Price 1996).

FMAD social scientists had determined that Japanese prisoners of war were valuable sources of information and effective propaganda. Clyde Kluckhohn argued that Japanese culture configurations viewed individuals within the context of larger groups, and when Japanese soldiers were captured, they became dead to the old collective. A prisoner could thus easily reformat his social existence to fit that of his captors. Kluckhohn wrote:

> An American prisoner of war still felt himself to be an American and looked forward to resuming his normal place in American society after the war. A Japanese prisoner, however, conceived of himself as socially dead. He regarded his relations with his family, his friends, and his country as finished. But since he was physically alive he wished to affiliate himself with a new society. To the astonishment of their American captors, many Japanese prisoners wished to join the American Army and were, in their turn, astonished when they were told this was impossible. They willingly wrote propaganda for us, spoke over loud speakers urging their own troops to surrender, gave detailed information on artillery emplacements and the military situation in general. In the last six months of the war some Japanese prisoners flew in American planes within forty-eight hours after their capture, spotting Japanese positions. Some were allowed to return within the Japanese lines and brought back indispensable information.
>
> From the American point of view there was something fantastic about all this. The behavior before and after capture was utterly incongruous. The incongruity, however, rests on a cultural point. The Judaic-Christian tradition is that of absolute morality—the same code is, at least in theory, demanded in all situations. To anthropologists who had steeped themselves in

Japanese literature it was clear that Japanese morality was a situational one. As long as one was in situation A, one publicly observed the rules of the game with a fervor that impressed Americans as "fanaticism." Yet the minute one was in situation B, the rules for situation A no longer applied. (Kluckhohn 1949: 154)

But few in civilian or military command circles seriously considered this or most of the other analyses coming from OWI anthropologists. Leonard Doob later described the situation as one in which "social scientists from academic institutions sometimes breezed into the offices of policy-makers not familiar with social science for the purpose of making a proposal which they considered sensational and important. They had to be treated politely for the sake of the OWI's budget and reputation. . . . The policy-maker would say 'how interesting,' and then pass it to a colleague whose desk was also littered with unread or undigested reports. Eventually the document was filed and only an efficient secretary could locate it, if anyone ever again asked to see it. Generally, nobody did" (Doob 1947: 665).

Alexander Leighton observed that, when OWI anthropologists' "conclusions reflected the prevailing ideas and beliefs of an important group of officials in the government, [their] reports were circulated widely and to the top. On the other hand, reports of a contrary nature had a limited circulation and traveled upward in the hierarchy only so far as the first line of disagreement" (Leighton 1949: 121).

OWI propaganda projects appeared to generate measurable results, but few outside the agency paid attention to these outcomes. Leighton observed that conditions were so dysfunctional that, when FMAD

> found that Japanese troops could be influenced toward surrender, there was agreement and enthusiasm on the part of policy makers who had all along been advocating psychological warfare. The reports of the Division were widely read by them and the contents used in speech and writing to support and justify their program. As previously noted the Division was given more funds, staff, office space and other such benefits. On the other hand, those who were opposed to psychological warfare found many opportunities for critical comment and objection.
>
> When the Division reported that Japanese attitudes toward the Emperor were not weakening as the war went along and that propaganda attacks on him were useless and dangerous, these findings did not fit with the views of many policy makers in psychological warfare. The suggestion that we tell the Japanese of our intention to leave the Emperor's fate in their hands was still

more distasteful. Numbers of those who had been supporting the Division's work were committed to an anti-Emperor program and they quickly fell · away as admirers. (Leighton 1949: 120)

There was little that owi anthropologists could do to affect decisions made in this heavily bureaucratic environment, where important decisions were usually made on the basis of preconceptions and evidence was used only when it fit those preconceptions.

owi *Propaganda and the Conditions of Unconditional Surrender*

By the war's end, the U.S. military had dropped more than three hundred fifty million owi leaflets over the Far East; most of them were dropped during the last nine months of the war (see table 2). In May 1945, ten million leaflets were dropped on Japan, and a series of owi shortwave propaganda messages were broadcast to the Japanese people (owi Leaflet News Letter 1945: 13).[13] In the spring of 1945, Taylor argued that Japanese morale was shattered, basic supplies were scarce, and the Japanese were ready to consider reasonable terms of surrender, but the White House and Pentagon saw no concrete evidence indicating that the Japanese were ready to surrender (Price 1996).[14]

Benedict, Gorer, and Morris Opler had argued that the emperor's symbolic status as the "sacred father" of Japan made his preservation a vital component of a peaceful postwar occupation. During the war, Benedict forcefully argued in owi reports that America's success in the postwar occupation would hinge on how it treated the emperor and other Japanese leaders once they surrendered:

Every act, every gesture on our part—and most of them would cost us nothing except self-control—which recognize [Japan] as a brave and reputable enemy even in defeat, will pay high dividends in the post war world. If we insist on degrading the Emperor, setting up humiliating terms of *mura* by *mura* [village by village] postwar occupation, and making conservative Japanese leaders, in their phrase, "crawl between our legs," Japanese reaction to these measures will be anger, vows of vengeance and righteous indignation. They will tend to become a nation of avenging ronin. They will certainly not learn conviction of sin out of the experience, though that is what, according to our ethic, we expect humiliation to teach. If law and order is to be achieved in the Far East in the next generations, such a nation of ronin must be avoided in Japan. No matter what the provocations—and they have been

Table 2. Office of War Information Leaflet Distribution in the Far East, 1945

TARGET	QUANTITY
China and Indochina	28,509,781
In Japanese	10,611,033
In Chinese	15,692,243
In Annamese-French	267,240
Language not reported	1,939,265
Japan	71,876,000
Disseminated by B-29s	58,648,000
Disseminated by MacArthur	13,228,000
Philippines	82,844,060
Language breakdown not available	
Northern Burma	8,660,783
In Shan, Kachin, and Burmese	2,526,773
In Japanese	3,734,236
Language not reported	2,399,774
Lower Burma	3,693,905
In Burmese	3,038,980
In Japanese	654,925
Siam	9,035,830
In Japanese	941,731
In Siamese	7,720,649
Language not reported	373,450
Formosa	1,652,000
Pacific Islands	26,042,900
TOTAL	354,091,558

Source: OWI Leaflet News Letter 1945: 26 (originally classified "confidential").
The Office of War Information's publication of this table noted that statistics for China and the Philippines were incomplete. The figures for the Pacific Islands were "a production rather than [a] dissemination figure," and the figures for leaflets dropped over Japan were likely "larger than indicated."

many and terrible—any treaty with Japan and any occupation of Japan can succeed only as we take some account of the desirability of not complicating her defeat with any unnecessary symbols of humiliation.

Japan will be able to salvage some self-respect out of the fact that, far from being defeated by a weak enemy like China, her defeat required the combined efforts of the United States, England and Russia. We would wisely not object to any ways in which she states this to her people and capitalize on it in negotiations. Japan's recognition that she was not ridiculed in the end-of-the-war arrangements is an asset which will be needed in the post-war world. (Benedict 1945: 59)

Other OWI anthropologists based arguments supporting the retention of the emperor on anthropological literature analyzing past episodes of cultural conquest. Morris Opler argued that previous American victories had been diminished by the troubles associated with the imprisonment, execution, and eradication of conquered peoples, when a coordinated campaign of co-optation would have gained more than the humiliations of militarized occupation. Opler reasoned that, during the U.S. government's past dealings with Indian tribes,

drastic measures were often taken to crush resistance against the method or precepts of our Government. Chiefs were deposed or imprisoned, specific types of government were substituted for the native forms, children were separated from their households so that the influence of their elders would be minimized. The results of this type [of] interference with tribal life have been disastrous in the extreme . . . because in an attempt to hit at what was supposed to be the sole or main function of the chief, his many other functions were overlooked, social balance was seriously disrupted and a disintegration for which we had not bargained took place. This is a national experience which could be documented endlessly from the files of the Office of Indian Affairs. (Quoted in Janssens 1995: 193)

After the war, Kluckhohn described American motivations for retaining the Mikado, reasoning that America had co-opted the Japanese power structure by keeping the emperor as a symbolic puppet who could carry out America's will with traditional Japanese movements. Kluckhohn explicitly linked the basis of this strategy to the British system of indirect rule:

Controversy raged in Washington over our propaganda treatment of the imperial institution in Japan. The liberal intellectuals in general urged that we should attack this as the prop of a fascist state. They maintained that it was dishonest and a betrayal of the deepest American ideals to allow the Japanese to assume from our silence that we would tolerate the monarchy after our victory. The anthropologists opposed this policy. They had the general objection that the solution to conflicts between the United States and other peoples can never rest on a cultural imperialism that insists upon the substitution of our institutions for theirs. But they had more immediately practical objectives. They pointed out, first, that if one examined historically the place of the imperial institution in Japanese culture it was clear that there was no inevitable linkage with the contemporary political attitudes and practices that we were bound to destroy. Second, since the imperial institution was the nucleus of the Japanese sentiment system, to attack it openly was to intensify and prolong enormously Japanese resistance, to give freely to the Japanese militarists the best possible rallying cry for morale. Third, the only hope for a unified Japanese surrender of all the forces scattered over Pacific Islands and on the continent of Asia was through this sole symbol that was universally respected.

Anthropologists showed that it is almost always more effective in the long run to preserve some continuity in the existing social organization and to work at reorganization from the established base. This had been demonstrated by the British anthropologists when they created the principle of "indirect rule." If the United States and its allies wished to abolish the monarchy it could be abolished eventually by the Japanese themselves if we handled the situation adroitly and adopted an astute educational program. When an institution is destroyed by force from without, there usually follows a compensatory and often destructive reaction from within. If a culture pattern collapses as a result of internal developments, the change is more likely to last. (Kluckhohn 1949: 153)

Since the First World War, indirect rule in Africa had proved a cost-effective way to extract wealth while pacifying local populations (see Kuper 1996). Anthropologists studying colonialism recognized that, through the procedures of indirect rule, Western conquerors found Africa to be "economical not only of the colonial power's cash resources, on which a large bureaucratic machine would have made heavy demands, but also of its military capacity. Emirs were offered a settlement of conquest without dishonor" (First 1970: 29). It was this same sort of "conquest without dishonor" that Benedict and others at the OWI advocated.[15]

Some of Benedict's OWI reports arguing for retention of the emperor also drew directly on anthropology's colonial literature. She argued:

One conclusion which is universally supported by these data is that frontal attacks by the dominant power upon the religion of the dominated are enormously expensive to the superordinate power and produce undesired results in the subordinate group. This is important when applied to Japan. Veneration of the Imperial House is a strict religious tenet of Japan and, however much it offends nations which espouse other tenets, it commands the deep loyalty of the Japanese. Every job to be done in rehabilitation will be less difficult according to the degree to which it has the sanction of the Emperor behind it, and more difficult in proportion to our requirements that he be eliminated.

This price, however, it would be desirable to pay it if were essential to future peace, and those who are concerned with war policy sometimes feel this is necessary. The crucial point to which Acculturation studies testify is that this is a misapprehension. Religion always takes its color and direction from the social life of the nation or community; as this social life changes, prayers, rituals and sacrifices of religion change along with it. It only compromises cooperation to legislate these changes, but they inevitably occur. Tribes which become warlike tailor their religion to war-making; tribes which become cut-throat in economic or social matters turn their religious rites toward sorcery uses. In peaceful tribes, or in those with more equitable distribution of goods, on the other hand, religious practices are means of achieving shared advantages—tribal health, fertility, rain, weather control, social solidarity, etc. Religions, being ways of using the supernatural realm for desired ends, inevitably seek the ends which are uppermost in that society. Their actual functioning is much more variable over time than religious historians are likely to stress. Religions change their role inevitably with changed conditions, but they cannot be changed on demand from outside without the gravest consequences. (Benedict 1945: 33)

Benedict's recommendation to retain the emperor thus was informed not only by her understanding of the cultural peculiarities of the Japanese, but also by a cost-benefit analysis based on her reading of successful colonial conquests. This analysis shows Benedict moving beyond the sort of psychological analysis found in much of her culture and personality writings.

Outside the owi, the Harvard anthropologist Earnest Hooton publicly proposed his own plan for Japan after the Allied victory. Hooton published his modest proposal in PM magazine with the disclaimer, "The following suggestions are offered by a physical anthropologist who has spent many years in the study of race, nationality, and the relation of individual biology to behavior. However, these suggestions represent no consensus of anthropological opinion; they have been endorsed by no one. The author, himself is not fully confident of the practicability of the measure outlined. He merely presents them for discussion" (Hooton 1943: 4). Hooton stated that the objective of this plan was "principally to remove for all time the menace of Japanese aggressiveness. The writer recognizes the industry, thrift, and mechanical skill of the Japanese, but doubts the desirability of perpetuating this stock as a national entity. He has no intimate acquaintance with the Japanese and feels ill-qualified to decide upon their genetic capacities" (Hooton 1943: 4). Hooton then listed five measures to be considered for the postwar period:

> Exile, imprison, and sterilize all members of the Japanese Royal family and all of the blood relations. The purpose of this measure is to extirpate the system of worship of the emperor.
>
> Actively propagate substitutes for the Japanese state religion (Buddhism, Islam, Christianity, and other types).
>
> Utilize present Japanese armies for rehabilitation of devastated Asiatic and Pacific areas. Under no circumstances permit the repatriation of Japanese males.
>
> Partially recolonize Japan with Chinese and other Asiatics. Forbid purely Japanese marriages.
>
> Entrust to the Chinese the task of supervising the Japanese population remaining in the homeland and of providing for the assimilation of Japanese by other Asiatic peoples.
>
> (Hooton 1943: 4)

But Hooton's proposals were too extreme. Fortunately, policymakers were moving away from retributional schemes and favoring plans designed to establish economic and social stability in postwar Japan.

Beyond anthropologists' recommendations concerning features of the conditions of unconditional surrender coming at the war's end, there were also momentous decisions regarding the war's end that might have been different had anthropological considerations not been unwelcome and routinely ignored.

Anthropologists Struggling on the Eve of Destruction

In George Taylor's papers and correspondence are copies of declassified intelligence reports with the codename "MAGIC—Diplomatic Summaries."[16] They are Japanese diplomatic intercepts that were secretly being decoded, translated, and read by American military intelligence during the war. A May 11, 1945, MAGIC intercept supports the views of Taylor and others at the OWI that the Japanese military was then ready to surrender:

> Report of peace sentiment in Japanese armed forces: On 5 May the German Naval Attaché in Tokyo dispatched the following message to Admiral Doenitz:
>
> "An influential member of the Admiralty Staff has given me to understand that, since the situation is clearly recognized to be hopeless, large sections of the Japanese armed forces would not regard with disfavor an American request for capitulation even if the terms were hard, provided they were halfway honorable."
>
> Note [by U.S. military intelligence]: Previously noted diplomatic reports have commented on signs of war weariness in official Japanese Navy circles, but have not mentioned such an attitude in Army quarters.[17]

Such "halfway honorable" terms of surrender were exactly why Ruth Benedict and other OWI anthropologists stressed the importance of retaining the emperor after Japan's surrender. However, the White House and War Department weighed the coming hundreds of thousands dead in Hiroshima and Nagasaki against the balance of specifying the conditions that did follow the unconditional surrender.

A July 20 MAGIC intercept revealed Japanese Ambassador Sato expressing his desire to surrender if the United States would assure him that the "Imperial House" would remain in existence.[18] In the days before the attacks on Hiroshima and Nagasaki, American intelligence had good evidence that Ambassador Sato was close to surrendering to the Americans, but neither the knowledge gleaned from these intercepts nor the work of social scientists at the OWI dissuaded the Americans from using nuclear weapons on Japanese civilians.[19]

The Potsdam Ultimatum, expressing the Allied forces' demand for Japan's unconditional surrender and threatening that "the alternative for Japan is utter destruction" was delivered July 26, 1945. But there were debates among American officials concerning whether or not the ultimatum should clarify that the emperor would be allowed to retain a symbolic position of power: "Some officials, like Undersecretary of State Joseph Grew, had argued that offering an explicit promise of Hirohito's continuation on the throne would greatly increase the chances of Japan's accepting Allied terms. Others, like Assistant Secretary of State Dean Acheson, felt that this kind of imperial guarantee would amount to an unconscionable form of appeasement toward a regime that bore direct culpability for all manner of atrocities and aggression" (Bess 2006: 211). Acheson's faction prevailed, but this view was counter to all of the findings of the OWI social scientists studying Japanese culture.

On the day following the Potsdam Ultimatum, the OWI broadcast a "Warning to All Cities" in Japan declaring that "leaflets falling on eleven Japanese cities warned the inhabitant that four of the eleven [cities] would be destroyed within the next few days." The OWI broadcast announced to the Japanese people:

> The broadcast you are now listening to may save your life or that of a friend or relative. American bombs will destroy at least four of the cities that we will now name within the next few days. Here are the cities on our list: Kurume, Uwajima, Tsu, Hakodate, Aomori, Ogaki, Ujiyamada, Nisfinomiya, Ichinomiya, Nagaoka, Koriyala. Military workshops and installations or factories making military supplies are found in these cities. Our determined resolution is to annihilate all the instruments of the military clique that are being used to lengthen this useless fight. Bombs have no eyes, unfortunately, so in conformity with the humanitarian policies of America, our air force has no desire that innocent people be injured and now wants to warn you to leave your cities in order that your lives may be spared. The United States is not waging war against the people of Japan but is battling the military machine which has enslaved the people of Japan. America will bring you a peace that will loose your bonds of oppression in which the military clique has you enmeshed and from the freedom will emerge a Japan that is new and better. Peace can be restored by you if you will demand new leaders that are good and will put an end to this conflict. No promise can be given that only these cities will be bombed, but at any rate, four cities at least will be attacked. So take heed of this warning, and immediately evacuate from these cities. (OWI Leaflet News Letter 1945: 20)

This broadcast emphasized the powerlessness of the Japanese leaders to prevent a coming American military victory. Similar messages continued in the days leading up to the bombing of Hiroshima and Nagasaki.

The anthropologists at OWI were unaware of the existence of the atomic bomb until they learned of the bombing of Hiroshima through public news sources. Once the bombing occurred, the OWI quickly adjusted its surrender leaflets to be dropped on the Japanese civilian home front. As unconfirmed reports of Japanese surrender were broadcast and circulated in Japan after the bombing of Nagasaki, Captain Zacharias advised that Japan should be left unharassed in order to prevent interference with the Emperor's efforts. There was no immediate need for a propaganda exploitation of the diplomatic note [from the Japanese government]. My apprehension of this period was fully confirmed some months later, when an OWI mission in Japan investigated the circumstances of the surrender. Frank Schuler of the OWI . . . discovered that the delay in acceptance of surrender was caused by a leaflet prepared in the field which informed the Japanese people prematurely of the surrender offer but after it was released in Washington.

The Japanese people who first learned of this fact from those leaflets were stunned. Moreover, there was no way for them to know that the Emperor was fully behind the offer. In their confused thinking they resorted to actions which made negotiations difficult for the imperial circle. But the leaflet did even greater damage. It incited certain Army officers of the palace guard to revolt against the Emperor and attempt large-scale assassinations to remove from the scene those who were in favor of the surrender. In the confusion created by this one leaflet there were hours when it seemed that the Emperor and his advisers would not be able to carry out their own surrender offer. (Zacharias 1946: 386)

While Zacharias viewed these leaflets as creating a disaster, Taylor saw them as persuasive tools. In 1952, the former OWI staff member Edward Barrett asked Taylor about his recollections of this OWI surrender-leaflet campaign at the war's end. Barrett wrote that he had just read Zacharias's account, and he wanted to know whether Taylor had "any clear recollection or conclusions regarding that particular leaflet which you and I sweated out at the suggestion of Byrnes, MacLeish and others?"[20] Taylor replied, "[My] impression of the leaflet story is that it was an important factor in bringing about the surrender. I recall asking Alexander Leighton about it when he returned from Japan after the war. He told me that the Japanese cabinet ministers picked up the leaflets on the way to the cabinet meetings. I have a very clear recollection of the leaflet and have always felt very strongly that it was an important factor in helping the Japanese to reach a conclusion."[21] These events were soon forgotten with the coming peaceful surrender, but this brief confusion and violence is one possible measure of the importance of retaining the emperor: When Japanese army officers did not know about the emperor's agreement to surrender, armed conflict emerged. This reaction suggests the sort of resistance that would have emerged if the emperor had been placed on trial at the war's end.

After the war, Captain Zacharias wrote that the impact of the Hiroshima and

Nagasaki bombings on the Japanese surrender were somewhat exaggerated. He believed the bombings were the least significant of three factors contributing to surrender; the other two being the long trail of American military victories throughout the Pacific and the "psychological offensive" launched by the OWI and others. Zacharias believed that it was "Japanese broadcasts which brought the Japanese emotionally and spiritually to their knees—and definitely hastened the implementation of the physical victory we had already won" (Zacharias 1946: 387).

It is possible that anthropologists and others at the OWI overestimated the impact of their propaganda on Japanese surrender rates. Certainly, the increase in surrenders among Japanese soldiers was contingent on successive military losses, and while it is difficult to unweave military outcomes from the impact of psychological-warfare campaigns, the latter depends on the former. Regardless of the reasons, beginning in 1944 Japanese soldiers surrendered at increased rates, and while the social scientists at the OWI realized the importance of this change, American military and civilian war planners were unwilling to link increased surrender rates with the intelligence findings that the Japanese government would surrender with a few simple assurances—assurances of conditions that they received at the war's end (Price 2004b).

Benedict and others at the OWI were ignored by a command structure that had it within its power to privately disclose to Japanese diplomats the conditions of unconditional surrender, allowing the emperor to surrender before the detonation of two atomic bombs on the civilian cities of Hiroshima and Nagasaki. It remains unclear what role, if any, OWI anthropologists played in the unfolding of the war's end. While the reports by Benedict, Opler, Gorer, and others at the OWI were circulated within and beyond the office, in the end "there is no evidence that the OWI's advice on the retention of the Japanese emperor was consulted in reaching the policy decision on the surrender terms" (Young 2005: 31).

When I interviewed Taylor about his memories of the war's end, he expressed some bitterness about the use of atomic bombs to bring unconditional surrender. Taylor's career credentials as a hawk—an ardent anti-communist conservative—made his voice an intriguing one in the chorus of those questioning the necessity of Truman's deployment of the atomic bomb.[22] Although he was outside the circle of those who decided to use the A-bomb, Taylor, and others at the OWI, knew that Japan was ripe for pseudo-unconditional surrender. Taylor later came to believe that Truman's decision to use nuclear weapons had more to do with "scaring the hell out of the Soviet Union" than it did with saving the

American lives that would have been lost in a U.S. invasion and occupation of the Japanese home islands (Price 1996).

In *The Decision to Use the Atomic Bomb*, Gar Alperovitz documented that while President Truman and his top civilian staff did not have the nuanced understanding of Japanese society that Benedict and others at the OWI did, they did realize that Japan was close to surrendering before atomic weapons were used. Alperovitz (1995: 35, 236, 334–35) wrote that many military commanders, such as Dwight Eisenhower, William D. Leahy, Curtis LeMay, and Henry H. Arnold, had misgivings about using such weapons on an enemy so close to surrendering.[23] The views of OWI anthropologists and others arguing that Japan was poised to surrender were ignored for a more expedient display of power.

Assessing FMAD Outcomes

Leighton's war experiences in the WRA and OWI led him to conclude skeptically that "the administrator uses social science the way a drunk uses a lamppost, for support rather than illumination" (Leighton 1949: 128). As with so many applied-anthropology projects, the work of social scientists at the OWI was embraced and used when its recommendations were of use to the immediate goals of patrons, and they were ignored when they went beyond institutional paradigms. In the case of the OWI, the military's decision to ignore the findings of anthropologists and others arguably contributed to the only uses of atomic weapons in warfare. But such selective uses of intelligence are not unique. Recurring concerns that members of the intelligence community selectively ignore intelligence data that do not support agency policies remain today. The CIA's practices of selectively ignoring and "cooking" intelligence to meet presidential policy needs has recurred during the Korean, Vietnam, and Iraq wars (Clarke 2004; McGehee 1983; Stockwell 1991). During the Second World War, anthropological intelligence was deployed only when its findings fit the narrow paradigms of civilian and military commanders, and it was neglected when its knowledge was outside these world-views, regardless of its usefulness.

It is important not to overestimate the value placed by military and civilian commanders on anthropologists at the OWI. It did not take a team of Ph.D.s to see that Japan was ready to surrender, or that the postwar occupation would go more easily if the emperor were retained. It did help to have such specialists supporting these policies, but in war, as in peace, policymakers occasionally consulted with anthropologists and then used whatever reports supported their views, ignored reports that contradicted their views, and undertook actions for their own reasons.

It is also possible that anthropologists at the OWI had only limited success in increasing surrender rates. While those rates did increase with OWI propaganda, Japanese soldiers surrendered not simply because more culturally appropriate leaflets were being distributed, but also because they were retreating and dying due to superior American resources and firepower. Accumulating military defeats created the conditions under which surrender became a viable option for Japanese soldiers. The shifting conditions of battle weakened the ideological pull of the Japanese state and opened the way for OWI propaganda to affect soldiers' decisions to surrender. In a war of bullets and leaflets, the leaflets can hold sway only after the bullets create conditions in which the enemy's words are worth considering.

Taylor, Benedict, and others at the OWI understood that, had the emperor not been retained, the postwar occupation would have been violent. Kluckhohn's contextualization of the logic of supporting the emperor's retention situated this policy within the tradition of British colonial indirect rule rather than as a compassionate act of cultural sensitivity. Benedict and Opler likewise anchored their recommendations in their anthropological reading of past colonial conquests.

Like most cogs functioning in large bureaucratic systems, the anthropologists at the OWI had little impact on what happened beyond their offices. At best, these anthropologists were offered a Hobson's choice; at worst, they were nothing more than window dressing. After the war, Margaret Mead noted that a general consensus emerged among wartime applied anthropologists that, after years of advising military policymakers, most of what had been said had simply fallen on deaf ears. A general feeling prevailed among many anthropologists during the war that "you can't advise an adviser" (Mead 1979: 153). The military's practice of selectively ignoring and selectively commandeering social scientists' recommendations allows for an ominous reading of Embree's optimistic postwar appeal that "it is imperative that our knowledge of the social sciences catch up with our ability to destroy the human race" (Embree 1946: 495). Embree assumed that advances in social science would provide enlightened means to curtail the causes of human conflict, but a more complete consideration of the uses and neglect of anthropology during the war suggests that the social sciences' catching up with the ability to destroy the human race could also mean that anthropology would be harnessed to hasten such an apocalypse.

The inability to influence what is done with recommendations is an inherent feature of anthropological contributions to warfare. This is no different from the

ANTHROPOLOGY AND *NIHONJINRON*   199

situation faced in other policy situations, though the potentially lethal outcomes of such work significantly raises the stakes for all involved. The inevitable risk of these limitations should caution anthropologists about the dangers of contributing their craft to such ends—even to projects that seem designed to preserve the lives of the populations under study. In the end, anthropologists have no say in how their research or recommendations will be applied in military contexts.

Even though the analyses by the OWI anthropologists were largely ignored during the war, some of them did catch the attention of important postwar military and intelligence agencies. The techniques used by OWI anthropologists to study remote cultures took on a growing importance in the coming Cold War. In the spring of 1946, the ONI awarded Ruth Benedict an annual grant of close to one hundred thousand dollars to carry out further culture and personality work. This was an incredible amount of money for the time—as Caffrey has noted, "Never had so much money been available to the Columbia-based anthropologists at one time" (Caffrey 1989: 329–30). Embree was being cleared by the FBI for sensitive government work after the war, when he suddenly died in an automobile accident (see Price 2004a), and Kluckhohn's work at Harvard's Russian Research Center found him secretly working with the CIA and other government agencies, a role that Kluckhohn used to recruit at least one anthropologist to work for the CIA (Coe 2006: 64; Diamond 1992). In many ways, the outcomes of these and other anthropological contributions found anthropologists facing constraints and dilemmas similar to those encountered at the OWI.

CHAPTER NINE

Archaeology and
J. Edgar Hoover's Special
Intelligence Service

> We likewise decided that the time had come when we would have to consider setting up a
> secret intelligence service—which I suppose every foreign office in the world has, but we
> have never touched.
> —ADOLF BERLE'S DIARY ENTRY AFTER MEETING WITH
> J. EDGAR HOOVER, June 3, 1940

J. Edgar Hoover's unchecked reign over the FBI made him one of the most
powerful Americans of the twentieth century. As the war expanded in Europe,
the Pacific, and Asia, Hoover felt his monopolistic grip on power threatened by
rumors of new intelligence agencies that would inevitably be born of America's
entry into the Second World War. During the years preceding the American entry
into the war, Hoover positioned himself to preemptively co-opt and manage
whatever international intelligence organizations might be created if America
took up arms. Hoover acutely realized the role that anthropologists could serve as
agents blending into the background in foreign countries.

On June 26, 1939, President Roosevelt signed a directive authorizing the FBI,
the Military Intelligence Division (MID), and the Office of Naval Intelligence
(ONI) to jointly oversee all U.S. intelligence operations throughout Central America
and South America. By the following spring, J. Edgar Hoover was using the FBI
to usurp the MID's and ONI's authority to conduct foreign intelligence operations
(Rout and Bratzel 1986: 33–34). At a May 31, 1940, inter-intelligence agency
meeting, Hoover outmaneuvered the MID's Brigadier-General Sherman Miles
and the ONI's Rear Admiral Walter S. Anderson by suddenly announcing a change
in the FBI's previous policy of refraining from conducting foreign intelligence
operations. Hoover declared, "Upon the instructions of the President, the Bureau

was arranging to detail men to Mexico City and Havana, but that this was the limit of the Bureau's operation in foreign countries" (quoted in Rout and Bratzel 1986: 33–34). Miles and Anderson were outraged by Hoover's move, and when they proposed that Adolf Berle (representing the Secretary of State) oversee intelligence operations conducted in Latin America, "The wily Hoover suavely suggested that Edward Tamm, the former's stand-in at previous meetings, be named as Berle's advisor and assistant in the selection process. The meeting ended, no blood having been spilt, but with the battle lines drawn" (Rout and Bratzel 1986: 35). Tamm used his position to protect Hoover's interests. Hoover later established a working relationship with Rear Admiral Anderson in which they colluded to keep decision-making power from Brigadier General Miles. Under this arrangement Hoover only needed to keep one organizational chief of the three-organization committee happy, so Miles was neutralized and Hoover expanded his reach into the arena of international intelligence.

In the spring of 1940, President Roosevelt authorized the creation of the Special Intelligence Service (SIS) within the FBI. The new agency was charged with coordinating all U.S. intelligence activities in Central and South America. President Roosevelt's secret authorization established the SIS as a covert organization with "an extensive program of counter-intelligence, utilizing the services of American business firms operating in Latin America, in operation for the purpose of maintaining a constant study of the Axis operations, propaganda, etc. in these countries" (Rout and Bratzel 1986: 40). Roosevelt's official authorization charging the SIS was a spoken directive, with the only written documentation being a memo from Berle. This arrangement meant that if SIS operatives were caught breaking the laws of foreign countries, President Roosevelt would be protected under a pretense of plausible deniability for covert actions (Rout and Bratzel 1986: 37).

Hoover's campaigns to expand the FBI's oversight of foreign espionage were more than simple battles over the rights to global intelligence. Recently declassified internal FBI memos indicate that Hoover was only interested in running these foreign intelligence operations if he was answerable to no other agency, because "Hoover wanted either all the authority to administer a given task or none of it" (Webb 2004 :46).[1]

Hoover and Miles continued to jockey for the administrative rights to conduct other foreign intelligence operations. As these power struggles intensified, President Roosevelt took decisive action at an April 4, 1941, cabinet meeting and announced that William J. Donovan would be appointed to a new position overseeing all international intelligence operations. Three months later (July 11,

1941), over the vigorous objections of Hoover, William "Wild Bill" Donovan was named Coordinator of Information (COI). Donovan was a successful Republican Wall Street lawyer and a law-school classmate of President Roosevelt. In 1940, Donovan had written an analysis of Britain's likelihood of withstanding a feared Nazi attack that proved to be prescient. The report led British diplomats to press Roosevelt to appoint Donovan to direct America's new intelligence agency (Jeffreys-Jones 1989: 15–16). The initial charge of the COI was to act as a centralized intelligence clearing house that would collect résumés and track intelligence desires to coordinate the needs of military and intelligence agencies with the availability of civilian and military personnel. The British helped mold the COI and OSS by lending to Donovan the British intelligence liaison Ian Fleming and other British agents who specialized in covert operations (Jeffreys-Jones 1989: 16). A year after the creation of the COI (July 13, 1942), Donovan used his base of power at the Office of the Coordinator of Information to direct the new and powerful spy agency as the COI was transformed into the Office of Strategic Services (OSS).

Hoover remained bitter over being outmaneuvered in his quest to control not only all domestic intelligence operations, but also international intelligence operations. But Hoover still controlled most U.S. intelligence operations in the Western Hemisphere.[2] While North America and South America did not have the active battle theaters of East Asia, the Pacific, Europe, and North Africa, there were plenty of political intrigue and Axis activities to be monitored, thwarted, and manipulated (Frye 1967).

Hoover established training programs where SIS operatives learned spycraft and the customs and cultural history of their assigned countries (Hilton 1981: 196–97). During the war, the SIS stationed approximately three hundred fifty agents throughout South America. They collected intelligence, subverted Axis intelligence networks, and, at times, assisted in the interruption of the flow of raw materials from South American Axis sources. More than a half million Germans lived in Argentina, Brazil, and Chile during the war, and more than a quarter million Japanese were in Brazil and Peru. Hoover used the SIS to install on-the-ground human sources gathering vital information for intelligence analysis. He used U.S. citizens and foreigners as operatives; in Brazil, he used a large number of members of the Basque government in exile as agents during the war.[3] Among those recruited by the SIS to collect intelligence in Central America and South America were American anthropologists. Some of their activities repeated the same sort of ONI intelligence-gathering operations that had so enraged Franz Boas during the First World War, and the archaeologist Samuel Lothrop reprised his First World War role as he became an SIS archaeologist-spy using fieldwork as a pretense for espionage.

Samuel Lothrop, Scholar and Spy

Samuel Lothrop's FBI file documents that he was one of several American anthropologists who had used archaeological fieldwork as a cover for espionage during the First World War. In 1940, the FBI reviewed records of Lothrop's past work with the intent of activating his spy services in the FBI's SIS division. An October 1940 memo from Quinn Tamm to J. Edgar Hoover reported that, during the First World War, Lothrop had spied for Naval Intelligence and performed "highly commendable" work in the Caribbean area, until "his identity as an Agent of Naval Intelligence became known. . . . [T]his so curtailed his effectiveness that he was removed from the area. Thereafter he was placed in a voluntary status with the Office of Military Intelligence in the capacity of the Reserve Officer."[4]

In October 1940, the New York socialite Vincent Astor sent Hoover a letter reporting on his recent meeting with Samuel Lothrop. Astor held an active interest in American intelligence and was a close friend of President Roosevelt.[5] Astor would soon be considered for the position of a national wartime intelligence czar, the position filled by William Donovan at what became the OCI (Office of Coordinator of Information). Astor wrote Hoover that he had ascertained that Lothrop was well suited to work as a spy in Latin America for the SIS. Astor had spent a portion of two days talking with Lothrop concerning the "capabilities and characteristics" of the men appearing on an undisclosed list of anthropologists deemed of use in foreign intelligence work. The full contents of this list have not yet been released under the Freedom of Information Act, but an ONI document released by the FBI indicates that Lothrop identified the anthropologists Junius Bird, Frans Blom, and Silvanus Morley "as being particularly well informed concerning different areas of Latin America." [6] After several censored pages of paragraph summaries of these individuals, Astor commented:

> [Lothrop] impressed me—and at this stage I can base my judgment only on what he told me, and how he expressed himself—as a competent, imaginative man, who is sincerely ambitious to serve the country. . . . When I asked him why he did not return to G-2 or O.N.I., both of which organizations he worked in the last war, he stated that he had left under somewhat of a cloud, due to the fact that he had uncovered one or two situations which had displeased the State Department; for which Department he certainly has no

great admiration. He is somewhat impulsive, and I believe is the type with whom one must strike "while the iron is hot," for if not, he might lose interest, or hope of being of service and go off on some other tangent. By and large, I feel that there is a decided possibility that the man would prove of real use, and might organize an effective group.[7]

Lothrop was a well-bred member of Astor's class. He was a man of independent means who came from a well-established New England family. As Gordon Willey once remarked, Lothrop came from "a distinguished family in the New England Brahmin intellectual tradition" (Willey 1976: 253). In his youth he had been a senior prefect at the Groton School who excelled in football and crew and received his undergraduate and doctorate degrees from Harvard. He had held a position at the Museum of the American Indian and had been a research associate and curator of Andean archaeology at the Peabody Museum. Lothrop was the American model of a gentleman spy.

A few weeks later, Hoover thanked Astor for his observations concerning Lothrop, informing him that Lothrop had already been to the FBI, and arrangements were being made to establish "as comprehensive a program as is possible in utilizing the services" of archaeologists who could work in Costa Rica, Guatemala, British Honduras, and Mexico.[8] It was soon decided that Lothrop would be stationed in Peru.[9]

Lothrop attended FBI espionage classes in Washington, D.C., where he was instructed in the use of secret codes, code keys, the proper employment of designated fictitious contact names, and U.S. mail drops to be used when mailing in reports from the field under assigned code names. With the assistance of S. J. Drayton, Lothrop's wife, Eleanor, made arrangements with the North American Newspaper Alliance "to write a series of articles on her travels" and to assist in the establishment of her husband's cover. Eleanor Lothrop's position as a journalist allowed her to collect needed information by conducting interviews of prominent Peruvians for the SIS.[10]

The Lothrops arrived in Lima in mid-December 1940. Samuel Lothrop initially reported to FBI headquarters by mail, sending letters to code-named letter drops in New York City and by using the embassy pouch. The FBI communicated with Lothrop by letters and telegrams under the pretext of discussing his archaeological work. For example, Lothrop wrote to the FBI that he had identified two local individuals he was considering hiring to assist him in his covert work. The FBI replied to this request by writing under a prearranged pseudonym, "With reference to your suggestion that your archaeological survey might be augmented by the use of several employees, you are informed that we will leave this to your discretion."[11]

Living in Lima allowed Lothrop to monitor Peruvian transportation centers as well as imports, exports, and political developments, but he was aware that in order to maintain his cover as an archaeologist without detection he needed to at least pretend to undertake archaeological investigations. He reported to FBI headquarters, "It is conspicuous to stay so long at a hotel and I should like to get an apartment or small house if I stay on. Also the nature of my archaeological work must change. In fact, I should put in a small dig (at least three weeks) and then return to Lima to work up the material. While I have made a number of short trips, I feel ashamed that I am not in a position to produce results of scientific value and this fact will be discussed sooner or later by local students."[12] After only a few months of residence in Peru, Lothrop, an FBI internal memo reported, had produced "valuable information," and the FBI extended his assignment in Peru beyond the few months initially agreed on.[13] In June 1941, the FBI decided to extend Lothrop's SIS mission in Peru indefinitely, and Lothrop was instructed to return to Washington, D.C., to receive advanced spycraft training. At FBI headquarters, he learned new code techniques and how to secure the specific intelligence information that the FBI desired. He was given "aminopyrin tablets and a supply of paper and was told to obtain a ball-point pen, an aspirin box to use as a container for the tablets" for writing invisible ink messages.[14]

From his first arrival in Peru onward, Lothrop was concerned that his communications with Washington, D.C., were being intercepted by British, Peruvian, Japanese, or German intelligence operatives. By August 1941, he was worrying that his lack of significant archaeological progress might lead to the discovery of his true work in Peru. Lothrop reported his concerns about being detected to FBI Headquarters:

> As regards the archaeological cover for my work in Peru, it was based on the understanding that I was to be in the country six months or less. It is wearing thin and some day somebody is going to start asking why an archaeologist spends most of his time in towns asking questions. This won't happen as soon as it might because the Rockefeller grant for research in Peru makes me a contact man between the field workers and the government. This setup should cover me for an additional couple of months. On the other hand, I do not think it would help a good-will project if my real job were suspected. Yet as an archaeologist of some standing it would have looked very phony if I had not taken some part in the project because I am a

member of the executive committee of the Institute of Andean Research [IAR] which is handling the finances.[15]

Lothrop reported that the Rockefeller Foundation would soon announce grants funding the fieldwork of archaeologists excavating in Central America, Chile, Colombia, Mexico, Peru, and Venezuela. Lothrop advised FBI headquarters that the program would "send about 20 Americans to various parts of Latin America. Among these men there might be some you could use."[16] In a July 25, 1941, letter to FBI headquarters, Lothrop reported that the "first of the people who will be working under me on the Andean Institute program sails next Friday and I have been busy getting them outfitted."[17]

Lothrop reported from Lima that he believed his home phone was tapped and that, "we are now expanding our activities here in several directions. ▬▬▬▬▬▬ has made contact with an anti-Nazi German and with a couple of Peruvians in touch with inner circles of the Government. . . . I hope we are beginning to penetrate into regions we could not touch before."[18]

At the time he joined the SIS, Lothrop was employed by the Carnegie Institution, which had a standing policy of paying the salaries of individuals who were working temporarily in government service. Lothrop began his work with the FBI under an agreement that the bureau would cover his travel and living expenses; later, after the United States' entry into the war, the FBI became one of many sources of income. A March 1942 memo from Lothrop to FBI headquarters indicated that he had received "income from four sources: the Bureau, the Rockefeller Foundation, the Carnegie Institute and one other source."[19] This "one other" funding source is identified not in the report but in a memo written seven months later, asking FBI headquarters for clarification of some income-tax-filing issues. Lothrop wrote, "Harvard University is keeping me on the pay roll in return for cover work I do for them here."[20]

Other institutions were funding and providing "legitimate" research covers for Lothrop's spying. A memo sent the following year from the Lima legal attaché to Hoover stated that Lothrop was "employed by the Institute of Andean Research, financed by the Coordinator of Inter-American Affairs."[21] A November 1943 internal FBI memo indicates that Lothrop later adopted "the cover of Peabody Museum c/o American Museum of Natural History" for his espionage assignment.[22] As Quetzil Castañeda's research clarifies, the Carnegie Institution has a long history of quietly supporting intelligence operations (Castañeda 2003, 2005).

Lothrop reported to the FBI that, when he returned to the Hotel Bolivar in

Lima, the management insisted on putting him back in his old hotel room, leading Lothrop to suspect that the room was bugged by a "Dictaphone" device.[23] During the fall of 1941, Lothrop reported progress in establishing well-placed intelligence contacts. His local operatives established contacts with "an anti-Nazi German and included a well placed Peruvian couple in touch with inner circles of the Government." At this point, Lothrop's most serious problems stemmed from his poor relationship with R. Henry Norweb, the U.S. ambassador to Peru. FBI records portray Norweb as a paranoid and controlling man obsessed with the notion that Lothrop and others were secretly reporting back to Washington about him and the workings of the embassy. Ambassador Norweb reportedly regularly opened and read mail sent out from the embassy. FBI documents record Norweb's anger over the FBI's decision to not brief him on the details of SIS operations in Peru. Later, a letter from Hoover to Assistant Secretary of State Adolf Berle reported that Ambassador Norweb had been overheard saying, "I will get S.K.L [Samuel K. Lothrop] if it is the last thing I do." Because of these concerns, Hoover requested that Lothrop and other FBI operatives be allowed to use a separate locked pouch when sending communiqués to Washington, D.C., but these procedures were not immediately undertaken at the embassy.[24]

A November 19, 1941, memo reported that Lothrop had secured important information on Peruvian politics and leading public figures of a nature usually difficult to secure. An FBI evaluation reported that headquarters "occasionally receive information of sufficient importance from Mr. Lothrop to transmit to the President."[25] In January 1942, Lothrop reported to headquarters that two Japanese officials had been making diplomatic calls to members of the Peruvian government and that "it is obvious that both the President and the Minister of Foreign Affairs deliberately lied to the U.S. Ambassador and got away with it."[26] In February 1942, Lothrop's cover was potentially compromised after an FBI employee in the United States inadvertently sent a signed letter discussing intelligence matters to Lothrop under his real name. Lothrop wrote to FBI headquarters complaining that this gave his position away to Peruvian censors who frequently sold such information to Nazi operatives:

> Since I last wrote you, the U.S. Ambassador summoned me to say that both British and Peruvian authorities had asked him whether he knew a certain "Joe Carson" and someone who signed himself "E.S.S." In other words, our correspondence has been followed by both Peruvian and British censorship. I have reason to believe that Peruvian censors sell information to the Nazis and I have sent you the name of at least one of the Peruvians involved.

(Knowing the Ambassador, I am not convinced that Peruvian censors *have* picked this up although it is certainly possible.) There seems to be no doubt, however, that the British censors have picked up my correspondence. Please note that my identity has been disclosed through US Government officials who presumably should be cooperating with me. British, Germans and Peruvians have presumably picked me up—through failure of your office to provide any regular means of communication except the open mails, which are known to be censored.[27]

At FBI headquarters, D. M. Ladd wrote a detailed memo to Edward Tamm summarizing Lathrop's concerns about security breeches, requests for new communication protocols, and approach to intelligence gathering. Ladd noted that Lothrop refused to use either coded communiqués or secret writing, adding:

Lothrop's assumption appears to be that he is the only representative of the Bureau in Peru, and that he is there to build an "organization." He does not give consideration to the fact that other under-cover men are in Peru and it is not intended that he should endeavor to cover all of Peru and every activity in Peru. It appears that Lothrop should not be permitted to "build an organization," together with ▇▇▇▇▇▇▇▇ but that he should cultivate informants in accordance with our regular practices and in accordance with the instructions that have been given him on more than one occasion. Lothrop lacks the investigative experience to organize and direct any kind of an intelligence organization.[28]

Ladd reported that Lothrop wanted to pay American anthropologist informants who assisted his intelligence work. In a section censored by FBI FOIA processors, Ladd described two individuals who he recommended be paid fifty dollars a month for their services. The first individual was described as a Russian-born male anthropologist who was an American citizen and a graduate of Columbia University. The second was an American citizen with an undergraduate degree from the University of California who was now a Harvard graduate student coming to Peru to "study the modern Indian economy" and who had married a woman from a prominent Boston family.[29] It is not clear whether these individuals were used for intelligence gathering, but it is possible that they were not because of growing concerns at FBI headquarters that Lothrop did not possess the skills needed to successfully manage an expanded spy network.

Although FBI censors have not released the identities of these individuals, some of the details appear to describe the anthropologists Bernard Mishkin and

Harry Tschopik Jr., but the FBI's limited release of records does not indicate that Mishkin or Tschopik worked for the SIS during the war.

Bernard Mishkin was born in Crimea in 1913, became a U.S. citizen in 1926, received his Ph.D. from Columbia University in 1937, and conducted fieldwork in South America in 1941 and 1942. However, Mishkin's released FBI file appears to have been created in 1953, and none of the records indicate that he worked for the SIS during the war.[30] Mishkin later served in the U.S. Navy during the war. Harry Tschopik earned his bachelor's degree from the University of California and his doctorate from Harvard (1951). He married Marion Hutchinson in August 1939, and she accompanied him to conduct fieldwork in Peru and Bolivia in the early 1940s.[31] The likelihood that Tschopik did spy for the SIS using archaeology as his cover is suggested by the proclamation in his *American Anthropologist* obituary: "In 1942 Harry undertook some intelligence work for the U.S. government, and the Tschopiks moved to Arequipa" (Rowe 1958: 134).

In late 1941, as the U.S. approached its entry into the Second World War, Bernard Mishkin traveled to Peru at the request of the National Museum of Peru, which had "arranged to send [Mishkin] to Peru under the auspices of the Nelson Rockefeller Committee, Coordinator of Commercial and Cultural Relations with the American Republics."[32] Mishkin's activities in Peru during this period are not fully understood. Tschopik had been excavating in Peru when the United States entered the Second World War, and after the Selective Service Act was passed, he was told to stay there. During the war, he undertook excavations "in Chuicuto and Puno near the Peru-Bolivian border in the highlands and was concerned with the activities of Germans in both countries."[33]

The SIS and Other Archaeologists in Peru

Lothrop was but one of many American archaeologists sponsored by the IAR working in South America during the war.[34] William Duncan Strong hired Gordon Willey to excavate to the south of Lima at Pachacamac, along with John M. Corbett and Marshall T. Newman. Alfred and Theodora Kroeber "had come to Peru in 1942 at the request of the U.S. State Department," where they worked on an IAR archaeology project (West 1982: 82). E. Wyllys Andrews IV, a Harvard-trained anthropologist, was working on archaeological excavations in Central America for the Carnegie Institution in 1941–42; he later joined the OSS, served in Morocco and Algiers, and became a career CIA officer.[35] It is interesting to find so many anthropologists and archaeologists leisurely undertaking archaeological tours in the midst of the war of the century.

Willey's excavations for the IAR during 1941–1942 were funded by grants secured by George Vaillant "through the US State Department as an attempt to consolidate and establish better relations with Latin American countries prior to the American entry into WWII. There were projects running all the way from Mexico down to Chile."[36] In Peru, Willey met several times with Lothrop, who was reportedly "studying museum collections rather than fieldwork."[37] Willey recalled that his meetings with Lothrop

> were essentially social occasions, casual encounters in the Hotel Bolivar Bar or dinners at Sam's house or mine. It was sort of widely known on the loose grapevine that Sam was carrying on some kind of espionage work, much of which seemed to be keeping his eye on German patrons of the Hotel Bolivar Bar. Up until Pearl Harbor, in December 1941, Peru had diplomatic relations with all the Axis as well as the Allied countries so there were plenty of Germans around.
>
> [Harry] Tschopik, who was doing ethnology in the Peruvian highlands then, although not [as] a part of the Institute of Andean Research Program, occasionally came down to Lima. [Bernard] Mishkin, living in Lima and doing some ethnology on the north Peruvian coast, was also around frequently. . . . Marshall Newman . . . was in the field with me, collecting skeletal material. Newman told me once that Sam [Lothrop] had asked him to keep his eye peeled for anything suspicious that he came across in our travels. While Newman was not quite sure just what this might be, it may be that he was one of those recommended to the FBI by Sam. Sam never attempted to enlist me, but then he didn't know me as well as he knew Newman, Mishkin, and Tschopik. . . .
>
> I doubt if Sam and his fellow "agents" carried out much serious espionage back then. For one thing, I wouldn't have thought there would have been a hell of a lot to spy on. On the lighter side, I remember seeing Sam limping around the Bolivar Hotel one day, and one of the boys, Newman or Mishkin probably, told me that a rival Nazi agent had stamped on his foot in the Bolivar Bar the night before. So you see there was a certain peril in what was going on.[38]

Lothrop reported to the FBI that he was expanding his espionage operation by putting American archaeologists and cultural anthropologists who had been assisting him with his work on the FBI's payroll.[39] William J. Clothier II, one of the "archaeologists" working on these programs, was no archaeologist; he was a career spy. Clothier came to Peru in September 1942, as he later reported to

J. Edgar Hoover, "in an undercover capacity as an archaeologist for Harvard University where I spent a year traveling in the more remote parts of the country."[40] After the war, Clothier established his career at the FBI and the CIA, and later worked at the CIA from 1952 to 1979. Clothier was the grandson of an American department-store magnate. He came from a prominent Philadelphia family and was known as a tennis star and international playboy (see Baltzell 2004: 270–71). During World War II, he spied for the SIS in Peru, Chile, and Cuba. After working in Peru, Clothier published a treatise on Peruvian Recuay pottery under his name, though it is doubtful that the article was actually written by him (see Clothier 1943). Clothier's *Times of London* obituary stated, "Few realized that while he was carrying on the family traditions of tennis and good works, Clothier was also operating clandestinely for the government. After taking an anthropology degree at Harvard, he worked during the Second World War, ostensibly as an archaeologist but really as an FBI special agent, in Peru, Chile and Cuba, where his fluent Spanish proved invaluable."[41]

In 1941, the archaeologist George Vaillant secured U.S. State Department funding through the IAR to undertake projects designed to improve political relations with Latin American countries. The projects were located throughout Central and South America . The sensitivity of the project required that the FBI conduct a background investigation of Vaillant, which found that Vaillant expressed isolationist and anti-British views and that he was involved with the America First Committee. One longtime acquaintance reported that his involvement in America First was in part due to his lifelong friendship with Anne Morrow Lindbergh. But after the Japanese attack on Pearl Harbor, Vaillant supported the American war effort without reservation, and he was appointed the American cultural attaché to Peru during 1943–44.[42]

Throughout the prewar period, archaeologists conducting fieldwork in Central America and South America were occasionally asked to report information of economic or military importance that they had observed during their travels. While most of the archaeologists only spent brief periods abroad, Lothrop's operation was designed as a long-term venture, but political and logistical problems created difficulties and kept him frustrated. In February 1942, Lothrop melodramatically submitted his resignation to the FBI, citing ongoing frustrations with his ability to communicate with FBI headquarters. He wrote to headquarters saying he wanted to use the diplomatic pouch to communicate directly with his FBI superiors. FBI headquarters responded by arranging for Lothrop to mail reports using the embassy pouch.[43]

A month later, an SIS operative was sent to Lothrop's "palatial house in the

Miraflores section of Lima" in the early hours of the morning for a debriefing and to assess the status of Lothrop's cover. A local source had reported to the SIS agent that, due to security lapses, "practically everyone in town suspects [Lothrop's] connections." The visiting SIS agent found Lothrop distraught and on edge:

> Immediately upon realizing who I was, [Lothrop] became greatly moved emotionally. There was a throb in his voice as he stated that he had waited for this moment for two years. He remarked with much emotion that everything was going wrong: the Bureau had "let him down," it had become impossible for him to continue working under the restraints imposed upon him by us; the problems of communication were overwhelming. He stated that that very day he had sent us an air-mail letter offering his resignation. He declared that when he was in Washington we promised him every cooperation . . . but they gave him only words, no help.[44]

Lothrop had become increasingly frustrated with the lack of contact and support he received from FBI headquarters. He found the secret ink messages to be overly cumbersome to use because he could not decipher the encoded messages he received from the bureau. He claimed that they were improperly encoded, but the bureau believed otherwise. Lothrop complained that if he did indeed resign, he had received offers from the ONI and MID and he would probably work for them, adding that "he had worked with them successfully during the previous war."[45] Lothrop was concerned about his wife, Eleanor, and made inquiries concerning the possibility of her receiving one hundred dollars per month in addition to their current salary.

FBI records indicated that the knowledge was widespread among the American expatriates and U.S. Embassy employees that the Lothrops were working for the FBI. As Lothrop's relationship with Ambassador Norweb deteriorated, Lothrop refused to send mail even in the embassy pouch out of a conviction that the ambassador would read it. A letter from an unidentified FBI source (apparently the embassy's legal attaché) dated March 17, 1942, indicated that the ambassador was so troubled by his perception that individuals were reporting to the State Department about his shortcomings that "he has lost 18 lbs during the past few months." Because the ambassador was so obsessed with these communiqués, FBI headquarters recommended that future reports to the FBI by this operative travel "through the pouch of the Military or Naval Attaché."[46]

Lothrop complained that, even though Norweb had been informed by Sumner Wells (an old college classmate of Lothrop's) of his position, he was made to wait "in the outer office just like any other American" when he had need to communicate with the ambassador. Lothrop reported that he had "no confidence in the Ambassador." The FBI was concerned that Lothrop had "spoken rather freely of his activities in this type of work during the previous war. He mentions often how he worked for both ONI and G-2. Since his activities now cause suspicion one can hardly draw any other conclusion than that he is working for us."[47]

Lothrop expressed "unlimited confidence in [Agent] Butler" and favored using Butler as the embassy contact for communication with FBI headquarters. "[Lothrop] was so thoroughly upset, almost on the verge of tears, that I promised to secure the Bureau's opinion on whether he should communicate through Butler and, in the meantime, I authorized him to communicate in this manner. The following day I gave our man in Santiago a coded telegram addressed to you, suggesting that the Bureau advise Eugene that in the future correspondence with him will be through the pouch."[48]

Lothrop had cultivated a network of informants who were separated from each other as self-contained cells, each knowing only the identity of the individual above him in the chain of information. When this SIS contact asked Lothrop for information on the identity of informants, he refused to reveal their identities to his SIS superiors. Lothrop insisted that the procedures used during the First World War in the ONI and G-2 to compartmentalize knowledge of informants' identities should be maintained. The FBI was not pleased, and FBI reports began to doubt the value of Lothrop as an intelligence source:

> [Lothrop] is supposed to have a wide circle of friends in high places. According to [Lothrop, his informant] can walk into the president's office at any time without a previous appointment, while even our Ambassador must wait for days to secure an appointment. However, in my discussion with [Lothrop], I did not see how these contacts have been of very much value to him. He obviously did not want to make out a list of his first generation [i.e., the informants whose identities were known directly to him], because he had sent it in some time ago, he said. Or, because he wouldn't think of putting their names down in writing. Apparently, he didn't even want to mention them to me as he stated that ONI and G-2 never ask for the sources of a man's information, when they are confidential.
>
> Perhaps it is a result of this hesitation on [Lothrop's] part to say who his informants are that I came to the conclusion that practically all of his work revolves around one man: the informant called "Churchill." How valuable

> this informant is, only the supervisor in charge of [Lothrop's] work can say.
> Fortunately under our new schedule, I visit Lima very often and I hope to go
> into this matter very fully with [Lothrop].[49]

There were discussions about the hiring of new informants. A local Goodrich Tire
agent was recommended as "an American of Polish descent, a research worker for
Harvard, who is living with his wife at Puno and who knows the Bolivian border
as well," and whom Lothrop had recommended for some time. The report's
author did not recommend hiring the informant. Lothrop continued to worry
that his intelligence information was being circulated within the FBI and State
Department without disguising his identity and that members of the embassy in
Lima could determine that he was the source of this information.[50]

The report by Lothrop's late-night SIS contact concluded by observing, "The
entire hours were given over to listening to his complaints, most of which were
immediately shown to be unwarranted. Perhaps [Lothrop] is discouraged easily
and needs encouragement from time to time. Due to the fact that he was upset
generally in regard to his work and progress, I gave him as much encouragement
as possible."[51]

Lothrop's insistence on protecting the identities of his informants irritated his
FBI superiors in Washington, D.C. His insistence contributed to the FBI's loss of
confidence in his ability to gather reliable intelligence. Lothrop had taken on a
central importance in the FBI surveillance operations in Peru, and despite headquarters' frustrations with him, he had become their central source of information in Lima. The FBI began to wonder about the intelligence that Lothrop was
not collecting: "Lima is one of the most important posts in South America.
Undoubtedly there is a great deal of Axis activity here but we are failing miserably
in securing it. With the [informant] in the police department, ▮▮▮▮▮▮▮▮ in the
Embassy, and [Lothrop] in his wide circle of friends, we should have had a very
productive organization."[52]

As the archaeological field projects associated with Lothrop's cover were concluding, the FBI felt that Lothrop should either return to the United States or
become involved in a research project that would "be good enough to warrant
approval by Peruvian technicians."[53] Lothrop doubted that he could develop a
research cover project of such a high caliber without consulting with resources
and contacts back in the United States. The FBI allowed Lothrop to return to
Washington, D.C., using a cover story that he was attending an academic conference. While in the States he concocted the details of a phony archaeological
project and a month later returned to Peru with a new research cover.

Lothrop's most important intelligence source was a confidential assistant to the Peruvian minister of government and police. In the spring of 1944, the informant resigned his government position and then began working under Lothrop's supervision. Lothrop's FBI file contained dozens of letters from 1943 to 1944 relating to the difficulties he was experiencing in filing his taxes from Peru, and Lothrop increasingly expressed concerns that members of the embassy were aware of his true reasons for being in Peru. During this period, the FBI's "annual efficiency report" characterized Lothrop "with the assistance of his wife [as having] been of particular assistance [to the SIS] in the investigation of local political matters. Both he and Mrs. Lothrop have a very extensive acquaintanceship with Peruvians who occupy high social positions, and as a result he is in a position to report on the observations and attitudes of this particular group of Peruvian society."[54]

A coded FBI radiogram dated May 14, 1944, from the embassy's legal attaché in Lima to FBI headquarters reported concerns that the principal informant and others were fully aware of Lothrop's connection to the SIS and the FBI. Lothrop's cover had apparently been compromised by "four Peruvian investigators" in the employ of the trusted informant. One of the four investigators had been overheard bragging to the "Peruvian police that he makes more by working for the United States Embassy than they make with the Peruvian Government."[55] These comments led the Peruvian police to investigate Lothrop and his work. The FBI's further investigations of Lothrop's primary informant "cast serious doubt upon both his veracity and good faith." Lothrop was instructed to immediately sever all contacts with the informant. Hoover notified the ambassador that the embassy was to do everything in its power to divert suspicions that there were any connections between the informant and Lothrop or American intelligence agencies.[56]

After the FBI report raised serious questions about the reliability of Lothrop's primary informant, the bureau decided to test the informant by assigning him to collect information on nonexistent events and individuals. The informant was given information about an upcoming anti-Jewish demonstration in another town that he was assigned to attend. The assignment included a list of individuals who would be attending. Even though the rally did not exist, the informant still produced a full report containing the list of individuals given to him in advance. The informant had previously provided information on a supposed meeting of one hundred fifty Japanese leaders at a small farm on December 7, 1943, to commemorate the anniversary of Japan's attack on Pearl Harbor. The FBI's investigation of the claim found that no such meeting had occurred and that "all Japanese have been removed from this area."[57]

The FBI further tested the informant by providing him with false information concerning a (nonexistent) German who had jumped ship and was supposedly hiding in Peru. The informant provided detailed but fictitious reports on this invented German. The FBI concluded that the "tendency on the part of [the informant] to include long and detailed accounts involving persons and circumstances which, in fact, were taken in whole or in part from his imagination has caused numerous investigations to be opened in the past which, in actuality, were unjustified and which, as has been observed in separate memoranda, appear to have been reported with a view to furthering [the informant's] private prejudices and ends."[58] But when Lothrop was confronted with these devastating findings, he refused to believe that his informant had produced false intelligence and would not sever contacts with him, even though the report indicated that the informant had invented reports of events and people that did not exist. In his report to the FBI's director, the legal attaché concluded that Lothrop's "loyalty to his informant outweighs that which he possesses for the Bureau."[59]

Lothrop was ordered to not tell the informant that his duplicity had been detected by the FBI. Instead, he was instructed to say that he was out of funds to pay for informants. With frustration, the embassy's legal attaché reported to Hoover that Lothrop's "association with [the informant] in Peru has influenced his good judgment regarding investigative matters in this country and . . . his further presence on behalf of the Bureau in Peru will ultimately seriously embarrass it. [Lothrop] has not actually offered his resignation as he threatened and I do not believe he will do so. It is my belief, which is shared by the other agents assigned to this office, that [Lothrop] should be recalled to Washington for conference and that he not be returned to Peru."[60]

Lothrop's frustration intensified. On June 6, 1944, he submitted a letter of resignation to J. Edgar Hoover using the stationary of the IAR.[61] On June 28, 1944, an encrypted radiogram from FBI headquarters notified the U.S. Embassy in Lima that Lothrop's resignation had been accepted and that the FBI would pay Lothrop's passage back to the United States.[62]

When he returned to the United States, Lothrop resumed his academic positions at Harvard's Peabody Museum and the Carnegie Institution. FOIA documents released by the CIA and FBI indicate that this terminated Lothrop's formal association with American intelligence agencies.

Wartime Uses of Fieldwork as an Espionage Front

The sis's use of archaeologist-spies pretending to conduct fieldwork resurrected the exact controversial practices that had been the basis of Franz Boas's 1919 complaint to the *Nation* (Boas 1919). That Lothrop was one of the same anthropologist-spies criticized by Boas during the First World War adds an extra layer of significance to Lothrop's decision to reprise his role as a spy posing behind his anthropological credentials. Boas's complaint had no behavioral impact on Lothrop's decision to again use fieldwork as a cover for wartime espionage. Lothrop rejected Boas's claim that these actions prostituted anthropology, and the American Anthropological Association's 1919 censure of Boas may well have helped empower Lothrop's choice to reuse archaeology as a cover for espionage during the Second World War.

Lothrop did not act alone in staging this duplicity. He had help from American funding agencies, research institutions, and institutions of higher learning. It remains difficult to know what to make of the covert roles played by private research foundations in aiding, abetting, and financing such duplicitous research. Private research institutions including the IAR, the Carnegie and Rockefeller foundations, and government bodies such as the CIAA made spying possible by providing funds for research and plausible cover for even implausible scholars working in Central America and South America during the war.[63] While these covert roles played by foundations like Carnegie and Rockefeller occurred in the distant past, the wall of silence preventing a straightforward accounting of the extent of such relationships continues to be maintained by these institutions in the present. We know that such relationships existed long before the Second World War (Castañeda 2005), but the extent of any such relationships after the war remains unknown.

This recurrent mixing of intelligence with legitimate funding foundations raises ongoing concerns about the legitimacy and independence of archaeologists, anthropologists, and foundations—concerns that span the past, present, and future. In the decades after the war, these relationships continued to undermine the credibility of claims of foundations' and research institutes' independence. In the 1970s, congressional hearings investigating private foundations' roles in allowing the CIA to covertly fund social-science research found that "the CIA's intrusion into the foundation field in the 1960s can only be described as massive" (U.S. Senate 1976: 182).[64] The roots of such relationships were established during the First World War, were strengthened during the Second World War, and grew throughout the Cold War. Some of the growth of these interactions during the Cold War was facilitated by relationships that emerged as former World War Two intelligence officers took on important peacetime leadership roles at academic foundations (see Roelofs 2003: 159–61).

Because the FBI has released only incomplete records on anthropologists' activities in the SIS, there is much that remains unknown about the details of Lothrop's espionage work and the reports he submitted. Even less is known about the extent to which other anthropologists conducted SIS espionage in Central America and South America during the war. Although Lothrop passed along the names of several other American archaeologists who could also serve as SIS agents, FOIA requests to the FBI for the files have not led to the release of records documenting SIS espionage work of the type engaged in by Lothrop. Even the FBI's released records of anthropologists apparently identified in Lothrop's files do not contain any records documenting any espionage for the SIS or other agencies.

Lothrop's war work was fundamentally different from that of most of the other anthropologists discussed in this book. His ongoing use of fieldwork as a cover for espionage moved beyond secret research to the realm of lying. Lothrop left no records expressing concern about the propriety or necessity of his duplicitous actions. His sense of patriotic duty seems to have precluded such second thoughts, and despite the damage done to his intelligence capacities by his overreliance on a compromised informant, at the end of his service Lothrop appeared convinced that he had accomplished a great service.

When we examine what Lothrop was able to accomplish through his deceit, it does not appear that the risks of his dishonesty (risks to future anthropologists) were anywhere near the value of the minor intelligence he generated. True, early in his service he produced intelligence of such importance that it was used to brief President Roosevelt, and he provided ongoing reports on political developments. But it is difficult to evaluate this information. Given what was later known about Lothrop being compromised by one of his own sources, it does not appear that he produced anything worth the damage that news of his actions could later bring to anthropology's reputation.[65]

While the details of how many other anthropologists conducted SIS espionage during the war are incompletely understood, released documents do clarify that many were considered and contacted for such work, and it appears that others undertook similar covert assignments while conducting (or pretending to conduct) South American fieldwork during wartime. The silences surrounding such actions maintained by former spies and spy agencies are understandable and not surprising. (Given spy agencies' natural pride in such successful operations, we can assume they are maintaining the silence for reasons of professionalism rather than regret). But the careful silences maintained—and, at times, *enforced*—by members acting within professional associations such as the Society for American Archaeology are another matter (see Baffi 1996; Roosevelt 1991, 1996), and the discipline's decisions not to investigate in a scholarly way the extent of such past relations or to clearly and unambiguously prohibit all such relationships in the present creates serious dangers for fieldworkers operating around the world. As more details about the extent of relationships are established in the scholarly literature, these dangers may possibly increase, not because scholars are making the secret history public, but because professional anthropologists have backed away from clarifying the impropriety of such actions.

Lothrop's deceit continues to damage the credibility and safety of fieldworkers. As information on connections between anthropologists and intelligence agencies spreads through settings where anthropologists conduct fieldwork, all anthropologists will be placed at risk—a risk exacerbated by professional anthropological and archaeological associations' refusal to clarify that such covert relationships between anthropologists and intelligence agencies are inappropriate.[66]

It is not just a dose of anachronistic presentist hindsight that emboldens critical evaluations of Lothrop's actions. There are historicist breadcrumbs leading to similar harsh conclusions. One need not have lived beyond the controversies of Project Camelot, the Thailand Affair, or the failures of other Cold War misappropriations of anthropology to be alerted to the dangers of Lothrop's action: Franz Boas saw it and expressed it clearly over two decades before Lothrop's SIS spying (Boas 1919). The fact that Lothrop was actually one of the anthropologists who garnered Boas's 1919 anger for "prostituting science" as a spy clarifies some deliberate awareness of action. If anything, Lothrop's repeated use of archaeological fieldwork as a front for spying exposes a certain sneering intentionality to his actions.

While J. Edgar Hoover's use of archaeological fieldwork as a front for espionage significantly pushed back traditional boundaries, it was the OSS that most significantly ran roughshod over the uncodified standards of anthropological propriety. The OSS prided itself on its unconventional approach to intelligence, and the talents of dozens of anthropologists were important formative elements used by the agency that was to become the institutional predecessor to the CIA.

CHAPTER TEN

Culture at War:

Weaponizing Anthropology

at the OSS

> During the war, we gladly used our professional techniques and knowledge to advance a
> cause, but I hope that no one believes that he had a scientific justification for doing so.
> —JULIAN STEWARD (1948a:352)

Beginning in July 1942, the Office of the Coordinator of Information (COI)
became America's national wartime clearinghouse charged with collecting the
applications and résumés of Americans thought to have specific or unusual skills
that could aid the war effort. The COI compiled these data and tried to match
individuals' talents with military and intelligence agencies that could best use
their skills. As the director of the COI, William Donovan sought individuals with
linguistic and cultural skills that could be useful in coming theatres of war. After
the COI was transformed into the Office of Strategic Services (OSS) on July 13,
1942, Donovan used the COI's collection of records to recruit the best operatives
and analysts he could find for the OSS.

While the OSS collected and analyzed intelligence from both the European
and Asian theaters of war, the field operations of the OSS in the war with Japan
were much more limited than those in Europe or North Africa. The OSS's Asian
field operations were primarily limited to India, China, Burma, and Indochina.
Because of the different approaches to battle operations between General Douglas MacArthur in the Pacific and General Bernard Montgomery in North Africa
and Europe, OSS operations did not occur in the Pacific islands occupied by
the Japanese. Despite the limits placed on the OSS in the Pacific, its Research
and Analysis Branch collected and analyzed intelligence data on Axis activities
around the world, including Japan.

The OSS was a fundamentally new type of military-intelligence agency—a multidisciplinary agency that relied on creative and unconventional means to collect intelligence and to undertake covert actions. The OSS prided itself on recruiting the best and brightest from elite academic and social circles for its ranks under a strategy characterized by Roger Hilsman as seeing whether "scholars could in some respects take the place of spies" (Trumpbour 1989: 54). It had a unique mix of American Ivy League scholars and brilliant unschooled operatives —people like Miles Copeland, whose Alabama roots provided him with unexpected improvisational advantages without the limits that can come with an Ivy League education (see Copeland 1989).

Scientists, artists, economists, poets, and adventurers were drawn to the ranks of the OSS. The office sought the skills of the economist William Parker, the Marxist philosopher Herbert Marcuse, the artist Ervin Ross Marlin, and the future chef Julia Child. The ornithologist S. Dillon Ripley coordinated British and American intelligence operations in Southeast Asia and eventually joined operations in Thailand in the final months of the war (Park 1984: 77). Well-traveled, linguistically savvy anthropologists were an obvious addition to such a broad mix of skills and backgrounds.

These anthropologists performed a variety of tasks that ranged from desk-bound research at the Library of Congress to covert field operations in West Africa or South Asia. The OSS anthropologists Gregory Bateson and Carleton Coon ran secret missions in South Asia and North Africa. The archaeologist Nelson Glueck mixed fieldwork with intelligence work. While stationed in Jerusalem, "He continued his surveys while scouting for the Office of Strategic Services." (David 2004: 90)[1] Derwood Lockard performed OSS duties while he was a U.S. Navy liaison officer stationed in Kenya in 1943–44 and later in Beirut.[2] Rhoda Métraux analyzed the impact of the war on civilian Germans' morale; using social-science methods, including reading "thousands of letters to German prisoners of war in America" (Mauch 2005: 126; cf. Mead 1953). Ruth Bunzel was in Spain during the Spanish Civil War, and she later monitored and translated Spanish broadcasts for the OSS from a base in England (Fawcett and McLuhan 1989: 33). Lloyd Cabot Briggs worked for the OSS with French intelligence units in Algeria and elsewhere in the northern Sahara (Briggs 1967). Alfred Tozzer directed the Honolulu OSS station, where he supervised radio broadcasts to eastern Asia and Indonesia and analyzed intercepted Japanese radio messages (Schmelz-Keil 1991: 705; see Price 1968: 117). David Mandelbaum directed the OSS's "Detachment 303" in New Delhi, where operational strategies for the daring OSS Detachment 101's operations in Burma were planned (McIntosh 1998: 191).

Over the course of the war, more than two dozen anthropologists were assigned to the COI and the OSS. Among the anthropologists working for the OSS were E. Wyllys Andrews IV, William Bascom, Gregory Bateson, Lloyd Cabot Briggs, Cora Du Bois, Alison Frantz, Anne Hutchinson Fuller, John P. Gillin, Nelson Glueck, Marcus S. Goldstein, Charlotte Gower, George M. Hanfmann, Jack Harris, Gordon Hewes, Frederick Seymore Hulse, Olov Robert T. Janse, Felix Maxwell Keesing, Alexander Lesser, Ralph Linton, Derwood Lockard, Edwin Meyer Loeb, David Mandelbaum, Leonard E. Mason, Mark A. May, Rhoda Métraux, David Rodnick, Morris Siegel, Richard Francis Strong Starr, David Stout, Morris Swadesh, Mischa Titiev, Alfred Tozzer, and T. Cuyler Young.[3]

The OSS understood that on-the-ground intelligence gathered by human operatives was the most valuable of intelligence commodities, and during the war, anthropologists with firsthand field experience in war regions were recruited as invaluable OSS resources. But the OSS also drew on anthropologists' academic research and writing skills to produce scholarly reports for strategists within the OSS, White House, and War Department. This chapter examines these anthropological contributions to the OSS first by discussing the OSS's Research and Anaylsis Branch reports, and then describing the OSS field activities of the anthropologists Cora Du Bois, Gregory Bateson, Jack Harris, and Carlton Coon.

The Research and Analysis Branch's Analysis of Japan

Like the OWI's Foreign Morale Analysis Division, the OSS's Research and Analysis Branch analyzed information on Japanese culture to track shifts in Japanese morale and estimate the best methods to wage psychological and armed warfare against Japan. Most OSS anthropologists applied their academic skills at the Research and Analysis Branch. Morris Siegel was a research analyst at the Research and Analysis Branch's African section, where he monitored the political situation in French and Spanish Africa and Ethiopia. At the end of the war, he transferred to the OSS's Near East Division.[4] David Stout left a teaching position at Vanderbilt University to serve as an analyst at the Research and Analysis Branch's Latin American Division.[5] Edwin Loeb wrote Research and Analysis Branch "background studies and reports relating to Sumatra and its adjacent islands," and he translated foreign-language materials into English, provided data for ethnographic maps, and "analyzed and organized current intelligence."[6] Gordon Hewes used his Japanese-language skills to compile data for the Research and Analysis Branch, tracking the Japanese food supply and food production, and he produced OSS reports on the Japanese fishing industry.[7] Felix Keesing left his professorship at the University of Hawaii for a desk job in Washington working as an analyst at the Research and Analysis Branch's Pacific Islands section. Keesing directed the compilation of information in Research and Analysis Branch reports by his staff on "all phases of psychological warfare, morale, politics, diplomacy, public administration, law personnel, and social affairs in the area of the Western Pacific, including Australia, New Zealand, the Philippines, New Guinea, the Bismarks, the Solomons, New Caledonia Fiji, and other Pacific Islands."[8] Keesing left the oss in June 1943 after accepting an appointment with the Military Administration Training Program.[9]

The Research and Analysis Branch produced a series of policy papers analyzing the role of the emperor in Japanese society that tried to predict such things as the outcome of America's bombing the Imperial Palace; the impact of food shortages; what events might trigger incidents of mass Japanese suicides; and what should be done with the emperor at the war's end. Some reports examined Japanese social structure, while others considered strategies for a postwar occupation. Many of the Research and Analysis Branch reports advocated no specific concrete action; they only analyzed elements of Japanese history and culture without recommending specific applications. One 1942 report analyzed the Eta Japanese minority group, describing how its members suffered from discrimination; however, this report did not advance any plan for using the Eta in a campaign against the Japanese government or military (oss 1942a). Another report on the structure of Japanese municipal governments was little more than a translation of a Japanese dictionary on jurisprudence, but even this legal document was presented with an eye toward finding exploitable wartime weaknesses (oss 1943b).

In September 1943, the Research and Analysis Branch produced the secret "Preliminary Report on Japanese Anthropology" (oss 1943a; Price 2005e). The report attempted to determine whether there were "physical characteristics in which the Japanese differ from others in such a way as to make these differences significant from the point of view of carrying on the war" (oss 1943a: 1). The report's author is not identified, but a list of forty-seven scholars consulted indicates the importance and depth of analysis the Research and Analysis Branch devoted to this study as America contemplated the effectiveness of using biological weapons against Japanese soldiers and civilians. Among those consulted were medical doctors, physiologists, psychologists, statisticians, geneticists, parasitologists, chemists, and anthropologists, including Clyde Kluckhohn, Fred Hulse, W. D. Strong, E. A. Hooton, C. M. Davenport, C. Wesley Dupertuis, Morris Steggerda, Otto Klineberg, and Stanley Lovell.

In considering possible biological weaknesses of the Japanese, the oss gathered scholarly materials organized under the headings "Anatomical or Structural; Physiological or Functional; Susceptibility to Disease; Constitutional and Nutritional" (oss 1943a: 1–2). The anthropologists and others working on the project were explicitly instructed to consider these questions "in a-moral and non-ethical terms," with an understanding that, "if any of the suggestions contained herein are considered for action, all moral and ethical implications will be carefully studied" (oss 1943a: 2). This record of simultaneous awareness and suspension of ethical responsibility records that the Research and Analysis Branch was aware of legal, ethical, and moral problems in the work being "theoretically" contemplated. This relegation of moral authority to unspecified others who would see to it that the "ethical implications [would] be carefully studied" appears to have eased the mind of most, but not all, of the report's potential contributors, as the report freely considers questions that could be put to deadly uses.

The desired outcomes of the study were clarified in a passage describing the supposed fundamental physical characteristics of the Japanese:

> It is common knowledge that anthropologists regard the Japanese as members of the Mongoloid division of mankind, who differ from other Asiatic Mongoloids chiefly by virtue of a long period of insular inbreeding and through intermixture with Ainus in the north and Indonesians in the south. As a group, the Japanese are characterized by yellowish-brown skin coloring, brown eyes, coarse, straight, black head hair, relatively hairless faces and bodies, short stature, broad heads, and fairly wide faces with prominent cheek-bones. Several other miscellaneous anatomical traits may be adduced. For example, the bones of the inner ear are located higher in the head than among other races; the eye orbits are longer; the intestines are lengthier than among Europeans; there are slight racial variations in the laryngeal musculature; they have fewer taste buds on the papillae; the liver is distinctive; and the arterial system differs somewhat from that of Europeans. As far as could be determined the bulk of these characteristics are only of academic interest and unimportant from the viewpoint of this study. (oss 1943a: 2–3)

It is unclear what recommendations would have been made if these physical characteristics had been recognized as *important*. If the oss team had had access to data on genotypic variation of the type compiled by the contemporary Human Genome Project, it, too, most likely would have been analyzed to see whether any genetic variations could be exploited to kill what was imagined to be Japanese racial stock.

The report observed a "relative frequency of Meckel's intestinal tract which renders it liable to inflammation or ulceration of the peptic type," noting that this defect was more common in Japanese men than women (OSS 1943a: 2–3). Elements of racial stereotyping crept into the examination of the Japanese medical and physiological literature. The Japanese were constructed as having "less sensitivity to pain," possessing small body frames that resulted in "increased efficiency," with widespread incidence of being "taste-blind" (OSS 1943a: 3–6). Such claims were presented without substantiation or references.

Potential weaknesses in Japanese immune systems were examined with hopes that a shortcoming could be identified that could be abused in a biological attack. The report stated:

> In a search for potential defects that could be exploited in the prosecution of the war, a mere record of diseases prevalent in Japan is of little consequence. Far more significant is a detailed knowledge of the principal causes of death among the Japanese; and a review of their vital statistics plainly reveals that they have outstanding weaknesses in their respiratory and gastrointestinal systems. Thus, tuberculosis, particularly of the pulmonary tract, is the greatest single cause of death; and the morbidity rate is exceptionally high from pneumonia, pleurisy, enteritis, dysentery, and related diseases. (OSS 1943a: 10)

There was keen interest in what was reported as the Japanese susceptibility towards bacillary dysentery. The possible military implications of this condition were suggested by a finding in occupied Poland in which an outbreak of dysentery among troops proved to be disastrous.

The use of anthrax and other biological agents was considered.[10] The OSS found that "the possibility of spreading infections of various kinds was briefly touched upon, and the conclusion was reached that anthrax bacilli which attack the respiratory tract, a known weak spot in the Japanese body, would probably be the most effective agent" (OSS 1943a: 23). Groups of anthropologists and medical doctors were consulted and were explicitly asked to forget the ethical or moral issues involved in biological warfare. For example:

> During the course of an interview at the Harvard Medical School one of the professors chanced to "think aloud" on the possibility of introducing some disease among enemy troops that might catch them by surprise, but against

which our own troops were well protected. Most ailments caused by flukes or protozoans he dismissed as impractical; plague virus he thought could be introduced by dropping infected mice or rats, possibly by parachute; typhus might be spread by the device of having louse-covered but immune volunteers submit to capture; and ticks infected with Rocky Mountain Spotted Fever might be released among our opponents, but this would scarcely be effective since the disease is not transmitted from man to man by contagion. The professor then launched into a spontaneous discussion of anthrax, whose introduction he regarded as entirely practical and highly effective, despite the fact that anthrax, too, is not contagious. In his opinion the enemy has no acquired immunity or tolerance for this disease, and if taken by surprise would have no available counteragent. Furthermore, it is possible to raise highly virulent strains of *Bacillus anthracis* and to spread them widely throughout any enemy concentration, as the spores of the bacillus are virtually indestructible and could even be distributed in bombs. In addition, the effects of anthrax are very rapid and dangerous since the bacilli enter into cuts, or abrasions, prevent wounds from healing, and induce pneumonia. (oss 1943a: 14–15)

The report noted with concern that the downside of unleashing anthrax on Japanese populations was that it could easily spread to livestock populations; thus, the region hit by such an attack would "remain dangerous for many years" (oss 1943a: 15). Indeed, it was the threat of such an uncontrolled spread of anthrax that led the oss to caution against its use as a weapon against the Japanese: "The anthrax bacillus is so potent that its use should not be contemplated unless our own forces and those of our allies can be guaranteed adequate protection. Similar precautions should, of course, be exercised before any disease-causing agent is employed in offensive warfare" (oss 1943a: 15).

The Harvard anthropologist Earnest A. Hooton recommended that the oss undertake a "constitutional study of Japanese prisoners or of native-born males of military age in the relocation centers [to] yield useful information regarding the weak spots of Japanese physique" (oss 1943a: 17). The anthropologist Carl Seltzer of Harvard's Grant Study Staff, which analyzed the physiques and constitutions of Harvard undergraduates, recommended means by which a wealth of useful information could be gained by using a team composed of a medical doctor, physiologist, hygienist, psychometrician, anthropologist, and psychologist or sociologist to examine a half dozen Japanese specimens looking for desired weaknesses that could be exploited in warfare (oss 1943a: 17).

Two anthropologists identified in the report opposed any such efforts: "There was by no means uniform agreement on the practical gains to be derived from a study of this sort, and men like Dr. [Ralph] Linton of Columbia and Dr. [Harry] Shapiro of the American Museum of Natural History . . . were decidedly against such an enterprise" (oss 1943a: 17).[11]

The oss also examined potential exploitations to be made of the general collapse of dietary and hygienic stability on the Japanese home front. The report found, "Practically all observers seem to agree that the bulk of the Japanese population lives on the ragged edge of dietary deficiency. If their opinions could be scientifically verified it would be of the greatest consequence to our study, since 'recently acquired knowledge in the field of nutrition, especially concerning the vitamins, shows that these substances are closely related to the hormones in many of their physiological activities including those related to natural resistance and susceptibility'" (oss 1943a: 18). Similar weaknesses among field soldiers were considered for possible attack:

The susceptibility of Japanese men of military age, especially under the strain of active warfare, to [beriberi] should be exploited to the full. Of course, it must be constantly borne in mind that under army supervision soldiers can be fed on diets that provide them with a fair degree of protection, regardless of what they customarily eat at home. Unquestionably, the rice which is served in the army is not deprived of vitamins; and the fighting forces are reported to be using a fish paste which utilizes every part of the animal, including bones, viscera and entrails. Nevertheless, Dr. Lu is firmly convinced that the diet of the enemy troops provides them only with minimum protection, and it is her sincere belief that Japanese soldiers cannot withstand *continuous*, exhaustive, physical strain, especially in very hot weather. Dr. Lu further contends that the Chinese have invariably been successful whenever they could keep the enemy on the go, day and night, for periods of over 72 hours. If Dr. Lu's observations can be indisputably verified, they would serve to provide our military strategists with a very valuable piece of knowledge.[12]

Another weakness of the Japanese diet arises from the extreme preference for rice and fish. No other foods, regardless of nutritional considerations, can compete in popular taste with these two staples. Consequently, irreparable physical and psychological damage could be done to the fighting forces and the civilian population, if ways could be found for destroying the sources of these key foods. It is by no means fantastic to assert that a continuing and concerted effort to sink every enemy fishing boat that is sighted, would contribute materially to our military success.

Equally important would be a planned attack on our opponent's rice supplies. Since stored rice tends to lose much of its Vitamin B the Japanese cannot readily build up large reserves, so that our energies should be directed towards the object of destroying growing crops that are about to mature. Furthermore, it would be more rewarding if rice fields in Japan proper were attacked whenever possible as this would force the enemy to rely more and more on imported rice, thus adding materially to his increasing shipping problems.

Several procedures for interfering with rice production may be suggested. Concentrations of rice fields might be subjected to bombing, particularly with missiles that spread laterally and tear up a good deal of ground; irrigating devices should be consistently destroyed; the acid concentration best suited to growing rice plants should be chemically upset whenever possible; and the introduction of rice-destroying diseases should be seriously considered. (OSS 1943a: 20–22)

The report identified a species of fungi (*Sclerotium oryzae*) that had attacked Japanese rice varieties in the early years of the twentieth century, finding that "the advisability of systematically destroying the enemy's rice plants, as well as his fish supplies, can scarcely be questioned" (OSS 1943a: 20).[13]

A 1942 Research and Analysis Branch study had already determined that the sinking of every sighted enemy fishing boat would significantly contribute to victory (OSS 1942c). This report, "The Fishing Industry of Japan," specified and mapped seasonal fishing grounds and provided detailed drawings, blueprints, and photographs of the vessels, gear, and ports used by Japanese fishermen. At the war's outbreak, Japan had the world's largest fishing industry, harvesting more than eleven million pounds of sea life annually (OSS 1942c: 5). The OSS estimated that the Japanese relied on almost half a million fishing vessels, of which almost three hundred thousand were powered without engines (OSS 1942c: 38). While this fishing industry report was a dry inventory of equipment and capacity, the military implications of this work give a purpose to the detailed accountings. A paragraph on "Tuna Catchers," for example, presents information ready to be used for targeting operations:

Of the motorized craft, the approximately 800 bonito and tuna boats are perhaps the most typical. These seaworthy vessels are now frequently all-steel, with wide cruising radii (up to 2000 miles). They carry the large crews necessitated by the angling technique for Scombroids, sometimes fifty and even seventy men. On a three-week trip 50,000 to 80,000 fish may be taken. Most of the modern tuna boats are equipped with cold-storage apparatus. The vessels range from 100 tons and 250 [horsepower] to 200 tons and 200 [horsepower], averaging about ten knots sped. The catch is stowed amidships, and live bait tanks are provided. These boats are common off Taiwan, Hainan, the Philippines, and the Bonins, as well as in tropical waters. They also fish the bonito and tuna grounds off the Pacific Coast of middle Honshu, and can be considered the most abundant Japanese fishing vessels on the high seas. (OSS 1942c: 39–42)

Thus, an overview of equipment and feeding capacity in wartime was easily transformed into an estimate of how much starvation and damage could be inflicted on the Japanese people with the sinking of single or multiple civilian fishing boats. In the military's hands, the report's accompanying photographs and shipbuilding plans became targeting guides.

The conclusion of "Preliminary Report on Japanese Anthropology" recommended that there was "no need of continuing the project in Japanese Anthropology as a permanent feature of the OSS," but it was recommended that occasional studies be undertaken (OSS 1943a: 24). The report identified "no significant structural, physiological, or constitutional variations on the part of the Japanese as compared with other races. Attempts to exploit such minor differences as do exist are almost certain to prove futile" (OSS 1943a: 23).

As the OSS and military personnel considered using biological agents against Japan, others considered using infected bats dropped from specially designed "bat bombs" (originally designed to carry incendiary devices that would be flown into Japanese farms, homes, and forests) to deliver such biological agents (see Couffer 1992: 208). At the Dougway Proving Ground at Tooele, Utah, plans for using biological, chemical, and Project X-Ray's incendiary weapons were tested on mock German and Japanese villages built using authentic materials to exact specifications of true German and Japanese structures. At Dougway, the "research for the construction and furnishings had been supervised by the most qualified anthropologists" (Couffer 1992: 208).

Morale in the Japanese Armed Services

The Research and Analysis Branch also studied Japanese troop morale. Half a year after the Japanese attack on Pearl Harbor, the branch's Psychology Division produced the report "Morale in the Japanese Military Services" (OSS 1942b).[14] It found that the Japanese military's resolve and morale were quite high, with deep devotion to the emperor. The report stressed the importance and power of the Japanese cultural commitment to spiritual training, but it also found that such powerful devotion carried potential threats to Japanese stability, as the "strong emphasis on morale and spiritual training in the Japanese military forces" could at some future date "lead Japanese forces into a disastrous situation" due to an "over-dependence" on these strong motivational forces if it appeared Japan was heading towards a military defeat (OSS 1942b: 2). The report examined the Spartan lifestyle and hardships endured by Japanese military conscripts, and the analysis stressed that such difficulties often produced group bonding and loyalty. The report analyzed the virtues and duties of soldiers and stressed that "the soldier is taught that to die in the battlefield for the Emperor is the reason for his being given life" (OSS 1942b: 11).

The details of training and cultural orientation were presented as influencing battle strategies to be used by Japanese forces in the war. For example, a passage discussing how troops' morale and discipline was affected by training stated, "At the end of a hard day some final command such as to march through a pond or to go double time around a building may be given in order to prove that the men's discipline is still good and also to show the men that they are not as exhausted as they may think. Thus in time of war they will be able to exert the one last effort that may win a battle" (OSS 1942b: 12).

An appendix reproduced the 1941 Code of the Japanese Army (OSS 1942b: 24–28). Several sections of the code on "Counsel Concerning Field Service" were specifically designed to thwart foreign propaganda efforts. Items four and five warned, "(4) Ideological warfare is an important phase in modern conflict. Destroy propaganda and fabrications of the enemy, by your unshakable faith in the cause for which the Empire stands, and endeavor to spread Kodo. (5) Rumors arise from a lack of confidence. Do not be misled; do not be agitated by them. Firmly believe in the strength of the Imperial Army and deeply trust your rulers" (OSS 1942b: 26). These precautions were identified by OWI staff as they designed propaganda leaflets that were dropped from planes on Japanese troops and civilians.[15]

Other Research and Analysis Branch reports examined social and economic forces in Japanese society. The 1942 report "Japanese Cliques: The 'Batsu'" de-scribed the distribution of wealth in Japan, noting that

> one family alone, the Mitsui, controls 15 percent of Japan's industry. Three houses, Misui, Mitusbishi, and Sumitono, together control 25 percent or more. If one adds the Imperial Household and the Ministry of Finance, about 10 groups perhaps control something like 70 percent of Japan's indus-try. Under present conditions it is inexpedient to refer to the Imperial Family in this connection in propaganda. Needless to say, the individuals and families which exercise this control enjoy incomes out of all proportion to those of the average Japanese laborer, government employee, army of-ficer, or professional man. (oss 1942e: 3)

Another report analyzed Japanese laborers as a force that could be used to disrupt Japan's domestic war effort and identified Japanese labor groups that could be used to install a different social order during the anticipated postwar occupation. One oss report stated that, while a quarter of the Japanese popula-tion were unemployed laborers, only a small minority were unionized. During the war, most unions had been disbanded and replaced with Industrial Patriotic Societies, organizations that fostered solidarity among workers for wartime pro-duction. This report outlined how propaganda campaigns contrasting the op-pression of Japanese labor with the American labor movement could undermine Japanese wartime productivity (oss 1942f).

The right to strike had been outlawed in Japan in 1900. Under wartime conditions, efforts to organize labor were further curtailed. The 1925 Peace Pres-ervation Law, known as the "Dangerous Thoughts Law," brought mandatory penalties ranging from five years in prison to death to anyone convicted of working to change the Japanese system of private property or labor relations, and it effectively suppressed any nascent Japanese labor movement (oss 1942f: 4). These anti-labor laws were exploited in propaganda using "some special tech-niques," such as making

> a special May 1st broadcast . . . to emphasize to the Japanese workers the suppression of their May Day holiday and of the whole labor movement. . . . Quotations from speeches of high American officials, particularly the Presi-dent, and from laws or Supreme Court Decisions guarding labor rights should be made. While American labor leaders might be quoted to show their sympathy with Japanese labor, advice should be sought in the selection of leaders respected in Japan. Finally, there should be no hesitancy about

appealing to Japanese labor as a "class" inasmuch as native tradition confirms the "class structure" of Japanese society. (oss 1942f: 11)

The report's appendix identified nine "memorable dates in Japanese labor history" from the previous thirty years. The list included the execution of a dozen anarchists in 1911, 1918 rice riots, and the murders of various socialist and communist activists for workers' rights.

The 1945 report "Japan's 'Secret' Weapon: Suicide" argued that the Japanese were culturally drawn to suicide because "the young Japanese early learned that hara-kiri traditionally has been the only honorable course in peace or war for the responsible person who has met failure" (oss 1945: 2). All Japanese were represented as uniformly conditioned to take such actions on request.

The report recounted tales of massive suicidal campaigns undertaken by defeated Japanese soldiers in Saipan, the Marianas, and Okinawa, where soldiers dove off cliffs to their deaths or killed Japanese field-hospital patients to avoid capture (oss 1945: 2). Beyond the kamikaze pilots crashing explosives-laden planes into ships, there were reports from Okinawa of attacks in which "miniature rocket planes," nineteen feet long with "2,500-pound explosive warheads" were launched from heavy Japanese bombers at high altitudes and flown into military targets twenty-five or more miles away (oss 1945: 5–6).

One can imagine how the report of "human mine suicide swimmers" hardened Pentagon policy against accepting owi reports arguing that the Japanese were ready to surrender. These suicide swimmers were reported to "swim under water in the direction of an approaching landing craft and they surface throwing mines until they explode in contact with the oncoming craft. The attack is generally made in the dark or when visibility is poor. In one such attack a small bamboo raft was used to transport demolitions. Other swimmers are reported to have had explosive charges strapped on their backs while some carried grenades, booby traps, and small explosive charges" (oss 1945: 4). The oss reasoned that, because suicide was so easily induced, it might be able to use the tendency as a weapon against the Japanese. This report identified a "tendency toward premature suicide" that was "causing the Japanese High Command to consider whether the Japanese soldier's carefully cultivated attitude toward death is not a military liability when Japanese troops are faced by superior Allied forces" (oss 1945: 3).

The report concluded, "The Japanese soldier's willingness to sacrifice his individual life in his country's interest is based in part on his strong feeling of the continuity of Japan's national life. Regardless of the current propaganda, should the continued existence of Japan as a nation be threatened by the possibility of

8

anything approaching the total extinction of its population, many Japanese soldiers and civilians might well come to prefer surrender to death" (OSS 1945: 6).

"Social Relations in Japan"

Although the COI and OSS reports rarely identified authors, it appears that John Embree wrote at least portions of the March 19, 1942, COI Psychology Division report "Social Relations in Japan" (COI 1942). Embree's authorship is suggested by the exact duplication of almost half of this report in *The Japanese* for the Smithsonian Institution's War Background Studies series (Embree 1943c). Embree's writing style is apparent, as is his detailed knowledge of village life in rural Japan. The COI report remarked on the class interests of Japanese soldiers, noting that "the majority of the soldiers come from rural villages and only a relatively small number from cities and from businessmen's and nobles' sons. To join the army in normal times one must pass a physical examination and on the whole more rural than city youths make fit soldiers. The army is thus closely allied in interest with the farmer as against either the nobility or the capitalists" (COI 1942: 18).

Some of the passages removed from the Smithsonian's published version of the report appear to have been dropped for editorial reasons, while others may have been removed because their criticism of Japanese society would have appeared out of place in a Smithsonian publication. For example, the Marx-inspired analysis of popular forms of Japanese Buddhism were well suited to internal circulation within intelligence and policy circles, but such analysis was inappropriate in such a scientific venue. The report stated, "Buddhist priests are subject to conscription just like anyone else. They have little political power . . . but indirectly they are important as they serve to soothe the common people with their talk of Amida's paradise and in this sense serve to make poor people satisfied with their lot. In Japan it may be said with some fairness that popular Buddhism serves as an opium for the people" (COI 1942: 20). The reforms of Prince Konoye were discussed, with special attention paid to Konoye's exclusion of Western influences and domestic control and consolidation of news sources. Beyond the control of industry and ideology, the report noted that "everything foreign has been Japanized." Included in this Japanization is the expulsion of Christian missionaries, but even further than this, it is reported that after the expulsions a Japanese subtext to Christianity was fostered as, "The Bible [was] revised to conform with Shinto mythology" (COI 1942: 28).

In writing about the intense emotional support among the Japanese people for the emperor's plans for Japan, Embree's anthropological orientation was apparent in the report's comparisons of religious revivalist movements: "Such a reaction serves to give the group a new feeling of social solidarity and to create new faith in the native beliefs which have been undermined by contact with western culture. This phenomenon has occurred among Bantu tribes in Africa, Indian tribes in North America and Melanesian tribes in New Guinea, but when it occurred, the non-western group had no definite means of getting rid of the foreigner and his influences" (COI 1942: 29–30).

Japanese Courtship of the Islamic World

The OSS produced two fascinating reports tracking Japan's efforts to gain Muslim allies in its fight against Soviet, American, and British foes (OSS 1943c, 1944). "Japanese Infiltration among the Muslims throughout the World" was a secret report on Japanese efforts during the previous decade to establish alliances with Muslims around the world (OSS 1943c). The OSS worried that the Japanese might successfully recruit combatants through these campaigns. It believed that Islam had an unusually high potential as a mobilizing force for political movements, and the report stressed the "outstanding significance of Islam as a theater for psychological warfare" (OSS 1943c: 3).

Japan staged several events supporting Islam as part of a strategy designed to build coalitions with Muslims. Japanese scholarship of Islam and Jewish studies intensified after the Japanese occupation of Manchuria in 1931 (Usuki 2004). The OSS recognized that Islamic minorities in the Soviet Union and China might be mobilized to assist Japan in its battles against these nations. The OSS also recognized that such alignments had significance beyond China and the USSR: "In the Philippines, Malaya, and particularly the Netherlands Indies, regions of immense economic importance, vast numbers of Muslims have lived under the rule of Western Powers. Political discontent in these territories could not but further avowed Japanese policy. India's huge Muslim minority would form the largest single group in the united Islamic front" (OSS 1943c: 4).

The OSS found that, with Shinto's flexibility, the Japanese state could fully embrace and encourage Japanese conversion to Islam if it became strategically beneficial. Shinto's demands were seen as being primarily political, and as long as Islam did not interfere with duties to the state, conversion could be welcomed. The possibility of such massive conversions worried OSS analysts, who believed that, "whether ostensible or real, [conversion] to other religions is meritorious from the standpoint of Shinto so long as such a step is in the interest of patriotism. Christianity is powerless to compete against this type of opposition" (OSS 1943c: 5). Japanese efforts to spread rumors throughout the Islamic world that the Mikado was considering converting to Islam were viewed by the OSS as threats to American interests. The report argued, "Because Islam is not only a creed but also a social and political body, Muslim solidarity is much stronger than Jewish, Christian, or Buddhist solidarity. This is due to a variety of factors. Islam is eminently a lay religion, free from the restrictive influence of a clerical hierarchy. It is also outspokenly democratic, untroubled by racial and social bias" (OSS 1943c: 5).

Japan had recognized the benefits of Muslim-friendly policies in the late nineteenth century. Japanese conversions to Islam illustrated that "political Shinto was awake to the limitless potentialities of a harnessed Islam" (OSS 1943c: 6). In 1906, the Japanese had cultivated rumors that "the Mikado is preparing to elevate Islam to the status of a state religion," and Japanese propagandists spread news stories that Japan was building mosques and Islamic centers in preparation for a surge of Japanese Muslim converts (OSS 1943c: 6). The OSS viewed these efforts as combining two threatening and powerful elements in "an ominous alliance between fanatical Japanese patriotism and Muslim ethno-religious fanaticism" (OSS 1943c: 7).

During the 1930s, Japanese universities recruited students from Egypt's Al-Azhar University, and in 1939, with great publicity in the Arab press, a leading Islamic scholar and imam had been sent from Al-Azhar to Tokyo (OSS 1943c: 9). The OSS believed that the Japanese alliance with Islam would bear fruit in the Muslim regions of the Soviet Union and China, where the Japanese were aiding Muslim ethic groups revolting against the nation-states surrounding them. The OSS reported that Indonesian Muslims "call in their prayers upon Allah to bless the imperial Japanese army and the imperial palace" (OSS 1943c: 14). In Afghanistan, Japan reportedly had "been able to capitalize on four fears: of Russia, Communism, England, and the Hindu Congress party. They are kept alive by the Japanese Legation at Kabul and by returning Afghan businessmen and students who had been entertained and indoctrinated in Japan" (OSS 1943c: 14–16).

In the spring of 1942, Japan targeted Latin American countries with radio broadcasts announcing, "The Bible has now become the Book of the Japanese"; the OSS wondered whether these were efforts inspired by "the Islamic venture to branch off into a Catholic policy" (OSS 1943c: 17). The report recommended that American policymakers and intelligence operatives counteract these Japanese

efforts by publicizing statements of prominent Islamic clerics denouncing totalitarian governments; distributing first-person accounts of Japanese oppression by
prominent Muslims; exposing the duplicity of similar Japanese campaigns to
attract Hindus, Buddhists, and Christians; and launching a publicity campaign
examining how similar claims of coming widespread Japanese conversions in the
early 1900s did not lead to massive numbers of converts (OSS 1943c: 18–19).[16]

Anthropology and the OSS in South Asia: Cora Du Bois

Anthropologists also contributed to the OSS's intelligence field operations
around the world. In 1942, Cora Du Bois's first OSS assignment was to establish
the Research and Analysis Branch for the Dutch East Indies section at headquarters in Washington, D.C. Her field experience among the Alorese and her extensive knowledge of the ethnology and history of Indonesia prepared her for this
task, but the Washington desk work left her with a desire to contribute more
actively to the war.

In 1943, Du Bois became the OSS's acting chief of the Research and Analysis
Branch's OSS Detachment 404, based in Kandy, Ceylon. Du Bois traveled from
Washington, D.C., to Ceylon with fellow OSS operatives Eleanor Thiry and Julia
McWilliams. (McWilliams later married fellow OSS agent Paul Child and became
the renowned chef, Julia Child.) As the group departed California for Bombay in
March 1943 on the SS *Mariposa*, they were joined by Gregory Bateson, who joined
McWilliams and Du Bois in shipboard Chinese-language lessons (Fitch 1999: 90;
cf. McIntosh 1998: 209–11). Ceylon later became the nerve center for OSS Southeast Asian operations, but when Du Bois arrived, there was "no material, no
reference books, no staff." Nonetheless, Du Bois built a sold operation with the
minimal support she was given (MacDonald 1947: 142).

In Ceylon, the regional OSS headquarters was stationed on an old tea planta-
tion's colonial estate, named Nandana, where the staff "worked in *basha* (palm-
thatched) huts connected by cement walks and surrounded by barbed wire"
(Fitch 1999: 91). Du Bois and the others at Nandana planned various guerrilla
campaigns to be undertaken against the Japanese in Malaysia, Burma, Siam, and
southern China. Fellow OSS operative Jane Foster wrote to a friend that "Ceylon
was an Elysium far removed from reality, where everyone had an academic
interest in the war but found life far too pleasant to do anything too drastic about
it. To the red-blooded Americans . . . Ceylon [was either] another form of British
tyranny-frustration without representation [or] . . . a palm-fringed haven of the

bureaucrat, the isle of panel discussions and deferred decisions" (quoted in Fitch 1999: 100). Elizabeth McIntosh wrote that Du Bois had

> something of a school teacher in her, trying to cope with military rigidity. Her acerbic cables to her Research and Analysis chief in Washington, requesting additional personnel, reveal both her frustration and her perspicacity: "24 August 1944: Research and Analysis is poorly staffed in comparison with other operational branches here. It may be an impertinence to tell you the SEAC [South East Asia Command] is the largest unexploited colonial region in the Far East and therefore a potential bone of contention between us and colonial powers in the future." And in an internal memo to her boss, Colonel Heppner, she had the temerity to suggest an improved modus operandi for the oss base in Ceylon involving more careful and integrated planning at all levels: "At present I feel that each branch operates in relation to any one project as though it were an isolated abstraction. The tendency for responsible people to gallop madly over the countryside should be controlled administratively." (McIntosh 1998: 212–13)

The realities of gender bias were not removed by the war's urgency, and such demands were likely doubly unwelcome from a woman. Colonel Heppner viewed Du Bois as a "sharp," "tactless," and "overbearing" woman, though he did implement most of the changes that she advocated. After the war, Heppner authorized that Du Bois be awarded the Exceptional Civilian Award (McIntosh 1998: 213).

Du Bois directed the compilation of waterproof intelligence field kits used by oss personnel during field missions. From Ceylon, Du Bois oversaw the Research and Analysis Branch's field operations in Siam. She managed intelligence and field operatives and a steady stream of supplies going to "jungle hideouts" and Bangkok (McIntosh 1998: 213). She also directed "document collecting teams, which later entered Rangoon ahead of the Allied armies to obtain some five thousand important documents including the minutes of the meetings of the Burmese Committee on Cooperation with the Quisling Ba Maw which showed the degree to which the Burmese interim government stalled off the Japs" (MacDonald 1947: 142).

In 1944, Du Bois criticized plans to increase military support for the war in China (Yu 1996: 106). She instead favored the support of British military campaigns in Malay and Sumatra. While other analysts argued that supporting the British efforts would damage American interests by becoming overly aligned with the neocolonial interests of the British empire, Du Bois countered:

Such involvement would put the USA in a position to have a role in determining the area's postwar future. Americans should participate, but their involvement should be based on a clear national policy.

Although Du Bois had not specifically mentioned Thailand, she took up that subject in a subsequent memorandum, referring to it as "our most important problem and, fortunately, the one which could promise most success." She described Thailand as "politically the most important postwar consideration in South East Asia," noting its strategic importance to Japan and pointing out its accessibility for oss operations because of its independent status. Du Bois believed that Detachment 404 had not acted decisively despite Thailand's obvious importance, a failure she attributed to a malaise of British origin, the "Singapore spirit." She called for the appointment of a special committee to plan and push oss operations aimed at Thailand. (Reynolds 2005: 221–22)

In August 1945, as the Asian war ended, Du Bois wrote a report that cast a prescient eye toward the Cold War future:

The Japanese, by breaking up the European colonial system, seem to be advancing the cause of nationalism in Southeast Asia. They have injected a new confidence in the natives and it will be next to impossible for them to go back to their old way of life. The British, French and Dutch have no positive program to offer these people, who witnessed the defeat of the European colonialists at the hands of the Japanese. The United States has a backlog of prestige over here now, but the generalities of our foreign policy must be made specific or we will soon lose this prestige. (Quoted in McIntosh 1998: 219; cf. MacDonald 1947: 143)

Du Bois viewed Siam, Burma, and Indonesia as nations primed to fight for independence from their colonial past. Du Bois returned from Kandy to Washington, D.C., in September 1945.[17] She later encountered problems in her postwar work at the U.S. Department of State for expressing these anticolonial views during the Cold War's McCarthy period, when views supporting colonial independence were suspiciously viewed as being aligned with communism.

Gregory Bateson and the oss

Gregory Bateson was a natural candidate for the oss. Since 1940, he and Margaret Mead, who was then his wife, had refined methods used in studies of "culture at a distance" (Yans-McLaughlin 1986b: 196). The oss was interested in using these techniques to understand and subvert foreign enemies.

Bateson began the war teaching pidgin English for the oss and U.S. Navy troops preparing to deploy in the South Pacific. He was later stationed in Ceylon and Burma (Yans-McLaughlin 1986b: 197). His friend Julia Child recalled that in Ceylon, Bateson spent much of his time away from the oss compound in villages studying local customs. While on one of these exploratory trips, Bateson learned of the Burmese belief that the color yellow portended the end of a period of foreign occupation (see MacDonald 1947: 144). Because Bateson "knew the Burmese superstition about the color yellow, he suggested that they drop yellow dye into the Irrawaddy River and have the MO [Morale Operations] branch spread rumors that when the Irrawaddy runs yellow, Japan will be kicked out. He won permission, according to Betty MacDonald, but the dye, which turns yellow in ocean salt water, just sank in the fresh water" (Fitch 1999: 100).[18]

In Burma, Bateson became the secretary of the Morale Committee and later was a civilian "member of a forward intelligence unit in the Arakan mountains of Burma from 1944 to 1945" (Bateson 1944; cf. USWDSSU 1976: 384). In Burma he "helped to operate an allied radio station that pretended to be an official Japanese station: it undermined Japanese propaganda by following the official Japanese line but exaggerating it" (Mabee 1987: 8).

Bateson's oss unit broadcast on a radio frequency adjoining that used by Tokyo Radio station JOAK, whose broadcasts could be heard in Burma. Japanese soldiers and others in Burma had difficulty distinguishing oss propaganda broadcasts from those of JOAK. Some of Bateson's black propaganda broadcasts resulted in intelligence blowback. In one instance, a Burmese-based broadcast "beamed to Siam, describing damage done to Japan by Allied bombing raids and the resultant instability of Japanese markets, was reprinted in Bangkok papers as a bona fide news story; and they credited it to the Siamese hour over JOAK in Tokyo" (MacDonald 1947: 144).

These were successful operations, but after the war, the uses of deceit bothered Bateson. In postwar years,

> even though both Mead and Bateson were disturbed by the use of deceit in psychological warfare, Mead was not as upset by it as Bateson was. During

the war and after, the naturally optimistic Mead never lost her basic faith that science, if responsibly applied, could contribute to solving the practical problems of society, whereas Bateson, more pessimistic by nature, and deeply upset by his wartime experience, emphasized that applying science to society was inherently dangerous, and that the most useful role of science was to foster understanding rather than action. These differences between them were reflected in the breakup of their marriage just after the war. (Mabee 1987: 8)

In Ceylon, Bateson analyzed intelligence and occasionally wrote oss policy papers. He was decorated for a dangerous ten-day secret mission during the final weeks of the war in which he "volunteered to penetrate deep into enemy territory in order to attempt the rescue of three agents believed to have escaped after their capture by the Japanese. Mr. Bateson shared all the very considerable dangers of this operation and in view of his civilian status, his courage in so doing [adds] greatly to his credit" (Mosgrip 1945). This "clandestine [operation] against the enemy, deep in enemy territory and beyond any possible support from Allied forces," was recognized as being above the call of duty as a civilian (Mosgrip 1945).

During the secret mission, Bateson led a team attempting to rescue three Indonesian oss operatives believed captured by the Japanese in the Batu Islands, to the southwest of Sumatra. oss directors were reluctant to launch a rescue mission because the end of the war was clearly at hand, but the oss agent Jane Foster pressed the point by arguing that, whatever became of the oss after the war (i.e., the CIA), it would have difficulty recruiting operatives if it did not at least try to rescue fallen comrades. Foster planned the rescue operation using a British transport ship. When she was forbidden from participating because she was a woman, Bateson volunteered to take her place and lead the rescue mission of "a dozen American commandos, mostly officers, who constituted the landing party" (Foster 1980: 134). Foster wrote:

> The party took off and, about ten days later, we received a radio flash saying that the ship had been attacked by a Japanese patrol plane. One can imagine how I felt, having mounted the whole operation. But shortly afterwards the ship limped back into Colombo harbour. We were all in the officers' club when the landing party arrived, dirty and unshaven with Gregory leading them.
>
> I threw my arms around him, kissed him and gushed, "Oh, Gregory, you don't know how glad I am to see you back."

He said in a rather nasty way, "Of course you are glad. You did not want *me* on your conscience for the rest of your life, did you?"

The landing party did find the charred remains of our agents' camp but could not locate the two missing men. Gregory's photographs were developed and they turned out to be mostly devoted to the defecation and nursing habits of the natives. Gregory, ardent anthropologist that he was, would go ashore at every possible place and take pictures of natives squatting and of mothers with babies at their breasts. It was important to him, it seems, to find out which breast mothers used for nursing and with which hand the natives wiped themselves! (Foster 1980: 134–35)

Bateson's oss duties did not usually involve the heroics of a field rescue. Most of his work involved analyzing shifting political conditions and writing analytical reports. One such report was a 1944 document pondering the long-term stability of British colonial control in South Asia. In that oss report, Bateson discussed the past importance of information that colonialists gathered through intimate contact with their local mistresses:

Another very important mechanism by which the white official came to know his people was the native mistress, who not only taught him the language but also taught him a great deal about native custom, native humor and native emotion. With the improvement of transportation, the discovery of quinine, the development of sanitation, mosquito control and public health measures generally, it has become increasingly easy for the white man to have his white wife and even children with him in the colonies. The presence of large numbers of white women relieves the official from the pinch of loneliness which formerly drove him to the native woman and at the same time the white women not unnaturally use their influence to build up strong moral sanctions against the taking of native mistresses—even to the point of ostracizing the guilty officials. As a result the more durable and more educative type of relationship with the native women has been reduced to a minimum and only the casual, impermanent—and education-al[ly] useless—types of relationship persist. (Bateson 1944: 3)

Bateson conceded that the days of learning about "native peoples" through village mistresses were gone and that there was "no likelihood that the native mistress [would] come back into her former influential position" (Bateson 1944: 6). He instead advocated that colonial authorities or other managers of native populations immerse themselves in "vernacular films" and literature. He recommended films because they "portray the day-dreams of the people—or at any rate day-dreams which the collaborating group of native writers and performers think will be acceptable to the native public" (Bateson 1944: 6).

Bateson contrasted differences in autonomy between British and American families to examine how the British colonial system was inherently training colonized people to need independence. Bateson's profile of the British family identified the psychological components underlying the structure of the colonial system, and these features were seen as being fundamentally different from those found in American families.[19] He wrote:

> The American family thus constitutes, in itself, a "weaning machine." It contains within itself a factor which pushes the child towards independent initiative and which breaks the child's earlier dependence upon the parents. The English family does not contain this machinery for making the child independent and it is necessary in England to achieve this end by the use of an entirely separate institution—the boarding school. The English child must be drastically separated from his parents' influence in order to let him grow and achieve initiative and independence.
>
> The British colonial office goes out to the tropics with a philosophy of life which he unconsciously learned during his childhood and during his public school education. He sees himself as a responsible parent and with the best intentions in the world considers himself and his institutions to be a model for the native people. He tries to show them how things should be done. He takes the exhibitionist role and leaves to the natives the role of spectator. He does not instinctively feel that it is appropriate for him to delegate initiative nor can he easily throw himself into admiration or constructive criticism of the natives' achievements. (Bateson 1944: 4)[20]

Bateson's comments on Soviet attempts to co-opt indigenous peoples' movements reveal how intelligence work channeled the thinking of oss anthropologists as they worked in settings that pressed them to view culture as a force to be studied and manipulated. With more than a trace of professional admiration for the Soviets' accomplishments, Bateson wrote:

> The most significant experiment which has yet been conducted in the adjustment of relations between "superior" and "inferior" peoples is the Russian handling of their Asiatic tribes in Siberia. The findings of this experiment support very strongly the conclusion that it is very important to foster spectatorship among the superiors and exhibitionism among the inferiors.

In outline, what the Russians have done is to stimulate the native peoples to undertake a native revival while they themselves admire the resulting dance festivals and other exhibitions of native culture, literature, poetry, music and so on. And the same attitude of spectatorship is then naturally extended to native achievements in production or organization. In contrast to this, where the white man thinks of himself as a model and encourages the native people to watch him in order to find out how things should be done, we find that in the end nativistic cults spring up among the native people. The system gets over-weighed until some compensatory machinery is developed and then the revival of native arts, literature, etc., becomes a weapon for use *against* the white man. (Phenomena, comparable to Gandhi's spinning wheel may be observed in Ireland and elsewhere.) If, on the other hand, the dominant people themselves stimulate native [revivalism], then the system as a whole is much more stable, and the nativism cannot be used against the dominant people.

oss can and should do nothing in the direction of stimulating native revivals but we might move gently towards making the British and the Dutch more aware of the importance of processes of this kind. (Bateson 1944: 6–7)

Here Bateson prefigured the sort of psy-war, culture-cracking counterinsurgency approach to conquest that was popularized by Edward Landsdale and others in the CIA in postwar Southeast Asia, and these ideas coalesced with those of OWI anthropologists considering the Mikado's postwar fate (see Jeffreys-Jones 1989).

Bateson seems to have pursued this and other OSS tasks with some zeal and interest, yet his biographer David Lipset found that in the years after the war, Bateson said he was "very disturbed with the O.S.S. treatment of the natives . . . [and according to Geoffrey Gorer] he felt that he was associated with a dishonest outfit" (Lipset 1980: 174; see also Yans-McLaughlin 1986b: 202–3). Carleton Mabee wrote that Bateson was bothered because during the war he had "engaged in deceitful propaganda, which made him even more uneasy" (Mabee 1987: 8). Bateson's postwar analysis of his OSS years was tinged with regret, and he came away concerned not about the failures, but about the successes of his OSS work (see Price 1998b).

Anthropology and the OSS in Africa: Jack Harris

OSS anthropologists working in Africa were sought for their linguistic and cultural expertise, and they became highly valued assets as the European front moved to Africa and the control of vital African resources took on increased importance. In the 1930s, Jack Harris had conducted fieldwork in Nigeria among the Ibo. After the Japanese attacked Pearl Harbor, Harris left his position at Ohio State University and went to Washington, D.C., where he looked up his friend Ralph Bunche, who was working at the COI.[21] Harris and William Bascom were soon recruited by the OCI and assigned to "go to the Gold Coast together under the cover of a phony anthropological expedition to West Africa. The cover was well prepared" (Edelman 1977: 11).

Even with Pearl Harbor fresh in his mind, Harris still felt some unease over the arrangement to use his anthropological credentials as a cover for espionage. Harris had been a student of Boas and had some general awareness that Boas had opposed such activities during the First World War. But despite these concerns, "Our feelings were so strong, I felt that whatever capabilities I could lend to the war effort in this war against infamy I was pleased to do" (quoted in Edelman 1977: 11). Harris reported that in January 1942, he and William Bascom

> were told that on reviewing our recent backgrounds of field work in Nigeria it was decided to send us to West Africa with covers as members of a joint Ohio State–Northwestern University Expedition for the study of "European and Native Culture Contact." The president of each university furnished us with appropriate letters requesting cooperation in our studies etc. They certainly knew that our mission was a cover for intelligence activities. I don't know who requested these letters but obviously it was someone in Washington with enough clout to get them to act quickly. In those early days the COI was composed of a fairly small group and, I was told, operating under direct authorization of the White House.
>
> West Africa became important in the spring of 1940 when the six-week German blitzkrieg forced the collapse of the French army. A call from de Gaulle to the French West African Colonial Forces to rally against the Vichy government was ignored. The four British colonies surrounded by the French were suddenly at peril—their reduced army, military installations and their exports: palm oil, tin, gold, cacao, lumber, rough diamonds etc.[22]

In February 1942, Harris and Bascom arrived on the Gold Coast with letters of introduction providing a cover that they were working on an archaeological expedition. Harris later reported that he and Bascom "were amateur bunglers in the field of intelligence. . . . [W]e had no prior training except for brief instruction in a simple code for our reports. . . . In early 1942 the level of intelligence knowledge and operations in the U.S. was very low. I recall Ralph Bunche telling me at that time the files at U.S. Army Intelligence on West Africa were composed almost completely of clippings from the *New York Times*" (quoted in Lawler 2002: 135).

After a few weeks, Harris and Bascom abandoned the pretense of working as archaeologists, and Harris "continued in West Africa more or less openly as an agent sent by Washington with liaison to the British Intelligence services. . . . In South Africa where my activities were more direct, my cover was traditional State Department with no connection to anthropology. Thus my wartime activities had little or nothing to do with the fact that I was an anthropologist except for those silly first few weeks."[23] Harris later recalled:

> The British, with a long tradition of intelligence activities, had been in West Africa for some 80 years with a network of informants in place reporting to trained agents. In the Gold Coast British Intelligence utilized the services of at least one anthropologist, Meyer Fortes, a South African, who after the war taught at Cambridge. . . . [24]
>
> It would have been foolish for us to undertake setting-up parallel sources of intelligence in the field and we did not. Since I had a recent history of comfortable and friendly working relationship with British colonial officials in Nigeria I quickly became the liaison with British Intelligence (soe [Special Operations Executive]) in Accra and later in Lagos and funneled to Washington reports that they made available to me. Although the number and contents of these reports were undoubtedly limited I was told later in Washington that the material I had sent was very much more than was being received directly from London. This modest achievement was the only worthwhile effort of our mission.
>
> As I recall, our instructions were to report on the situation in the surrounding Vichy colonies (Ivory Coast to the west of the Gold Coast and Togoland to the east), and especially military information. We were also to advise on conditions in the British colonies that might affect the course of the war and, in general, any other intelligence that we thought might be of interest to Washington.
>
> After some months Bascom returned to Washington. . . . I was told to proceed to Lagos where I assumed the cover of Special Assistant to the

American Consul. At that time American civilians, mostly women and children, were being evacuated from India and neighboring countries to be flown to the States via Cairo–Khartoum–Lagos. PanAm passenger planes and pilots were used under military supervision. We were involved in minor security matters concerning this traffic since passengers had to wait in the Lagos area for a week or more for the transatlantic flight to the U.S. via Belem, Brazil.

After the landing of U.S. troops in North Africa I was directed to go to the French Cameroons to see whether the colonial administration there might abandon Vichy and join the Free French. I went to Douala but I had no briefing and I was ill-prepared. I held conversations with the French officials but it was a fruitless mission and, under the circumstances, a stupid one.

We were not asked to contact native chiefs in the Vichy territories. It was just as well; any attempt on our part to do so would have been resented by the British who were far better prepared for such a task.

I did interview the Emir of Kano at his palace but that was on my own initiative, motivated by anthropological interest and not for intelligence purposes.[25]

After a few months working at a desk assignment in Washington while recuperating from malaria, Harris was dispatched to South Africa in August 1943 under U.S. State Department cover as special assistant to the American minister to the Union of South Africa. South Africa was an important assignment because it

had entered the war on the side of the Allies with the barest majority in its Parliament. The pro-Nazi sentiment was strong and provided a hospitable base for anti-Allied activities and I was charged with reporting on such activities and to create an organization to that end. It was understood that I would engage in or foment activities consistent with these goals.

South African industrial diamonds were being smuggled into Germany; clandestine radio stations were sending information to a Nazi submarine base on the French coast on the movements of troop ships and freighters proceeding through the Mozambique Channel. We had almost no success with the diamond smuggling but we did manage to break up some of the clandestine radio stations. I went on two of those raids. I also had Washington send more modern and sophisticated D/F [Direction Finding] equipment to replace what the British had been using.[26]

In South Africa, Jack Harris tracked and disrupted South African fascists' efforts to smuggle industrial diamonds to Nazi Germany. At the war's end, the OSS operative Kermit Roosevelt wrote of Harris's operation:

> In the Union of South Africa one OSS agent, cooperating with an OWI representative, uncovered evidence of pro-Axis activities on the part of the Ossewa Brandwag. This widespread local Fascist organization was strong enough to prevent Marshal Smuts from taking serious repressive action. By the fall of 1943, however, U.S. and British espionage services had accumulated sufficient evidence so that the British Foreign Office might approach General Smuts in London and thereby enable him to take action against the Ossewa Brandwag. It was learned later that the report, submitted by the OSS agent, on an interview with the Ossewa Brandwag leader, had played an important part in the South African cabinet decision to adopt a firm policy against that organization. (USWDSSU 1976: 43)[27]

Harris recalled meeting the leader of Ossewa Brandwag (OB)

> at their country headquarters where pistol and rifle practice were going on as we talked. He was cheerfully boastful and described many of the OB activities—cultural, sports, youth movements, Afrikaner nationalist rallies and their private army. His pro-Nazi feelings were open and evident. Although he may not have known my OSS affiliation, my thin diplomatic cover as Special Assistant to the American Minister established me as an official of the U.S. Government and he seemed anxious that I report to Washington the wide-spread and genuine popular support of the OB organization.
>
> Of course he did not speak of the sabotage by the Ossewa Brandwag storm trooper units. That knowledge came to us from informers, from our undercover activities, and from British and South African Government Intelligence sources. The sabotage included the blowing up of bridges, cutting telephone lines, derailing trains, burning post offices etc. to force retention of some army units for security purposes and thus reduce the number of South African soldiers engaged in combat with the German army in North Africa.
>
> The report of this meeting to Washington was followed by several others on OB activities. We had no doubt that OB officials were in direct contact and collaborated with German agents in subversive activities in South Africa. [28]

After the war, Harris declined an offer to join the CIA "partly because of promises which the US broke to certain of his contacts—people whom he owed a debt of gratitude for helping him out of some difficult situations" during World War II (Melvern 1995: 55). Harris later worked for the United Nations' Division of Trusteeship Territories until he was fired after aggressively advocating for the decolonization of Africa and being identified as a target in a congressional committees hunting for communist influences at the United Nations (see Price 2004a: 154–63).

Carleton Coon and the OSS

Carleton Coon's account of his recruitment to the OSS on the eve of the Yale–Harvard game depicted the old-school networks that the OSS revered and the CIA sustained in the postwar years. Before the game, Wallace Phillips of the U.S. Navy, "a tall, dignified, elderly gentleman wearing a blue serge suit and black shoes," visited Coon at his home. In a scene right out of a John le Carre spy novel, Coon wrote, "He swore me to utter secrecy, then he told me more about myself than I had dreamed anyone else could know. He asked me if I wanted to serve my country. I told him that I was already in the Massachusetts State Guard at Sudbury, but that was not enough. He then informed me that I had been chosen to be the Lawrence of Morocco. . . . [He] told me that the Germans planned to drive through Spain from Vichy France and then to conquer Morocco, reinforcing Rommel and taking over the whole Middle East" (Coon 1981: 162). Coon was instructed to not tell his wife, Mary, what he was doing. He soon left for Washington for training in the art of signals and other elements of spycraft and then went to Canada, where he was issued a Canadian army uniform and a false identity and was trained in the arts of "unarmed combat, street fighting and particularly demolition" at the OSS's "Camp X" (Coon 1981: 163; Stafford 1987).

A flurry of correspondence between Donovan's office and the Department of State transpired in the spring of 1942 relating to Coon's leaving for North Africa.[29] While processing Coon's security clearance, the OSS discovered that the State Department was reluctant to provide a cover for his presence in Morocco because he had left Ethiopia in 1933 under a cloud of accusations of wrongdoing. Coon later claimed that Donovan had gotten President Roosevelt to direct the State Department to destroy its report on his troubles in Ethiopia (Coon 1981: 164).[30]

A secret OSS memo listing the "job description in the case of Carelton Stevens Coon" described the OSS's plans for him:

[He will] be sent to the Near East Theater for special subversive and demolition work. He will be responsible for physical subversion in enemy or enemy occupied or controlled territory. He will promote, organize and equip partisan groups and operational nuclei for guerrilla warfare, will instruct and use allied agents in modern methods of sabotage and will furnish the necessary implements and weapons of resistance. . . . The applicant in civilian life is a noted anthropologist and is an authority on native tribes in the theater to which he will be assigned. He knows various tribal leaders in this theater as a result of his scientific research expeditions.[31]

In the months before the American invasion of French North Africa, the OSS placed a handful of covert operatives in Morocco and Gibraltar to make contact with sympathetic locals who helped them launch a pre-invasion propaganda campaign. As the American invasion got under way, President Roosevelt broadcast radio messages to French citizens, then under Vichy control, proclaiming America's history of solidarity with France and asking for their assistance. Coon, Gordon Browne, and the local Moroccan OSS operative Randolph Mohammed Gusus "translated" ("composed" is a more accurate description) a message from President Roosevelt to the Moroccans broadcast in a highly stylized form of Arabic. The broadcast mimicked Coon's, Browne's, and Gusus's conception of Quranic Arabic and had Roosevelt calling the American military campaign the "great Jihad of freedom" and American troops "American Holy Warriors." Coon later recalled:

One of the few useful things which we did in this cover job was to translate the President's Flag Day speech into Arabic. Browne and I would reword the English in a more Arabic sounding way, and Gusus would sing out an Arabic poetical version and then write it down. Every time Mr. Roosevelt mentioned God once, we named Him six times; and the result was a piece of poetry which might have come out of the Koran. It was a free translation, but it caught Mr. Roosevelt's sense perfectly, and the original English lent itself well to this treatment. Finally we had it checked by the British Arabic expert at their Legation, and gave it to Geier to have several thousand copies printed. We mailed it all over the Spanish Zone, and some copies got (by mistake) into the French Zone. There the French announced that any native found with it in his possession would receive three months imprisonment.

Since the landing [of American forces] this document has been read several times over the Rabat radio. More than anything else it gave the natives the idea that we would come across the sea to set them free; this influenced many of them in our favor, particularly those who had been wavering in an Axis direction, and it was very hard to explain to these natives, after the landing, why their condition had not immediately changed for the better. (Coon 1945: 14)

The following English version of Coon's, Browne's, and Gusus's Arabic broadcast shows the liberty that Coon and his assistants took in "translating" the meaning of President Roosevelt's speech. They had Roosevelt proclaiming in classical Arabic:

Praise be unto the only God. In the name of God, the Compassionate, the Merciful. O ye Moslems. O ye beloved sons of the Moghreb. May the blessing of God be upon you.

This is a great day for you and for us, for all the sons of Adam who love freedom.

Behold. We the American Holy Warriors have arrived. Our numbers are as the leaves on the forest trees and as the grains of sand in the sea.

We have come here to fight the great Jihad of Freedom.

We have come to set you free.

We have sailed across the great sea in many ships, on many beaches we are landing, and our fighters swarm across the sands and into the city streets, and into the wide countryside, and along the highways.

Light fires on the hilltops; shout from your housetops, and from the high places, and say the sound of the drum be heard in the land, and the ululation of the women, and the voices even of small children. Assemble along the highways to welcome your brothers.

We have come to set you free.

Speak with our fighting men and you will find them pleasing to the eye and gladdening to the heart. We are not as some other Christians whom ye have known, and who trample you under foot. Our soldiers consider you as their brothers, for we have been reared in the way of free men. Our soldiers have been told about your country and about their Moslem brothers and they will treat you with respect and with a friendly spirit in the eyes of God.

Look in their eyes and smiling faces, for they are Holy Warriors happy in their holy work. Greet us therefore as brothers as we will greet you, and help us.

If we are thirsty, show us the way to water. If we lose our way, lead us back to our camping places. Show us the paths over the mountains if need be, and if you see our enemies, the Germans or Italians, making trouble for us, kill them with knives or with stones or with any other weapon that you may have set your hands upon.

Help us as we have come to help you, and rich will be the reward unto you as all who love justice and righteousness and freedom.

Pray for our success in battle, and help us, and God will help us both.

Lo. The day of freedom hath come.

May God grant his blessing upon you and upon us.—Roosevelt (Brown 1982: 252–53; see also Pipes 2000)

Coon gave fifty thousand francs to a prominent mullah who was raising funds to expand a mosque in Tangier, and Coon recruited the mullah and his associates "for intelligence, for propaganda, and for armed revolt among all the tribes of the Ghomara confederacy, and many of these of the Jebala" (Coon 1945: 17).

One of Coon's first assignments in Tangiers was to translate articles from a local newspaper—a task beyond his limited Arabic-language skills (Coon 1981: 164). When the OSS assigned Coon the task of compiling a forty-page text on Moroccan propaganda, he borrowed heavily from his textbook, "*Principles of Anthropology*, and padded it with enough technical terms to make it ponderous and mysterious, since [he] had found out in the academic world that people will express much more awe and admiration for something complicated which they do not quite understand than for something simple and clear" (Coon 1945: 10). But Coon's limited Arabic was sufficient to instruct locals in the techniques of sabotage and terrorism:

> Before receiving a major assignment, my first job was to teach some Arabs to blow up railroad tracks, a form of academic instruction of which the French took an exceedingly dim view, for they were thinking of the postwar future. I managed to teach two men adequately, and to sew the needed explosives and other equipment into an Arab packsaddle. Off they went with a load of grain, fruit, or something equally innocent, to the railroad track between Bizerte and Tunis. At a place where it ran over an embankment between two bodies of water, they set it, assuring the Germans of a salty bath. I was told that it worked. (Coon 1981: 175–76)

Coon operated a covert radio station, monitored the local political scene, and took notes on the strategic lay of the countryside. One day while traveling on rural roads, Coon and Browne were looking for something suitable to be used as an antitank explosive device when they

> observed that the one constant factor on all roads was mule turds, large enough for our purpose, uniform in size, fat and greenish brown, depend-

ing on the animal's feed—but the color differences were of little importance because they fade. Gordon and I picked up as many as we could without being observed, for why should two Christians in an American car be picking up mule turds.

Carefully wrapped, these turds made their way to London in a British diplomatic pouch, and were returned via Gibraltar in plastic facsimile, the mule's revenge on a motor vehicle. The plastic turds were used in at least one battle. They were not camel turds, as has been reported in several books and *Time* magazine. In 1942 there weren't enough camels on the roads in northern Morocco. (Coon 1981: 165–66)

The turd bombs were deployed to stop the advance of German tanks after the battle of Kassarine Pass (Coon 1981: 179).

Coon managed a small ring of local intelligence informants who usually met with him in the dead of night or during the day using disguises. Coon later wrote about his work with a Muslim operative using the code name "Tassels," whom Coon had arranged to meet at a clandestine oss radio station on the rural estate of Mrs. Bertram Thomas:

> [I] was stationed to lie under the rose bushes near the entrance to [Mrs. Thomas's] garden, to lead [Tassels] in when he should appear at the gate. Colonel Eddy, Mrs. Thomas, and [Gordon] Browne were on the roof. I lay in the bushes next to a reed fence, and spiders and ants crawled over me and spun webs over me. Meanwhile a pair of Spanish lovers lay down on the other side of the fence; I was treated to all their physiological noises as well as their periodic and inane conversation. Finally, after what seemed to me a distinguished effort (compared to the graph describing sexual intercourse published by Boas and Goldschmitt in "The Heart Rate," *American Journal of Physiology*), they left, and I was able to move and brush off a few cobwebs. I retired to the roof and Gordon made a sortie, finally picking up Tassels, who was wandering about lost several blocks away. (Coon 1945: 21–22)

Coon found Tassels to be an excellent intelligence source, at times providing four or five hours of reports on military and political matters (Coon 1945: 23). Coon's operatives "Tassels" and "Strings" became key contacts for American forces in North Africa, important enough that Kermit Roosevelt mentioned Coon and his work with them as a vital component of oss operations in the North African campaign (Roosevelt 1976: ix). According to the oss's postwar final evaluation of these operations,

Members of the "Strings" group number tens of thousands of Moors from every walk of life, ready to obey unquestioningly the will of their divine leader. "Strings" reports to COI came from caids and sheiks, holy men who penetrated areas forbidden by the French authorities to the general populace, and from farmers and shepherds who relayed pertinent items of intelligence in comparative anonymity.

The Riffs under "Tassels," on the other hand, were Berber adventurers, willing to carry out any job regardless of the danger involved, and highly adept at avoiding detection by Spanish or French police. These men knew how to handle arms and conduct guerilla warfare in difficult terrain.

COI handled both groups with caution, letting neither know of the other's cooperation. Secret meetings were held at regular intervals with "Tassels" and "Strings"; or their leg-men, at frequently changed rendezvous. Here were reported at length detailed combat intelligence—Spanish battle orders, troop movements, fortifications, etc.—and significant political events. Appropriate information was turned over by COI to G-2, ONI, the State Department and the British. (USWDSSU 1976: 13–14)

On Christmas Eve 1942, one of Coon's operatives, Fernand Bonnier de la Chapelle, assassinated Admiral Darlan, Vichy's North African administrator. Coon's role as one of de la Chapelle's "teachers" created serious problems for him, and Coon was forced to flee to Tunisia (see Coon 1981; O'Donnell 2004: 39). When he arrived in Tunisia, Coon used the "nom de guerre Captain Retinitis and dressed in a British Army uniform with a phony officer's pipes cut from the green felt of a billiard table. 'Now,' a fellow saboteur observed, 'the company of rogues and cutthroats is complete'" (Atkinson 2003: 276–77).

Coon led a group of fifty commandos who planted mule-turd bombs, blew up a railroad trestle, and seized and held local children as hostages. Coon's commandos' use of kidnapping was a successful tactic, as "boys were imprisoned in the Cap Serrat lighthouse until their fathers provided authenticated information about enemy positions" (Atkinson 2003: 277). In January and February 1943, Coon "trained two Arabs and sent them through the enemy lines to blow up a train full of German troops between Tindja and Ferryville. This operation was successfully carried out and the Arabs returned. During these operations, Major Coon suffered concussion and injuries to his head when a building into which he had gone after the aerial machine-gunning was dive-bombed."[32]

Coon was later sent to Cairo to help plan an invasion of Albania—a plan that was later dropped in favor of the liberation of Corsica.[33] He was in the first landing of the French liberation of Corsica on September 13, 1943, where he "remained in a forward combat position with his men and personally directed their activities."[34]

Coon made remarkable claims about his skills to negotiate various wartime arrangements. Among them was his successful effort "to persuade the Pope in German-held Rome to desanctify a putative parachute landing field located on papal property" (Coon 1981: 188). Coon later bragged that the war's leaders had fought for his abilities: "General MacArthur, who had heard of me as a rouser of rebel Moslem tribes, demanded that I be released to him to be dropped among the Moros. He and [Bill] Donovan had been great rivals in the First World War, and three stars stood between them. But Bill kept me out of it" (Coon 1981: 189).

The citation for Coon's Distinguished Service Cross (awarded in September 1945) described his OSS work, listing his travels in civilian clothing in German-controlled areas of North Africa, "smuggling firearms, explosives, hand grenades, flares, and other incriminating material to the French resistance groups in the invasion ports for their use on D-Day. During the same period he also collected military intelligence from native sources, which he transmitted to Washington, and which were of great value to our forces in planning the details of the North African landings." It also cited Coon's crucial work in Tunisia, where he "[won] over the native population to the allied cause, whereas before most of them had been hostile; in going alone on nightly expeditions in no-man's land to set booby traps and signal devices, to assure the safety of the garrison."[35]

Coon had neurological problems after he was knocked in the head during battle in early 1943. His injury reportedly required surgery and led him to end his field activities.[36] On November 18, 1944, Coon wrote a memo describing plans to write a history chronicling his involvement in OSS operations. The memo argued that social scientists should have an increasing role in the OSS's management and operation: "I believe that history can approach the status of a science, in that functional relationships between variables can be learned and future behavior predicted, and that like other forms of science it can be put to practical use. The greatest single task which confronts all of us, once the war is won, is to prevent its recurrence; if the OSS history can do its share in giving guidance, this project will well be worth the effort, time and expense."[37] Coon's proposal to be reassigned to write this history hit a bureaucratic snag,[38] but eventually he was authorized to undertake some of the work, which resulted in his OSS manuscript "Torch Anthropology" (Coon 1945). It was partially published later as *A North Africa Story: The Anthropologist as OSS Agent, 1941–1943* (Coon 1980).[39]

When Coon returned to Harvard in March 1945, the OSS made arrangements to secretly maintain his services as a consultant. He earned seven thousand dollars a year as he continued to write a historical summary of the OSS's North African activities—the effort that produced his "Torch Anthology" document. The CIA released records under FOIA listing Coon as working as a "scientific consultant" in 1948, 1949, and 1950.[40] Coon's consultancy was canceled on January 19, 1951.

Coon's Postwar Vision of the "Invisible Empire"

Carleton Coon's years in the OSS gave him some sense of what had been unleashed with the establishment of an agency waging unconventional warfare, operating outside of the law and the public's knowledge. This experience made him interested in the prospects that such an agency presented to American interests in the postwar world. In a postscript to his 1945 historical analysis of OSS North African operations, titled "The World after the War: OSS–SOE, the Invisible Empire," Coon speculated on what could be done with the OSS in the postwar period.[41] This postscript was withheld from publication when Coon's war memoir, *A North Africa Story*, was published in 1980.[42]

The postscript is reprinted in its entirety here because it offers a clear view into the wartime conception held by Coon and others in the OSS of the uses of the OSS's "objective social science." The postscript captures Coon's confidence in the usefulness of intelligence operations and his vision of a natural role for academics in intelligence. It also shows Coon advocating for America to increasingly rely on the OSS's skills (or the CIA's) to maintain a "secret empire" in the postwar period:

VIII: POSTSCRIPT: THE WORLD AFTER THE WAR:

OSS–SOE, THE INVISIBLE EMPIRE

One of the commonest topics of discussion heard in OSS and SOE messes and in other gatherings where agents of these two organizations convene is, "What will you do after the war? How can you ever go back to teaching—life insurance—banking—the advertising business—or whatever?" The general opinion is that a return to these occupations will be difficult. One British [Lieutenant] Colonel said that he was going to start an organization called "Piracy Unlimited"; another agent wishes to become an international financial crook.

Most of us, however, seriously wish to see our British and American organizations continued, either separately or in combination, and our present type of work carried on in some way. Probably the heads of our organization have already made plans, and certainly a number of us who serve in minor capacities have formulated, at least tentatively, individual schemes. In the next few pages I would like to revert for a moment to my long neglected academic role, and try to view the situation from the standpoint of an objective social scientist insofar as my present knowledge permits me to do so.

As matters seem to be working out, we agents will be called upon neither to police nor to administer occupied countries. The CIC [Counter Intelligence Corps] will presumably take the former, and the new corps of Civil Administrators which is in training, the latter, task. This in my opinion is to our advantage, because most of us would not be content with either type of work.

We have, by a combination of historical accident and of selection, assembled a group of versatile and bold individuals the like of which has not been brought together for many centuries. We are furthermore living in a period of history which has never been anticipated or equaled, and of which only the most imaginative of authors have dreamed.

We are at length on the brink of an era in which technology, man's control over the natural forces of the world, has neared the stage of completion. We have discovered new metals, new techniques of processing materials which will place all kinds of material objects at the disposal of everyone if our social relations can be adequately arranged; and we have developed techniques of transportation which, as everyone knows, have made the world a small and closely interwoven unit. In short, our technological advances have brought us to the stage where human relations can no longer be permitted to exist on a trial and error basis. Just as we have learned the principles of technology, so must we learn those of human relations.

Just as we have applied the principles of technology which we have learned, so must we apply the social principles which we are tardily discovering. If we do not apply these latter principles the process of evolution of which we are latest, and most complex stage must come to an end.

Let us review for a moment the history of this evolutionary process. The earth, when it broke loose from the sun and finally cooled, was a body of chemical elements, both pure and arranged in relatively simple combinations. As it continued to cool and the land, sea, and atmosphere were separated, more complex combinations arose, and some of these resulted in life. From the simpler forms of life arose ultimately the vertebrates and mammals on the one hand, the land-living plants and the angiosperms on the other.

Out of one relatively unspecialized kind of mammal, the primates, evolved creatures with nervous systems competent to do more than react directly to external impulses; these nervous systems developed the mechanism for memory and a complex association of symbols, which we call "thinking" or "reason."

Beyond the level of the apes came the half-brained Pithecanthropi and Sinanthropi, and also the full brained Neanderthal and Sapiens men. These men developed social systems through the division of labor, and this division of labor gave an opportunity for specialization, and specialization led to the discovery of technological principles through the mechanism of trial and error. The advanced nervous system of these men permitted a greater conditioning process than that found in any other animal. Whereas the bulk of behavior in most animals is directly genetic in inspiration, in man conditions play a predominant role, and as each generation moves on we have more and more to learn.

Most of the principles which we have learned have come to us through the old process of trial and error, and this process is simply an [extension] into the social field of what Darwin called the survival of the fittest, or natural selection. However, once we had acquired a sufficient corpus of principles, we could see how to discover new principles directly by the application of others previously known, and this process is called science. We can at length become aware of the existence of a new principle, and then look for it, just as an astronomer knows that a star which no one has yet seen must exist in a certain place in the universe of time and space with which he deals.

So far most attempts to apply our knowledge of principles to the field of human relations have led us astray. The Nazis for example have developed a false body of science, based on too little knowledge, or rather on the false use of what they consider to be science as a set of symbols in terms of which they can rationalize, to build up a social system which cannot work.

Thus they have used the false science of Freud to furnish them with a variety of excuses, and the puerile physical anthropology of Gunther and Fischer, and the speculation of Gobineau, along with a misapprehension of Darwin, to name but a few, in the synthetic construction of a "Herrenvolk." As a scientist during the twenties and thirties, I among many others was able to observe the gradual twisting of German science, to note how the Germans would collect great masses of data which they did know how to interpret; how they then warped this body of facts and figures to produce the rationalizations required by their state of national disequilibrium.

The social sciences can, however, and must, be used objectively and compassionately to adapt our human relations to the new technological world, and if this is not done we shall join the other forms of life which have become overspecialized and destroy themselves. We must see that no major mistakes are made, for the world is now too small and too tight to permit a continuation of the process of trial and error. A mistake made in one quarter will of necessity spread rapidly all over the world, for all our apples are now in one barrel and if one rots the lot is destroyed.

All charges in human social systems require leadership. The type of personality which gives leadership is not always the type which is capable of producing or even understanding progressive social change. Men with large oral cavities and silver tongues, men with sparkling personalities and boundless energy, men who know how to act as clearing houses of goods and human relations, are not always scholars. Our greatest thinkers have seldom been temporal leaders as well.

Therefore we cannot be sure that the clear and objective scholars who study the existing social systems and who draw up the blueprints for a society to suit our technology will always be heard, or that their plans will be put into operation. We can almost be sure that this will not be the case. Therefore some other power, some third class of individuals aside from the leaders and the scholars must exist, and this third class must have the task of thwarting mistakes, diagnosing areas of potential world disequilibrium, and of nipping the causes of potential disturbance in the bud. There must be a body of men whose task it is to throw out the rotten apples as soon as the first spots of decay appear. If such a body had existed in 1933 its members could have recognized the potential danger of Hitler and his immediate disciples and have killed this group. This would have prevented the rise of a Nazi state in the peculiarly lethal form which it has taken.

A body of this nature must exist undercover. It must either be a power unto itself, or be given the broadest discretionary powers by the highest human authorities.

The only organizations in existence today which have even the rudiments of what is needed in the formation of such a body of men are the oss and soe. Agents of these two organizations are trained to act under cover, to act ruthlessly and without fear. We include objective scientists in our midst, and men of the widest experience in the political, economic and diplomatic fields.

It seems therefore to me not too wild, too visionary, or too improbable a thought to suppose that from these two groups a smaller can be selected; a group of men, sober-minded and without personal ambition, men competent to judge the needs of our world society and to take whatever steps are necessary to prevent this society from a permanent collapse. (Coon 1945: 171–77)

Coon envisioned the postwar world being saved by "some third class of individuals aside from the leaders and the scholars," a "third class" of covert philosopher kings who could secretly and decisively act to save the world from slipping into a disastrous state of "disequilibrium" and to "throw out the rotten apples" at the "first spots of decay." This record captures the self-assured milieu of the OSS. Coon believed that an organization like the OSS could have prevented the rise of Nazis by recognizing potential threats and preemptively killing them in their political infancy. But Coon appears to have been unconcerned that his confident vision of unchecked decisive action for a believed betterment of humanity shared basic beliefs with the Nazis and other totalitarians he wished to exterminate.

Evaluating OSS Trajectories

In the laboratory, the library, and the field, the OSS prided itself on using unorthodox approaches to problems of war and intelligence. While OSS operatives' daring and panache are unassailable, some have questioned the actual wartime outcomes of the OSS, and there are clearly reasons to question some of the OSS's own claims. As Alexander Cockburn observed, the OSS loved to promote a romantic public vision of secret agents: "Fortified [by] boyish fantasies, the officers of OSS never wrought much damage to the foe, but, from Donovan and his subordinate Allen Dulles downwards, learned to exploit romantic public fantasies of what a secret service should be. Thus they ensured their survival, if not in the field then in the crucial bureaucratic battlegrounds of Washington" (Cockburn 1987: 50). From concocting mule-turd bombs and attempting to dye rivers to contemplating anti-Japanese biological weapons, anthropologists played important roles in establishing these "boyish fantasies." The fantasies sometimes delivered results; sometimes, they only added to a pose of intrigue; and at other times they were best kept classified secret so as to not publicly reveal failures or depravities. But tales of these exploits were vital justifications later used to argue for the establishment of the CIA (Winks 1987: 112). In most ways, the anthropologists at the OSS were just like the other scholars working at the agency—although at times, the practice of using cultural information they collected *against* those they studied raised ethical issues that were substantially different from those raised by the activities of other OSS employees (Price 2004c).

The OSS's 1943 "Preliminary Report on Japanese Anthropology" encouraged the sort of "no-holds barred" approach for which the OSS was so famous, although this effort found anthropologists contemplating frightening genocidal options. While a few anthropologists refused to contribute to this project, the lack of any codified anthropological ethical guidelines made such decisions purely personal ones, without any linkage to the duties or responsibilities of anthropologists. Without ethical guidelines and in an atmosphere of pressing war needs, some anthropologists acted as if there were no limits to what was allowed.

Bateson's and Coon's experiences as OSS field operatives serve as interesting contrasts. Coon seems to have deeply enjoyed his time in North Africa running covert operations and teaching terrorist tactics to local operatives. That his anthropological skills could assist him in these tasks seems to have been viewed as a bonus to him and the OSS. In his reports and his OSS historical writings, Coon appears comfortable using kidnapping as a method of extorting intelligence from Tunisian locals, and he does not appear to have had second thoughts about operating a terrorist training school. For Coon, these were the necessities of warfare.

Unlike Coon, after the war Gregory Bateson came to regret some of the means he undertook in the field. Perhaps Bateson's actions were undertaken with the sort of dynamics that were examined by the sociologists Solomon Asch, Irving Janis, Stanley Milgram, and Philip Zimbardo in which institutional and group forces converge to get individuals to undertake role-based acts that they otherwise would not. The professional and scientific codes of ethics that evolved in the postwar period are marked by different specific contents, but each is designed to remove social scientists from such institutional pressures.

Bateson recognized the necessity of the war, but he also worried about the outcomes of anthropology's tactical wartime contributions and its alignments with colonial forces. In 1944, Bateson wrote a letter to his wife, Margaret Mead, recounting a brief encounter on an Indian train with a British colonial character right out of the pages of Kipling. After discussing some negative impacts of British colonialism in India, Bateson wrote about a long train journey with a real old style Blimp—a lt. Col. in one of the crack native regiments. And he was grand. Two or three times he spotted troops from some regiment that he had served with and he would then hop out of the train and go and get the latest gossip of his old regiment—using the native languages for rapport purposes—very broken evidently but unusually good cadence. And then he would tell me stories of training his troops— every story would show (and perhaps boast of) his human understanding of his men—and several times when he had demonstrated his human under- standing of them he would feel a need to cover himself and interject, "You see—just animals—that's what these people are—just animals."

And perhaps there is some truth in it—that to him his soldiers are trained animals—dogs or horses—entitled therefore to all the love and understand- ing which he would lavish on an animal which he had trained. Certainly his knowledge and understanding of the civilian population was much slighter —and he lacked not only knowledge but also any sort of interest in them— but still there was a warmth about his behavior which made it tolerable— gust, blustering and violent, and I felt that his violence was forgiven and even enjoyed by the recipients.[43]

These contacts and subordinate relations with military men such as this colonel simultaneously amused and bothered Bateson. It was this lending of anthropol- ogy to those who saw "his" conscripted colonized troops as "just animals" that troubled him during and after the war (Price 1998b).

Coon's vision of the role of postwar intelligence and covert operations proved prescient. The oss was disbanded in on October 1, 1945—but, more accurately, its unique form and many of its personnel (along with those of agencies such as the Central Intelligence Group) were essentially transformed into the CIA under the National Security Act of 1947. Some anthropologists who had worked for the oss during the war and a new generation of postwar anthropologists made careers at the new agency, some of them secretly straddling the worlds of academe and government intelligence. Scholarly work that reveals the revolving door between the intelligence community and academe during the Cold War suggests that many of the connections established during the war continued to function quietly as many intelligence veterans took on increasingly prominent roles in public and private institutions (Price 2003a, 2003b; *Studies in Intelligence* 1983; Winks 1987).

CHAPTER ELEVEN

Postwar Ambiguities:

Looking Back at the War

> The crisis consists precisely in the fact that the old is dying and the new cannot be born;
> in this interregnum, morbid phenomena of the most varied kind come to pass.
> —ANTONIO GRAMSCI (1937: 32–33)

The world that emerged after the war was changed in ways both obvious and subtle. Those who waged the war were not the only ones whose worlds were transformed. Cultures around the world were profoundly affected. The impacts of the war on the populations of warring nations are well and thoroughly documented; the effects on the indigenous peoples traditionally subjected to the anthropological studies of the mid-twentieth century, however, tended to be minimized in the postwar period's classic ethnographies.[1] The war brought changes to a global economic system that had already been transformed by the Depression. Disruptions of shipping routes and shortages of ores, petroleum, rubber, and other natural resources affected populations that owned, procured, or lived in proximity to these vital commodities. Anthropologists were not just observers or recorders of these changing conditions. In some instances, anthropologists studying these commodities used their professional training to gain advantages for their nations. It was oil that had brought the Japanese army to Java, and rubber, oil, and other natural resources helped bring American anthropologists to South America after the war.

American soldiers returning home were also transformed. Some tried to return to the lives they knew before the war; others enrolled in colleges under the generous provisions of the GI Bill of Rights, itself a program designed to alleviate the economic, social, and political difficulties of suddenly introducing millions of workers into an economy still damaged by the Great Depression. Campus enrollments bulged as veterans taking advantage of the GI Bill enrolled en masse.

Most anthropologists left their colleagues at the oss, owi, sis, and wra and headed back to campus, where they tried to return to roles left behind when duty called.[2] But the war and its legacy were not easily left behind.

The war not only transformed—in some cases, ended—the lives of those who fought it. It also transformed the disciplines that waged it. Such changes were obvious in fields such as biology, physics, chemistry, and medicine, where tangible products like aviation improvements, penicillin, rocketry, and radar provided evident milestones. The social sciences and humanities were equally altered by the challenges anthropologists faced during the war. The arts and humanities amplified the chaos of the post–Holocaust world, and the social sciences spread out to account for the world of culture in ways old and new. In the decades after the war, some strands of American anthropology reacted to the madness of the world of warfare, turning toward escapist, authorial-heavy narratives that focused on structural and poststructural analysis that stepped back from acknowledging the primacy of economic forces. But such descriptive approaches necessarily diminished anthropologists' responsibility to acknowledge the political economy of fieldwork settings, even acts of genocide (Price 2003b).

America emerged from the war not only as a victor, but also as the most prominent nation among the Allied forces not to have sustained significant battle damage at home. America's spoils of victory were acquired not as the traditional looted plunder of war but in the nation's ability to dominate the global patron–client relations that more fully emerged in the postwar period. One importance to anthropology of America's new role in the postwar world was that wartime trajectories of sponsored research continued in new ways. During the war, anthropologists had learned to perform directed research tasks, and these developments were not lost on private and government research funding agencies as funding opportunities rose to a new prominence after the war. Anthropologists crossed over the lines separating war and peace—or, more accurately, wartime and Cold Wartime—and they brought with them attitudes concerning duty, service, and the pursuit of funding-directed research that they learned during the war. As Eric Wolf and Joseph Jorgensen observed, anthropologists' transitions in the 1940s were crucial because, "as World War II slipped imperceptibly into the Cold War of the late Forties, anthropologists found that they could build readily upon the varieties of experience gained during the shooting war" (Wolf and Jorgensen 1970: 32). Cross-cultural studies were given a boost as the Human Relations Area File emerged from George Murdock's Cross-Cultural Survey. Area-study centers were awash in funds, generating interest and new possibilities to study what had previously been remote languages from around the world. Statistical analyses took on new importance beyond the subdiscipline of physical anthropology as linguistic anthropologists, archaeologists, and cultural anthropologists began to infuse elements of statistical analysis that had been used in wartime, and culture and personality studies blossomed with hitherto unimaginable funding from military and other government sources (Price 2003b).

The primacy of the wartime economy not only shifted the patriotic fervor of soldiers and their families, it shifted all ideological components of American life. Anthropological theory was no less or more immune than other ideational features. Some of the ways that American anthropology's theoretical developments grew from a political economy of total warfare were clear; others were more easily concealed by an overgrowth of wartime ideology.[3] The theories and methods refined to study culture at a distance and the methods used to collect and catalogue culture-trait data for the IHR's Cross-Cultural Survey had obvious roots in the war. While American anthropologists had pioneered culture and personality studies back in the 1930s, the war revived and propagated the spread of culture and personality studies throughout the discipline, and derivative, psychologically idealized culture studies spread after the war. Applied anthropology's wartime birth launched many of its practitioners on seldom considered, undemocratic trajectories that accepted the propriety of manipulating the public for the promise of a greater good rather than developing applied strains that stressed advocacy over manipulation. All of these developments spilled over into the "peacetime" world in which postwar anthropology thrived—even as the McCarthyistic limits of postwar anthropological theory cajoled anthropologists to eliminate studies of class and inequality or avoid incorporating openly materialist analysis, and the militant advocacy for racial, economic, or gender equality (Price 2004a, 2008).

American anthropologists quickly positioned themselves and their discipline to adapt to the postwar world, and they used the skills they had honed during wartime as anthropology changed to meet postwar opportunities. In 1945, the AAA once again held its annual meeting in an open academic setting, meeting at the Museum of the University of Pennsylvania. At this first postwar meeting, the AAA "voted that, given the great influence of anthropologists in enemy countries on the thinking of the post-war population of these countries, a committee, chaired by Carleton Coon, along with members Gregory Bateson, Earl Count, Melville Herskovits and Alfred Métraux, be appointed to investigate the possibility of strengthening the hands of non-Nazi anthropologists in enemy countries."[4]

To assist American anthropologists' adjustment to peacetime, the Social Science Research Council administered "Demobilization Awards" fellowships and grants to anthropologists younger than thirty-six who held Ph.D.s to help the scholars resume their professional careers after the war.[5] In 1945–46, David Aberle, Joseph Casagrande, Albert Damon, George Fathauer, Joseph Greenberg, George Harris, Jack Harris, Marion Levy, Horace Miner, Marvin Opler, Morris Opler, John Roberts, Dimitri Shimkin, Allan Smith, and Evon Vogt received Demobilization Awards. The John Simon Guggenheim Memorial Foundation sponsored "Post-Service Fellowships" to help veterans make smooth transitions from the war to academia.[6]

Ralph Beals and Julian Steward sought funds from the National Research Council to compile a history of American anthropology's contributions to the war efforts.[7] Steward suggested that the NRC might fund about fifteen thousand dollars for the project, but focused considerations of wartime anthropology were not forthcoming as the postwar uses of the discipline took on a growing importance.[8] The National Research Council convened a meeting at the war's end to discuss the coming roles for anthropology and other social sciences in the postwar world. Margaret Mead, Father John Cooper, Ruth Benedict, Regina Flannery, Clyde Kluckhohn, and Julian Steward represented the field as they used wartime anthropology's contributions to campaign for postwar research funds.[9] It soon became obvious that the Allied forces' victory would provide to anthropologists the sort of pelf befitting victors of such a global struggle. The AAA was reorganized to better position itself to receive the new levels of postwar funding that were soon to be disbursed to all who would direct their research in ways of interest to public and private funding agencies (Frantz 1974). Anthropology quickly positioned itself for the rapid funding developments and prosperity that came at the war's end, but like that of other veterans, anthropologists' writings of this period seldom publicly looked back at the war in any depth.

Ethnographies set in recent battle theaters tended not to mention the recent violence, and whatever traumas affected these communities were often ignored or represented as part of the culture's baseline. The filters modulating the scientific tenor of the ethnographic voices removed former soldiers' personal wartime experiences or flashbacks from the ethnographies produced in the postwar years. In the worlds of most postwar ethnographies, it was almost as if the war had not happened, and the "natural laboratories" where many cultural anthropologists conducted research were represented as lands that time forgot, untouched by the ravages of the modern age. Questions remained about the impact of the war on the development of anthropology and anthropologists. In 1953, Frederick Johnson mused, "World War II probably had a profound effect upon Anthropology but the generalizations coming from the many personal experiences which are the sources of knowledge concerning diversion, expansion and distortion are not available and present records in the science cannot be fully understood" (Johnson 1953: 3). Such open ponderings were rare and seldom publicly addressed. But even if the imprint of the war was not explicitly acknowledged, it was always there.

Anthropology: What Is It Good For?

Given the nature of the war and the range of anthropologists' skills, the tasks undertaken by American anthropologists during the war were logical ones. But this observation does not clarify whether anthropologists should have undertaken all of these tasks, nor does it address later questions asking whether ethical limits should govern the uses of anthropology.

Fieldwork is such a natural cover for espionage that, over the past century, countless innocent researchers have aroused suspicion. Using anthropologists to train native peoples to fight as guerrillas was also a logical and effective application of anthropologists' skill sets. Edmund Leach's use of the Kachin in Burma, Tom Harrisson's training of the Sarawakan Kelabit, and Carleton Coon's use of trained assassins in North Africa each contributed to the Allied victory over the Axis. Gregory Bateson used his cultural knowledge to spread lies under oss black-propaganda operations. John Embree used ethnographic knowledge gained in peacetime against his host nation during the war.[10] Dozens of anthropologists used their ethnographic skills to observe imprisoned Japanese Americans, writing reports to be read by those who designed and managed these shameful camps. Anthropologists informed the oss's efforts to develop anti-Japanese biological weapons.

These anthropological contributions were all useful to the American war effort, but some of them had long-term costs that were not considered at the time. It is not that the choices made by these World War Two anthropologists were necessarily wrong choices (perhaps some were and some were not)—most of them may well have been *necessary*, given the bad choices faced in wartime. But these decisions changed American anthropology—or, at a minimum, they openly reconnected American anthropology to its international colonial roots and to the larger economic forces that were exerting an influence on the manufacture and consumption of American social science. Some of these choices inevitably contributed to a desensitization that changed anthropology during and after the war (see Nader 2001: 167). During the war, few anthropologists considered what would be done with their contributions after they were made. In dynamics similar to those experienced by Robert Oppenheimer and others consumed with working on the Manhattan Project, the immediate challenges at hand consumed their attention, and only later were questions raised about the propriety of some actions.

What does it mean that anthropologists used their professional backgrounds to do such things as generate propagandistic lies or train local operatives to kill or kidnap? Perhaps it only means that this is what all people find themselves doing in times of war. Perhaps these acts revealed the lurking potential uses of an ethnographic knowledge that passively justified the funding of such a seemingly impractical discipline. That such acts were undertaken during times of total war—or during what has become for so many the last "*Good War*"—comforts some, but those who find comfort have little hope of identifying consistent means of determining when such acts are acceptable. Perhaps the Nazis provided all the identification that is needed, but the acceptance of such practices in one circumstance opens the possibility that such practices can occur in *any* circumstance.

But even conceding these points, I remain troubled by some of what American anthropologists did in the war. Anthropologists faced hard decisions, and some of the ones they made were dead wrong. While my presentist reading finds that only a small percentage of anthropology's contributions to the war clearly violated coming postwar ethical norms, such actions by these few damaged American anthropology's credibility, and American anthropologists' refusal to critically examine these events continues to provide justifications for a wide range of interactions with military and intelligence agencies that are seldom openly examined.

My reading of anthropological contributions to the war leaves me ambivalent. Using anthropology to combat and defeat fascism seems, in retrospect, to have been not only logical but also a noble undertaking under conditions of total warfare. But even conditions of total war do not mean that anthropologists should have done everything they did. While these actions are understandable from a historicist point of view, if we are to learn from this past to contemplate present and future calls to war, historicism fails to help us learn from this past in ways that presentism can. While most of the anthropological applications to the war seem appropriate for their time, some uses of anthropology seem, from the present, to have crossed lines of propriety, even under conditions of total warfare.

The OSS's emphasis on the use of unorthodox means created an institutional environment that fostered some amoral practices. When anthropologists joined the oss, their work damaged the credibility of anthropology in ways that are not easily repaired. Coon's use of his anthropological experience to train assassins and kidnappers was wrong, and his visions of a postwar American empire using covert operations to maintain hegemonic control prefigured where such unbridled acts would later lead the CIA as it thwarted international law to launch coups, develop plans to assassinate world leaders, and subvert democratic movements that were not to its liking. Even the deskbound anthropologists and other social scientists within the oss's Research and Analysis Branch were encouraged to follow depraved paths. The genocidal fantasies of "Preliminary Report on Japanese Anthropology" left American anthropology positioned but one step removed from complicity in genocide. Although there is comfort in finding that some anthropologists cautioned against such pursuits, it remains disturbing to find *any* anthropologists complying with such degenerate requests. The cocksure environment at the oss nurtured such dreams, and this free-for-all environment pushed Bateson and others to use anthropology in ways that they came to regret after the fever of war cooled.

Given the AAA's 1919 censure of Boas, it was logical that Samuel Lothrop reprised his role as one of the spies who "prostituted science by using it as a cover for their activities as spies" (Boas 1919). Lothrop did not give a damn about Boas's complaint, and the AAA's official stance invited his duplicity. But Lothrop, Clothier, and unidentified others used respectable museums, research institutes, funding foundations, and universities (some of which wittingly participated in this fraud), to falsely establish pretenses of archaeological fieldwork to facilitate spying for the sis, and this duplicity created problems for future archaeologists. Lothrop's well-established institutional backers knowingly assisted the fraud. That they have never publicly described, much less renounced, their participation in such espionage schemes raises serious questions in the present.

Anthropological studies of interned Japanese Americans were used for differing ends, but instances of anthropologists working in the camps secretly informing on internees betray basic assumptions of trust assumed between ethnographers and the people they study. The varied studies in the WRA camps also articulated an ongoing feature of anthropological projects' occurring in settings featuring military occupation. Such research blurs the lines that demarcate when anthropologists studying cultures under military control are helping groups adjust to each others' differences (thereby arguably lessening risks or increasing the quality of life) and when they are enabling military conquest or subjugation (see Rubinstein 2003a, 2003b). These remain troubling issues today, as anthropologists—or, more frequently, military or intelligence personnel who have co-opted anthropological cultural conceptions for their own uses—are brought into war zones to instruct soldiers on the basic cultural features of those they are occupying or conquering. This information that can simultaneously reduce civilian casualties (by sensitizing edgy troops, with fingers on hair triggers, to understand that "suspicious" actions might have different cultural meanings) and enable unjust or illegal military occupations. These are old issues. As John Embree observed at the Second World War's end, when "helping military government to govern a population without bloodshed one is aiding a dictatorship to avoid trouble with the masses, but—and this is the applied anthropologist's point of view—one is also helping to avoid the sorts of decisions that not only will lead to more trouble and expense for the administrators, but that will also lead to greater harshness of treatment of a people by the temporary governors" (Embree 1946: 494). Assuming that all of American anthropologists' contributions to the Second World War were wrapped in glory prevents us from understanding how complicated such anthropological interactions were and are.

But even though some Americans applied anthropology in ethically questionable ways during the war, these acts were not as egregious as were those of their enemies. As the historian Michael Bess has observed, Hermann Goering was wrong in his arguments at the Nuremberg Trials when he claimed that in war all nations and actors equally shared in the atrocities. Bess correctly rejected the logic of Goering's defense, writing, "Each nation, each people, has to deal with its own measure of accountability for the moral transgressions it committed. We need to make detailed, exacting distinctions among the barbaric behaviors of wartime, assigning proper responsibility to each perpetrator in due proportion to the gravity of the deeds done and the policies pursued" (Bess 2006: 8–9). And just as each nation must deal with such accountings, anthropologists need to account for its field's actions and inactions in World War Two and the wars that followed.

That the Nazis were such evil enemies made it inviting to use anthropology in the war, but this invitation did not obliterate questions about whether ethical problems are inherent in using anthropology for warfare. If anything, it clarified them. Cultures do not only establish taboos and prohibitions for things that are repellent; such limits are most frequently established for things that hold ongoing attractions. It is because of the natural attractions of using anthropology for intelligence work or warfare that ethical limits for the uses anthropology are necessary. Without limits, anthropology too easily becomes, as Laura Thompson warned, nothing more than a tool for the highest bidder. If this is all that anthropology is to become, then the world's people had best be warned when they see anthropologists coming. The uses of anthropology in wartime clarify why the field needs something like a Plimsoll line to demarcate the limits of appropriate anthropological contributions to war.

Even if it is successfully argued that it was necessary for anthropologists to undertake everything they did during the war, arguments of necessity do not set limits on the future applications of such practices, and precedents are always seen by some as invitations. Anthropologists' involvement in World War Two's guerrilla campaigns opened the door for anthropologists to play a surprising number of supportive roles in future ventures in American capitalism's Cold War proxy battles with communism. Most of those undertaking these roles justified their actions under the precedents established in the Second World War, just as the latest wave of anthropologists supporting President Bush's "war on terrorism" justify their positions using the same arguments claiming an indiscriminate sanctity of World War Two's anthropological contributions (McFate 2005; Moos 2002; Simons 2003; Wax 2002; cf. Price 2005d, 2005e). American anthropologists need to begin to carefully examine this past before using it to justify contemporary actions.

Because anthropologists' Second World War contributions were so routinely ignored by their superiors, it can be difficult to establish how significant their contributions to the war really were. Anthropologists are not to blame for the failures of the War Department and the White House as they ignored evidence that the Japanese were ready to surrender prior to the atomic bombing of Hiroshima and Nagasaki, or for the ignored recommendations at the owi, oss, White House, and other agencies. Conditions of warfare necessarily intensify the problems of clients' not listening to anthropologist-consultants, an ongoing problem that is common to applied anthropological work in any setting. As Delmos Jones observed, "When policy makers don't listen, this could mean [applied anthropologists] are not telling them what they want to hear" (Jones 1976: 227).

As anthropologists find themselves in recurrent advisory roles in which their advice is ignored or unwelcome, questions are raised about the wisdom of continuing to take on such roles. The failures of anthropologists at the owi to cut through civilian and military prejudices concerning the Japanese raised serious questions for all anthropological interactions with military and intelligence agencies. Anthropologists should question the wisdom of such advisory relationships when there is so little evidence that military and intelligence agencies actually use anthropologists to expand their understanding of such situations. The owi seemed to be looking for anthropologists to justify decisions that had already been made or to more easily implement policies. One lesson for contemporary anthropologists to learn from the experiences of OWI anthropologists might be that anthropologists have an equal, if not better, chance to influence policy decisions by remaining outside the military and intelligence organizations. Working for military or intelligence agencies diminishes anthropologists' abilities to speak out to the press, to other scholars, to Congress, and in other public venues, and internal pressures limit internal critiques.

Today, we should question anthropology's disciplinary intelligence as it repeatedly submits its knowledge to military and intelligence agencies with hopes that these agencies will somehow do something more than selectively use the knowledge for their own predetermined purposes, while discarding vital anthropological analyses at odds with deeply rooted institutional features. Such repeated transactions have been fueled by a general lack of historical considerations of relationships between anthropologists and such organizations, as well as ideographic mixtures of individual anthropologists' sense of patriotic duty, naïveté, employment needs, or cynicism.

During the war, American anthropologists' work conformed to the demands of the U.S. wartime political economy. This occurred in several ways. Some war agencies, such as the CIAA, the IHR, and the ISA, focused anthropologists' attention on specific cultural areas of research tied to war needs. Other war agencies, such as the OSS, M Project, and SIS, undertook research or collected information in ways that would have been unacceptable during times of peace, and anthropologists were asked to think toward specific ends. While most of the data used by anthropologists during the war were available at leading American university libraries, secrecy was a central element in all of this work, and conditions of secrecy warped some of the results produced by war anthropologists.

While secrecy is an important component of military and intelligence endeavors, it is antithetical to the academic production of knowledge and the functioning of a scientific environment that fosters falsifiability or debate. In a number of instances, wartime secrecy created conditions that helped anthropologists produce work that would not have survived the scrutiny of a peer-review process. Mission-centered social-science applications were susceptible to reduced self-criticism and skepticism, but the addition of secrecy to such pursuits disabled basic "self-corrective" features of academic processes. Because secrecy removed the institutional checks and balances of humanistic or normal scientific endeavors, anthropologists pursued some ideas long after they would have perished in an environment that required oversight (see Merton 1968: 611). Obvious examples of these failures included the Research and Analysis Branch's investigation into possible biological weaknesses of the Japanese and the M Project's base assumptions that the world was full of "empty" places where refugees should or could be moved at the convenience of American policymakers.[11]

Even with these limitations, the Second World War demonstrated to military and intelligence agencies that anthropologists had knowledge, intelligence, and skills that could contribute to the waging of war. The war's demonstration of these uses expanded anthropology's horizons. But this expansion did not clarify anthropology's *purpose(s)*, as some learned to see the discipline as a tool not only for understanding culture, but also for manipulating it. Perhaps it was because Americans had fought against such clearly oppressive forces during the Second World War that postwar anthropologists had such unrealistic expectations that their future applied-anthropology military projects would be directed for honorable ends such as freedom and liberation. The optimism accompanying the Allied victory dangerously curtailed skepticism of the outcomes that might come from a social science more directly harnessed to the desires of state and corporate powers.

Nazi and Japanese threats made anthropology's total cooperation a natural act, and the war atrocities of Axis nations made it easy to ignore the nosocomial complications that lingered on the *corpus anthropology* as it emerged from the war. The anthropologists who went on to make careers at the CIA in the late 1940s through 1960s often entered the agencies through doors opened in the Second World War, with little thought of the complications. The Second World War should have warned anthropologists that their discipline had applications beyond those perceived or intended by most ethnographic fieldworkers, but there are but scattered traces of such findings in postwar anthropological writings. The hitching of science to warfare under conditions of secrecy transformed the scientific process—or, at least, it laid bare how outcome-based science could easily be used to harm others. The needs of warfare muted ethical debates during the war, and after the victory, some time passed before most anthropologists were willing to reconsider the ethics of contributing anthropology to warfare. As American anthropologists later considered anthropological ethics, their field's contributions to World War Two were often in their minds, although the specific details of the contributions remained unexamined.

Ethics, Smethics?

The Second World War was not the first time American anthropologists faced pressures to contribute their ethnographic skills and knowledge to warfare, but it was the first war in which they joined the fight with such impact and unanimity.

James Mooney's actions during the previous century established important precedents for ethically disengaging anthropological research from military campaigns, but such considerations were rarely discussed during the war. I raise this point not to impugn those who applied anthropology during the war, but to add a historicist clarity underlining that ethical notions maintaining a primal responsibility to protecting the interests of studied populations over those of the nation's military interests had previously been articulated by anthropologists. Thus, it is not overly presentist to inquire of the ethical questions raised by anthropologists' using their discipline for the war. It may simply be that principles of a "just war" or the seriousness of the Nazi threat overrode such concerns, but these questions were generally left unanswered or unaddressed during the war.

In 1917, Boas argued not that anthropology should never be used in support of war. Instead, he argued that anthropologists' "first duties are to humanity as a whole, and that, in a conflict of duties, our obligations to humanity are of higher value than those toward the nation; in other words, that patriotism must be subordinated to humanism" (Boas 1945 [1917]: 156). It follows that a vital question in considering a consistent Boasian view of the anthropological uses of the Second World War might be: Did the Axis threat align American anthropologists' Boasian vision of "obligations to humanity" with their obligations toward their nation (thereby folding the calls of patriotism within the larger envelope of "obligations to humanity")? While the answer to this question appears clearly to be yes, the resolution of this point does not address Boas's fundamental complaint that anthropology must not serve as a cover for espionage.

Logically, there are deeper fundamental questions embedded within Boas's 1919 position that anthropology must not serve as a front for espionage. One such question concerns the propriety of anthropology's serving not as a *front* for intelligence work, but as a *back*. This question asks whether it is proper to take cultural information (or analytical techniques) anthropologically collected openly during times of peace and use this information against this culture later, during times of war. If Boas's position is temporally unbound (if the order in which anthropologists conduct fieldwork and become spies is seen as insignificant), then the issues of secretly using anthropology as a war weapon become much more complicated. At a minimum, anthropologists should protect those who share their lives with them when political winds shift against those studied. Ethnographic relationships of trust assume that some level of secrecy should be used to shield those whom anthropologists study. If such relationships can so easily be brushed aside during times of war, then it is incumbent on all contemporary fieldworkers to inform those they meet in the field of the apparently dangerously fickle nature of these interactions.

If, as Peter Pels has argued, "it is easy to unmask the ethical policies of colonialism by referring to their practical politics," then it should be similarly easy to unmask the "ethical policies" embedded in anthropological activities during the Second World War (Pels 1999: 106). But the Axis threat made the "practical politics" of the Second World War simultaneously simple and complex —simple because total warfare was the only way to combat the Nazis, and complex because an anthropology without limits invites unknown future evils. Before and during the Second World War, American anthropologists had not yet developed explicit ethical codes of conduct, so individual anthropologists found themselves negotiating the ethical demands of wartime anthropology without much professional guidance. This kept things pretty uncomplicated for most wartime anthropologists. Some later anthropologists came to view the Second World War era's lack of professional ethics as securing some sort of state of un-Mirandized bliss, wherein anthropologists' wartime actions could not be critically evaluated later under conditions of *nullum crimen sine lege*. This position is logical but unsatisfying. Without wrestling with Dostoyevsky's Grand Inquisitor, it can be argued that stating nothing was forbidden is not the same thing as stating that everything was permitted.

In the decades before the war, uncodified informal professional standards of practice had emerged among American anthropologists. These practices included such basic things as not tying anthropological outcomes to the needs of state, not using native informants to kill other people, not kidnapping people, not meticulously designing and spreading lies to trick people into taking desired actions. But the needs of war swept aside these uncodified standards of practice. The feeling observed in the weeks after Pearl Harbor "among the younger generation that the Association had dragged its feet in giving active support" to the war appears to have marked a hesitation that signified some awareness that American anthropology was poised to cross a murkily identified ethical Rubicon (Stocking 1976: 37).

Even as anthropologists in great numbers committed themselves to the war effort, some, such as Laura Thompson and Gregory Bateson, questioned whether there might be something wrong with using anthropology as a means toward ends that were to be determined by others. In the years after the war, as an outcome of the Nuremberg Trials, professional anthropological societies slowly developed ethical codes. The SFAA was the first American anthropological professional association to codify an ethics statement. The effort grew directly out of the questions raised by American anthropologists serving in the war. In 1947, the SFAA's membership was sent a draft of the proposed "Statement on Ethics," and while the code clarified some of the responsibilities and limits of anthropologists working in commercial or government settings, most questions about wartime anthropology were left unresolved.

But given the issues raised by the use of anthropology in the war, some anthropologists found elements of the SFAA's postwar ethics code to be lacking. In early 1947, Thompson raised concerns that the proposed ethics code did not address fundamental issues pertaining to the ethical limits of anthropological activities. Thompson complained to the SFAA committee drafting the ethics statement that the scope of activities it addressed had not been fully explored by the membership. She worried that the presentation of such a finalized draft would limit informed discussions of what constituted the proper limits of applied anthropology and how such limits might be regulated or delineated:

> My contention is that we should first, at least, make explicit the problem so far as possible, with the help of scientists who have been trained in philosophy and ethics and also the various types of applied anthropologists. Before even drawing up a code of ethics, it seems to me that we should consider the problem of whether our role is to be social engineers whose basic function is developing techniques for the more effective manipulation of human beings in the interest of government, pressure groups, or in the lines of group social therapy. These are two entirely different lines of development and the code of ethics, which is being circulated, is a code for social engineers and not for social therapists. If we accept this code, we may influence the cultural trend along the road toward more and more efficient social engineers and social manipulation, rather than social therapy. This, I think, will be almost inevitable.
>
> The difficulty which faces us now that we have been asked to comment on the code is that no amount of changing of this word and that will change the basic implication underlying the present tentative code.[12]

As the primary author of the draft, Margaret Mead replied somewhat defensively to Thompson's complaints that the SFAA's membership would discuss these concerns at the upcoming meeting before voting on the proposal. But Thompson believed a floor discussion would be a difficult place to seriously address her core issues of concern. Such meetings by their nature tend to adopt and advance or reject outright policy matters, and such settings are not conducive to thoughtful discussions. Mead wrote to Thompson that these concerns could be raised at the upcoming SFAA meetings, but Mead objected to constructing the sort of ethics code limiting anthropology's scope that Thompson was proposing. Mead wrote,

"It is at this discussion that I think your suggested statements should be presented. I hope you will also have them in writing so that the Committee will be able to cover them."[13]

Following Mead's suggestion, Thompson drafted a document titled "Suggestions and Additions to the Draft of the 'Preliminary Report of the Committee on Ethics'" and sent it to the SFAA Committee on Ethics. Thompson identified several problems in the draft code, the most significant of which concerned the committee's decision to leave decisions about applying anthropology in warfare up to individuals. Thompson was disappointed that "the Committee felt that whether anthropology was to be applied destructively in the interests of a national state was a matter which must be left up to the conscience of the individual member and upon which the Society could not presume to make recommendations."[14]

As Thompson foresaw, discussions of such fundamental issues proved futile in a meeting intent on passing the document forged by a committee. Thompson was bothered by the way that the code was railroaded through the committee. After the SFAA approved the ethics code, Thompson wrote a letter to *Commentary* criticizing the association for ignoring questions concerning the proper limits of anthropological applications:

> During the war most of the social scientists of this country were mobilized toward the immediate task of winning a speedy victory. Their efforts were oriented toward a single practical goal. But now that the war is over, we are squarely faced with a dilemma. Is applied social science to develop into a set of skills for the more precise manipulation of people in the interests of management? Or is it to become a scientific discipline of social therapy in the interests of group hygiene and social welfare? Are practical social scientists to become technicians whose skills are on the market for sale to the highest bidder? Or are they to develop a code of professional ethics which will orient them to strive toward long-range humanitarian goals? On the resolution for this issue hangs not only the practical function and developmental trend of the social sciences but also, it may be, the personal welfare of millions.[15]

After two and a half years of meetings and several revisions, the SFAA adopted the ethics code at its Philadelphia meeting in 1948 (Mead et al. 1949: 20). The code stressed anthropologists' responsibilities "for the effects of his recommendations . . . to promote a state of dynamic equilibrium within systems of human relationships." It made vague commitments to holism and declarations of good work, and it encouraged social responsibility and honesty (Mead et al. 1949:20).

One section the code did generically address issues of relevance to wartime anthropological applications, stating, "The applied anthropologist should recognize a special responsibility to use his skill in such a way as to prevent any occurrence which will set in motion a train of events which involves irreversible losses of health or the loss of life to individuals or groups or irreversible damage to the natural productivity of the physical environment" (Mead et al. 1949: 21). But even this general statement not to bring "losses of health or the loss of life to individuals or groups" skirted Thompson's questions of limits for wartime anthropology.

The SFAA's 1963 revised ethics statement focused primarily on the contractual obligations of applied anthropologists, but the statement bluntly declared, "If an anthropologist has reason to believe that his work will be used in a manner harmful to his fellow men or to science, then he must decline to make his services available" (Human Organization 1963 22: 237). This proclamation, if taken literally, would have precluded many anthropologists' activities during the Second World War—although baroque arguments could always be constructed maintaining that apparently harmful acts were in the long run not harmful but "helpful."

The AAA did not issue a code of ethics until after the public disclosure of Project Camelot, a non-classified Defense Department program that used anthropologists and other social scientists to study counterinsurgency in Latin America (see Horowitz 1967). Strong public reactions to Project Camelot pressed the AAA to produce its first "Statement on Problems of Anthropological Research and Ethics" in 1967 (FNAAA 1967). The statement declared, "Constraint, deception, and secrecy have no place in science" and that, unless a declaration of war was declared by Congress, anthropologists should not undertake clandestine or classified research (FNAAA 1967).[16] The negotiated distinction that covert military and intelligence research was allowable under conditions of declared war was influenced by senior anthropologists who had contributed to the Second World War. But such distinctions were unsatisfying to some. As one critic of this wartime-ethics-reprieve clause observed, this simply meant that anthropologists were to "turn off [their] ethics during wartime . . . and turn them on again during the interim" (Frucht 1967: 8).[17] This was an indecisive solution to the issues raised by using anthropology for harm.

In 1971, the AAA adopted a new "Statement of Professional Responsibility," which proclaimed that all anthropologists' reports should be available to the public, anthropologists had primary responsibilities to those they studied, and covert research should not be conducted. This statement was crafted in the shadows of

America's military misadventures in Southeast Asia and revelations that anthropologists were covertly contributing to these wars (Hickey 2003; Wakin 1992). The 1971 statement was so radical in its pronouncements that arguably a great many of anthropology's contributions to World War Two would have been deemed unethical by its standards.

In the 1980s, pressure from increasing numbers of anthropologists working for corporations and government and nongovernmental agencies led to an effort to significantly revise the code of ethics, but these efforts were rejected by the AAA's membership in a 1984 vote (see Fluehr-Lobban 2003: 13–15). In 1990, the AAA membership voted to revise the ethics code. Among the approved changes was language removing explicit condemnations of clandestine research. This significant change was enacted primarily because of concerns expressed by anthropologists producing proprietary reports in corporate and government settings, but the decision opened the doors to the CIA and other agencies that wanted to hire anthropologists (Fluehr-Lobban 2003: 12–14). Amid these changes there emerged some widespread confusion regarding the appropriate use of secrecy to protect sponsors under standards of secrecy developed to protect research subjects (Price 2006a, 2007).

Far more than the proprietary pressures of industry, or laissez-faire arguments about academic freedom, it has been anthropologists' contributions to the Second World War that have silently loomed large in the background of American anthropologists' periodic reexaminations of their professional ethics.[18] The decided silence self-imposed by members of the generation that waged this war with anthropology has made it difficult to evaluate the range of anthropological contributions to the war, much the less the meaning of those contributions. This silence not only limits our understanding; it damages anthropologists' ability to process and understand the past so they can act with wisdom in the present. Some of this silence appears not to be accidental. The work of a few scholars who have critically examined anthropologists' contributions to World War Two has met with hostility and unusually defensive rebuttals for breaking the negotiated silence.[19] But waiting so long to address these issues leaves anthropology in a World War Two–generation inquorate state. It is as if the legitimacy of individual anthropologists' claims to historically analyze disciplinary contributions to the war have become subjected to a twisted tontine, where reduced numbers of surviving war-era anthropologists remain to speak for those who applied anthropology in the war. And those who were not living during the war are left to understand recurrent calls to again weaponize anthropology through the broken frames of their incomplete understanding of that vital war.

Some anthropologists have suggested that the issues raised by Allied anthropological contributions to World War Two negate the possibility of constructing meaningful anthropological ethics codes. In supporting Pels's thesis that anthropology ethics codes are inherently futile enterprises, Antonius Robben has argued that American and British anthropologists' contributions to World War Two constitute one of the strongest arguments "against devising a general code of ethics" (Pels 1999; Robben 1999: 122). For Robben, these anthropologists' war-research agendas were "defined by political objectives that superseded ethical concerns. Anthropologists were applying their professional skills to defeat the very peoples they had studied in prewar times" (Robben 1999: 122). But Robben mentions only a limited summary of World War Two culture-and-personality and national-morale work to characterize anthropological contributions to the war. Such simplistic characterizations avoid the complications of anthropologists' advising the oss on race-based weapons and assisting the detention of Japanese Americans, or the long-term effects of using fieldwork as a cover for espionage or to train soldiers for enhanced military action or occupation.

Examinations of anthropological contributions to World War Two should complicate anthropologists' approach to research ethics, but these examinations should not reduce commitments to establishing ethical guidelines. Ethical codes do not descend on stone tablets from mountaintops. They are built by human hands, hearts, and minds living in particular political worlds. If ethical codes are nothing more than shifting statements of what anthropologists should and should not do, then they are useful announcements and warnings for the world anthropologists work in, and they can occasionally serve as guideposts to remind anthropologists and employers of what anthropologists should be doing.

If ethical statements always betray latent and manifest political agendas, then anthropologists cannot do better than to clearly construct ethical statements that clarify their agendas to those they study under conditions of war and peace. Anthropologists often work in worlds at war, and ethical codes can help clarify anthropology's relationships to conflict. Some anthropologists have worked to produce ethnographic work that acknowledges and documents conflicts but does not support or justify attacks, while other anthropologists have learned to more comfortably align their research with the aims of state. Anthropological ethical codes generally allow either approach, although the influence of funding opportunities increasingly favors the syncopation of research with state interests (Fisher 1983; Roelofs 2003).

The War's Transmuted Meanings:
The Cold War as a Second World War Ricochet Formation

While American anthropologists' wartime actions can be documented, sum-marized, and described, the *meanings* of those acts necessarily remain contested. The meanings are complicated not only by our historical distance from these events, but also by the ways popular understandings of the Second World War framed the events that followed.

The war's fight against fascism was a noble one, but those who committed anthropology to warfare in this context were unaware that their actions were releasing a genie from a bottle, unleashing forces they could not control in new, unimagined Cold War contexts. Once released and the wishes exhausted, the genie made its own demands in this new war, where the fight for free markets and client states supplanted the fight for freedom. The lines of ethical propriety already blurred in the Second World War were pushed aside as many anthropologists explained their contributions to the Cold War with rationalizations from World War Two without acknowledging how much had changed.

The poet John Ciardi coined the phrase "ricochet formations" to describe "the inevitable process by which language gives rise to language, a word or phrase called into being by another without which it could make no sense" (Ciardi 1987: 244). Ciardi saw the ricochet formation as a recurrent force responsible for birthing new words (like "software" or "implosion") out of preexisting, well-established words (hardware, explosion) in ways that misconstrued the mor-phological roots of the new words. Such back-constructions build on previously established morphologies and alter and aim resulting neologisms in ways that are consistent with the word's form, but they can also alter future speakers' under-standing of the antecedent term. Ciardi saw this process as largely directionless, as if extant structures roamed aimlessly, were reworked as root forms were re-cognated in ways that conformed to present and future uses, with little fidelity to root forms (though the aimlessness of these constructions remains an open question).

From a post–World War Two and post–Cold War perspective, the activities of anthropologists during the Second World War can be difficult to disentangle from the ricochet formations that emerged later. In the years after the Axis surrenders, American anthropology's optimistic wartime sense of direction was not easily shaken, even as the U.S. national-security state shifted America's international posture from a defensive one to an increasingly offensive imperial stance. For Americans who had lived through the war, anthropologists' contributions to the

"Good War" could be difficult to disarticulate from anthropological contributions to the Cold War that soon followed. Like other ricochet formations, many Cold War views were spawned by the Second World War, "without which it could make no sense" (Ciardi 1987: 224). But these were fundamentally different formations, and while the Cold War made old, familiar claims of fighting for freedom against tyranny, its victories supported more imperial ends as patron and client leverage, proxy wars, covert actions, and coups replaced the Second World War's blitzkriegs and massive counteroffensives. Later, in the 1960s and 1970s, increasing numbers of anthropologists would view Cold War interactions with intelligence agencies as problematic; a view emerged that "anthropologists who served in the Office of Strategic Services in the declared war were accepted as contributing to victory. Anthropologists who worked for the OSS's successor, the Central Intelligence Agency, were considered to be misusing their skills and compromising their profession" (Woodbury 1993: 31). But the impact of the Second World War was so strong that such views were rare in the first decade of the Cold War.

The war opened doors between the academy and the intelligence community. In the late 1940s and throughout the 1950s, few alumni of the OSS and other wartime intelligence agencies gave second thoughts to answering calls (or encouraging their students to answer such calls) for assistance from the CIA and other strategic government agencies. Their experiences in the Second World War framed such Cold War uses of anthropology, and while the threats of Nazism and Japanese expansion had long subsided, the honorable uses of anthropology for military and intelligence goals were rarely reconsidered in the early Cold War. But reconsidered or not, applying anthropological knowledge to defeat fascism and applying it to the CIA's efforts to achieve global hegemony were categorically different undertakings, although such applied-anthropology undertakings at times shared methodological bonds.

With the waves of Cold War funding for basic and directed research came other, less obvious ways to keep anthropology in harness. And while such vast funds financed far too diverse a range of anthropological projects to claim anything approaching direct hegemonic control, between the lines of the funding ledgers one could at times detect the strained tune or cadence of the Garryowen.

Preface

1 The most famous of such croppings is that acknowledged by Clifford Geertz in his book *After the Fact*. Almost three decades after the fact, Geertz uncomfortably acknowledged that his classic Balinese fieldwork transpired in the midst of genocidal warfare that he had hidden with his thick descriptions (cf. Geertz 1995; Price 2003b; Reyna 1998).

2 There are some striking exceptions to this trend. Charles Harris's and Louis Sadler's account of the archaeologist Sylvanus Morley's Central American espionage documents fascinating episodes of anthropological espionage—but as historians, Harris and Sadler's lack of concern with anthropological ethics diminishes their analysis (Harris and Sadler 2003). A few sources examined Vietnam War–era controversies (Hickey 2003; Wakin 1992), and there are a few memoirs and duty accounts of World War Two veteran-anthropologists (Coon 1980; Mead 1979). Except for Wakin's groundbreaking work, these books tend to examine—or, more often, *justify*—specific incidents while ignoring larger systemic issues of American anthropology's historical assistance in U.S. foreign wars.

3 Some anthropologists and historians have examined American anthropologists' activities during World War Two, but none has tried to synthesize a picture of the full range of anthropological activities undertaken by these applied servants of the state. Most of these works either quickly summarize the entire field's contributions to the war or they gloss over uncomfortable situations in which individuals used anthropological techniques to bring harm to people (see Mabee 1987; Yans-McLaughlin 1986b). George W. Stocking's 1976 introduction to a collection of essays published in the interwar years in the *American Anthropologist* remains an important statement of how American anthropology viewed its involvement in this war (Stocking 1976). Among the essential considerations of American anthropology during World War Two are Bennett 1947; Coon 1980; Cooper 1947; Doob 1947; Drinnon 1987; Embree 1943a; Katz 1989; Linton 1945; Price 1998b; Starn 1986; Stocking 1976; Suzuki 1981; Yans-McLaughlin 1986b.

4 The "Preface to the Phoenix Edition" of *Culture and Evolution* finds Stocking retreating from earlier statements (in a 1968 book review in *Science* 1986a) criticizing Marvin Harris's "presentivist" stance in considering the history of anthropology. Stocking's

lengthy review of *The Rise of Anthropological Theory* in *Science* had harshly criticized Harris for judging past theoretical analyses from the perspective of the present. After some reconsideration, Stocking wrote,

> I am . . . much more inclined today than when I first read Marvin Harris' *Rise of Anthropological Theory* to grant the historical utility of a strongly held present theoretical perspective. However one may feel about the reading of particular figures which seem to be required to align ancestors in the two moieties of "techno-environmental determinism" and "idealism," it seems to me that Harris not only provided a productive synthetic interpretation but in fact directed attention to problems which are historically significant, but which were not likely to be raised so long as one tried to work from within the perspective of the historical actors. (Stocking 1982 [1968]: xvii)

1 American Anthropology

1   "Preserving our Ideas" was later republished under the title "Patriotism." Ironically, during the attacks of the McCarthy period, Melville Herskovits wondered how Boas's essay "could ever have been regarded as other than a tightly-argued, intellectual presentation of idealistic principles" (Herskovits 1952: 116).

2   By this time, Mooney's advocacy for native rights had so marginalized him that his protests provided no assistance to Frachternberg (see Moses 1984: 199).

3   Hoffman's recommendations to the NRC and the National Academy of Science were also signed by W. H. Holmes, C. B. Davenport, G. M. Kober, Aleš Hrdlička, Madison Grant, E. A. Hooton, and Tom Williams (Hoffman 1918: 28). Hoffman found in Chicago in 1913 "11,920 applicants for enlistment, with 9,342 rejections, or 78.4 per cent.; in New York, 17,055 applicants for enlistment, with 13,758 rejections, or 80.6 per cent.; in Savannah, New Orleans and Little Rock, 3,855 applicants for enlistment, with 3,011 rejections or 781 per cent.; in San Francisco, 5,504 applicants for enlistment, with 4,443 rejections, or 80.7 per cent" (Hoffman 1918: 22). Between 1913 and 1915, more than 75 percent of the army's volunteers were rejected (Hoffman 1918: 22–23), but once America entered the war, the army relaxed its recruiting standards.

4   V. M. Kaikini's "Anthropological Observations on Indian Troops during the World War" was published in the *Journal of the Anthropological Society of Bombay*. These observations consisted of Kaikini's personal evaluations of the fighting capacities of ethnic, caste, and tribal groups of India, such as various Sikh groups, Marathas, Gharwalis, and the Gurkha (Kaikini 1953).

5   Leslie White's experience of the destructiveness of war left him with deep questions of how humankind could do such things. William Peace wrote,

> Undoubtedly the war was a shock to men and women of [White's] generation, as it destroyed their preconception about the nature of civilization. Before the war many believed civilization had advanced beyond warfare and the wanton de-

struction of life and property. World War I provided graphic proof this was not the case.... Although White did not participate in any battle when in the navy, he became adamantly opposed to all warfare, writing: "I was awed and appalled by the war; I could not understand it. And I had the sickening feeling that our verbal explanations and professions did not really account for our behavior. I wanted to know *why* millions of men should murder and mangle each other, when the full realization that everything is not as it pretends to be, struck me; almost everything seemed out of joint. (Peace 2004: 8–9)

6 While interned, Graebner still read and conducted research that shaped his later work on Indo-European, African, Polynesian, and Asiatic comparative mythologies and calendar systems.

7 Woolley was later traveling on a ship sunk by a sea mine in the eastern Mediterranean. He was captured and spent two and a half years as a prisoner of war (Woolley 1962: 110–13).

8 The Cosmos Club occasionally served as a drop spot for espionage reports (Harris and Sadler 2003: 109).

9 Farabee and Saville did not use fieldwork as a cover for espionage, but they did collect intelligence during the First World War (Sullivan 1989: 241, n. 12).

10 Boas did not identify these "at least four men," and scholars have identified different individuals as these spies (cf. Harris and Sadler 2003; Price 2001b; Sullivan 1989).

11 Leslie Spier later recalled that Charles Walcott, secretary of the Smithsonian, was among those leading the charge against Boas. Spier, a witness to the censure vote, described Walcott as "Boas' bitter enemy (because Boas challenged Walcott's smooth glad-handing). Walcott saw his opportunity in *The Nation* letter: [Neil] Judd was his willing stooge. Judd backed by [Aleš] Hrdlička, presented the resolution printed in the 1919 proceedings" (Price 2001b).

12 See "Referendum for Uncensoring Boas," AAA website, available online at http://www.aaanet.org/committees/nom/05comments/05_ref_boas.htm (accessed April 20, 2005); Glenn 2004.

13 See Glenn 2005; Gusterson and Price 2005; Moos 2002; Price 2005a, 2005b, 2005d; Wax 2002.

2 *Professional Associations*

1 Prior to America's entry in the war, more than seven hundred Americans had already fought fascists with the Abraham Lincoln Brigade in the Spanish Civil War. The anthropologists Clifford Amsbury, John Murra, Angel Palerm, and Elman Service fought with the Lincoln Brigade.

2 A decade later, the CIA covertly collaborated with the AAA's Executive Board to compile a detailed roster of anthropologists' expertise of interest to the CIA (see Price 2003a).

3 Fred Eggan to Bella Weitzner, August 28, 1942, AAA. Shimkin became a Cold War

adviser to various military agencies and to the CIA (see Price 2004a:190–92; FOIA MORI ID 3082, CIA; FOIA MORI ID 34176, CIA; FOIA 121-HQ-43855, FBI). Citations that contain the abbreviations CIA, FBI, OSS, and NAVY signify that the records were released to me under the Freedom of Information Act; the numbers and letters are agency record designations (see Price 1997, 2004a: 355–61).

4   Fred Eggan to George Murdock, January 3, 1943, AAA.

5   Fred Eggan to Verne Ray, January 25, 1942, AAA.

6   Esther Goldfrank noted that Boas's involvement in numerous "Communist-dominated and Communist front organizations" increased in 1939. Goldfrank was uneasy that Boas's statements denouncing totalitarian states did not identify which states he was referring to in his famous defense of academic freedom published in *New Masses*, which stated that "a bigoted democracy may be as hostile to intellectual freedom as a modern totalitarian state" (Goldfrank 1978: 114–15; see also Boas 1939). Goldfrank stopped short of accusing Boas of being a communist, but she believed that Boas was a fellow traveler because his position on the Stalin–Hitler Pact had "interesting analogues in the Communist Party line of the time" (Goldfrank 1978: 118). George Stocking found that Boas privately

> acknowledged that the methods the Soviets used to achieve the socialist ideal of "equal rights for every member of humanity" had "much in common" with those of fascist totalitarianism . . . , and he was painfully aware of the limitations of intellectual freedom in a land where "anthropology must be Marxian and Lewis Morgan, otherwise it is not allowed." . . . Publicly, however, his posture was that of the "united front"—even in the period of the Nazi Soviet pact and even to the jeopardy of funding that the American Jewish Committee had been providing for his research on race. (Stocking 1979b: 44)

When the Stalin–Hitler Pact ended on June 22, 1941, Goldfrank detected Boas engaging in more vocal expression of his anti-Nazi criticisms, dampening his critical remarks regarding French, English, and American domestic problems (Goldfrank 1978: 119).

7   Hook first suspected that Boas was influenced by Communist Party dogma when he observed Boas's work with the New York College Teachers Union—an organization Hook believes was "completely in the hands of the Communist Party" (Hook 1987: 257).

8   Stocking observed that, despite his opposition to the Nazis and his support for various organizations thwarting Hitler, Boas rejected the notion of setting aside science to combat Nazism. Instead, Boas "retained all his life a rather idealized and absolutistic conception of science. At the very end he rejected the idea that scientists must lay aside their studies to devote themselves full-time to the anti-Nazi struggle: 'the ice-cold flame of the passion for seeking the truth for truth's sake must be kept burning.' And despite the frequently utilitarian tone of his appeals for research funds, he had—or came to have as he grew older—a rather limited conception of the practical utility of anthropological research" (Stocking 1979b: 46).

9 Some of Boas's students later explained their use of anthropology for the war effort by evoking claims of Boas's support for the war and by making anthropological justifications for the melding of anthropology with warfare. Decades after the war, Margaret Mead even claimed that Boas stayed alive for an extended period just to help defeat Hitler. Later, Mead claimed necrodictive pronouncements of Boas's view on warfare to justify using anthropology in the war. Mead insisted,

> In considering the success of anthropologists during World War II in making a substantive contribution to national politics, it is important to realize that we faced a unique situation at that time, which may never recur. Because in World War II the deepest paradigm of cultural anthropology—the psychic unity of humankind—was violated by Nazism and because of the geopolitical accidents that made the Soviet Union and the United States temporary allies, it was possible to encompass all the normal divergences of ideology between left and right, pacifism and militancy, and sympathies with country of origin among anthropologists themselves in an almost 100% commitment to the importance of defending Hitler. Those of us who were close to Professor Boas felt that he stayed alive longer than might have been expected to make certain that Hitler was defeated. (Mead 1979: 146)

10 FOIA MORI 199920, March 23, 1942, CIA.
11 Among the American anthropologists who belonged to the Cosmos Club during the war years were David L. Bushnell, Edward S. C. Handy, Neil M. Judd, Alfred V. Kidder, Samuel K. Lothrop, Sylvanus G. Morely, Earl H. Morris, Oliver G. Ricketson, Frank M. Setzler, H. Jermain Slocum, Mathew W. Stirling, William D. Strong, Alfred M. Tozzer, and Clark Wissler (Cosmos Club 1941).
12 The Committee on Anthropology and the War Effort was later established, with Ralph Beals (chairman), Margaret Mead, and David Mandelbaum discussing coordinating anthropological contributions to warfare at home and abroad (Frantz 1974: 8).
13 Fred Eggan to Bella Weitzner, January 3, 1943, Box 24, AAA.
14 Eggan to Melville Herskovits, January 3, 1943, Box 23, AAA.
15 Eggan to Murdock, January 3, 1943, AAA.
16 Regina Flannery to Melville Herskovits, October 29, 1943, Box 23, AAA.
17 Flannery to Leslie Spier, December 11, 1943, Box 23, AAA.
18 *American Anthropologist* 46, no. 4 (1944): 473.
19 Melville Herskovits to Villard, January 26, 1945, Box 23, AAA.
20 *Applied Anthropology* 1, no. 3 (1941): 65.
21 During the war, Eliot Chapple (the SFAA's president in 1941–42) was a research fellow at the Harvard Medical School (Herskovits 1950: 30). Conrad Arensberg (president, 1942–43) was a BSR consultant at the Poston Camp, helped decode Japanese communications for the army's Special Security Group, and was an analyst at the Strategic Bombing Survey (Comitas 2000). John Provinse (president, 1943–46) was the chief of the Community Management Division, Washington, D.C.

22 Malamud's and Stephenson's work looked beyond psychological explanations accounting for recovery from what we would now term post-traumatic stress disorder and examined the impact of cultural factors such as upbringing, conflicts at home, deviance, sexual orientation, and the environment inhabited by patients after leaving the hospital (Malamud and Stephenson 1944: 10).

23 Future scholarship should examine the importance that Thompson's fieldwork and her marriage to U.S. Commissioner of Indian Affairs John Collier played in the formation of her sensitivities to anthropological ethics.

24 Anthropology was not the only American social science that contributed its scholars and methods to the Second World War (see Herman 1995). The sociologist Samuel Stouffer directed the professional staff at the Research Branch of the War Department; this work led to the production of his classic book *The American Soldier*. Harry Stack Sullivan's work with traumatized veterans of World War One affected the development of his theories, and during this war, Sullivan was a consultant to the Selective Service (Stanton 1968: 398). J. P. Guilford and other psychologists used their skills to help the military sort and classify recruit draftees in useful and hurried (if not also devastatingly inaccurate) ways. Rensis Likert refined the Likert scale and other surveying techniques that measured public opinions of the war. The sociologist John Dollard interviewed veterans of the Abraham Lincoln Brigade concerning the mechanisms of fear in battle; this research led to the 1943 book *Fear in Battle*, which was used in the training of American soldiers during World War Two (Dollard and Horton 1943). the social psychologist David Krech worked for the oss (Petrinovich 1979), and the pollster Elmo Roper developed pioneering work in quantitative sampling methods at the coi and the oss (Lindzey 1979). Henry A. Murray applied his research on personality types at the oss, where he screened agents before sending them off on secret missions to see if they could endure the stresses and strains of such clandestine work. This evaluative work led to his contributions to the oss's book *Assessment of Men* (oss 1948). Carl Rogers was appointed the director of counseling services at the uso (IEssBS). The social psychologist Daniel Katz served at the owi and the U.S. Strategic Bombing Survey.

25 Late in the First World War, the Army's Thirty-Sixth Division successfully used fourteen Choctaw Indians as code talkers to transmit vital battlefield intelligence with field telephones. Because this operation had been so successful in the First World War, Navajos, Comanches, and code talkers speaking twelve other Indian languages were deployed during World War Two. In 1939, German scholars posing as anthropologists reportedly were caught by the FBI studying Comanche, and during the 1930s "foreign diplomats were found to have been among the chief customers of the Bureau of Indian Affairs for the purchase of publications" (Meadows 2002: 65). American anthropologists appear not to have been involved in the use of code talkers during World War Two. The use of Navajo code talkers by the Marine Corps occurred largely because of the efforts of Technical Sergeant Philip Johnston, who had learned Navajo as a child living on the Navajo Reservation with his missionary parents (Meadows 2002: 74).

26 Mason's role in connecting Agogino with military intelligence suggests the possibility

that Mason's World War One espionage work led to sustained contacts with the American military intelligence community.

27 Leighton listed David Aberle as a propaganda analyst at the Sociological Branch, Military Intelligence Service, but Aberle stated that he did not work in that capacity (Leighton 1949: 223–25; David Aberle to the author, December 6, 2000).

28 Clellan Ford straddled several agencies during the war. He also assisted George Murdock in preparing military government handbooks (Lonergan 1991a: 205).

29 After the war, Starr became a Middle East analyst at the CIA (Owen 1996: 5).

30 The British physical anthropologist Solly Zuckerman conducted ballistic experiments, developed bombardment plans used by Allied headquarters to disrupt German and French rail lines, and studied the impact of bombardments on North Africa and the United Kingdom (McArthur 1990: 143; Zuckerman 1978).

31 Goldschmidt studied agencies organized under the Farm Bureau and the Associated Farmers. Some of these organizations coordinated the shared use of farm machinery; other agencies oversaw the Air Raid Warning System, fire-fighting programs, the Aircraft Warning Service, and even local militias of "unofficial guerrilla organizations" of armed farmers (Goldschmidt 1943: 16). John Bennett was a field researcher in the Bureau of Agricultural Economics' Division of Program Surveys and later was a field director in the OWI's Domestic Intelligence Branch (John Bennett to the author, June 12, 1997).

32 In a letter written to his brother Dick soon after his liberation from Los Banos, Roy Barton recounted his liberation, some of his losses, and his plans to continue on with his research in the postwar period. He wrote that he was

> rescued by parachutists & amphibian tanks, operating at daybreak in cooperation with Filipino guerillas, conveyed in the tanks 40 km across a lake, thence by truck to present location. We would have been killed—according to a story generally believed, on evening of same day—if not rescued. . . . I lost everything except 3 [manuscripts], two of which were the ones, fortunately, that cost me [the] most work. I had about 10 volumes as well as several shorter papers & notes but aside from fact that Japs [who] were interning me allowed me to pack only 1 suitcase & a suitcase wouldn't have held these, the volumes, with exception of those mentioned, were in the storehouse of a mine, the Japs came unexpectedly on us first of all the many mines around Baguio, and the Filipino keeper of the storehouse ran away with the key. I had duplicates left with an Ifugao teacher in Burney where I was working & the Japs burned his village and house after bombing it, and I've heard he was killed. So I have no hope with resp. these other ms. I saved one on Religion, Ifugaos,—English workbook & one on mythology. (Roy F. Barton to J. R. Barton, March 4, 1945, RFB)

33 *Euphoria*, vol. 2, no. 4 (1945), 11.

34 Though Bowles spent much of his youth and early career in Japan, his anthropological training had not focused on Japan before the war. His dissertation and early research

focused on south-central Asian physical anthropology of northern India, Burma, Tibet, and China (Mayo 1982).

35 Gene Weltfish's FBI file records that the FBI viewed her and Benedict's views on racial equality as dangerously disruptive to America's socioeconomic status quo (see Benedict and Weltfish 1943; Price 2004a: 109–35).

36 FOIA 77-HQ-28923–8 9/17/43, FBI.

37 FOIA 77–2474–4, FBI.

38 FOIA 77–29387, FBI.

39 FOIA 101–6392, FBI; Price 2004a: 237, 254.

40 FOIA 100-HQ-212233, FBI.

41 FOIA HQ-65–39058, FBI.

42 FOIA 65-HQ-39058, FBI; see Theoharis 1991: 15–34.

43 FOIA 65-HQ-8857, FBI.

44 *Time* 78, no. 22, December 1, 1961, 92.

45 All FBI reports need to be read with skepticism, as innuendo and speculation are mixed with facts, and Axel Wenner-Gren's file is no exception. Such provisions notwithstanding, the FBI did gather some evidence indicating ongoing interactions with Nazis. The following excerpts from a 1961 summary of past ongoing inquiries outlines some of the accusations investigated by the FBI:

> It was reported that Wenner-Gren claimed he had induced a group of Swedish financiers to purchase a German interest in Bofors and he, Wenner-Gren, had a controlling fifty percent of stock. It has also been alleged that Wenner-Gren purchased a large share of Bofors stock and at the same time the Krupp Munitions Trust of Germany purchased a thirty-five percent interest in this concern. Reportedly, this purchase by the Krupp interests was contrary to a Swedish law which prohibited foreigners from holding an interest in a Swedish corporation in excess of twenty percent. It was reported that in 1934 Wenner-Gren purchased the Krupp interest in Bofors. However, it was also stated that although this interest was purchased in Wenner-Gren's name, in reality this interest was held as a proxy for Krupp. Although proof of this allegation was lacking. Wenner-Gren allegedly denied that this stock had been purchased by him on behalf of the Krupp interests.
>
> It was further reported that Wenner-Gren's brother, Hugo had resided in Germany for many years where he operated a bakelite factory and could not leave Germany during the 1930's because of his financial holdings in that country. It was reported that Wenner-Gren claimed his brother had no political affiliations and that his brother's wife, in fact, had been incarcerated in a concentration camp because of opposition to Adolph Hitler. . . .
>
> A confidential source who has furnished reliable information in the past, advised that he recalled hearing Goering say in 1933 that Wenner-Gren was one of the most powerful instruments which the Nazis would be able to use in their economic operations with important people in England, France, and the United States.

It was reported that in June, 1945, Hermann Goering admitted having had a limited acquaintanceship with Wenner-Gren which was initiated during the 1930s. Goering allegedly claimed that Wenner-Gren mentioned important connections in the United States and England, claimed he was personally acquainted with the President of the United States and indicated he might negotiate a peace settlement. Goering allegedly stated that Wenner-Gren's peace plan was regarded by Hitler as a very confused project and was rejected. Goering further was reported to have stated that he personally believed Wenner-Gren was an opportunist, who, when in Berlin, was very flattering concerning the National Socialist system and its successes, but undoubtedly was just as critical of the National Socialism when he was talking with persons not sympathetic to Nazism. (FOIA 100-HQ769–33538, January 16, 1961, FBI)

46 Gordon Bowles was born and raised in Japan, and his Quaker beliefs led him to avoid combat-related contributions to the war. Bowles served at the Board of Economic Warfare and the Special Areas Branch (Mayo 1982: 104). The future anthropologist Victor Turner's pacifism found him in the British Army serving "in the lowly rank of a conscientious objector, digging up unexploded bombs" (Turner 1985: 1; see Harris 1998 for a treatment of the Society for the Psychological Study of Social Issue's advocacy for pacifism in World War Two).

47 "McGuffin" (sometimes rendered "macguffin") was a term originated by Alfred Hitchcock for the element in a story whose primary purpose is to advance the plot development. Sometimes it is an object sought by the story's principal characters and their enemies, such as the titular statue in *The Maltese Falcon* or the plans for the Death Star in *Star Wars* (for more on McGuffin, see Gottlieb and Hitchcock 2003: 62–63; Žižek 1992: 5–10). I thank Milo W. Price for his knowledgeable exegesis on the importance of McGuffins in narrative history.

48 In 1975, Sol Tax wrote, "If applied anthropology presupposes a body of scientific knowledge—competent empirical propositions—developed by theoretical anthropologists and awaiting application to particular situations when we are asked to do so by management, government, administrator, or organization, the action anthropology is far different. For one thing, the action anthropologist can have no master; he works as a member of the academic community" (Tax 1975: 515).

49 In the wake of the Vietnam War, Robert Murphy wrote, "It may be apposite for younger members of the American Anthropological Association to learn that there was no debate among anthropologists, nor were there significant reservations, about the role of the profession in the conduct of the [Second World War]" (Murphy 1976: 4).

3 Allied and Axis Anthropologies

1 "Mr. Philip Corder, Curator of the Verulamium Museum, pointed out that the old Roman city lies twelve feet below the present surface, thus giving the present-day archaeologist an unparalleled opportunity for excavation. The catch is that it is abso-

lutely impossible to obtain excavators, as every man from eight to eighty, who is not directly concerned in the war effort, [was] used to repair the million or more damaged homes" (Phillips 1945: 476). The widespread aerial bombing and shelling of civilian areas also damaged uncounted archaeological sites throughout Europe, Asia, and North Africa.

2 The volumes I consulted have stickers glued to the back leaf of the title page that read: "The volume was produced and printed for official purposes during the war 1939/45." When one holds the page up to the light, the original text beneath the sticker is visible. It reads, "This book is for the use of persons in H.M. service only and must not be shown, or made available, to the Press or any member of the public" (see, e.g., Naval Intelligence Division 1943: ii).

3 Banks was a Japanese prisoner of war interned in Kuching, where he remained until 1945 (Durrans 1991: 24).

4 As payment for this, the Japanese allowed the Tagal to keep the American soldiers' heads as trophies (Harrisson 1959: 241).

5 Many Japanese soldiers died fighting, while others were pushed to abandon strongholds, surrender, and retreat to weakened positions. Some Japanese soldiers retreating into the jungles committed suicide. Other retreating Japanese soldiers reportedly died after their intestinal tracts exploded from eating unhusked rice found in rural storage huts (Harrisson 1959: 299–300).

6 Due to Japanese incursions in 1942, Leach lost all of his field notes and photos and a draft monograph on his Hpalang fieldwork. This work was later re-created from memory (Tambiah 2002:42).

7 Tindale also researched Japanese use of the little understood global jet stream to send incendiary balloon bombs that killed American civilians and started forest fires in the American West. Tindale determined where the balloon bombs were manufactured and released, information that allowed American bombers to destroy the plants manufacturing them (Jones 1995).

8 Elkin's journal *Oceania* was threatened by the war as funds and paper became scare, but the Carnegie Corporation funded a small-font version during the war years (Wise 1985). Elkin lobbied the government to appoint him to create an Australian Department of Propaganda (Wise 1985: 151).

9 Waves of European scholars found a safe haven in American universities during the war. Among those who came to the United States were Róheim Géza, Roman Jakobson, Max Horkheimer, and Herbert Marcuse (who joined the OSS). The New School in Exile provided a haven for scholars such as Paul Leser, Claude Lévi-Strauss, and Karl Wittfogel (Krohn 1993). After the Dutch paleontologist G. H. R. von Koenigswald was liberated from a Japanese prison camp, he came as a refugee to New York, bringing with him Javanese *Pithancanthropus* fossils (Washburn 1968: 503). The French anthropologist Paul Rivet was an outspoken socialist who was fired from the Musée de l'Homme in 1940 "by the Vichy government and hunted by the Gestapo." He found refuge in South America (Jamin 1991: 585). As Nazis advanced on France, Jean Rouch

bicycled through the countryside, blowing up bridges to slow the invasion and later screening films banned by the Vichy government. He eventually traveled to Niger to join the Batallion de Génie (Stoller 1992: 27). Georges Friedmann joined the French Resistance and fought the Nazi occupation of France in the underground (Dofny 1979: 206). Malinowski's student Stanislaw Ossowski was an active member of the Polish underground, and "at the risk of his life, he lectured in the then-underground University of Warsaw" (Nowak 1968: 346).

10 William Peace to the author, July 2, 2006.

11 Some American and Allied anthropologists held views of racial hierarchies and eugenics that were aligned with Nazi views. Harvard was home for numerous scholars who embraced eugenics, and E. A. Hooton even proposed establishing an American national breeding bureau that would determine who could reproduce with whom (FOIA 62-HQ-73410, FBI; Price 2002a). George H. L. F. Pitt-Rivers (grandson of A. H. L. F. Pitt Rivers) espoused pro-Nazi racial views and was "held as a political prisoner by the [British] Home Office" during the war (Barkan 1988: 193).

12 A notable exception to this trend is the series of seminars on East Asian anthropology and Japanese colonialism (see Shimizu and van Bremen 2003: 1; Chun, ed., 2004: 2–7). Conferences examining Japanese anthropological contributions to the war and colonialism have been held in Leiden in May 1995 (see van Bremen and Shimizu 1999); in Osaka in 1999 (see Shimizu and van Bremen 2003); and in Seoul in 2002 and 2004 (see Chun, ed., 2004: 2–7).

13 The Sino-Japanese War also affected Chinese ethnographic research. When the Japanese occupied eastern China, the Chinese ethnologist Ling Shun-Sheng, who had been trained at the University of Paris, relocated his field research site to western Hunan Province (Huang 1991: 412). The Japanese occupation also launched a first wave of Chinese rural sociology, as Chinese "scholars who had previously spent their lives with no contact whatever with the common people in dilapidated temples and peasant huts" (Fei 1979: 27). Some of these displaced scholars discovered fieldwork, and after the war they helped established a Maoist flavor of Chinese sociology (Fei 1979). The war disrupted paleontological excavations at Choukoutine, where the Peking Man skulls were excavated; the skulls were being shipped by the U.S. Embassy to safety in 1941 when they were "lost in the confusion following the bombing of Pearl Harbor. . . . They have not been heard of since" (Chang 1984: 135).

14 Gregory Bateson to Ian Hogbin, July 2, 1943, in GB.

4 The War on Campus

1 This passage comes from a pamphlet entitled, "Intensive Language Program's Opportunities for the Intensive Study of Unusual Languages, During the Autumn of 1942," located in Melville Jacobs's papers (MJ Box 1–10). The *American Anthropologist* announced the ILP in its "Notes and News" section in 1942, 44: 729–30.

2 Cowan's statement that the mission of the ILP was to gather all available American

linguists to contribute to the program is in contrast to the anthropologist and linguist Melville Jacobs's efforts to write to well-placed friends and associates offering his unique skills as a linguist to the war effort—to no avail. While the reasons for Jacobs's failure to secure a position are unknown, entries in his FBI file indicate that the FBI's knowledge of his past membership in the Communist Party may have led to the loss of his, and others', unique contributions (see Price 2004a: 34–49). Jacobs complained to Margaret Mead about the selective preferences being shown by the military to some anthropological views over others: "The thought that members of the Hooton–Harvard bunch, with their racist slantings, should get in on any army or governmental services that may be already or might in the future be set up to do a job with a racial bearing gives me the itch" (Melville Jacobs to Margaret Mead, July 19, 1942, MJ Box 1–10). Other left-leaning anthropologists had problems finding government positions; when Eleanor Leacock volunteered, she hit some political roadblocks (Gailey 1988: 216).

3 Jay Swadesh to the author, August 26, 2002.

4 MJ Box 1, Folder 10.

5 Powdermaker also taught classes on Pacific cultures to army personnel at Yale (Silverman 1989: 293).

6 Box M25, MM. Mead's "Proposal" is undated; another document in Box M25, MM, titled "Memorandum for Colonel Beukema" is a less developed but similar document dated January 1943.

7 Ibid.

8 During the Cold War, the Institute for Intercultural Studies undertook studies of increasing interest to the national-security state, but it was during World War Two that Mead established relationships with national security and intelligence figures that would have importance during the Cold War. For example, Mead's first contact with Harold G. Wolff, who would later become infamous for receiving funding from the CIA, was in March 1943 as she was using the council to integrate social science into the war effort (E. Embree to Margaret Mead, March 5, 1943, Box M1, MM). These relationships took on increased importance during the Cold War (see Marks 1979:159; Price 1998a, 2003b).

9 CIR Army Project, February 13, 1943, Box M25, MM.

10 Dalia Hagan has observed that it is remarkable that Mead failed even to mention gender as one of the primary influences for students to observe (Dalia Hagen to the author, February 1, 2006).

11 Before returning to Columbia, Linton had worked in Washington, D.C., as a consultant to British military liaisons planning maneuvers in Madagascar.

12 *Euphoria*, vol. 2, no. 4 (1945), 2.

13 Ibid., vol. 1, no. 2 (1942), 1–2.

14 Ibid., vol. 1, no. 2 (1943), 3.

15 Ibid., vol. 1, no. 2 (1943): 5.

16 Ibid., vol. 1, no. 5 (1943), 10.

17 Ibid., vol. 1, no. 5 (1943), 1.

18 Ibid., vol. 2, no. 4 (1945), 21.

19 Ibid., vol. 2, no. 4 (1945), 13.

20 Ibid., vol. 1, no. 5 (1943), 13.

21 Ibid., 19–20.

22 Ibid., vol. 2, no. 4 (1945), cover.

5 *The Wartime Brain Trust*

1 Murdock's earliest work on the survey was assisted by Clellan Ford, Alfred Hudson, Raymond Kennedy, and John Whiting (Ford 1971: 184, n. 1).

2 According to Mel Ember, "The CIA was an Associate Member of the HRAF consortium between 1979 and 1983, and I don't think that the Board of Directors was told about it" (Mel Ember to the author, July 18, 1995).

3 For example, the OPNAV *Civil Affairs Handbook: West Caroline Islands* stated that, "Although prostitution in the usual sense did not exist in the Western Carolines before the coming of Europeans, there were native customs on Yap and Palau which some-what resembled it. In these islands it was the practice for each men's club to maintain several unmarried girls at the clubhouse to perform the work and to bestow their favors upon club members. The girls, known as mespil on Yap and as armengol on Palau, were obtained almost entirely from neighboring villages because of the pre-vailing taboos against sexual intercourse with members of one's own clan" (OPNAV 1944b: 46).

4 This image of knowledge withdrawals is reminiscent of Paulo Freire's notion of educa-tors' roles as bankers in anti-dialogical education settings (Freire 1970).

5 Swanton's essay on the evolution of nations had several emotive passages marking it as a war-era piece, but they stood apart from the main essay, which was clumsily framed to hide the state's natural brutality.

6 Cochran recognized that the war presented opportunities for the Smithsonian to increase its herpetological knowledge and collections, and she ended her monograph with a concise paragraph subtitled, "Directions for Making Scientific Collections," which instructed readers destined for "little-explored regions" how to preserve and ship (using readily available materials such as a penknife, paper, or straw and an empty gasoline tin) specimens back to the U.S. National Museum (Cochran 1943: 36–37). Addison Wynn of the Smithsonian's Amphibians and Reptiles Division informed me that no scholar has formally examined the impact of Cochran's wartime efforts to get soldiers to ship her reptile specimens, but more than three thousand specimens were apparently shipped to the Smithsonian from military units (Addison Wynn to the author, January 19, 2006). Some of these specimens represented important discoveries. Wynn wrote, "Six of the specimens are holotypes for new species or subspecies and over 200 are paratypes for new species or subspecies (although most of these are specimens donated by the research units), and the large number of specimens we

received from such places as Papua New Guinea and the Solomons are an important part of our research collections" (Wynn to the author, January 19, 2006).

7 EB Box 15, Folder 29.

8 AAA to Carlson, June 19, 1944, Box 24, AAA.

9 EB Box 3, Folders 1–10.

10 Some rosters listing anthropologists were compiled before the war. Examples of such rosters include the AAA's annually published membership lists (e.g., *American Anthropologist* 41 [1939]: 174–87) and the NRC's *International Directory of Anthropologists* (NRC 1938). However, none of these rosters was the cross-indexed, multi-trait work of the type designed by the Ethnogeographic Board's Area Roster Group.

11 EB Box 4.

12 EB Box 10.

13 Searches for such records were ongoing. Anthropologists' correspondence from this period records instances of military personnel requesting maps and other region specific documents. Typical of these requests was one received by Gregory Bateson in July 1943 from the Army Map Service asking for any topographical maps, foreign-city plans, "guide books, travel folders containing city plans, gazetteers, survey notes and maps, and aerial photographs" pertaining to the Bismarck Archipelago of the New Guinea Lesser Sundas Islands (MM Box 2, Viohla Klipell to Gregory Bateson, July 24, 1943). The Army Map Service made similar requests to Margaret Mead for any available maps of "the Islands of the South Pacific" (Army Map Service to Margaret Mead, December 15, 1943).

14 The other recorded meetings were mostly held at the Cosmos Club and included the Far Eastern Geographers (October 5, 1942), Netherlands East Indies Dinner (October 12, 1942), Near East Dinner (October 19, 1942), dinners honoring Paul Rivet (December 30, 1942) and Lord Hailey (February 13, 1943), postwar needs of anthropology (April 12, 1943), land-tenure problems (April 28, 1943), and the Colonial Questions Conference (May 4, 1943; Bennett 1947: 69–71).

15 This recommendation stands in contrast to the advice given in the "Native" section recommending caution in eating the natives' foods because they can make one sick.

16 This passage apparently provided the inspiration for a scene in Neal Stephenson's *Cryptonomicon* in which the Japanese solider Goto Dengo performs this exact maneuver to escape a sea of flaming diesel (Stephenson 1999: 401–404). *Survival on Land and Sea* appeared in Martha Johnson's 1945 wartime adventure novel *Ann Bartlett Returns to the Philippines*. When the novel's heroine nurse, Ann Bartlett, ends up in a raft in the western Pacific off the coast the Philippines, she notices one of the men on the raft studying a book: " 'Survival on Land and Sea,' she read aloud. 'Was that book on the raft, too?' 'You bet, and it's our Bible from here on in. We've got to begin planning some definite course of action. We've checked the water supply from our canteens and have enough to last out the night. . . . The food situation is tough. Just a handful of biscuits in the compartment. But this book says a man can survive for several weeks without

food'" (Johnson 1945: 91). Bartlett's party followed *Survival*'s instructions on keeping dry, conserving water, and navigating, and once they reached shore, it helped them identify taro and other edible foods (Johnson 1945: 92–116).

17 The Division of Cultural Relations and the Inter-Departmental Committee on Cooperation with American Republics had both been established by the U.S. State Department in 1938, while the Institute of Social Anthropology was established in 1943 at the Smithsonian's Bureau of American Ethnology.

18 As was the case with Charles Wagley, who had studied rubber and other natural resources in Brazil during the war.

19 The CIAA also occasionally backed more covert activities. An August 19, 1943, memo from the Peruvian legal attaché to FBI Director J. Edgar Hoover reported that the archaeologist Samuel Lothrop's SIS espionage was being "financed by the Coordinator of Inter-American Affairs" (see chapter 9), but the frequency of such occurrences is now poorly understood (67-HQ-384224–30, 67-HQ-384224–31, both in FBI).

20 FOIA document, U.S. Department of State, January 11, 1946.

21 Foster left the IIAA after four months to work for Julian Steward at the ISA (Foster 2000: 124).

22 F94–01317/6/43, CIA.

23 Julian Steward to Abbot, January 5, 1944, Box 1, Folder 1, ISA.

24 In June 1942, Steward wrote to Charles Wagley that he had made inquiries about such funding with members of the Rockefeller's Planning and Analysis Division and learned "that they had a scheme to connect social science with many of their field projects. They agree that my plan would be helpful, especially in that it would emphasize training local personnel in basic concepts and research procedure, as well as adding to the number of people who would do field research in connection with Rockefeller projects" (Julian Steward to Charles Wagley, June 10, 1942, Box 11, ISA).

25 "Loyalty Data," Box 2, ISA. After the war, Gordon Willey became the acting director of the ISA. Richard N. Adams also joined the ISA and worked in Guatemala and elsewhere in Central America.

26 "Paraguay" and "Information on Anthropologists," Box 1, ISA. This report is undated, but it appears to have been written around 1943.

27 Steward to Abbot, January 5, 1944, Box 1, Folder 1, ISA.

28 Ibid.

29 Ibid.

6 White House War Projects

1 Margaret Mead to Eleanor Roosevelt, January 21, 1943, MM.

2 The U.S. Navy Liberty ship the ss *Ales Hrdlicka* (Maritime Commission hull no. 2817) was launched on October 7, 1944.

3 Aleš Hrdlička to Franklin D. Roosevelt, December 18, 1937, HRD. In 1933, Hrdlička wrote to President Roosevelt:

Americans have never been, in dealing with the Asiatic peoples and Japan in particular, unfair, dishonest, hypocritical, or more than legitimately selfish. I saw further, that the future of human relations, commercial, educational, scientific, and many others, lies more and more in the Pacific. This naturally creates the hope that this country and people, as the most advanced and most just, should become the dominant power for human progress in the Pacific.

To this there has been arising an ever more threatening obstacle, which is Japan. Not the Japanese people, who have enough good in them, but that something utterly egotistic, tricky and ruthless to the weaker, which is the governing clique of the country. This power since fifty years is working steadily towards the exclusion of all and particularly the white man from the Pacific, towards the domination, by hook or crook, of all it can reach, and towards a reign backed by brute force and all other means, moral or immoral, over all eastern Asia and the whole great ocean. (Hrdlička to Roosevelt, February 25, 1933, HRD)

4 Roosevelt at times crudely expressed his dislike of the Japanese. Greg Robinson wrote, "William Hassett, recounted in August 1942 that 'the President related an old Chinese myth about the origin of the Japanese. A wayward daughter of an ancient Chinese emperor left her native land in a sampan and finally reached Japan, then inhabited by baboons. The inevitable happened and in due course the Japanese made their appearance'" (Robinson 2001: 119–20).

5 Hrdlička to Roosevelt, September 21, 1942, HRD.

6 Ibid., October 20, 1942, HRD.

7 Ibid., October 29, 1942, HRD.

8 Ibid., December 23, 1942, HRD.

9 Ibid.

10 Carter brought Hanfstaengl to the United States from Canada to better understand the inner workings of the German government and to gather information that could be used for anti-German propaganda (as part of the S Project). Field helped arrange Hanfstaengl's housing, and Field was used to leak information on Hanfstaengl to the British Embassy (Morrissey 1966: 20–21).

11 Field's account is partially supported by Frances Perkins's claim that Roosevelt planned to spend his post-presidential years "redeveloping that area from the Sahara to the Tigris-Euphrates Valley" (Field 1962: 329).

12 Carter praised Field's contributions to the M Project, but he did not believe Field's claims of direct presidential directives, saying, "Field did a hell of a good job . . . and he has taken a lot of credit to himself for it. I'm not going to argue against it because he is entitled to a great deal of credit for it. But by God, he was not ever employed by Roosevelt. He was employed by me with Roosevelt's knowledge and approval on a number of projects, including [the M Project] and including the 'S' Project. He was my second in command; he did a hell of a good job in many ways, and in some ways he fell flat on his face, but, who doesn't?" (Morrissey 1966: 22). Carter argued that "having seen [Field's 1962 book] make the general inference that he was called on by Roosevelt

to do this great thing, which he wasn't—although Roosevelt knew he was doing it, he thought it was a good selection, and he did a good job. I am a little hesitant to trust anything that Henry Field would write along these lines because I think he cannot help himself" (Morrissey 1966: 29).

13 In early 1943, the FBI undertook an extensive "Espionage" investigation of Henry Field (Roach to Ladd, FOIA 65–47510, January 21, 1943, FBI). The investigation was launched after Field received a letter from France from Marcel Coste containing information that the FBI believed could threaten the United States' wartime national security interests. Coste's letter was checked for secret writing (FOIA 65–47510–3, February 22, 1943, FBI). The FBI's suspicions grew when agents interviewed a number of Field's Dumbarton Avenue neighbors and learned he had several Russian friends (FOIA 65–47510–6, February 23, 1945, FBI). The FBI's investigations later uncovered Field's involvement in the M Project, though the nature of the project was unknown to the FBI.

14 It is unclear how much of these reports was written by Field and how much by his staff. John Carter did not think that Field "wrote a word of it. It was all done by other people. He organized it. Isaiah Bowman was the man who is responsible for the overall policy" (quoted in Morrissey 1966: 21–22).

15 Reports were identified by the letter "R," followed by a dash and a number designating a report number. A total of 163 reports were issued. Translation Series reports were identified with the letter "T," followed by a dash and a number designating a report number. A total of 122 translations were produced. Memorandum Series documents were identified with the letter "M," followed by a number indicating a report number. Three-hundred and forty-five memoranda were produced. Lecture Series documents were identified with the letter "L"; Administrative Series reports were identified with the letter "A."

The Translation Series comprised a broad range of materials, including translations of Japanese-language articles on the occupation of Manchuria and Soviet city planning; economic and demographic reports on regions of the Soviet Union; and natural-resource reports from around the world. The Translation Series collected and translated reports on the relocations—often *forcible* relocations—of peoples from cultures all over the world. One report (T-71) based on a rare book by Petr Korolevich documented a failed effort in the 1920s to resettle two hundred Cossacks in the Apurimac River region of eastern Peru. The report examined how the improper selection of participants and poor planning contributed to a disastrous resettlement.

16 R-38; R-59; Field 1962: 44.

17 R-106

18 R-48

19 Steve Niva to the author, July 18, 2006.

20 Government officials recognized more than an opportunity to offer humanitarian relief in these measures. From its inception, the CIA saw opportunities to bring "useful" Nazis to the United States and had language inserted into a 1949 statute authorizing the creation of the CIA, which allowed the Director of Central Intelligence, the attorney general, and the commissioner of immigration to declare:

The entry of a particular alien is in the interest of national security or essential to the furtherance of the national intelligence mission, such alien and his immediate family shall be given entry into the United States for permanent residence without regard to their admissibility under the immigration or any other laws and regulations pertaining to admissibility: *Provided*, That the number of aliens and members of their immediate families entering the United States under the authority of this section shall in no case exceed one hundred persons in any one fiscal year. ("Administration of the Central Intelligence Agency," June 29, 1949, 63 Stat. 208, sec. 8)

21 HQ121–12261–18.
22 Nash later wrote:

All of these fears of a repetition of 1919[-like riots] were borne out in 1946, the first year after WWII. There was little we could do about it. The riots did not occur in plants but in public places. We could ask the FBI to investigate, but in some flagrant cases of daytime violence no one was willing to testify, though there must have been dozens of witnesses. . . . The military in WWII was not the best place in the world for Black servicemen, but when they returned to a rural and suburban South, they acted too assertively and violence often erupted. Black people were no longer willing to stand aside in such instances, and violence quickly became major.

Late in the war, we had begun to classify riots and had a scale: words, words and blows; words, blows and missiles. We also scaled to size: crowds less than 25, 25–99 and 100 and over. The riots in 1946 steadily went to the top of the scale. (Nash 1986: 192–93)

Nash's role as an adviser to President Truman on racial integration later brought attacks by Senator Joseph McCarthy and the surveillance of the FBI (see Price 2004a: 263–77).

23 As Neil Smith observed, "Bowman's scientific interest lay more with the social and physical environment of the receiving country than with any concern for the refugees individually or collectively. They were faceless, and considerable effort was made to keep them so, while the places to which they would be resettled brimmed with personality" (Smith 2003: 312).

7 Internment Fieldwork

1 President Roosevelt's decision to treat Japanese Americans differently from other Americans whose ancestors came from Axis nations was a decision influenced by racial prejudice. Greg Robinson found that, "Roosevelt's past feelings toward the Japanese Americans must be considered to have significantly shaped his momentous decision to evacuate American citizens from their homes. FDR had a long and unvaried history of viewing Japanese Americans in racialized terms, that is, as essentially Japanese in their

identity and emotional allegiance, and of expressing hostility toward them on that basis. In the years before World War II, Roosevelt considered immigration part of the Japanese threat to the West Coast" (Robinson 2001: 118–19).

2 The WRA used Orwellian language to refer to all aspects of internment. The make-shift camps at fairgrounds and racetracks where Japanese Americans were forced to report after abandoning or selling off their homes, land, and other possessions were called "reception centers" as if hostesses were greeting them as guests. The camps were called "relocation centers" not detention centers, concentration camps, or internment camps. The imprisoned Japanese Americans were not referred to as "prisoners," "in-mates," or even "internees," they were instead called "evacuees" as if they had been saved from some natural disaster and temporary relocated to higher ground for their own safety. Those refusing to sign the loyalty question became "disloyals."

3 Japanese Americans were not the only North Americans to be evacuated from their homes during the war. American military also evacuated Aleuts living to the west of the Unimak Islands after Japanese attacks in the summer of 1942. These Aleuts were relocated to makeshift camps in "abandoned fish canneries on the mainland without proper medical treatment or adequate food," conditions that led to a ten percent mortality rate during the war (Madden 1992: 55–56).

4 Peter Suzuki to the author, November 14, 2006.

5 Starn noted that while Morris Opler assisted Korematsu's attorneys and "privately criticized" policies requiring internees to answer question 28, he "never published his oppositional views. His silence exemplified the public role anthropologists defined for themselves as advisers to the WRA, a role that responded compliantly to pressure for an ethnography validating the internment centers in functionalist form" (Starn 1986: 710).

6 In later years, Fay-Cooper Cole criticized Roosevelt's move to detain and relocate Japanese Americans as "a response to self-interested pressure groups rather than to the needs of national security" (quoted in Stocking 1979a: 31).

7 Leighton and Spicer later admitted that the BSR's choice of a name was a poor one, because "the term Bureau turned out to have connotations of the FBI for some among the evacuees" (quoted in Leighton 1945: 479).

8 Spicer transformed the community analyst bureaucracy, having analysts report di-rectly to administrators in the camps where they were deployed rather than to WRA headquarters in Washington, D.C.

9 Hankey, Spencer, and Tsuchiyama worked for JERS, and Arensberg, Colson, Leighton, Spicer, and Thompson worked for the BSR. All other listed anthropologists worked for the WRA.

10 Female detainees were asked noncombatant versions of these questions (Thomas and Nishimoto 1946: 56–58).

11 Mike Salovesh to the author, July 9, 2004.

12 Salovesh wrote that, when faced with such gruesome conditions, Hansen "came up with a solution of sorts. He crawled into a bottle and didn't come out for decades after the war" (ibid.).

13 Washington CAS, "Community Analysts Section Annual Report," July 1-December 31, 1943, Washington, D.C., 1944, 9.

14 Robert Lowie was initially involved in recruiting anthropologist fieldworkers for JERS, but he left the program in 1943 because of obligations in the ASTP.

15 Thomas had separate field researchers make individual observations in the same camps—although generally this did not occur at identical points in time, so some confounds emerged in the implementation of this method.

16 Suzuki to the author, November 14, 2006; Suzuki 1986b.

17 Suzuki to the author, January 14, 2006.

18 Hankey was miserable and became stoic about her hardships, taking "a masochistic satisfaction in them, naively hoping that [her] misery would increase [her] rapport with the Japanese Americans" (Wax 1971: 72). She first coped with these hardships by eating her way through the PX's meager offerings, putting on thirty pounds in three months.

19 Tsuchiyama wrote to Thomas on April 6, 1943, "I do not care what you do with my reports provided they do not fall into the hands of the Tenney Committee, the F.B.I., the Senate Investigation Committee, the NSGW [Native Sons of the Golden West], and other governmental and non-governmental agencies which may utilize them for propaganda purposes" (Hirabayashi 1999: 119).

20 It is known that the FBI's release of files on Hankey, Tsuchiyama, and Thomas is incomplete because Hankey's released files make no mention of her work at Gila or Tule Lake and have gaps in other reported activities. Hirabayashi has noted that the FBI did not release files on Tsuchiyama's efforts to brief the FBI on Japanese religious beliefs.

21 Tsuchiyama was not the only JERS fieldworker whose fieldwork materials Thomas tried to control and publish (see Murray 1991).

8 Anthropology and Nihonjinron

1 Under the pseudonym Cordwainer Smith, Linebarger wrote some of the most influential works of science fiction's great golden age of the 1950s, pushing the genre beyond confrontations with bug-eyed monsters to social experiential science fiction. As Cordwainer Smith, Linebarger influenced such science-fiction writers as Philip K. Dick, Ursula LeGuin, and Harlan Ellison. Linebarger's principles of psychological warfare established a firm reliance on culturally specific propaganda at the OWI that shaped the direction of the agency throughout the war (see Linebarger 1948).

2 Leighton also used OWI and BSR data to prepare reports on the coming American occupation of Japan. Protests at the camps, strikes, and disruptions were studied as demonstrations of what could occur when American forces occupied postwar Japan. The OWI "planners of the occupation saw the community analysis section as essential to the occupation's smooth governance and prevention of trouble" (Hayashi 2004: 205).

3   As Talcott Parsons and Evon Vogt recalled, Kluckhohn's work at the OWI

> showed that it was possible, by careful use of social science methods, to achieve a substantially higher level of understanding, precisely in the areas most relevant to policy, than could even the best interpretations of the empirical, policy-oriented "experts" operating within the traditional framework of government. Specifically, the progressive deterioration of Japanese morale from early 1944 on, and the importance of the role of the Emperor, were matters on which the usual experts did not have clear, certainly not agreed opinions, but the relevant findings of research were unequivocal. The important point here is that the directors of the research, though they made liberal use of experts on Japan, were not themselves such experts at the beginning, but were general social scientists. (Parsons and Vogt 1962: 146–47)

4   As Marvin Harris noted in "The Case of the Japanese Sphincter," the speculative theories on Japanese toilet training and compulsiveness during wartime were concocted by social scientists who had never been to Japan. Anthropologists who conducted Japanese fieldwork in the postwar period found no basis for what turned out to be racist wartime speculation (Harris 1968: 443–44; cf. Lindesmith and Strauss 1950). But the lack of evidence for such complex fantasies about the nature and meaning of Japanese toilet training did not stop Gorer from speculating at some length on the topic. According to Gorer, "A Japanese baby's toilet training begins at four months, and is likely to be the most painful experience of his life. He is held out over the balcony or road at frequent intervals. For every lapse, he is ferociously punished—by his mother's scoldings (in a tone of disgust), by shaking, sometimes by beating. Training is made more difficult by the fact that Japanese babies are habitually overfed. . . . Nonetheless, a baby is almost invariably perfectly housebroken by the time he can toddle"(quoted in La Barre 1945: 329).

5   A January 12, 1942, COI memo described Embree as "a distinguished social anthropologists who has the unusual qualification of having made extensive field studies in Japan. One could find no one superior to him in ability to make psycho-social reports on the people of this enemy country" (FOIA F94–0128, January 12, 1942, CIA).

6   FOIA 124-HQ-5221, FBI.

7   Other government and private agencies used culture and personality studies to analyze and anticipate Japanese actions during the war. On December 16–17, 1944, the Institute of Pacific Relations sponsored the conference "Japanese Character Structure," which brought social scientists together to analyze the Japanese personality type. Most of those who attended the meeting had no firsthand knowledge of Japan, and all but a few had ever studied Japanese culture before the war. Among those attending were Gordon Bowles and Douglas Haring (two anthropologists who had spent years in Japan), as well as Margaret Mead, Talcott Parsons, and Frank Tannenbaum. Dower claims that Embree's 1945 complaints about sloppy culture and personality analysis from non-specialists was directed at the products of this conference (Dower 1986:131; Embree 1945a).

8 Although the OWI's internal distribution date of "Japanese Behavior Patterns" was September 15, 1945, the report was written before Japan's surrender. In her foreword, Benedict clarified that "this study of Japanese ethics, now made available in mimeographed form, was distributed in typescript before the capitulation of Japan and is reproduced here as written in the early summer" (Benedict 1945: ii).

9 GT, September 15, 1945, Box 18, Folder 12.

10 Rudolf Janssens claimed, "The only additions she made to 'Japanese Behavior Patterns' to transform it into *The Chrysanthemum and the Sword* were an overview of Japanese domestic history since the *Meiji* Restoration in 1867, and a chapter about child rearing practices," but there were other minor editorial changes, too (Janssens 1995: 212). Many of the changes reflected the sensitivities of a peacetime audience. For critical evaluations of *Chrysanthemum* and its impact on postwar Japanese society, see Bennett and Nagai 1953; Bowles 1947; Fukui 1999; Kent 1996, 1999; Lie 2001; Lummis 1982; Ryang 2004.

11 See Price 2002a: 18–19 for an account of Taylor's futile efforts to convince General Joseph Stilwell of the utility of propaganda campaigns.

12 GT Box 18, Folder 7, undated.

13 Zacharias's broadcasts to Japan began on May 8, 1945 (V-E Day) using scripts designed by the OWI. The OWI reported, "These broadcasts were evaluated by John K. Fairbanks, Acting Deputy Director of Area III on Sept. 10th [after the war], as being one of the most effective weapons in Area II's psychological warfare armament. He further points out that 'at the moment of surrender, even though the purpose might have had a propaganda slant, Captain Zacharias' name was mentioned in the same breath as the surrender' " (OWI Leaflet News Letter 1945: 13).

14 Leighton wrote that, after the FMAD "concluded that Japanese homefront morale was declining, there were apparently few policy makers who were already convinced of this. As a result, policy directives in psychological warfare lagged behind the changes occurring among the Japanese people and were altered only when the war was almost over" (Leighton 1949: 121).

15 Kluckhohn's analysis connected Benedict's proposals with a generation of British functionalists who aligned their anthropology with indirect rule. But this alignment complicates our evaluation of this work. As Stocking observed, some have argued that, "whereas evolutionism had served primarily as the ideological legitimation of the initial conquest of 'savage races' by 'civilized' Europeans, the 'function of functionalism' was to sustain an established and routinized colonial order by clarifying the principles of traditional native systems through which 'indirect rule' could be carried on" (Stocking 1995: 368). Given the application of the culture and personality approach during the war, this reasoning could be extended to argue that these studies helped administrations install a form of indirect rule that preserved elements of traditional social forms and values. More recently, Katsumi Nakao examined similarities between Twentieth Century British and Japanese colonial anthropologists' experiences and found shared means and goals (Nakao 2004).

16 Notations in Taylor's papers indicate that he received these documents from the National Security Agency under the Freedom of Information Act in 1978.

17 GT SRS-1164, May 11, 1945, Classified "TOP SECRET, ULTRA" Box 18, Folder 11.

18 Ibid.

19 For a treatment of the literature discussing the American intelligence community's intercepts of MAGIC communications indicating the Japanese desire to surrender, see Alperovitz 1995: 23–29, 54–55, 464–65.

20 Edward W. Barrett to George Taylor, October 28, 1952, Box 2, Folder 1, GT.

21 George E. Taylor to Edward W. Barrett, November 18, 1942, Box 2, Folder 1, GT.

22 In the months and years following the use of atomic bombs against the Japanese, there was a swell of partisan criticism of the decision by conservative Republicans (see Alperovitz 1995: 437–43).

23 Leahy publicly criticized Truman's decision to use the atomic bomb, saying that it "was of no material assistance in our war against Japan. The Japanese were already defeated and ready to surrender" (Alperovitz 1995: 3). Even General Douglas MacArthur was critical of using nuclear weapons without clarifying that America's conditions of surrender would include the retention of the emperor. William Manchester wrote that MacArthur "knew that the Japanese would never renounce their Emperor, and that without him an orderly transition to peace would be impossible anyhow, because his people would never submit to Allied occupation unless he ordered it. Ironically, when the surrender did come, it was conditional, and the condition was a continuation of the imperial reign. Had the General's advice been followed, the resort to atomic weapons at Hiroshima and Nagasaki might have been unnecessary" (Manchester 1978: 512). When Norman Cousins asked MacArthur about the decision to use the atomic bomb, he "was surprised to learn he had not even been consulted. What, I asked, would his advice have been? He replied that he saw no military justification for the dropping of the bomb. The war might have ended weeks earlier, he said, if the United States had agreed, as it later did anyway, to the retention of the institution of the Emperor" (Cousins 1987: 70–71).

9 Hoover's Special Intelligence Service

1 Hoover tried to pass off his control over the SIS because of his dislike of having to work under the supervision of others. In the spring of 1941, Hoover wrote to Attorney General Jackson asking the SIS to be reassigned to the ONI or the MID (Webb 2004). Webb argues that Hoover was primarily worried about the liability of running such widespread operations: "Even if Hoover's motivations for guarding his authority over the SIS were selfish, as they undoubtedly were, his concern lay in minimizing his liability for the foreign-intelligence responsibilities he already possessed and not in seizing greater influence for himself and the FBI" (Webb 2004: 51).

2 On January 1, 1942, President Roosevelt "issued a directive specifically ordering Donovan to keep his operative north of the Rio Grande" (Rout and Bratzel 1986: 39).

3 See FOIA 64-HQ-23119, FBI, and FOIA 65-HQ-41922, FBI, for records on the SIS's use of
   the Basque Intelligence Service and the Basque SIS operatives Antonio de Irala, Jose
   Marie de Lasarte, and Jose Antonio de Aguirre Lecube.

4 FOIA 67-HQ-384224–1, FBI.

5 For more on Aston's and Hoover's power struggles, see Powers 1987: 267–69.

6 FOIA 67-HQ-384244–1X, FBI. FOIA requests for SIS records on Bird, Blom, and Morley
   produced no records; it is not clear whether this indicates the FBI's failure to comply
   with FOIA or that no records exist. This ONI memo indicates that Lothrop also listed
   the following organizations or individuals as "well informed" and potentially useful to
   the FBI and SIS: American Smelting and Refining Company, Juan Palett (San Salvador),
   Bethlehem Steel Company, William Bridges (Estancia Viamonte), G. P. Chittenden
   (United Fruit Company), International Telephone and Telegraph, Ralph Jenkins (Bo-
   gotá, Colombia), Lambert Perrson (Guatemala City), Lewis Riley (Wells Fargo, Mexico
   City), Schufeldt (Guatemala), Ledward Smith (Carnegie Institution), Roger Stone
   (New Orleans; FOIA 67-HQ-384224–1X, FBI).

7 FOIA 67-HQ-384224–4, October 24, 1940, FBI.

8 Ibid., November 2, 1940, FBI.

9 FOIA 67-HQ-384224–10, FBI.

10 FOIA 67-HQ-384224–14X2, December 2, 1940, FBI.

11 FOIA 67-HQ-384224–14X12, FBI.

12 FOIA 67-HQ-384224–14X13, FBI.

13 FOIA 67-HQ-384224–15X, FBI.

14 FOIA 67-HQ-384224–16, FBI.

15 FOIA 67-HQ-384224, May 22, 1941, FBI.

16 Ibid.

17 FOIA 67-HQ-384224–15X2, FBI.

18 FOIA 67-HQ-384224–16X3, FBI.

19 FOIA 67-HQ-384224, March 4, 1942, FBI.

20 FOIA 67-HQ-384224–21, FBI.

21 FOIA 67-HQ-384224–30, FBI.

22 FOIA 65-HQ-384224–35X, FBI.

23 FOIA 67-HQ-384224–16X2, FBI.

24 FOIA 67-HQ-384224, April 20, 1942, FBI.

25 FOIA 67-HQ-384224–17, November 19, 1941, FBI.

26 FOIA 67-HQ-384224, January 13, 1942, FBI.

27 FOIA 67-HQ-384224–17X5, FBI.

28 FOIA 67-HQ-384224–17X10, February 17, 1942, FBI.

29 Ibid.

30 FOIA 100-HQ-154696, FBI.

31 *American Antiquity* 7, no. 1 (1941): 83.

32 FOIA 100-HQ-28041–2, September 25, 1953, FBI.

33 Tom Patterson to the author, January 24, 2000.

34 During the war, the IAR undertook research in Venezuela and the West Indies (B. I. Rouse, George Howard), Colombia (W. C. Bennett, James A. Ford), northern Peru and Ecuador (S. K. Lothrop, Marshall Newman, A. I. Kroeber, Theodore McCown), southern Peru and northern Chile (Gordon Willey, Junius Bird), and southern Peru and the Bolivian highlands (A. Kidder, John Rowe; *American Antiquity* 7, no. 1 [1941]: 83).

35 See FOIA F-1994–00037, CIA.

36 Gordon Willey to the author, April 29, 2000.

37 Ibid.

38 Ibid.

39 FOIA 67-HQ-384224–17X10, FBI.

40 FOIA 67-HQ-227981–127, March 14, 1946, FBI.

41 *Times* (London), November 23, 2002, 44.

42 Vaillant committed suicide in 1945 while he was preparing to move with his family to run the U.S. OWI's operations in Madrid (Kidder 1945: 596; see also Lothrop and Price 1968: 278).

43 FOIA 67-HQ-384224–17X13, FBI.

44 FOIA 67-HQ-384224–17X18, March 9, 1942, FBI.

45 Ibid.

46 FOIA 67-HQ-384224–17X20, FBI.

47 FOIA 67-HQ-384224–17X18, FBI.

48 Ibid.

49 Ibid.

50 Ibid.

51 Ibid

52 Ibid.

53 One internal FBI memo indicated that Lothrop also used the Peabody Museum and the American Museum of Natural History as part of his cover (FOIA 67-HQ-384224, November 12, 1943, FBI).

54 FOIA 67-HQ-384224–35, FBI.

55 FOIA 67-HQ-384224–36, FBI.

56 FOIA 67-HQ-384224, May 20, 1944, FBI.

57 FOIA 67-HQ-384224–38, FBI.

58 Ibid.

59 Ibid.

60 Ibid.

61 FOIA 67-HQ-384224–43, FBI.

62 FOIA 67-HQ-384224–39, FBI.

63 The 1944 IAR letterhead, listed the following individuals as board members: A. L. Kroeber (University of California, Berkeley), M. Tozzer (Harvard), A. V. Kidder (Carnegie), F. C. Cole (University of Chicago), A. Means (Pomfret, Conn.), S. K. Lothrop (Peabody Museum), Leslie Spier (Santa Cruz, Calif.), C. Vaillant (American Museum of Natural History), W. C. Bennett (Yale), W. D. Strong (Columbia), and A. Kidder

(Peabody Museum). In 1997 and 1998, I wrote to the IAR several times asking about its records or correspondence from the 1940s, but I received no replies.

64 The Senate Select Committee to Study Governmental Operations with Respect to Intelligence Activities found that, in the 1960s, "excluding grants from the 'Big Three'— Ford, Rockefeller, and Carnegie—of the 700 grants over $10,000 given by 164 other foundations during the period 1963–66, at least 108 involved partial or complete CIA funding. More importantly, CIA funding was involved in *nearly half* the grants the non-'Big Three' foundations made during this period in the field of international activities. In the same period more than one-third of the grants awarded by non-'Big Three' in the physical, life, and social sciences also involved CIA funds" (U.S. Senate 1976: 182).

65 This is not to argue that his duplicitous use of fieldwork as a shield for espionage would have been worth it if he had produced highly valued research. Instead, it highlights how cheaply anthropology was exploited at great risk with little return.

66 Nancy Howell (1990) has discussed the dangers faced by archaeologists falsely accused of being spies; Geoffrey Ross Owens has recounted his experiences conducting fieldwork in Zanzibar, where he was "treated as an American political gent working to undermine a revolutionary government" (Owens 2003); and Payson Sheets has described a field-research setting where locals believed that CIA operatives were operating under claims that they were archaeologists (Sheets 2001). Professional associations could best protect their members from such accusations by instating clear language in their ethical codes clarifying that anthropologists must not conduct secret research for military or intelligence agencies.

10 Culture at War

1 FOIA MORI 199920, March 23, 1942, CIA.

2 FOIA, May 4, 2001, NAVY.

3 References for these examples are: Andrews (Stirling 1973); Bascom (Herskovits 1950: 11); Briggs (Briggs 1967); Coon (Coon 1980); Du Bois (Davis 1991); Frantz (*Anthropology Newsletter*, vol. 36, no. 4 [1995], 68); Fuller (*Anthropology Newsletter*, vol. 25, no. 6 [1983], 4); Gillin, who was only briefly with the OSS (140-HQ-6951, May 20, 1943, FBI); Glueck (Aronson 2004: 150–51; MORI 199920, CIA; Winks 1987: 137); Goldstein (Newman 1991: 246); Gower (Lepowsky 2000: 162); Hanfmann (*Anthropology Newsletter*, vol. 27, no. 5 [1986], 3); Harris (Edelman 1997); Hewes (Herskovits 1950: 79); Hulse (Herskovits 1950: 85); Hutchinson (*Anthropology Newsletter*, vol. 25, no. 6 [1984], 4); Janse (Herskovits 1950: 89); Keesing (Siegel and Spindler 1962); Lesser (Belmonte 1985); Linton, who was briefly an OSS consultant to the Research and Analysis Branch (FOIA 801–43, December 7, 1942, OSS); Lockard (*Anthropology Newsletter*, vol. 18, no. 7 [1977], 3); Loeb (Teffelmeir 1967: 200–203); Mandelbaum (Berreman et al. 1988:410); Mason (Herskovits 1950: 122); May (Winks 1987); Métraux (Herskovits 1950: 125); Murdock (Linton and Wagley 1971: 61); Rodnick (Herskovits 1950: 154); Siegel (Joffee 1964: 395–

96); Starr (Owen 1996: 45); Stout (Trager 1974:72–75); Swadesh (McQuown 1968: 755–56); Tozzer (Schmelz-Keil 1991: 705); Titiev (Lonergan 1991b); and Young (Winks 1987: 497). Some of these anthropologists served at the OSS for short periods on loan from other government agencies; other anthropologists also worked for the OSS during the war. This list is a sample; it is not meant to be comprehensive.

4 FOIA, September 29, 1943, August 12, 1945, CIA.

5 FOIA F94–0125, February 15, 1943, CIA.

6 FOIA, May 30, 1944, February 7, 1945, CIA.

7 FOIA 61–554, 68, October 26, 1942, January 30, 1942, CIA.

8 FOIA, April 17, 1943, CIA.

9 FOIA, May 18, 1943, May 25, 1943, CIA.

10 While even the consideration of using anthrax as a weapon was ethically reprehensible, Japanese scientists working in the Manchukuo Unit 731 (and its predecessor organization, the Epidemic Prevention Department of the Kwantung Army, also known as the Ishii Unit) had already been working on such applications of biological warfare. At Unit 731,

> various methods were developed for dispersal of biological weapons. One was to introduce the pathogen to a local water supply or food supply. Another was to use airborne means, and Unit 731 developed a bomb specifically designed for dispersing pathogens from aircraft. In 1939, when Japanese and Russian forces clashed in the battle of Nomohan on the Mongolian–Manchurian border, Unit 731 introduced the typhoid-fever pathogen into rivers in the area. In 1940 and 1941 the unit used aircraft to spread cotton and rice husks contaminated with the black plague at Changde and Ningbo, in central China. (Tanaka 1996: 137)

After 1940, the Japanese used a series of biological weapons in battle, including anthrax-bacillus bombs; bomb shrapnel coated in bacillus; experiments with cholera, typhoid, and paratyphoid bacilli; and plague-carrying fleas and rats to be dropped from aircraft on enemy territories (Tanaka 1996: 136–38; see also Harris 2000). Unit 731 used Chinese and Russians in biological-weapons tests in Pingfan, where some of the Chinese who resisted the Japanese occupation were used as human "guinea pigs" (Tanaka 1996: 138).

11 A footnote stated that the author was unable to "to confer with Drs. Draper and Dupertuis . . . two of the most enthusiastic workers in the constitutional field, as they were both on vacation while I was in New York" (OSS 1943a: 17).

12 The footnote for this passage argued: "Another aspect that should not be overlooked by our strategists is the fact that beri-beri is a high temperature disease, being most virulent in the summer and early fall. The highest death rate, if one can trust an article in the *Japan Medical World*, VI, 1926, p. 8, occurs among breast fed infants and males aged 15 to 30 from cities in the northern districts of the Empire" (OSS 1943a: 21, n. 1).

13 The report's footnote cautioned: "Care must be taken to protect our rice-eating allies from retaliation by the enemy" (OSS 1943a: 21, n. 2).

14 The report was later redesignated oss Research and Analysis Branch report 614.

15 John Embree's authorship of this report is suggested by the bibliography listing "John Embree's *Suye Mira, A Japanese Village* (Unpublished Field Notes)."

16 The lengthy 1944 oss report "Japanese Attempts at Infiltration among Muslims in Russia and Her Borderlands" examined in further detail the extent of Japanese alliances in Soviet territories (oss 1944).

17 MORI 225413–2, September 1, 1945, CIA.

18 MacDonald observed that the original legend linking the prophesized yellow river with an occupation's end most likely referred to the British, not the Japanese occupation, but Bateson figured that the prophesy could still be of use (MacDonald 1947: 144).

19 Bateson's theories that Americans generated independence in their children and protectorate colonies were negated in the Cold War, as American forms of indirect rule and debt dependence accomplished control while maintaining illusions of independence (Frank 1967).

20 Bateson expounded on his analysis of British parenting and colonial models in a letter to Mead in which he reminded her of his theory that

> the English as colonists would adopt the complete responsible-parental attitude towards native people and that therefore, specializing in being *models* for behavior, they would never be able to "wean" their colonies because the colony as a whole cannot be "sent to school" to learn independence.
>
> Well—it's tragic, heartbreaking, to watch the relations between the responsible, model Englishman and the Indians with whom he works in his office. He just dare not delegate responsibility and they just dare not take it up themselves— a self-propagating vicious circle. Built into the notion of white prestige is the notion that we are here to *show* the Indian how to behave and how to govern. And the act of showing him is dignified and the Englishman feels that he is doing his duty by the Indian and at the same time is not being as domineering as he would be if he ordered the Indian to do the job while he sat by and watched. (Bateson to Mead, June 1, 1944, Box A1, MM)

In this more private, personal presentation of the issues, Bateson blankly expressed his personal dislike of the relationships that colonialism bred.

21 MORI 43862, CIA.

22 Jack Harris to the author, February 7, 2005.

23 Harris to the author, January 28, 2005.

24 For an overview of Harris's troubles at the United Nations, see Price 2004a: 154–63.

25 Harris to the author, February 7, 2005.

26 Harris to Jonathan Harris, October 24, 2004.

27 Roosevelt compiled a comprehensive report evaluating oss "intelligence and unorthodox warfare" operations. This top-secret report was completed in 1947 and was published in 1976 with limited redactions as *War Report of the* oss (see Roosevelt 1976: vii).

Harris confirmed to me that he was the OSS agent mentioned in the passage (Harris to the author, July 16, 2005).

28 Harris to the author, July 16, 2005. When he read passages on OSS intelligence operations in South Africa in *War Report of the* OSS, Harris wrote, "It is with great interest and some satisfaction that I now read from your quote of the Roosevelt paper that my report 'played an important part in the South African decision to adopt a firm policy against that organization.' I never knew that!" (ibid.).

29 FOIA 93–01068R, CIA.

30 For Coon's account of the problems that arose because of his association with Makonnen Desta during this Ethiopia visit, see Coon 1981: 96–98.

31 FOIA 93–01068R, 7/456, July 10, 1943, CIA.

32 Ibid.

33 FOIA 93–01068R, 7/456, August 4, 1943, CIA.

34 FOIA 93–01068R, 7/456–88, April 24, 1945, CIA.

35 Ibid.

36 On October 30, 1947, Major F. N. Arnoldy wrote to Coon asking him to come to Fort Riley to help with the development of a training course for paramilitary operatives. Coon declined, writing, "I received a medical discharge and am officially insane. Therefore, there is little likelihood of my regaining my commission" (Carleton Coon to F. N. Arnoldy, November 4, 1947, CC). The CIA released some documents under FOIA recording Coon's failed efforts in the late 1970s to establish benefits for the injuries he sustained in the OSS (MORI 394981, April 6, 1979, CIA). Included in this paperwork is an undated World War Two–era affidavit reporting that, on January 12, 1942, Coon received a concussion when a roof tile fell on his head (FOIA MORI 394981, 1996, CIA).

37 FOIA 93–01068R, 7/456–69, CIA.

38 FOIA 93–01068R, 7/456–72, December 5, 1944, CIA.

39 FOIA 93–01068R, 7/456–81, February 20, 1945, CIA. In April 1944, the anthropologist E. Wyllys Andrews IV conducted OSS operations in North Africa and later traveled to Italy and France, where he "further expanded [an underground resistance] group's activities to include, in addition to its several hundred secret intelligence agents, one hundred and fourteen foreign saboteurs with experience in guerilla warfare." In April 1945, Andrews led a group of operatives across France and delivered vital intelligence (FOIA docs., memorandum, September 25, 1945, CIA). The citation awarding Andrews the Legion of Merit award stated:

> As a result of Lieutenant Andrews's initiative, planning, and personal work, sometimes under the most difficult conditions, one of the most productive sources of intelligence and sabotage, consisting of hundreds of well organized, daring, and well trained secret intelligence agents and saboteurs, was expanded and integrated into a working unit to bear more directly against the enemy in Europe, and made available to the United States Government's intelligence services. (FOIA docs., Wash-PPB-Pers 1, CIA, received February 8, 1999)

The month after the disillusion of the oss, the War Department's Strategic Services Unit was already making secret arrangements to secure "special funds" for Andrews to continue government operations. He later made a career at the CIA (FOIA, CIA, received February 8, 1999; Stephen Penrose to Douglas Dimond, November 23, 1945).

40 FOIA MORI 395505–394406, CIA.

41 The SOE was a clandestine British warfare-intelligence unit that undertook several coordinated operations with the oss during the war (see Smith 1983).

42 Anthony Brown published a few paragraphs of Coon's postscript in his 1982 biography of William Donovan, *The Last Hero*, explaining that he could not locate the document in Donovan's papers, "nor was it part of Coon's memoirs, *North Africa Story*. According to Coon, it was excised by his editor. Coon voluntarily sent this segment of his report to the author" (Brown 1982: 846, n. 8).

43 Bateson to Mead, June 1, 1944, Box A1, MM.

11 *Postwar Ambiguities*

1 For example, while anthropologists began to directly confront the impact of the war on peoples of the Pacific in the 1960s and '70s, a few anthropologists wrote against the trends of disciplinary silence in the decade following the war. Notable among them were Ian Hogbin's *Transformation Scene: The Changing Culture of a New Guinea Village* (1951) and Cyril Belshaw's *The Great Village* (1957), which examined a New Guinea village destroyed during the war and later rebuilt and reinhabited. Various studies of the cargo-cult movement later examined the war's impact as a central feature of analysis (Lawrence 1964; Worsley 1968). Margaret Mead's longitudinal fieldwork with the Manus (Mead 1956) examined postwar changes more in terms of modernization than as a direct effect of the war. In later decades, the impact of the war became a theme of anthropological consideration (e.g., Robinson 1981). For more on the war's impact on communities traditionally studied by anthropologists, see Foerstel and Gilliam 1992; Gray 2005; Hogbin 1949; Newton 1996; Read 1947; Ritzenthaler 1943.

2 Other anthropologists stayed behind and began careers at the State Department, CIA, and other agencies, although the politics of the Cold War narrowly limited the range of intelligence views that were welcome in those agencies (Price 2004a, 2004d).

3 As Frederick Engels observed at Marx's graveside: "Marx discovered the law of development of human history: the simple fact, hitherto concealed by an overgrowth of ideology, that mankind must first of all eat, drink, have shelter and clothing, before it can pursue politics, science, art, religion, etc.; that therefore the production of the immediate material means of subsistence and consequently the degree of economic development attained by a given people or during a given epoch form the foundation upon which the state institutions, the legal conceptions, art, and even the ideas on religion, of the people concerned have been evolved, and in the light of which they must, therefore, be explained, instead of *vice versa*, as had hitherto been the case" (Engels 1970 [1883]: 162).

4 *American Anthropologist* 48 (1946): 308, 319.

5 Ibid. 47 (1945): 327.

6 Ibid. 48, no. 1 (1946): 146–47, 167.

7 Ralph Beals to Julian Steward, October 10, 1945, Box 4, ISA.

8 Ibid., October 25, 1945, Box 4, ISA.

9 Margaret Mead to Robert Redfield, October 5, 1945, Box 175, ST.

10 The application of peacetime ethnography for military purposes raises an unexplored but fundamental ethical question. Before the war, John Embree was hosted by a rural village that fed him, sheltered him, and answered his probing questions—all with the understanding that the venture was undertaken simply to increase Embree's knowledge of Japanese culture, which, at the time, it was. While the principles of "informed consent" for research subjects were not codified until after the war, troubling questions remain about obtaining information from willing cultural informants in one context and using it to harm them in another.

It is not that the Japanese military was completely unaware of the potential intelligence risks of allowing foreigners to study in Japan before the war. Embree writes in his preface to *Suye Mura* that military suspicions about ethnographic work were serious enough that Suye Mura was selected because of its distant proximity from military installations. Embree wrote, "Suye is far from any military zone, and thus our work did not come under undue suspicion by the military. In any field work by foreigners in Japan this is an important consideration" (Embree 1939: xxii). Given the U.S. military's uses of Embree's ethnographic data during the war, such concerns should be seen as well warranted rather than as xenophobic or needlessly paranoid.

11 However, lack of secrecy does not guarantee the quality of work produced. The problematic war research of Geoffrey Gorer and Weston La Barre was published in peer-reviewed journals during and after the war (see Gorer 1943a, 1943b; La Barre 1945).

12 Laura Thompson to Maria Rogers, February 11, 1947, Box 23, LT.

13 Margaret Mead to Laura Thompson, May 21, 1947, Box 23, LT.

14 Laura Thompson, "Suggestions and Additions to the Draft of the 'Preliminary Report of the Committee on Ethics,'" May 30, 1947, Box 23, LT.

15 Idem to *Commentary*, August 14, 1946, Box 23, LT.

16 It also declared, "Except in the event of a declaration of war by the Congress, academic institutions should not undertake activities or accept contracts in anthropology that are not related to their normal functions of teaching, research, and public service. They should not lend themselves to clandestine activities. We deplore unnecessary restrictive classifications of research reports prepared under contract to the Government, and excessive security regulations imposed on participating academic personnel" (FNAAA 1967: 382). It noted that Department of Defense and funding from "other mission-oriented" government agencies created hazardous field-research conditions. It stated that even the impression that anthropologists were involved in intelligence work damaged anthropology, and it declared, "Academic institutions and individual members of the academic community, including students, should scrupulously avoid both involve-

314 NOTES TO CHAPTER 11

ment in clandestine intelligence activities and the use of the name of anthropology, or the title of anthropologist, as cover for intelligence activities" (FNAAA 1967: 382).

17 *Fellows' Newsletter*, vol. 8, no. 6 (1967), 8. Outside of anthropology, other social scientists have made more general arguments concerning the propriety of social-science contributions to the waging of wars. The political scientist Bruce Cumings has argued that, for academics not to compromise their academic integrity by contributing their skills to military and intelligence agencies, they must meet three criteria:

> 1. The war is one of total mobilization against an enemy clearly determined to take away all our freedoms, including academic ones.
> 2. One takes a leave of absence from the classroom to serve this war effort, establishing a clear difference between the two domains of the state and the university.
> 3. Classified work does not continue after reentry to the university.
> (Cumings 2002: 175)

Most of the actions taken by American anthropologists during the Second World War meet Cumings's ethical criteria. For Cumings, the acceptability of academics' contributing their skills to military or intelligence agencies is determined by a consideration of the nature or justness of the fight that they are joining:

> Working for the government against Hitler was different from doing the same type of thing during the cold war; the difference, it seems to me, is that between a crisis that drew nearly every American to the effort against the Nazis and Japan in conditions of total war to Washington and overseas posts distinct from campus positions, and the very different requirements placed on scholars and universities in peacetime to uphold their independence and academic freedom and to make full disclosure of possible biases deriving from clandestine sponsorship and privileged access to research funds. (Cumings 2002: 175)

Cumings's distinctions are attractive, but there are no clear criteria for determining national threats, and his approach invites partisan applications of anthropology. Today there is a significant division among American anthropologists concerning the nature of the threats posed by the "war on terror," as well as the propriety of anthropological contributions to the current war, with justifications calling back to anthropology's contributions to the Second World War.

18 In 1948, as a reaction to McCarthyistic attacks on Melville Jacobs and Richard Morgan, the AAA's membership endorsed a statement of academic freedom proclaiming that all anthropologists should have "complete freedom to interpret and publish findings without censorship or interference" (*American Anthropologist* [1949]: 370). These principles of academic freedom would later be used by anthropologists who wished to engage in military and intelligence research.

19 When Anna Roosevelt discussed in passing the Second World War activities of Clifford Evans and other archaeologists associated with the *Handbook of South American In-*

dians, a letter of complaint from 188 archaeologists was published in the *Society for American Archaeology Bulletin* (see Baffi et al. 1996; Price 2002c: 17; Roosevelt 1991, 1996). Peter Suzuki has had difficulty publishing research that was critical of anthropologists' work in the WRA camps (Suzuki 1986b: 6–8). Gretchen Schafft's documentation of Nazi anthropology generated attacks from German anthropologists displeased with the light it cast (cf. Schafft 2006; Streck 2006). The strong reactions in opposition to Starn's analysis of anthropologists' activities at the WRA convey similar efforts to establish rights of analytical cabotage (see Opler 1987; Sady 1987 and 1988).

Archival and Manuscript Sources

AAA   Papers of the American Anthropological Association. National Anthropological Archives, Smithsonian Institution, Washington, D.C.

CC   Carleton S. Coon Papers. National Anthropological Archives, Smithsonian Institution, Washington, D.C.

EAH   E. A. Hooton Papers. Peabody Museum of Archaeology and Ethnology, Harvard University, Cambridge, Mass.

EB   Ethnogeographic Board Records, Washington, D.C., 1942–1945. Smithsonian Institution, Washington, D.C.

EG   Esther Goldfrank Papers. National Anthropological Archives, Smithsonian Institution, Washington, D.C.

FB   Franz Boas Papers, 1858–1942. American Philosophical Society, Philadelphia.

FDRL   Franklin Delano Roosevelt Presidential Library Papers, Hyde Park, New York.

FE   Fred Eggan Papers. Department of Special Collections, University of Chicago Library.

FJ   Frederick Johnson Papers. National Anthropological Archives, Smithsonian Institution, Washington, D.C.

GB   Gregory Bateson Correspondence, 1937–1943. In "Papers of Margaret Mead and the South Pacific Ethnographic Archives," Margaret Mead Papers, Manuscript Division, Library of Congress, Washington, D.C.

GT   George Edward Taylor Papers. University of Washington Library Manuscripts, Special Collections, University Archives, Seattle, Washington.

HB   Homer Barnett Papers. National Anthropological Archives, Smithsonian Institution, Washington, D.C.

HF   Henry Field Papers. University of Miami, Otto G. Richter Library, Archives and Special Collections Department, Collection No. 72, Miami, Fla.

HRD   Aleš Hrdlička Papers. National Anthropological Archives, Smithsonian Institution, Washington, D.C.

ISA   Papers of the Institute of Social Anthropology. National Anthropological Archives, Smithsonian Institution, Washington, D.C.

LT   Laura Thompson Papers. National Anthropological Archives, Smithsonian Institution, Washington, D.C.

MJ   Melville Jacobs Papers. University of Washington Library Manuscripts, Special Collections, Seattle, Washington.

MM   Margaret Mead Papers, Manuscript Division, Library of Congress, Washington, D.C.

NA   National Archives and Records Administration. College Park, Md.

PSF   Papers of the Pacific Survey File. National Anthropological Archives, Smithsonian Institution, Washington, D.C.

PN   Philleo Nash Papers. Harry S. Truman Library, Independence, Mo.

RB   Ralph Beals Papers. National Anthropological Archives, Smithsonian Institution, Washington, D.C.

RFB   Roy Franklin Barton Select Correspondence. Correspondence collected and held by John W. Barton.

ST   Sol Tax Papers. University of Chicago, Special Collections.

Books, Journals, Reports, and Interviews

AA (*American Anthropologist*). 1920. "Anthropology at the Cambridge Meeting and Proceedings of the American Anthropological Association." *American Anthropologist* 22: 85–96.

———. 1942. "Report: Proceedings of the American Anthropological Association for the Year Ending December, 1941." *American Anthropologist* 44, no. 2: 281–93.

Aberle, David F. 1967. "Correspondence." *Fellows' Newsletter of the American Anthropological Association*, vol. 8, no. 5, 7.

Agin, Dan. 2006. *Junk Science*. New York: Thomas Dunne.

Aginsky, B. W. 1942. "Social Science and the World Situation." *American Anthropologist* 44: 521–25.

Alinsky, Saul D. 1971. *Rules for Radicals*. New York: Vintage.

Allied Geographical Section. 1943. *You and the Native: Notes for the Guidance of Members of the Forces in Their Relations with New Guinea Natives*. Allied Geographical Section, Southwest Pacific Area (reproduced in Brown 2004).

Alperovitz, Gar. 1995. *The Decision to Use the Atomic Bomb and the Architecture of an American Myth*. New York: Alfred A. Knopf.

Arensberg, Conrad M. 1942. "Report on a Developing Community, Poston, Arizona." *Applied Anthropology* 2, no. 1: 1–21.

Arnold, Bettina. 1990. "The Past as Propaganda: Totalitarian Archeology in Nazi Germany." *Antiquity* 64: 464–78.

Aronson, Schlomo. 2004. *Hitler, the Allies, and the Jews*. Cambridge: Cambridge University Press.

Asad, Talal, ed. 1973. *Anthropology and the Colonial Encounter*. London: Ithaca Press.

Ashley, David, and David Michael Orenstein. 1995. *Sociological Theory: Classical Statements*, 3d ed. Boston: Allyn and Bacon.

Atkinson, Rick. 2003. *An Army at Dawn: The War in North Africa, 1942–1943*. New York: Henry Holt.

Baffi, E. I., et al. 1996. "Letter to the Editor." *Society for American Archaeology Bulletin* 14, no. 1: 4–5.

Baltzell, Digby. 2004. *Philadelphia Gentlemen: The Making of a National Upper Class*. New Brunswick, N.J.: Transaction Publishers.

Barclay, Paul David. 2001. "An Historian among the Anthropologists: The Inō Kanori Revival and the Legacy of Japanese Colonial Ethnography in Taiwan." *Japanese Studies* 21, no. 2: 117–36.

Barkan, Elazar. 1988. "Mobilizing Scientists against Nazi Racism, 1933–1939." Pp. 180–205 in *Bones, Bodies, Behavior: Essays on Biological Anthropology, Volume 5: History of Anthropology Series*, ed. George W. Stocking. Madison: University of Wisconsin Press.

Bateson, Gregory. 1942a. "Announcement: Council on Human Relations." *Applied Anthropology* 1, no. 2: 66–67.

———. 1942b. "Morale and National Character." Pp. 71–91 in *Civilian Morale*, ed. Goodwin Watson. New York: Cornwell Press.

———. 1944. Gregory Bateson to Dillon Ripley, OSS Southeast Asia Command, memorandum, November 15, 1944. Released by CIA under FOIA in August 1994.

Bateson, Gregory, and Margaret Mead. 1941. "Principles of Morale Building." *Journal of Educational Sociology* 15: 206–20.

Beals, Ralph. 1946. *Cherán: A Sierra Tarascan Village*. Washington, D.C.: Government Printing Office.

———. 1967. "Background Information on Problems of Anthropological Research and Ethics." *Fellows' Newsletter of the American Anthropological Association* 8, no. 1, 2–13.

Beals, Ralph, Pedro Carrasco, and Thomas McCorkle. 1944. *Houses and House of the Sierra Tarascans*. Institute of Social Anthropology, Publication No. 1, Washington, D.C.: Government Printing Office.

Beals, Ralph L., F. L.W. Richardson, Julian H. Steward Jr., and Joseph E. Weckler. 1943. "Anthropology during the War and After." Memorandum Prepared by the Committee on War Service of Anthropologists, Division of the Anthropology and Psychology National Research Council, March 10, 1943, box 3, "Manuscript and Data Files," EAH.

Belmont, Thomas. 1985. "Alexander Lesser." *American Anthropology* 87 (3): 637–44.

Belshaw, C. 1957. *The Great Village*. London: Routledge and Kegan Paul.

Bendix, Reinhard. 1968. "Otto Hintze." Pp. 366–68 in *International Encyclopedia of the Social Sciences*, vol. 6. New York: Free Press.

Benedict, Ruth. 1934. *Patterns of Culture*. New York: Houghton Mifflin.

———. 1945. "Japanese Behavior Patterns." OWI Area III, Overseas Branch, Foreign Morale Analysis Division, report no. 25, September 15, box 18, folder 12, GT.

———. 1946. *The Chrysanthemum and the Sword: Patterns of Japanese Culture*. Boston: Houghton Mifflin.

———. 1950. *Race: Science and Politics*. Revised Edition. New York: Viking Press.

Benedict, Ruth, and Gene Weltfish. 1943. *The Races of Mankind*. New York: Public Affairs Committee.

Bennett, John W. 1996. "Applied and Action Anthropology: Ideological and Conceptual Aspects." *Current Anthropology* 36 (supple.): s23–s53.

Bennett, John W., and Michio Nagai. 1953. "The Japanese Critique of the Methodology of Benedict's 'Chrysanthemum and the Sword.'" *American Anthropologist* 55: 404–11.

Bennett, Windell Clark. 1947. *The Ethnogeographic Board*. Washington D.C.: Smithsonian Institution.

Berleant-Schiller, Riva. 1989. "Gitel (Gertrude) Poznanski Steed." Pp. 331–36 in *Women Anthropologists, Selected Biographies*, eds. Ute Gacs et al. Urbana: University of Illinois Press.

Berreman, Gerald D., Elizabeth Colson, and Milton Singer. 1988. "David G. Mandelbaum, 1911–1987." *American Anthropologist* 90, no. 2: 410–15.

Bess, Michael. 2006. *Choices under Fire: Moral Dimensions of World War II*. New York: Alfred A. Knopf.

Bishop, Carl Whiting. 1942. *Origin of the Far Eastern Civilizations: A Brief Handbook*. War Background Studies, no. 1. Washington, D.C.: Smithsonian Institution.

Black Book Committee. 1976 (1946). *The Black Book: The Nazi Crime against the Jewish People*, reprint. ed. New York: Nexus Press.

Boas, Franz. 1919. "Scientists as Spies." *Nation*, December 20, 797.

——. 1939. "Intellectual Freedom." *Masses* 30, no. 8, 17.

——. 1945 (1917). "Patriotism." Pp. 156–59 in Franz Boas, *Race and Democratic Society*. New York: J. J. Augustin.

Bock, Philip K. 1991. "Stanley S. Newman." Pp. 504–505 in *International Dictionary of Anthropologists*, ed. Christopher Winters. New York: Garland Publishing.

Bomb, P.A. 1981. *From Asininity to Assassination: A Biography about a Peripatetic Presidential Candidate*. Portland, Ore.: Metropolitan Press.

Boswell, Sharon. 1996. Interview with George Taylor, May 16, box 10, folder 24, GT.

Bowles, Gordon T. 1947. "Review of *The Chrysanthemum and the Sword*." *Harvard Journal of Asiatic Studies* 10: 237–41.

——. 1964. "Douglas G. Haring, Early Years and Scholarly Career," Pp. 9–23 in *Fact and Theory in Social Science*, eds. Earl W. Count and Gordon T. Bowles. Syracuse, N.Y.: Syracuse University Press.

——. 1991. "Douglas Gilbert Haring." Pp. 269–70 in *International Dictionary of Anthropologists*, ed. Christopher Winters. New York: Garland Publishing.

Briggs, Lloyd Cabot. 1967. "Letter to the Editor." *Fellows' Newsletter of the American Anthropological Association* 8, no. 6, 8.

Browman, David L. 2005. " 'Uncensuring' Boas." *Anthropology News* 46, no. 1: 3.

Brown, Anthony Cave. 1982. *The Last Hero, Wild Bill Donovan*. New York: Time Books.

Brown, G. Gordon. 1945. "War Relocation Authority Gila River Project. Rivers, Arizona Community Analysis Section. May 12 to July 7, 1945." *Applied Anthropology* 4, no. 4: 1–49.

Brown, Malcolm. 2003. *T. E. Lawrence*. New York: New York University Press.

Brown, Paula. 2004. "Appendix II. 'You and the Native.'" Pp. 129–44 in *The Chibu: A Study of Change in the New Guinea Highlands*. London: Routledge.

Bullen, Ripley P. 1942. "An Anthropological World." *American Anthropologist* 44: 525–26.

Burleigh, Michael. 1988. *Germany Turns Eastwards*. Cambridge: Cambridge University Press.

Caffrey, Margaret M. 1989. *Ruth Benedict: Stranger in This Land*. Austin: University of Texas Press.

Carey, Frank. 1942. "It's Anthropologist's Plan to Prevent Future Wars." *Washington Post*, April 19, 1942, p. L6.

Castañeda, Quetzil. 2003. "Stocking's Historiography of Influence: Boas, Gamio and Redfield at the Cross 'Road to Light.' " *Critique of Anthropology* 23, no. 3: 235–62.

——. 2005. "The Carnegie Mission and Vision of Science: Institutional Contexts of Maya Archaeology and Espionage." Pp. 37–74 in *History of Anthropology Annual*, vol. 1, eds. Regna Darnell and Frederic Gleach. Lincoln: University of Nebraska Press.

Chabon, Michael. 2007. *The Yiddish Policemen's Union*. New York: Harper Collins.

Chang, Gordon H. 1993. " 'Superman Is about to Visit the Relocation Centers' and the Limits of Wartime Liberalism." *Amerasia Journal* 19, no. 1: 37–60.

Chang, W. C. 1984. "W. C. Pei, 1904–1982." *American Anthropologist* 86, no. 1: 115–18.

Chapple, Eliot D. 1943. "Anthropological Engineering: Its Use to Administrators." *Applied Anthropology* 2, no. 2: 23–32.

Chomsky, Noam. 1978. *Intellectuals and the State*. Baarn: Het Wereldvenster.

——. 1991. *Deterring Democracy*. New York: Hill and Wang.

Chun, Kyung-soo. 2004. "Opium and Emperor with the Context of Colonialism and the War in Imperial Japan." Paper presented at the East Asian Anthropology and Japanese Colonialism Forum, Third Conference, Seoul National University, November 13.

Chun, Kyung-soo, ed. 2004. "Abstracts and Papers Presented at the East Asian Anthropology and Japanese Colonialism Forum, Third Conference." Seoul National University, November 13.

CIAA (Office of the Coordinator of Inter-American Affairs). 1947. *History of the Office of the Coordinator of Inter-American Affairs*. Historical Reports on War Administration. Washington, D.C.: Government Printing Office.

Ciardi, John. 1987. *A Third Browser's Dictionary*. Pleasantville, N.Y.: Akadine.

Clark, Austin Hobart. 1943. *Iceland and Greenland*. War Background Studies, no. 15. Washington, D.C.: Smithsonian Institution.

Clarke, Richard. 2004. *Against All Enemies: Inside America's War on Terror*. New York: Free Press.

Clothier, William J. 1943. "Recuay Pottery in the Lower Santa Valley." *Revista del Museo Nacional* 12, no. 2: 235–38.

Cochran, Doris M. 1943. *Poisonous Reptiles of the World: A Wartime Handbook*. War Background Studies, no. 10. Washington, D.C.: Smithsonian Institution.

Cockburn, Alexander. 1987. *Corruptions of Empire*. London: Verso.

——. 2005. "Anthropologists, Internment and Complicity: Executive Order 9066 as Opportunity." Paper presented at the annual meeting of the American Anthropological Association, Washington, D.C., December 2.

——. n.d. *Internment: Who Said No*. Unpublished ms.

Coe, Michael D. 2006. *Final Report: An Archaeologist Excavates His Past*. New York: Thames and Hudson.

Cogan, Frances B. 2000. *Captured: The Japanese Internment of American Civilians in the Philippines, 1941–1945*. Athens: University of Georgia Press.

Cohn, Bernard S. 1987. *An Anthropologist among the Historians and Other Essays*. Delhi: Oxford University Press.

COI (Coordinator of Information). 1942. "Social Relations in Japan." Psychology Division, report no. 17. March 19.

Colby, Gerard, and Charlotte Dennett. 1995. *Thy Will Be Done: The Conquest of the Amazon: Nelson Rockefeller and Evangelism in the Age of Oil*. New York: Harper Perennial.

Cole, Sally. 2003. *Ruth Landes: A Life in Anthropology*. Lincoln: University of Nebraska Press.

Collins, Henry Bascom. 1945. *The Aleutian Islands: Their People and Natural History*. War Background Studies, no. 21. Washington, D.C.: Smithsonian Institution.

——. 1946. "Anthropology during the War, II. Scandinavia." *American Anthropologist* 48: 141–44.

Comitas, Lambros. 2000. "Conrad Arensberg, 1910–1997." *American Anthropologist* 101, no. 4: 810–13.

Cook, S. F. 1945. "Demographic Consequences of European Contact with Primitive Peoples." *Annals of the American Academy of Political and Social Science* 237: 107–11.

Coon, Carleton S. 1945. *Torch Anthology*. (Section 22, Copy 1). North Africa, May 1942–May 1943, My Part in the OSS Operations during that Period. OSS Archives, National Archives and Records Administration, College Park, Md.

——. 1980. *A North Africa Story: The Anthropologist as OSS Agent, 1941–1943*. Ipswich, Mass.: Gambit.

——. 1981. *Adventures and Discoveries: The Autobiography of Carleton S. Coon, Anthropologist and Explorer*. New York: Prentice Hall.

Cooper, John M. 1946. "Anthropology during the War: III. Italy." *American Anthropologist* 48: 299–301.

——. 1947. "Anthropology in the United States during 1939–1945." *Société des Americanistes des Paris Journal* 36: 1–14.

Copeland, Miles. 1989. *The Game Player: Confessions of the CIA's Original Political Operative*. London: Aurum Press.

Coser, Lewis A. 1968. "Max Scheler." Pp. 39–42 in *International Encyclopedia of the Social Sciences*, vol. 14. New York: Free Press.

Cosmos Club. 1941. *Membership of the Cosmos Club*. Washington, D.C.: Cosmos Club.

Couffer, Jack. 1992. *Bat Bomb: World War II's Other Secret Weapon*. Austin: University of Texas Press.

Cousins, Norman. 1987. *The Pathology of Power*. New York: W. W. Norton.

Cowan, J. Milton J. 1975. "Peace and War." *Linguistic Society of America Bulletin* 64 (March): 28–34.

———. 1979. "Linguistics at War." Pp. 158–68 in *The Uses of Anthropology*, ed. Walter Gold-schmidt. Washington, D.C.: American Anthropological Association.

Crawford, O. G. S. 1955. *Said and Done: The Autobiography of an Archaeologist*. London: Weidenfeld and Nicolson.

Crowley, Daniel, and Alan Dundes. 1982. "William Russel Bascom, 1912–1981." *Journal of American Folklore* 95, no. 378: 465–67.

Cumings, Bruce. 2002. *Parallax Visions: Making Sense of American–East Asian Relations*. Dunham: Duke University Press.

Daniels, Roger. 2004. *Guarding the Golden Door: American Immigration Policy and Immigrants since 1882*. New York: Hill and Wang.

Darnell, Regna. 1998. *And Along Came Boas: Continuity and Revolution in Americanist Anthropology*. Philadelphia: John Benjamins Publishing.

———. 2002a. "Fred Eggan." Pp. 145–48 in *Celebrating a Century of the American Anthropological Association*, eds. Regna Darnell and Frederic Gleach. Lincoln: University of Nebraska Press.

———. 2002b. "Frederica de Laguna." Pp. 201–4 in *Celebrating a Century of the American Anthropological Association*, eds. Regna Darnell and Frederic Gleach. Lincoln: University of Nebraska Press.

———. 2002c. "Conrad M. Arensberg." Pp. 253–56 in *Celebrating a Century of the American Anthropological Association*, eds. Regna Darnell and Frederic Gleach. Lincoln: University of Nebraska Press.

Datta-Majumder, N. 1948. "Anthropology during the War: VI. India." *American Anthropologist* 49: 159–64.

Davenport, Charles Benedict. 1919a. *Naval Officers, Their Heredity and Development*. Washington, D.C.: Carnegie Institution.

———. 1919b. *Defects Found in Drafted Men: Statistical Information Compiled from the Draft Records under the Direction of the Surgeon General, M. W. Ireland* (with A. G. Love). Washington, D.C.: Government Printing Office.

David, Thomas. 2004. *Shifting Sands: The Rise and Fall of Biblical Archaeology*. Oxford: Oxford University Press.

Davis, Elmer. 1943. "OWI Has a Job." *Public Opinion Quarterly* 7, no. 1: 5–14.

Davis, Eric. 1991. "Cora du Bois." *Anthropology News* 36 (6): 5.

Deignan, Herbert Girton. 1943a. *Siam—Land of Free Men*. War Background Studies, no. 8. Washington, D.C.: Smithsonian Institution.

———. 1943b. *Burma, Gateway to China*. War Background Studies, no. 17. Washington, D.C.: Smithsonian Institution.

DeVos, George. 1996. "A Cloak of Competence or an Opened Kimono: Ruth Benedict on the Cultural Psychology of the Japanese." Paper presented at the Annual Meeting of the American Anthropological Association, San Francisco, November.

Diamond, Sigmund. 1992. *Compromised Campus: The Collaboration of Universities with the Intelligence Community, 1945–1955*. New York: Oxford University Press.

Doak, Kevin M. 2003. "Nakano Seiichi and Colonial Ethnic Studies." Pp. 109–29 in *Wartime*

Japanese Anthropology in Asia and the Pacific, Senri Ethnological Studies No. 65, eds. Akitoshi Shimizu and Jan van Bremen. Osaka: National Museum of Ethnology.

Dofny, Jacques. 1979. "Georges Friedmann." Pp. 205–8 in *International Encyclopedia of the Social Sciences, Biographical Supplement*, vol. 18. New York: Free Press.

Dollard, John, and Donald Horton. 1943. *Fear in Battle*. New Haven, Conn.: Institute of Human Relations.

Donald, Leland. 2006. "David Friend Aberle." *American Anthropologist* 108, no. 1: 263–67.

Doob, Leonard W. 1947. "The Utilization of Social Scientists in the Overseas Branch of the Office of War Information." *American Political Science Review* 61, no. 4: 649–67.

Dorwart, Jeffery. 1979. *The Office of Naval Intelligence: The Birth of America's First Intelligence Agency, 1865–1918*. Annapolis, Md.: Naval Institute Press.

Dower, John W. 1986. *War without Mercy: Race and Power in the Pacific War*. New York: Pantheon.

Drinnon, Richard. 1987. *Keeper of Concentration Camps: Dillon S. Meyer and American Racism*. Berkeley: University of California Press.

Dufour, Darna L. 1989. "Alice Mossie Brues." Pp. 23–28 in *Women Anthropologists, Selected Biographies*, eds. Ute Gacs et al. Urbana: University of Illinois Press.

Durrans, Brian. 1991. "Edward Banks." Pp. 23–25 in *International Dictionary of Anthropologists*, ed. Christopher Winters. New York: Garland Publishing.

Dutton, Lee. 1991. "H. Otley Beyer." Pp. 56–57 in *International Dictionary of Anthropologists*, ed. Christopher Winters. New York: Garland Publishing.

Edelman, Marc. 1997. "Anthropologist, Secret Agent, Witch-Hunt Victim, Entrepreneur: An Interview with Jack Harris ('40)." *Anthrowatch* 5: 8–14.

Eggan, Fred. 1942. "Ethnic Relations in Guatemala." *America Indigena* 2 (October): 43–47.

——. 1943. "[Report on] the American Anthropological Association." *American Association for the Advancement of Science Bulletin* 2, no. 5: 38.

——. 1974. "Among the Anthropologists." *Annual Review of Anthropology* 3: 1–19.

Eggan, Fred, and R. F. Barton. 1947. "Anthropology during the War, IX. The Philippines." *American Anthropologist* 49: 352–53.

Embree, John F. 1939. *Suye Mura: A Japanese Village*. Chicago: University of Chicago Press.

——. 1943a. "Dealing with Japanese-Americans." *Applied Anthropology* 2, no. 2: 37–41.

——. 1943b. "Resistance to Freedom." *Applied Anthropology* 2, no. 4: 10–14.

——. 1943c. *The Japanese*. War Background Studies, no. 7. Washington, D.C.: Smithsonian Institution.

——. 1944. "Community Analysis: An Example of Anthropology in Government." *American Anthropologist* 46, no. 3: 277–91.

——. 1945a. "Applied Anthropology and Its Relationship to Anthropology." *American Anthropologist* 47: 635–37.

——. 1945b. *The Japanese Nation: A Social Survey*. New York: Rinehart.

——. 1946. "Anthropology and the War." *Bulletin of the American Association of University Professors* 19: 485–95.

——. 1948. "Anthropology during the War, X. Anthropology in Indochina since 1940." *American Anthropologist* 50: 714–16.

——. 1949. "American Military Government." Pp. 207–25 in *Social Structure: Studies Presented to A. R. Radcliffe-Brown*, ed. Meyer Fortes. New York: Russell and Russell.

Emory, Kenneth P. 1943. "South Sea Lore." Special Publication No. 36. Bishop Museum: Honolulu.

Engels, Frederick. 1970 (1883). "Speech at the Graveside of Karl Marx." Pp. 162–63 in *Karl Marx and Frederick Engels, Selected Works*, vol. 3. Moscow: Progressive Publishers.

Ethnogeographic Board. 1944 (1943). *Survival on Land and Sea*. Washington, D.C.: Publications Branch, Office of Naval Intelligence.

Euphoria. 1942–1945. "Euphoria" Newsletter of the University of Chicago, Department of Anthropology. Archival Serials Collection. Special Collections Research Center. University of Chicago Library.

Evans, Andrew D. 2002. "Anthropology at War: World War I and the Science of Race in Germany." Ph.D. diss., Indiana University, Bloomington.

——. 2003. "Anthropology at War: Racial Studies of POWs during World War I." Pp. 198–229 in *Worldly Provincialism: German Anthropology in the Age of Empire*, eds. H. Glenn Penny and Matti Bunzl. Ann Arbor: University of Michigan Press.

Fagan, Brian. 1979. *Return to Babylon*. Boston: Little, Brown.

Farago, Ladislas. 1947 "Refugees: The Solution as FDR Saw It." *United Nations* 1, no. 5, 14–15.

Farish, Matthew. 2005. "Archiving Areas: The Ethnogeographic Board and the Second World War." *Annals of the Association of American Geographers* 95, no. 3: 663–79.

Fawcett, David M., and Teri McLuhan. 1989. "Ruth Leah Bunzel." Pp. 29–36 in *Women Anthropologists, Selected Biographies*, eds. Ute Gacs et al. Urbana: University of Illinois Press.

Fei, Xiaotong. 1979. "The Growth of Chinese Sociology." Pp. 19–31 in *Fei Hsiaopt: The Dilemma of a Chinese Intellectual*, ed. J. P. McGough. New York: Sharpe.

Fellowes-Gordon, Ian. 1957. *Amiable Assassins: The Story of the Kachin Guerrillas of North Burma*. London: Robert Hale.

Fenton, William N. 1946. "Integration of Geography and Anthropology in Army Area Study Curricula." *American Association of University Professors Bulletin* 32, no. 4: 696–706.

——. 1947a. "Anthropology during the War, VII. The Arab World." *American Anthropologist* 49: 342–43.

——. 1947b. *Area Studies in the American University*. Washington, D.C.: American Council on Education.

Ferguson, R. Brian. 1995. *Yanomami Warfare: A Political History*. Santa Fe, N.M.: School of American Research Press.

Feuer, Lewis S. 1979. "Arthur O. Lovejoy." Pp. 464–69 in *International Encyclopedia of the Social Sciences, Biographical Supplement*, vol. 18. New York: Free Press.

Field, Henry. 1962. *"M" Project for F.D.R., Studies on Migration and Settlement*. Ann Arbor, Mich.: Edwards Brothers.

———. 1967. *The Track of Man*. New York: Dell.

———. 1982. *The Track of Man, Volume 2: The White House Years, 1941–1945*. Miami: Banyan Books.

First, Ruth. 1970. *Power in Africa*. New York: Pantheon Books.

Fisher, Donald. 1983. "The Role of Philanthropic Foundations in the Reproduction and Production of Hegemony: Rockefeller Foundations and the Social Sciences." *Sociology* 17, no. 2: 206–33.

Fitch, Noël Riley. 1999. *Appetite for Life: The Biography of Julia Child*. New York: Anchor Books.

Fluehr-Lobban, Carolyn. 2003. "Ethics and Anthropology 1890–2000: A Review of Issues and Principles." Pp. 1–28 in *Ethics and the Profession of Anthropology: Dialogue for Ethically Conscious Practice*, 2d ed., ed. Carolyn Fluehr-Lobban. Walnut Creek, Calif.: AltaMira.

———. 2005. " 'Uncensuring' Boas." *Anthropology News* 46, no. 1: 3.

FNAAA (Fellows Newsletter, American Anthropological Association). 1967. "Statement on Problems of Anthropological Research and Ethics." *Fellows Newsletter* 69, no. 3, 381–82.

Foerstel, Lenora, and Angela Gilliam, eds. 1992. *Confronting the Margaret Mead Legacy: Scholarship, Empire and the South Pacific*. Philadelphia: Temple University Press.

Fogelson, Raymond D. 1979. "Fred Eggan." Pp. 163–66 in *International Encyclopedia of the Social Sciences, Biographical Supplement*, vol. 18. New York: Free Press.

Ford, Clellan S. 1966. "The Role of HRAF in the Organization of Knowledge about Behavior and Mankind." *Behavior Science Notes* 1: 3–6.

———. 1970. "Human Relations Area Files: 1945–1969." *Behavior Science Notes* 5: 1–27.

———. 1971. "The Development of the *Outline of Cultural Materials*." *Behavior Science Notes* 3: 173–86.

Fortes, Meyer. 1945. "The Impact of the War on British West Africa." *International Affairs* 21, no. 2: 209–19.

———. 1957. "Siegfried Frederick Nadel, 1903–1956: A Memoir." Pp. ix–xvi in *The Theory of Social Structure*, ed. S. F. Nadel. London: Cohen and West.

———. 1968. "C. G. Seligman." Pp. 159–62 in *International Encyclopedia of the Social Sciences*, vol. 14. New York: Free Press.

Foster, George M. 1967a. "The Institute of Social Anthropology of the Smithsonian Institution, 1943–1952." *Annuario Indigenista* 27: 173–92.

———. 1967b. *Tzintzuntzan: Mexican Peasants in a Changing World*. Boston: Little, Brown.

———. 1979. "The Institute of Social Anthropology." Pp. 205–16 in *The Uses of Anthropology*, ed. Walter Goldschmidt. Washington, D.C.: American Anthropological Association.

———. 2000. "An Anthropologist's Life in the Twentieth Century: Theory and Practice at UC Berkeley, the Smithsonian, in Mexico, and with the World Health Organization." Oral-history interview conducted in 1998 and 1999 by Suzanne B. Riess, Regional Oral History Office, Bancroft Library, University of California, Berkeley.

Foster, Jane. 1980. *An UnAmerican Lady*. London: Sidgwick and Jackson.

Fox, Margalit. 2005. "Paul Ricoeur, 92, Wide-Ranging French Philosopher, Is Dead." *New York Times*, May 24.

Frank, Andre Gunder. 1967. *Capitalism and Underdevelopment in Latin America*. New York: Monthly Review Press.

Frantz, Charles. 1974. "Structuring and Restructuring of the American Anthropological Association." Paper presented at annual meeting of the American Anthropological Association, Mexico City, November 22.

Freilich, Morris. 1968. "S. F. Nadel." Pp. 1–3 in *International Encyclopedia of the Social Sciences*, vol. 11. New York: Free Press.

Freire, Paulo. 1970. *Pedagogy of the Oppressed*. New York: Continuum Press.

Frese, Pamela R., and Margaret C. Harrell, eds. 2003. *Anthropology and the United States Military: Coming of Age in the Twenty-First Century*. New York: Palgrave.

Friedmann, Georges. 1968. "Maurice Halbwachs." Pp. 304–306 in *International Encyclopedia of the Social Sciences*, vol. 6. New York: Free Press.

Friedmann, Herbert. 1942. *The Natural-History Background of Camouflage*. War Background Studies, no. 5. Washington, D.C.: Smithsonian Institution.

Frucht, Richard. 1967. "Letter." *Fellows Newsletter of the American Anthropological Association* 8, no. 6: 8.

Frye, Alton. 1967. *Nazi Germany and the American Hemisphere, 1933–1941*. New Haven, Conn.: Yale University Press.

Fukui, Nanako. 1999. "Background Research for *The Chrysanthemum and the Sword*." *Dialectical Anthropology* 24: 173–80.

Gacs, Ute. 1989. "Camilla Hildegarde Wedgwood." Pp. 367–71 in *Women Anthropologists, Selected Biographies*, eds. Ute Gacs et al. Urbana: University of Illinois Press.

Gailey, Christine W. 1988. "Eleanor Burke Leacock." Pp. 215–21 in *Women Anthropologists*, eds. Ute Gacs et al. New York: Greenwood Press.

Geertz, Clifford. 1995. *After the Fact: Two Countries, Four Decades, One Anthropologist*. Cambridge, Mass.: Harvard University Press.

Gellman, Irwin F. 1979. *Good Neighbor Diplomacy: United States Policies in Latin America, 1933–1945*. Baltimore: Johns Hopkins University Press.

Gilbert, William Harlen. 1944. *Peoples of India*. War Background Studies, no. 18. Washington, D.C.: Smithsonian Institution.

Giles, Eugene. 1996. "Frederick Seymour Hulse, February 11, 1906–May 16, 1990." *Biographical Memoirs* 70: 174–89.

Gillin, John. 1944. "Cultural Adjustment." *American Anthropologist* 46, no. 4: 429–47.

——. 1947. *Moche, A Peruvian Coastal Community*. Washington, D.C.: Government Printing Office.

Gleach, Frederic W. 2002a. "E. Adamson Hoebel." Pp. 161–64 in *Celebrating a Century of the American Anthropological Association*, eds. Regna Darnell and Frederic Gleach. Lincoln: University of Nebraska Press.

——. 2002b. "Alexander Spoehr." Pp. 193–96 in *Celebrating a Century of the American Anthropological Association*, eds. Regna Darnell and Frederic Gleach. Lincoln: University of Nebraska Press.

——. 2002c. "John Gillin." Pp. 197–200 in *Celebrating a Century of the American Anthropo-*

logical Association, eds. Regna Darnell and Frederic Gleach. Lincoln: University of Nebraska Press.

———. 2002d. "Fay-Cooper Cole." Pp. 65–68 in *Celebrating a Century of the American Anthropological Association*, eds. Regna Darnell and Frederic Gleach. Lincoln: University of Nebraska Press.

Glenn, David. 2004. "Anthropologists Act to Revoke 1919 Censure of Franz Boas, a Key Figure in the Field." *Chronicle of Higher Education*, Internet ed., December 17. Available online at http://chronicle.com/temp/email.php?id=e7xkv13q13qob01r9pds1jk61zyrfs08 (accessed December 22, 2004).

———. 2005. "Cloak and Classroom." *Chronicle of Higher Education*, March 25, 2005, A14–15.

Goldfrank, Esther S. 1978. *Notes on an Undirected Life: As One Anthropologist Tells It*. Queens College Publications in Anthropology No. 3. Flushing, N.Y.: Queens College Press.

Goldman, Jan. ed. 2006. *The Ethics of Spying: A Reader for the Intelligence Professional*. Lanham, Md.: Scarecrow Press.

Goldschmidt, Walter R. 1943. *A Study of the Methods of Mobilizing Rural People for War Emergencies, Tulare County, California*. Berkeley, Calif.: Bureau of Agricultural Economics, U.S. Department of Agriculture.

———. 1977. "Anthropology and the Coming Crisis: An Autoethnographic Appraisal." *American Anthropologist* 79: 293–308.

Goldschmidt, Walter R, and John S. Page. 1943. *A Study of the Methods of Mobilizing Rural People for War Emergencies, San Joaquin County, California*. Berkeley, Calif.: Bureau of Agricultural Economics, U.S. Department of Agriculture.

Gorer, Geoffrey. 1942. "Themes in Japanese Culture and Propaganda," 2d ed. Mimeograph distributed by the Institute for Intercultural Studies, New York.

———. 1943a. "Themes in Japanese Culture." *Transactions of the New York Academy of Sciences* 5: 106–24.

———. 1943b. "The Special Case of Japan." *Public Opinion Quarterly* 7, no. 4: 567–82.

———. 1943c. *Japanese Character Structure and Propaganda: A Preliminary Study*. New Haven, Conn.: Yale University, Institute of Human Relations.

Gottlieb, Sidney, and Alfred Hitchcock. 2003. *Alfred Hitchcock: Interviews*. Jackson: University of Mississippi Press.

Gough, Kathleen. 1968. "Anthropology and Imperialism." *Monthly Review* (April): 12–27.

———. 1993 " 'Anthropology and Imperialism' Revisited." *Anthropologica* 35, no. 2: 79–289.

Gramsci, Antonio. 1937 [1967]. *Prison Notebooks*. Ed. and trans. Joseph A. Buttigeg. New York: Columbia University Press.

Gray, Geoffrey. 2000. "Managing the Impact of War: Australian Anthropology and the Southwest Pacific." Pp. 187–210 in *Science and the Pacific War: Science and Survival in the Pacific, 1939–1945*, ed. R. M. MacLeod, 187–210. London: Kluwer.

———. 2005. "Australian Anthropologists and World War II." *Anthropology Today* 21, no. 3: 18–21.

———. 2006. "The Army Requires Anthropologists: Australian Anthropologists at War, 1939–1946." *Australian Historical Studies* 37, no. 127: 156–80.

Greenberg, Joseph H. 1986. "On Being a Linguistic Anthropologist." *Annual Review of Anthropology* 15: 1–24.

Gusterson, Hugh, and David Price. 2005. "Spies in Our Midst." *Anthropology News* 46, no. 6: 39–40.

Guthe, Carl. 1943. "The Ethnogeographic Board." *Scientific Monthly* 57, no. 2: 188–91.

Hall, Edward T. 1992. *An Anthropology of Everyday Life: An Autobiography*. New York: Doubleday.

Halle, Louis J. 1948. "Significance of the Institute of Inter-American Affairs in the Conduct of U.S. Foreign Policy." Department of State Publication 3239, Inter-American Series 36. Washington, D.C.: Government Printing Office.

Hancock, Graham. 1989. *Lords of Poverty: The Power, Prestige and Corruption of the International Aid Business*. New York: Atlantic Monthly Press.

Hansen, Arthur A. 1995. "Oral History and the Japanese American Evacuation." *Journal of American History* 82, no. 2: 625–39.

Hansen, Asael T. 1946. "Community Analysis: An Example at Heart Mountain Relocation Center." *Applied Anthropology* 5, no. 3: 15–25.

Haring, Douglas. 1943. *Blood on the Rising Sun*. Philadelphia: Macrae Smith.

——. 1946a. "Religion, Magic, and Morale." Pp. 209–58 in *Japan's Prospect*, ed. Douglas Haring. Cambridge, Mass.: Harvard University Press.

——. 1946b. "The Challenge of Japanese Ideology." Pp. 259–85 in *Japan's Prospect*, ed. Douglas Haring. Cambridge, Mass.: Harvard University Press.

Haring, Douglas. ed. 1956. *Personality Character and Cultural Milieu*. Syracuse, N.Y.: Syracuse University Press.

Harris, Benjamin. 1998. "The Perils of a Public Intellectual." *Journal of Social Issues* 54, no. 1: 79–118.

Harris, Charles H., and Louis R. Sadler. 2003. *The Archaeologist Was a Spy*. Albuquerque: University of New Mexico Press.

Harris, Chauncy. 1997. "Geographers in the U.S. Government in Washington, D.C., during World War II." *Professional Geographer* 49: 245–56.

Harris, Jack. 1947. "Anthropology during the War, VIII. South and British Central Africa." *American Anthropologist* 49: 350–52.

Harris, Marvin. 1968. *The Rise of Anthropological Theory*. New York: Thomas Crowell.

Harris, Sheldon H. 2000 "The American Cover-up of Japanese Human Biological Warfare Experiments, 1945–1948." Pp. 253–69 in *Science and the Pacific War: Science and Survival in the Pacific, 1939–1945*, ed. Roy M. Macleod. Dordrecht: Kluwer Academic Publishing.

Harrisson, Tom. 1959. *World Within: A Borneo Story*. London: Cresset Press.

Hauser, R. M., D. Mechanic, A. O. Haller, and T. S. Hauser. 1982. "William H. Sewell: A Biographical Note." Pp. xxix–xxxii in *Social Structure and Behavior: Essays in Honor of William Hamilton Sewell*, eds. R. M. Hauser and S. W. Hamilton. New York: Academic Press.

Hayashi, Brian M. 2004. *Democratizing the Enemy: The Japanese American Internment*. Princeton: Princeton University Press.

Haynes Jr., C. Vance 2004. "Memorial: In the Field with my Friend and Colleague George A. Agogino." *Plains Anthropologist* 49: 299–310.

Henson, Pamela M. 2000. "The Smithsonian Goes to War: The Increase and Diffusion of Scientific Knowledge in the Pacific." Pp. 27–50 in *Science and the Pacific War: Science and Survival in the Pacific, 1939–1945*, ed. Roy M. Macleod. Dordrecht: Kluwer Academic Publishers.

Herbert, Frank. 1965. *Dune*. Philadelphia: Chilton Books.

Herge, Henry C., and Consultants to the Commission. 1948. *Wartime College Training Programs of the Armed Services*. Washington, D.C.: American Council on Education.

Herman, Ellen. 1995. *The Romance of American Psychology*. Berkeley: University of California Press.

Herskovits, Melville J. 1936. "Applied Anthropology and the American Anthropologist." *Science* 83: 215–22.

——. 1946. "Anthropology during the War, IV. Belgium and Holland." *American Anthropologist* 48: 301–304.

——. 1952. *Franz Boas: The Science of Man in the Making*. New York: Scribner's.

Herskovits, Melville J., ed. 1950 *International Directory of Anthropologists*, 3d ed. Washington, D.C.: Committee on International Relations in Anthropology.

Hess, Jerry N. 1973. "Oral History Interview with Philleo Nash." On file in Philleo Nash Papers, Harry S Truman Library, Independence, Mo.

Hickey, William. 2003. *Window on a War: An Anthropologist in the Vietnam Conflict*. Lubbock: Texas Tech University Press.

Hilton, Stanley E. 1981. *Hitler's Secret War in South America, 1939–1945*. Baton Rouge: Louisiana State University Press.

Hirabayashi, Lane Ryo. 1999. *The Politics of Fieldwork: Research in an American Concentration Camp*. Tucson: University of Arizona Press.

Hockett, Charles F. 1968. "Leonard Bloomfield." Pp. 95–99 in *International Encyclopedia of the Social Sciences*, vol. 2. New York: Free Press.

Hoffman, Frederick L. 1918. *Army Anthropometry and Medical Rejection Statistics*. Newark, N.J.: Prudential Press.

Hogbin, H. Ian. 1949. "Government Chiefs in New Guinea." Pp. 189–206 in *Social Structure: Studies Presented to A. R. Radcliffe-Brown*, ed. Meyer Fortes. New York: Russell and Russell.

——. 1951. *Transformation Scene: The Changing Culture of a New Guinea Village*. London: Routledge and Kegan Paul.

Holbrook, Wendell P. 1985. "British Propaganda and the Mobilization of the Gold Coast War Effort, 1939–1945." *Journal of British History* 26: 347–61.

Homans, George C. 1946. "The Small Warship." *American Sociological Review* 11, no. 3: 294–300.

——. 1984. *Coming to my Senses: The Autobiography of a Sociologist*. Somerset, N.J.: Transaction Press.

Honigsheim, Paul. 1945. "Voltaire as Anthropologist." *American Anthropologist* 47, no. 1: 104–18.

Hook, Sidney. 1987. *Out of Step: An Unquiet Life in the Twentieth Century.* New York: Carroll and Graf.

Hooton, Earnest. 1943. "Let Chinese Run Japan." *PM*, February 8, 4.

Horowitz, Irving Louis, ed. 1967. *The Rise and Fall of Project Camelot.* Cambridge, Mass.: MIT Press.

Howell, Carol L., ed. 1998. *Cannibalism Is an Acquired Taste, and Other Notes: From Conversations with Anthropologist Omer C. Stewart.* Niwot: University Press of Colorado.

Howell, Nancy. 1990. *Surviving Fieldwork.* Special Publication No. 26. Washington, D.C.: American Anthropological Association.

Hrdlička, Aleš. 1942. *The Peoples of the Soviet Union.* War Background Studies, no. 3. Washington, D.C.: Smithsonian Institution.

Huang, Shu-min. 1991. "Ling Shun-Sheng." Pp. 411–12 in *International Dictionary of Anthropologists*, ed. Christopher Winters. New York: Garland Publishing.

Hurley, G. V. ca. 1944. "Pocket Guide to the Philippines" Lieutenant-Commander G. V. Hurley, Enemy Bases Section, typescript, University of Washington library system.

Hutchinson, Charles F. 2000. "John Wesley Powell and the New West." *Cosmos 2000.* Available online at www.cosmos-club.org/web/journals/2000/hutchinson.html (accessed February 5, 2006).

Hyatt, Marshall. 1990. *Franz Boas, Social Activist: The Dynamics of Ethnicity.* New York: Greenwood Press.

Hyneman, Charles S. 1945. "The Wartime Area and Language Courses." *Bulletin of the American Association of University Professors* 31: 434–47.

Jamin, Jean. 1991. "Paul Rivet." Pp. 584–85 in *International Dictionary of Anthropologists*, ed. Christopher Winters. New York: Garland Publishing.

Janis, Irving L. 1972. *Victims of Groupthink.* Boston: Houghton Mifflin.

Janse, Olov Robert Thure. 1944. *The Peoples of French Indochina.* War Background Studies, no. 19. Washington, D.C.: Smithsonian Institution.

Janssens, Rudolf V. A. 1995. *"What Future for Japan?" U.S. Wartime Planning for the Postwar Era, 1942–1945.* University of Amsterdam Monographs in American Studies No. 5. Amsterdam: Rodopi.

———. 1999. "Toilet Training, Shame, and the Influence of Alien Cultures." Pp. 285–304 in *Anthropology and Colonialism in Asia and Oceania*, eds. Jan van Bremen and Akitoshi Shimizu. Surrey: Curzon Press.

Jeffreys-Jones, Rhodri. 1989. *The CIA and American Democracy.* New Haven, Conn.: Yale University Press.

Joffe, Natalie F. 1964. "Morris Siegel." *American Anthropologist* 66: 395–96.

Johnson, Frederick. 1953. "A Study of the Anthropological Profession." *Bulletin of the American Anthropological Association* 1, no. 3: 2–4.

Johnson, Martha. 1945. *Ann Bartlett Returns to the Philippines.* New York: Thomas Y. Crowell.

Jones, Delmos. 1976. "Applied Anthropology and the Application of Anthropological Knowledge." *Human Organization* 35: 221–29.

Jones, Philip G. 1995. "Norman B. Tindale, 12 October, 1900–19 November, 1993." *Records of the South Australian Museum* 28, no. 2 (December): 159–76.

Jordan, James B. 1992. "Christianity in the Science Fiction of 'Cordwainer Smith.' " *Contra Mundum* 2 (Winter): 1–8.

Junker, Klaus. 1998. "Research under Dictatorship: The German Archaeological Institute 1929–1945." *Antiquity* 72, no. 2: 282–92.

Kaempffert, Waldemar. 1940. "Science in the News: Brain Waves." *New York Times*, July 7, D5.

Kahin, George M. 2003. *Southeast Asia: A Testament.* London: Routledge Curzon.

Kaikini, V. M. 1953. "Anthropological Observations on Indian Troops during the World War." *Journal of the Anthropological Society of Bombay* 7, no. 2: 45–60.

Katz, Barry M. 1989. *Foreign Intelligence: Research and Analysis in the Office of Strategic Services, 1942–1945.* Cambridge, Mass.: Harvard University Press.

Keefer, Louis E. 1988. *Scholars in Foxholes: The Story of the Army Specialized Training Program in World War II.* Jefferson, N.C.: McFairland.

Keen, Mike. 1999. *Stalking the Sociological Imagination: J. Edgar Hoover's FBI Surveillance of American Sociology.* Westport, Conn.: Greenwood Press.

Keith, Arthur. 1918. "Anthropological Activities in Connection with the War in England." *American Journal of Physical Anthropology* 1, no. 1: 91–96.

Kennedy, Raymond. 1943. *Islands and Peoples of the Indies.* War Background Studies, no. 14. Washington, D.C.: Smithsonian Institution.

Kent, Pauline. 1996. "Misconceived Configurations of Ruth Benedict." *Japan Review* 7: 33–60.

———. 1999. "Japanese Perceptions of *The Chrysanthemum and the Sword.*" *Dialectical Anthropology* 24: 181–92.

Kerns, Virginia. 2003. *Scenes from the High Desert: Julian Steward's Life and Theory.* Urbana: University of Illinois Press.

Kidder, A. V. 1942. "Annual Meeting." *American Anthropologist* 44: 730.

———. 1945. "George Clapp Vaillant." *American Anthropologist* 47: 589–97.

Kilsūng, Ch'oe. 2003. "War and Ethnology/Folklore in Colonial Korea: The Case of Akiba Takashi." Pp. 169–87 in *Wartime Japanese Anthropology in Asia and the Pacific*, Senri Ethnological Studies No. 65, eds. Akitoshi Shimizu and Jan van Bremen. Osaka: National Museum of Ethnology.

King, Russell, and Guy Patterson. 1991. "Charlotte Gower Chapman." Pp. 105–106 in *International Dictionary of Anthropologists*, ed. Christopher Winters. New York: Garland Publishing.

Kluckhohn, Clyde. 1943. "On the Use of Culture Contact Situations in Regional Training." Suggested materials for training of Regional Specialists Army Program, prepared in Collaboration with the Council on Intercultural Relations. Copy in Box M25, MM.

———. 1949. *Mirror for Man.* New York: Whittlesey House.

——. 1954. "Paul Reiter, 1909–1953." *American Anthropologist* 56, no. 4: 1085–87.

Kluckhohn, Clyde & O. H. Mowrer. 1944. " 'Culture and Personality': A Conceptual Scheme." *American Anthropologist* 46, no.1: 1–29.

Krieger, Herbert W. 1942. *Peoples of the Philippines*. War Background Studies, no. 4. Washington, D.C.: Smithsonian Institution.

——. 1943. *Island Peoples of the Western Pacific, Micronesia and Melanesia*. War Background Studies, no. 16. Washington, D.C.: Smithsonian Institution.

Krohn, Claus-Dieter. 1993. *Intellectuals in Exile: Refugee Scholars and the New School for Social Research*. Amherst: University of Massachusetts Press.

Kuper, Adam. 1986. "An Interview with Edmund Leach." *Current Anthropology* 27, no. 4: 375–81.

——. 1996. *Anthropology and Anthropologists: The Modern British School*. New York: Routledge.

Kurashige, Lon. 2001. "Resistance, Collaboration, and Mazanar Protest." *Pacific Historical Review* 70, no. 3: 387–417.

La Barre, Weston. 1945. "Some Observations on Character Structure in the Orient: The Japanese." *Psychiatry* 8: 319–42.

Lagemann, Ellen C. 1989. *The Politics of Knowledge: The Carnegie Corporation, Philanthropy and Public Policy*. Chicago: University of Chicago Press.

Lawler, Nancy. 2002. *Soldiers, Airmen, Spies, and Whisperers*. Columbus: Ohio University Press.

Lawrence, Peter. 1964. *Road Belong Cargo*. Manchester: Manchester University Press.

Leach, Edmund. 1954. *Political Systems of Highland Burma*. Boston: Beacon.

——. 1977. "In Formative Travail with Leviathan," *Anthropological Forum* 4, no. 2: 190–97.

——. 1979. "Raymond Firth." Pp. 186–92 in *International Encyclopedia of the Social Sciences, Biographical Supplement*, vol. 18. New York: Free Press.

Leahey, Thomas H. 1991. *A History of Modern Psychology*. Englewood Cliffs, N.J.: Prentice Hall.

Leighton, Alexander H. 1942. "Training Social Scientists for Post-War Conditions." *Applied Anthropology* 1, no. 4: 25–30.

——. 1945. *The Governing of Men: General Principles and Recommendations Based on Experience at a Japanese Relocation Camp*. Princeton, N.J.: Princeton University Press.

——. 1949. *Human Relations in a Changing World: Observations on the Use of the Social Sciences*. New York: E. P. Dutton.

Leighton, Alexander, and Morris Opler. 1967. "Psychological Warfare and the Japanese Emperor." Pp. 250–60 in *Personalities and Cultures: Readings in Psychological Anthropology*, ed. Robert Hunt. New York: Natural History Press.

Lepowsky, Maria. 2000. "Charlotte Gower and the Subterranean History of Anthropology." Pp. 123–70 in *Excluded Ancestors, Inventible Traditions, Volume 9: History of Anthropology Series*, ed. Richard Handler. Madison: University of Wisconsin Press.

Lesser, Alexander. 2003. "Franz Boas." Pp. 1–23 in *Totems and Teachers: Key Figures in the History of Anthropology*, ed. Sydel Silverman. Walnut Creek, Calif.: AltaMira.

Lewis, Martin, and Karen Wigen. 1997. *The Myth of Continents: A Critique of Metageograpy*. Berkeley: University of California Press.

Ley, Ronald. 1990. *A Whisper of Espionage*. Garden City, N.J.: Avery.

Lie, John. 2001. "Ruth Benedict's Legacy of Shame: Orientalism and the Occidentalism in the Study of Japan." *Asian Journal of Social Science* 29, no. 2: 249–61.

Lindesmith, Alfred R., and Anselm L. Strauss. 1950. "A Critique of Culture and Personality Writings." *American Journal Review* 15: 587–600.

Lindzey, Gardner. 1979. "Henry A. Murray." Pp. 566–71 in *International Encyclopedia of the Social Sciences Biographical Supplement*. New York: Free Press.

Linebarger, Paul Myron Anthony. 1948. *Psychological Warfare*. Washington, D.C.: Infantry Journal Press.

Linton, Adelin, and Charles Wagley. 1971. *Ralph Linton*. New York: Columbia University Press.

Linton, Ralph. 1924. "Totemism in the A.E.F." *American Anthropologist* 26, no. 2: 296–300.

——. 1945. *The Science of Man in the World Crisis*. New York: Columbia University Press.

Lipset, David. 1980. *Gregory Bateson : The Legacy of a Scientist*. Englewood Cliffs, N.J.: Prentice Hall.

Lofquist, Lloyd H. 1968. "Walter Bingham." Pp. 78–79 in *International Encyclopedia of the Social Sciences*, vol. 2. New York: Free Press.

Loftus, John, and Mark Aarons. 1994. *The Secret War against the Jews: How Western Espionage Betrayed the Jewish People*. New York: Saint Martin's Griffin.

Lonergan, David. 1991a. "Clellan Stearns Ford." Pp. 205–206 in *International Dictionary of Anthropologists*, ed. Christopher Winters. New York: Garland Publishing.

——. 1991b. "Mischa Titiev." P. 701 in *International Dictionary of Anthropologists*, ed. Christopher Winters. New York: Garland Publishing.

Loomis, Charles P. 1942. "Wartime Impacts upon the Schools." *Applied Anthropology* 2, no. 1: 29–32.

——. 1943. "Applied Anthropology in Latin America: Developing a Permanent and Stable Supply of Needed Agricultural Materials." *Applied Anthropology* 2, no. 4: 15–16.

——. 1945. "Rural Sociologists in Latin America." *Applied Anthropology* 4, no. 4: 50–51.

Loomis, Charles, and Nellie H. Loomis. 1942. "Skilled Spanish–American War-Industry Workers from New Mexico." *Applied Anthropology* 2, no. 1: 33–39.

Lothrop, Samuel K., and Barbara J. Price. 1968. "George C. Vaillant." Pp. 277–79 in *International Encyclopedia of the Social Sciences*, vol. 16. New York: Free Press.

Lummis, C. Douglas. 1982. *A New Look at The Chrysanthemum and the Sword*. Tokyo: Shohakusha.

Luomala, Katherine. 1946. "California Takes Back Its Japanese Evacuees." *Applied Anthropology* 5, no. 3: 25–39.

——. 1947. "Community Analysis by the War Relocation Authority outside the Relocation Centers." *Applied Anthropology* 6, no. 1: 25–31.

Lyon, Gabrielle H. 1994. "The Forgotten Files of a Marginal Man: Henry Field, Anthropology, and Franklin D. Roosevelt's 'M' Project for Migration and Settlement." Master's thesis, Department of History, University of Chicago, November 17.

Lyotard, Jean-François. 1984. *The Postmodern Condition: A Report on Knowledge*, trans. Brian Massumi. Minneapolis: University of Minnesota Press.

Mabee, Carleton. 1987. "Margaret Mead and Behavioral Scientists in World War II: Problems in Responsibility, Truth, and Effectiveness." *Journal of the History of the Behavioral Sciences* 23: 3–13.

MacDonald, Elizabeth P. (a.k.a. E. P. McIntosh). 1947. *Undercover Girl*. New York: Macmillan.

MacFarlane, Alan. 2006. "Elizabeth Colson Interviewed by Alan Macfarlane." Available online at www.dspace.cam.ac.uk/bitstream/1810/183616/3/colson.txt (accessed May 22, 2006).

Madden, Ryan. 1992. "The Forgotten People: The Relocation and Internment of Aleuts during World War II." *American Indian Culture and Research Journal* 16, no. 4: 55–76.

Malamud, Irene T., and Rachel B. Stephenson. 1944. "A Study of the Rehabilitation of Neuro-Psychiatric Casualties Occurring in the Armed Forces." *Applied Anthropology* 3, no. 2: 1–15.

Manchester, William. 1978. *American Caesar: Douglas MacArthur 1880–1964*. Boston: Little, Brown.

Mann, Thomas L. 1991. "Kenneth Pike Emory." Pp. 181–82 in *International Dictionary of Anthropologists*, ed. Christopher Winters. New York: Garland Publishing.

Marks, John. 1979. T*he Search for the "Manchurian Candidate": The CIA and Mind Control*. New York: Times Books.

Marks, Jonathan. 2002. "Harry Shapiro." Pp. 125–28 in *Celebrating a Century of the American Anthropological Association*, eds. Regna Darnell and Frederic Gleach. Lincoln: University of Nebraska Press.

Matthew, Robert John. 1947. *Language and Area Studies in the Armed Services: Their Future Significance*. Washington, D.C.: American Council on Education.

Mauch, Christof. 2005. *The Shadow War against Hitler: The Covert Operations of America's Wartime Secret Intelligence Service*. New York: Columbia University Press.

May, Mark A. 1971. "A Retrospective View of the Institute of Human Relations at Yale." *Behavioral Science Notes* 6: 141–72.

Mayo, Marlene J. 1982. "Psychological Disarmament: American Wartime Planning for the Education and Re-Education of Defeated Japan, 1943–1945." Pp. 21–127 in *The Occupation of Japan: Educational and Social Reform*. Norfolk, Va.: Gatling.

McArthur, Charles. 1990. *Operations Analysis in the U.S. Army Eighth Air Force in World War II*. Providence, R.I.: American Mathematical Society.

McCartney, Allen P. 1998. "Alvin R. Cahn: World War II Aleutian Archaeologist." *Arctic Anthropology* 35, no. 2: 136–46.

McFate, Montgomery. 2005. "Anthropology and Counterinsurgency: The Strange Story of Their Curious Relationship." *Military Review* (March–April): 24–38.

McGehee, Ralph W. 1983. *Deadly Deceits: My Twenty-Five Years in the* CIA. New York: Sheridan Square Publications.

McIntosh, Betty. 2004. "Famed French Chef Julia Child Remembered by her OSS Colleagues." *The O.S.S. Society, Inc.,* Fall, 1–3.

McIntosh, Elizabeth P. 1998. *Sisterhood of Spies: The Women of the* OSS. Annapolis, Md.: Naval Institute Press.

McIntyre, Jerrie. 1989. "Mary Douglas Nicol Leakey." Pp. 222–30 in *Women Anthropologists, Selected Biographies,* eds. Ute Gacs et al. Urbana: University of Illinois Press.

McQuown, Norman A. 1968. "Morris Swadesh." *American Anthropologist* 70: 755–56.

Mead, Margaret. 1941. "On Methods of Implementing a National Morale Program." *Applied Anthropology* 1, no. 1: 20–24.

——. 1942. *And Keep Your Power Dry: An Anthropologist Looks at America.* New York: William Morrow.

——. 1943a. "Food and Feeding in Occupied Territory." *Public Opinion Quarterly* 7, no. 4: 618–28.

——. 1943b. "On the Use of Living Sources in Regional Studies: General Considerations." Suggested materials for training of Regional Specialists Army Program, prepared in collaboration with the Council on Intercultural Relations, n.d., MM, Box 25.

——. 1943c. "News of Developing Research Methods." *Applied Anthropology* (January–March): 35–37.

——. 1953. "Four Applications of End-Linked Analysis." Pp. 379–93 in *The Study of Culture at a Distance,* eds. Margaret Mead and Rhoda Métraux. Chicago: University of Chicago Press.

——. 1956. *New Lives for Old: Cultural Transformation, Manus, 1929–1953.* New York: Morrow.

——. 1979. "Anthropological Contributions to National Policies during and Immediately after World War II." Pp. 145–57 in *The Uses of Anthropology,* ed. Walter Goldschmidt. Washington, D.C.: American Anthropological Association.

Mead, Margaret, Eliot D. Chapple, and G. Gordon Browne. 1949. "Report of the Committee on Ethics." *Human Organization* (Spring): 20–21.

Meadows, William C. 2002. *The Comanche Code Talkers of World War II.* Austin: University of Texas Press.

Melvern, Linda. 1995. *The Ultimate Crime: Who Betrayed the* UN *and Why.* London: Allyn and Busby.

Merton, Robert. 1968. *Social Theory and Social Structure.* New York: Free Press.

Métraux, Alfred 1948. "Anthropology during the War, XI: Anthropology in Germany." *American Anthropologist* 50: 717.

Mintz, Sidney. 2005. "Picking Sides: 1939–1945 and beyond." Paper presented at the annual meeting of the American Anthropological Association, Washington, D.C., December 2.

Miyazaki, Kōji. 2003. "Colonial Anthropology in the Netherlands and Wartime Anthropology in Japan." Pp. 223–37 in *Wartime Japanese Anthropology in Asia and the Pacific,* Senri

Ethnological Studies No. 65, eds. Akitoshi Shimizu and Jan van Bremen. Osaka: National Museum of Ethnology.

Modell, Judith Schachter. 1983. *Ruth Benedict: Patterns of a Life*. Philadelphia: University of Pennsylvania Press.

Momose, Hibiki. 2004. "The Internal Colonization of Hokkaido and the Ainu Policy." Paper presented at the East Asian Anthropology and Japanese Colonialism Forum, Third Conference, Seoul National University, November 13.

Mooney, James. 1896. "The Ghost-Dance Religion and the Sioux Outbreak of 1890." Pp. 651–1136 in *Bureau of American Ethnology Annual Report, 1893*. Washington, D.C.: Government Printing Office.

Moos, Felix. 2002. "The Stark Reality: Anthropology and Warfare." Paper presented at the annual meeting of the American Anthropological Association, New Orleans, November 20, 2002.

Morawski, J. G. 1986. "Organizing Knowledge and Behavior at Yale's Institute of Human Relations." *Isis 77*: 219–42.

Morgenstern, Oskar. 1968. "Karl Schlesinger." Pp. 51–52 in *International Encyclopedia of the Social Sciences*, vol. 14. New York: Free Press.

Morrissey, Charles T. 1966. "Oral History Interview with Mr. John Franklin Carter." February 9. On file at Franklin Delano Roosevelt Presidential Library, Hyde Park, New York.

Moses, Lester George. 1984. *The Indian Man: A Biography of James Mooney*. Urbana: University of Illinois Press.

Mosgrip, Amos. 1945. "Affidavit of Amos Mosgrip, Operations Officer, HQ, OSS, IBT," August 13, 1945, released by the CIA under FOIA in August 1994.

Mosse, David. 2005. *Cultivating Development*. London: Pluto.

Movius, Hallam L. 1956. "Teilhard Pierre de Chardin, 1881–1955." *American Anthropologist* 58, no. 60: 147–50.

Murdock, George P. 1949. *Social Structure*. New York: Macmillan.

———. 1971. *Outline of Cultural Materials*. 4th Revised Edition. New Haven: Human Relations Area Files, Inc.

Murphy, Robert F. 1976. "Introduction: A Quarter Century of American Anthropology." Pp. 1–22 in *Selected Papers from the American Anthropologist*, ed. Robert Murphy. Washington, D.C.: American Anthropological Association.

———. 1991. "Anthropology at Columbia: A Reminiscence." *Dialectical Anthropology* 16: 65–81.

Murray, Florence. 1945. "White Superior to Natives, General Advises in Pamphlet." *People's Voice*, February 17, 3.

Murray, Stephen O. 1991. "The Rights of Research Assistants and the Rhetoric of Political Suppression." *Journal of the History of the Behavioral Sciences* 27, no. 2: 130–56.

Nader, Laura. 1972. "Up the Anthropologist—Perspectives Gained from Studying Up." Pp. 284–311 in *Reinventing Anthropology*, ed. Dell Hymes. New York: Pantheon.

———. 1997. "The Phantom Factor: Impact of the Cold War on Anthropology." Pp. 107–46 in *The Cold War and the University*. New York: New Press.

——. 2001. "Breaking the Silence—Politics and Professional Autonomy." *Anthropological Quarterly* 75, no. 1: 161–69.

Nader, Laura, ed. 1996. *Naked Science: Anthropological Inquiry into Boundaries, Power and Knowledge*. New York: Routledge.

Nakao, Katsumi. 1999. "Japanese Colonial Policy and Anthropology in Manchuria." Pp. 245–65 in *Anthropology and Colonialism in Asia and Oceania*, eds. Jan van Bremen and Akitoshi Shimizu. Surrey: Curzon Press.

——. 2003. "Mabuchi Tōichi in Makassar." Pp. 239–79 in *Wartime Japanese Anthropology in Asia and the Pacific*, Senri Ethnological Studies No. 65, eds. Akitoshi Shimizu and Jan van Bremen. Osaka: National Museum of Ethnology.

——. 2004. "Japanese Colony and Anthropology: Comparison with European Colonialism." Paper presented at the East Asian Anthropology and Japanese Colonialism Forum, Third Conference, Seoul National University. November 13.

Nash, Edith. 1989. "Philleo Nash and Georgetown Day School." Pp. 34–41 in *Applied Anthropologist and Public Servant: The Life and Work of Philleo Nash*. National Association for the Practice of Anthropology, Bulletin, no. 7. Washington, D.C.: American Anthropological Association.

Nash, Philleo. 1980. "Philleo Nash." Pp. 52–56 in *The Truman White House*, ed. Francis Heller. Lawrence: Regents Press of Kansas.

——. 1986. "Science, Politics, and Human Values: A Memoir." *Human Organization* 45, no. 3: 189–201.

——. 1989. "Anthropologist in the White House." Pp. 3–6 in *Applied Anthropologist and Public Servant: The Life and Work of Philleo Nash*. National Association for the Practice of Anthropology, Bulletin, no. 7. Washington, D.C.: American Anthropological Association.

Nature. 1941. "National Character." *Nature*, vol. 148, no. 3741, 31–33.

Naumann, Hermann. 1968. "Fritz Graebner." Pp. 240–41 in *International Encyclopedia of the Social Sciences*, vol. 5. New York: Free Press.

Naval Intelligence Division. 1943. *Admiralty Handbook, Algeria*. London: Naval Intelligence Division.

Needham, Rodney. 1979. "Robert Hertz." Pp. 295–97 in *International Encyclopedia of the Social Sciences, Biographical Supplement*, vol. 18. New York: Free Press.

Neiburg, Federico, and Marcio Goldman. 1998. "Anthropology and Politics in Studies of National Character." *Cultural Anthropology* 13, no. 1: 56–81.

Newman, Stanley M. 1967. "Morris Swadesh." *Language* 43: 948–57.

——. 1991. "Marcus S. Goldstein." Pp. 246–47 in *International Dictionary of Anthropologists*, ed. Christopher Winters. New York: Garland Publishing.

Newton, Janice. 1996. "Angels, Heroes and Traitors: Images of Papuans in the Second World War." *Research in Melanesia* 20: 141–56.

Nie, Lili. 2003. "Studies of Chinese Peasant Society in Japan: Before and during World War II." Pp. 209–21 in *Wartime Japanese Anthropology in Asia and the Pacific*, Senri Ethnological Studies No. 65, eds. Akitoshi Shimizu and Jan van Bremen. Osaka: National Museum of Ethnology.

Nobayashi, Atsushi. 2003. "Physical Anthropology in Wartime Japan." Pp. 143–50 in *Wartime Japanese Anthropology in Asia and the Pacific*, Senri Ethnological Studies No. 65, eds. Akitoshi Shimizu and Jan van Bremen. Osaka: National Museum of Ethnology.

Nordstrom, Carolyn. 2004. *Shadows of War: Violence, Power, and International Profiteering in the Twenty-First Century*. Berkeley: University of California Press.

Nowak, Stefan. 1968. "Stanislaw Ossowski." Pp. 245–47 in *International Encyclopedia of the Social Sciences*, vol. 11. New York: Free Press.

NRC [National Research Council]. 1938. *International Directory of Anthropologists*. Washington, D.C. NRC.

O'Donnell, Patrick K. 2004. *Operatives, Spies, and Saboteurs: The Unknown Story of the Men and Women of World War II's OSS*. New York: Free Press.

Ohnuki-Tierney, Emiko. 2002. *Kamikaze, Cherry Blossoms, and Nationalisms: The Militarization of Aesthetics in Japanese History*. Chicago: University of Chicago Press.

Opler, Marvin K. 1945. "A 'Sumo' Tournament at Tule Lake Center." *American Anthropologist* 47, no. 1: 134–39.

Opler, Morris Edward. 1943. "Studies of Segregants at Manzanar." WRA Community Analyst Section.

——. 1945. "Social Science and Democratic Policy." *Applied Anthropology* 4, no. 3: 11–15.

——. 1987. "Comment on 'Engineering Internment.'" *American Ethnologist* 14, no. 2: 383.

OPNAV (U.S. Office of Naval Operations). 1943. *Civil Affairs Handbook: Marshall Islands*. OPNAV P22–1. U.S. Navy Department. August 17.

——. 1944a. *Civil Affairs Handbook: East Caroline Islands*. OPNAV P22–5. U.S. Navy Department. February 21.

——. 1944b. *Civil Affairs Handbook: West Caroline Islands*. OPNAV P22–7. U.S. Navy Department. April 1.

——. 1944c. *Civil Affairs Handbook: Mandated Marianas Islands*. OPNAV P22–8. U.S. Navy Department. April 15.

——. 1944d. *Civil Affairs Handbook: Marshall Islands Statistical Supplement*. OPNAV 50E-1S. U.S. Navy Department. May 20.

——. 1944e. *Civil Affairs Handbook: Ryukyu (Loochoo) Islands*. OPNAV 13–31. U.S. Navy Department. November 15.

——. 1944f. *Civil Affairs Handbook: Administrative Organization and Personnel of the Japanese Mandated Islands*. OPNAV 50E-4. U.S. Navy Department. January 1.

OSS (Office of Strategic Services). 1942a. "The Eta: A Persecuted Group in Japan." OSS Research and Analysis Branch report 202 (originally released as COI Research and Analysis Branch, Psychology Division, report 12), February 5, OSS Archives, NARA, College Park, Md.

——. 1942b. "Morale in the Japanese Military Services." OSS Research and Analysis Branch report 614 (Originally released as COI Research and Analysis Branch, Psychology Division, report 26), April 1. Classified "Restricted." OSS Archives, NARA, College Park, Md.

——. 1942c. "The Fishing Industry of Japan (Excepting Tropical Waters)." OSS Research and

Analysis Branch report 586, June 25. Classified "Confidential. oss Archives, NARA, College Park, Md.

———. 1942d. "Preliminary Survey of Japanese Social and Psychological Conditions: Background for the Formulation of Plans for Psychological Warfare." oss Research and Analysis Branch Report 679, October 13. Classified "Confidential." oss Archives, NAA.

———. 1942e. "Preliminary Studies of the Social Structure of Japan, Japanese Cliques: The 'Batsu.'" oss Research and Analysis Branch report 117, n.d. Classified "Confidential." oss Archives, NAA.

———. 1942f. "Preliminary Studies of the Social Structure of Japan, Japanese Labor: The Labor Union Movement." oss Research and Analysis Branch report 118, n.d. Classified Confidential." oss Archives, NAA.

———. 1942g. "Draft of Certain Sections of a Strategic Survey of Japan." oss Research and Analysis Branch report 715, February 28. Classified "Confidential." oss Archives, NAA.

———. 1943a. "Preliminary Report on Japanese Anthropology." oss Research and Analysis Branch report 1605, September 29. Classified "Secret." oss Archives, NAA.

———. 1943b. "Municipal Government in Japan." oss Research and Analysis Branch report 941, June 30. Classified "Restricted." oss Archives, NAA.

———. 1943c. "Japanese Infiltration among the Muslims throughout the World." oss Research and Analysis Branch report 890, May 15. Classified "Secret." oss Archives, NAA.

———. 1944. "Japanese Attempts at Infiltration among Muslims in Russia and Her Borderlands." oss Research and Analysis Branch report 890, August 2. Classified "Confidential." oss Archives, NAA.

———. 1945. "Japan's 'Secret' Weapon: Suicide." Current Intelligence Study Number 31, oss Research and Analysis Branch report 3301S, July 20. Classified "Secret." oss Archives, NARA, College Park, Md.

———. 1948. *Assessment of Men: Selection of Personnel for the Office of Strategic Services.* New York: Rinehart.

owi Leaflet News Letter. 1945. "owi Propaganda against Japan: A Summary, Section I: 1944–May 1945." *owi Area III Far East Leaflet News Letter.* Classified "Confidential," vol. 1, no. 11, September 1, box 8, no. 19, GT, 3–25.

Owen, David I. 1996. "R. F. S. Starr, 1990–1994." *Studies on the Civilization and Culture of Nuzi and the Hurrians* 8: 3–7.

Owens, Geoffrey Ross. 2003. "What! Me a Spy? Intrigue and Reflexivity in Zanzibar." *Ethnography* 4, no. 1: 122–44.

Park, Edwards. 1984. "Secretary S. Dillon Ripley Retires after Twenty Years of Innovation." *Smithsonian* 15: 76–85.

Parsons, Talcott. 1943. "The Kinship System of the Contemporary United States." *American Anthropologist* 45: 22–38.

———. 1986. "Social Science: A Basic National Resource." Pp. 41–112 in *The Nationalization of the Social Sciences*, eds. S. Klausner and V. Lidz. Philadelphia: University of Pennsylvania Press.

Parsons, Talcott, and Evon Z. Vogt. 1962. "Clyde Kay Maben Kluckhohn." *American Anthropologist* 64, no. 1: 140–51.

Partridge, William L., and Elizabeth M. Eddy. 1978. "The Development of Applied Anthropology in America." Pp. 3–48 in *Applied Anthropology in America*, eds. Elizabeth M. Eddy and William L. Partridge. New York: Columbia University Press.

Pastore, Nicholas. 1990. "Review of Ley's *A Whisper of Espionage*." *Journal of the History of the Behavioral Sciences* 26: 366–70.

Patai, Raphael. 1946. "Anthropology during the War, V. Palestine." *American Anthropologist* 48: 477–82.

Patterson, Thomas 2001. *A Social History of Anthropology in the United States*. Oxford: Berg.

Peace, William J. 2004. *Leslie A. White: Evolution and Revolution in Anthropology*. Lincoln: University of Nebraska Press.

——. 2005. "V. Gordon Childe and World War II." Paper presented at the annual meeting of the American Anthropological Association, Washington, D.C., December 2.

PEER (Public Employees for Ethical Responsibility). 2006. "How Old Is the Grand Canyon? Park Service Won't Say: Orders to Cater to Creationists Makes National Park Agnostic on Geology." Press release, December 28. Available online at www.peer.org/news/news_id.php?row_id=801 (accessed December 28, 2006).

Pels, Peter. 1996. "The Pidginization of Luguru Politics: Administrative Ethnography and the Paradoxes of Indirect Rule." *American Ethnologist* 24, no. 3: 738–61.

——. 1999. "Professions of Duplexity: A Prehistory of Ethical Codes in Anthropology." *Current Anthropology* 40, no. 2: 101–14.

Peri, David W., and Robert W. Wharton. 1965. "Samuel Alfred Barrett, 1879–1956." *Kroeber Anthropological Society Papers* no. 33, 3–28.

Petrinovich, Lewis. 1979. "David Krech." Pp. 391–93 in *International Encyclopedia of the Social Sciences Biographical Supplement*. New York: Free Press.

Phillips, Wendell. 1945. "Anthropology in the British Empire during the War." *American Anthropologist* 47: 474–79.

Pipes, Daniel. 2000. "FDR Addresses the Arabs." *Middle East Quarterly* 7, no. 1: 93–94.

Powers, Richard Gid. 1987. *Secrecy and Power: The Life J. Edgar Hoover*. New York: Free Press.

Poznanski, Gitel. 1946. "The Strategy of Decimation." Pp. 111–240 in *The Black Book: The Nazi Crime Against the Jewish People*, eds. Jewish Black Book Committee and Ursula Wasserman. New York: Duell, Sloan and Pearce.

Price, Barbara J. 1968. "Alfred M. Tozzer." Pp. 116–17 in *International Encyclopedia of the Social Sciences*, vol. 16. New York: Free Press.

Price, David H. 1996. Interview with George E. Taylor, Seattle, Wash., July 17.

——. 1997. "Anthropological Research and the Freedom of Information Act." *Cultural Anthropology Methods* 9, no. 1: 12–15.

——. 1998a. "Cold War Anthropology: Collaborators and Victims of the National Security State." *Identities* 4, nos. 3–4: 389–430.

——. 1998b. "Gregory Bateson and the oss." *Human Organization* 57, no. 4: 379–84.

——. 1998c. "Population Models, Development Anthropology and Cold War Funding." Paper presented at the annual meeting of the American Anthropological Association, Philadelphia, December.

——. 2000. "Anthropologists as Spies." *Nation*, vol. 271, no. 16 (November 20), 24–27.

——. 2001a. "Fear and Loathing in the Soviet Union: Roy Barton and the NKVD." *History of Anthropology Newsletter* 28, no. 2: 3–8.

——. 2001b. " 'The Shameful Business': Leslie Spier on the Censure of Franz Boas." *History of Anthropology Newsletter* 28, no. 2: 9–12.

——. 2002a. "Lessons from Second World War Anthropology: Peripheral, Persuasive and Ignored Contributions." *Anthropology Today* 18, no. 3: 14–20.

——. 2002b. "Reply to van Bremen, Kopytoff and Hardiman." *Anthropology Today* 18, no. 4: 22.

——. 2002c. "Interlopers and Invited Guests: On Anthropology's Witting and Unwitting Links to Intelligence Agencies." *Anthropology Today* 18, no. 6: 16–21.

——. 2002d. "Secrecy, Betrayal and Past, Present and Future Uses of Anthropology." Paper presented at the annual meeting of the American Anthropological Association, New Orleans, November 23.

——. 2003a. "Anthropology *Sub Rosa*: The AAA, the CIA and the Ethical Problems Inherent in Secret Research." Pp. 29–49 in *Ethics and the Profession of Anthropology: The Dialogue Continues*, 2d ed., ed. Carolyn Fluehr-Lobban. Walnut Creek, Calif.: AltaMira.

——. 2003b. "Subtle Means and Enticing Carrots: The Impact of Funding on American Cold War Anthropology." *Critique of Anthropology* 23, no. 4: 373–401.

——. 2004a. *Threatening Anthropology: McCarthyism and the FBI's Surveillance of Activist Anthropologists*. Durham: Duke University Press.

——. 2004b. "In the Shadow of Hiroshima and Nagasaki: The Cultural Conditions of Unconditional Surrender." *CounterPunch*, http://www.counterpunch.org/price0806 2004 .htm. Accessed April 20, 2007.

——. 2004c. "Weaponizing Anthropology: American Anthropologists at the Office of War Information during the Pacific War." Paper presented at the East Asian Anthropology and Japanese Colonialism Forum, Third Conference, Seoul National University, November 13.

——. 2004d. "Standing up for Academic Freedom: The Case of Irving Goldman." *Anthropology Today* 20, no. 4: 16–21.

——. 2005a. "The CIA's University Spies." *CounterPunch* 12, no. 1, January 1–15: 1–6.

——. 2005b. "From PRISP to ICSP: Skullduggery among the Acronyms." *CounterPunch*, vol. 12, no. 5, March 1–15, 3–4.

——. 2005c. "How U.S. Anthropologists Planned 'Race-Specific' Weapons against the Japanese." *CounterPunch*, vol. 12, no. 11 (June 1–15), 1–3.

——. 2005d. "America the Ambivalent: Quietly Selling Anthropology to the CIA." *Anthropology Today* 21, no. 5: 1–2.

——. 2005e. "Anthropology as Weapon: The Uses and Abuses of Anthropology at the oss's

Research and Analysis Division." Paper presented at the annual meeting of the American Anthropological Association, Washington, D.C., December 2.

——. 2006a. "Critiquing Silence: On the Ethical Impropriety of Secret Research and Covert Ties to Intelligence Agencies." Paper presented at the annual meeting of the American Anthropological Association, San Jose, Calif., November 17.

——. 2006b. "American Anthropologists Stand up against Torture and the Occupation of Iraq." *CounterPunch*, http://www.counterpunch.org/price11202006.html. November 20.

——. 2007. "The Wages of Secrecy" *Anthropology News* 48, no. 2, in press.

——. 2008. "Materialism's Free Pass: Karl Wittfogel, McCarthyism and the 'Bureaucratization of Guilt.' " In *Anthropology at the Dawn of the Cold War*, ed. Dustin Wax. London: Pluto, forthcoming.

Prins, Herbert H. T., and Harald E. L. Prins. 2005. "From Tropical Africa to Arctic Sandanavia: A. H. J. Prins as Maritime Anthropologist." *Circumpolar Studies* 2: 21–28.

Proctor, Robert. 1988. "From *Anthropologie* to *Rassenkunde* in the German Anthropological Tradition." Pp. 138–79 in *Bones, Bodies, Behavior: Essays on Biological Anthropology, Volume 5: History of Anthropology Series*, ed. George W. Stocking. Madison: University of Wisconsin Press.

Provinse, John H. 1943. "Anthropology in Program Planning." *Applied Anthropology* 3, no. 1: 1–5.

Provinse, John H., and Solon T. Kimball. 1946. "Building New Communities during War Time." *American Sociological Review* 11: 396–410.

Pützstück, Lothar. 1991. "Julius Ernst Lips." Pp. 415–16 in *International Dictionary of Anthropologists*, ed. Christopher Winters. New York: Garland Publishing.

Rauch, Jerome. 1955. "Area Institute Programs and African Studies." *Journal of Negro Education* (Fall): 409–25.

Read, K. E. 1947. "Effects of the Pacific War in the Markham Valley, New Guinea." *Oceania* 18, no. 2: 95–116.

Redfield, Robert. 1943. "The Japanese-Americans." Pp. 143–64 in *American Society in Wartime*, ed. William Ogburn. Chicago: University of Chicago Press.

Reyna, Steve. 1998. "Right and Might: Of Approximate Truths and Moral Judgments." *Identities* 43, nos. 3–4: 431–65.

Reynolds, E. Bruce. 2005. *Thailand's Secret War: The Free Thai, oss and soe during World War II*. Cambridge: Cambridge University Press.

Richardson, Dorothy E. 1957. *U.S. Naval Administration of the Trust Territory of the Pacific Islands*. Vol. 3. Washington, D.C.: Office of the Chief of Naval Operations.

Ritzenthaler, Robert. 1943. "The Impact of War on an Indian Community." *American Anthropologist* 45, no. 2: 325–26.

Robben, Antonius C. G. 1999. "Comments on Peter Pels' 'Professions of Duplexity.' " *Current Anthropology* 40, no. 2: 122.

Roberts, Frank H. H. 1943. *Egypt and the Suez Canal*. War Background Studies, no. 11. Washington, D.C.: Smithsonian Institution.

Robinson, Greg. 2001. *By Order of the President: FDR and the Internment of Japanese Americans*. Cambridge, Mass.: Harvard University Press.

Robinson, N. K. 1981. *Villagers at War: Some Papua New Guinea Experiences in World War II*. Canberra: Australian National University Press.

Roelofs, Joan. 2003. *Foundations and Public Policy: The Mask of Pluralism*. Albany: State University of New York Press.

Roosevelt, Anna C. 1991. "Determinismo ecológico na interpretação do desenvolvimento social indígena da Amazônia." Pp. 103–41 in *Origens, Adaptacoes, e Diversidade Biologica do Homen Nativo da Amazonia*, ed. W. Neves. Balem: Museu Goeldi.

———. 1996. "Reply to Baffi et al." *Society for American Archaeology Bulletin* 14, no. : 5.

Roosevelt, Kermit. 1976. "Introduction to the 1976 Edition." Pp. vii–xix in *The Overseas Targets: War Report of the OSS*, vol. 2, ed. Kermit Roosevelt. U.S. War Department Strategic Services Unit History Project. New York: Walker.

Ross, Eric B. 1998. *The Malthus Factor: Poverty, Politics and Population in Capitalist Development*. New York: Zed Books.

———. 1999. "Axel Wenner-Gren, the Nazi Connection and the Origins of the Viking Fund." Paper presented at the annual meeting of the American Anthropological Association, Chicago, November 19.

———. 2003. "Anthropology, the Cold War and the Myth of Peasant Conservatism." Paper presented at the annual meeting of the American Anthropological Association, Chicago, November 21.

———. 2005. "World War Two: Development Theory and the Professionalization of Anthropology." Paper presented at the annual meeting of the American Anthropological Association, Washington, D.C., December 2.

Rossiter, Margaret W. 1995. *Women Scientists in America: Before Affirmative Action, 1940–1972*. Baltimore: Johns Hopkins University Press.

Rout Jr., Leslie B, and John F. Bratzel. 1986. *The Shadow War: German Espionage and American Counterespionage in Latin America during World War II*. Frederick, Md.: University Publications.

Rowe, David Nelson. 1943. "OWI's Far Eastern Outposts: Some Proposals." *Public Opinion Quarterly* 7, no. 2: 90–99.

Rowe, John Howland. 1958. "Harry Tschopik, Jr. 1915–1956." *American Anthropologist* 60: 132–38.

Rowen, Herbert H. 1979. "Geyl S. Pieter." Pp. 232–36 in *International Encyclopedia of the Social Sciences, Biographical Supplement*, vol. 18. New York: Free Press.

Rubinstein, Robert. 2003a. "Politics and Peace Keepers: Experience and Political Representation among United States Military Officers." Pp. 15–27 in *Anthropology and the United States Military: Coming of Age in the Twenty-First Century*, eds. Pamela R. Frese and Margaret C. Harrell. New York: Palgrave.

———. 2003b. "Cross Cultural Considerations in Complex Peace Operations." *Negotiation Journal* 19, no. 1: 29–49.

Ryang, Sonia. 2004. "Chrysanthemum's Strange Life: Ruth Benedict in Postwar Japan."

Japan Policy Research Institute Occasional Paper No. 32. July. Available online at www
.jpri.org/publications/occasionalpapers/op32.html. Accessed April 20, 2006.

Sady, Rachel. 1987. "Comments on 'Engineering Internment.'" *American Ethnologist* 14, no.
3: 560–62.

——. 1988. "Further Comment on 'Engineering Internment.'" *American Ethnologist* 15, no.
2: 385.

Sasaki, Shirō. 2003. "Anthropological Studies of the Indigenous Peoples in Sakhalin in Pre-
Wartime and Wartime Japan." Pp. 151–68 in *Wartime Japanese Anthropology in Asia and
the Pacific*, Senri Ethnological Studies No. 65, eds. Akitoshi Shimizu and Jan van Bremen. Osaka: National Museum of Ethnology.

Schafft, Gretchen. 2004. *From Racism to Genocide: Anthropology in the Third Reich*. Urbana:
University of Illinois Press.

——. 2005. "Meshing Nazi Anthropology with Public Health in Occupied Poland during
WWII: The Case of Herbert Grohmann." Paper presented at the annual meeting of the
American Anthropological Association, Washington, D.C., December 2.

——. 2006. "Commentary on Bernhard Streck's Review of *From Racism to Genocide*."
American Anthropologists 108, no. 4: 930–31.

Schaffter, Dorothy. 1948. *What Comes of Training Women for War?* Washington, D.C.: American Council on Education.

Schmelz-Keil, Lynne M. 1991. "Alfred Tozzer." Pp. 704–706 in *International Dictionary of
Anthropologists*, ed. Christopher Winters. New York: Garland Publishing.

Schneider, David M. 1946. "The Culture of the Army Clerk." *Psychiatry* 9: 123–29.

——. 1947. "The Social Dynamics of Physical Disability in Army Basic Training." *Psychiatry*
10: 323–33.

——. 1995. *Schneider on Schneider*. Durham: Duke University Press.

Science. 1939. "The New York Meeting of the American Anthropological Association" *Science*, vol. 89, no. 2298, January 13, 1939, 29–30.

Sekimoto, Teruo. 2003. "Selves and Others in Japanese Anthropology." Pp. 131–41 in *Wartime Japanese Anthropology in Asia and the Pacific*, Senri Ethnological Studies No. 65,
eds. Akitoshi Shimizu and Jan van Bremen. Osaka: National Museum of Ethnology.

——. 1943b. *A Pocket Guide to Burma*. Washington, D.C.: U.S. War Department and U.S.
Navy Department.

——. 1943c. *A Pocket Guide to India*. Washington, D.C.: U.S. War Department and U.S. Navy
Department.

——. 1943d. *A Pocket Guide to New Caledonia*. Washington, D.C.: U.S. War Department and
U.S. Navy Department.

——. 1943e. *A Pocket Guide to Netherlands East Indies*. Washington, D.C.: U.S. War Department and U.S. Navy Department.

——. 1943f. *A Pocket Guide to Egypt*. Washington, D.C.: U.S. War Department and U.S. Navy
Department.

——. 1943g. *A Pocket Guide to North Africa*. Washington, D.C.: U.S. War Department and
U.S. Navy Department.

Selden, Mark. 1995. "Before the Bomb: The 'Good War,' Air Power, and the Logic of Mass Destruction." *Contention* 5, no. 1: 113–32.

Sheets, Payson. 2001. "The CIA." *Anthropology News* 42, no. 1: 3.

Shimizu, Akitoshi. 2003. "Anthropology and the Wartime Situation of the 1930s and 1940s: Masao Oka, Yoshitarō Hirano, Eiichirō Ishida and Their Negotiations with the Situation." Pp. 49–108 in *Wartime Japanese Anthropology in Asia and the Pacific*, Senri Ethnological Studies No. 65, eds. Akitoshi Shimizu and Jan van Bremen. Osaka: National Museum of Ethnology.

Shimizu, Akitoshi, and Jan van Bremen, eds. 2003. *Wartime Japanese Anthropology in Asia and the Pacific*. Senri Ethnological Studies No. 65. Osaka: National Museum of Ethnology.

Siegel, Bernard J., and George D. Spindler. 1962. "Felix Maxwell Keesing." *American Anthropologist* 64: 351–53.

Silberman, Neil Asher. 1982. *Digging for God and Country: Exploration, Archaeology, and the Secret Struggle for the Holy Land, 1799–1917*. New York: Alfred A. Knopf.

———. 1989. *Between Past and Present: Archaeology, Ideology, and Nationalism in the Modern Middle East*. New York: Henry Holt.

Silverman, Sydel, ed. 1989. "Hortense Powdermaker." Pp. 291–96 in *Women Anthropologists, Selected Biographies*, eds. Ute Gacs et al. Urbana: University of Illinois Press.

———. 2004. *Totems and Teachers: Key Figures in the History of Anthropology*. Walnut Creek, Calf.: AltaMira.

Simons, Anna. 2003. "The Military Advisor as Warrior-King and Other 'Going Native' Temptations." Pp. 113–34 in *Anthropology and the United States Military: Coming of Age in the Twenty-First Century*, eds. Pamela R. Frese and Margaret C. Harrell. New York: Palgrave.

Simpson, Christopher. 1994. *Science of Coercion: Communication Research and Psychological Warfare, 1945–1960*. New York: Oxford University Press.

Slobodin, Richard. 1978. *W. H. R. Rivers*. New York: Columbia University Press.

Sluka, Jeff. 2000. *Death Squad: The Anthropology of State Terror*. Philadelphia: University of Pennsylvania Press.

Smith, Bradley F. 1983. *The Shadow Warriors: O.S.S. and the Origins of the C.I.A.* New York: Basic Books.

Smith, Neil. 2003. *American Empire: Roosevelt's Geographer and the Prelude to Globalization*. Berkeley: University of California Press.

Spicer, Edward H. 1946. "The Use of Social Scientists by the War Relocation Authority." *Applied Anthropology* 5, no. 2: 16–36.

Spicer, Edward H., Asael T. Hansen, Katherine Luomala, and Marvin Opler. 1969. *Impounded People: Japanese-Americans in the Relocation Centers*. Tucson: University of Arizona Press.

Spitzer, Herman M., and Ruth Benedict. 1945. "Bibliography of Articles and Books Relating to Japanese Psychology." OWI Area III, Overseas Branch, Foreign Morale Analysis Division, report no. 24, August 25. box 18, folder 12, GT.

SSD (Special Service Division). 1943a. *A Pocket Guide to West Africa*. Washington, D.C.: U.S. War Department and U.S. Navy Department.

Stafford, David. 1987. *Camp X: OSS, "Intrepid," and the Allies' North American Training Camp for Secret Agents, 1941–1945*. New York: Dodd, Mead.

Stanton, Alfred H. 1968. "Harry Stack Sullivan." Pp. 396–98 in *International Encyclopedia of the Social Sciences*, vol. 14. New York: Free Press.

Starn, Orin. 1986. "Engineering Internment: Anthropologists and the War Relocation Authority." *American Ethnologist* 13, no. 4: 700–720.

——. 1987. "Reply to Opler." *American Ethnologist* 14, no. 2: 383–84.

Stegner, Wallace. 1992 (1954). *Beyond the Hundredth Meridian: John Wesley Powell and the Second Opening of the West*. New York: Penguin.

Steinmetz, George. 2005. "Introduction." Pp. 1–56 in *The Politics of Method in the Human Sciences: Positivism and Its Epistemological Others*, ed. George Steinmetz. Durham: Duke University Press.

Stephenson, Neal. 1999. *Cryptonomicon*. New York: Avon.

Steward, Julian H. 1948a. "Comments on the Statement on Human Rights." *American Anthropologist* 50: 351–52.

Steward, Julian H., ed. 1948b. *Handbook of South American Indians: Volume 3, The Tropical Forest Tribes*. Smithsonian Institution Bureau of American Ethnology, Bulletin 143. Washington, D.C.: Government Printing Office.

Stirling, Matthew W. 1943. *The Native Peoples of New Guinea*. War Background Studies, no. 9. Washington, D.C.: Smithsonian Institution.

——. 1973. "Edward Wyllys Andrews IV." *American Anthropologist* 75: 295–97.

Stocking, George W. 1968a. "A Historical Brief for Cultural Materialism." *Science* 162 (October): 108–10.

——. 1968b. "The Scientific Reaction against Cultural Anthropology, 1917–1920." Pp. 270–307 in *Race, Culture, and Evolution: Essays in the History of Anthropology*, ed. George W. Stocking. Chicago: University of Chicago Press.

——. 1976. "Ideas and Institutions in American Anthropology: Toward a History of the Interwar Period." Pp. 1–54 in *Selected Papers from the American Anthropologist*, ed. George W. Stocking. Washington, D.C.: American Anthropological Association.

——. 1979a. *Anthropology at Chicago: Tradition, Discipline, Department, an Exhibition Marking the Fiftieth Anniversary of the Department of Anthropology*. Chicago: Joseph Regenstein Library, University of Chicago.

——. 1979b. "Anthropology as Kulturkampf: Science and Politics in the Career of Franz Boas." Pp. 33–50 in *The Uses of Anthropology*, ed. Walter Goldschmidt. Special Publication No. 11. Washington, D.C.: American Anthropological Association.

——. 1982. *Race, Culture and Evolution: Essays in the History of Anthropology*, reprint. ed. Chicago: University of Chicago Press.

——. 1985. "Yours Affectionately Rex: Radcliffe-Brown, during and after World War II." *History of Anthropology Newsletter* 12, no. 2: 3–11.

——. 1995. *After Tylor: British Social Anthropology 1888–1951*. Madison: University of Wisconsin Press.

Stockwell, John. 1991. *The Praetorian Guard*. Boston: South End Press.

Stoller, Paul. 1992. *The Cinematic Griot*. Chicago: University of Chicago Press.

Streck, Bernhard. 2006. "Review of *From Racism to Genocide*." *American Anthropologist* 108, no. 1: 257–58.

Studies in Intelligence (author's name classified by the CIA). 1983. "The CIA and Academe." *Studies in Intelligence* (Winter): 33–42.

Sullivan, Paul. 1989. *Unfinished Conversations: Mayas and Foreigners between the Wars*. New York: Alfred E. Knopf.

Sullivan, William C. 1979. *The Bureau: My Thirty Years in Hoover's FBI*. New York: Norton.

Suzuki, Peter T. 1980. "A Retrospective Analysis of Wartime 'National Character' Study." *Dialectical Anthropology* 5, no. 1: 33–46.

——. 1981. "Anthropologists in the Wartime Camps for Japanese Americans." *Dialectical Anthropology* 6, no. 1: 23–60.

——. 1986a. "The University of California Japanese Evacuation and Resettlement Study: A Prolegomenon." *Dialectical Anthropology* 10: 189–213.

——. 1986b. "When Black Was White: Misapplied Anthropology in Wartime America." *Man and Life* 12, nos. 1–2: 1–13.

Swanton, John R. 1942. *The Evolution of Nations*. War Background Studies, no. 2. Washington, D.C.: Smithsonian Institution.

——. 1943. *Are Wars Inevitable?* War Background Studies, no. 12. Washington, D.C.: Smithsonian Institution.

Tabachnick, Stephen E. 1997. "Lawrence of Arabia as Archaeologist." *Biblical Archaeology Review* 23, no. 5: 40–71.

Tambiah, Stanley J. 2002. *Edmund Leach, an Anthropological Life*. Cambridge: Cambridge University Press.

Tanaka, Yuki. 1996. *Hidden Horrors: Japanese War Crimes in World War II*. Boulder, Colo.: Westview Press.

Tax, Sol. 1950. "Action Anthropology." *América Indígena* 12: 103–109.

——. 1975. "Action Anthropology." *Current Anthropology* 16: 514–17.

Teffelmier, Gertrude. 1967. "Edwin Meyer Loeb." *American Anthropologist* 69: 200–203.

Terkel, Studs. 1984 *"The Good War": An Oral History of World War Two*. New York: Pantheon.

Textor, Robert B. 1967. *A Cross-Cultural Summary*. New Haven, Conn.: HRAF Press.

Theoharis, Athan, ed. 1991. *From the Secret Files of J. Edgar Hoover*. Chicago: Ivan R. Dee.

Thomas, Dorothy Swaine, and Robert Nishimoto. 1946. *The Spoilage*. Berkeley: University of California Press.

Thomas, Dorothy Swaine, Charles Kikuchi, and James Sakoda. 1952. *The Salvage*. Berkeley: University of California Press.

Thomas, Norman. 1942. *Democracy and Japanese Americans*. New York: Post War World Council.

Thompson, Laura. 1938. "Nordics under the Nazis." Paper presented to the Anthropological Society of Honolulu, March, box 5, LT.

——. 1944. "Some Perspectives on Applied Anthropology." *Applied Anthropology* 3: 12–16.

Thompson, Raymond. 2002. "Archaeological Innocence at Pecos in 1917–1918." *Kiva* 68, 2: 123–27.

Torgovnick, Marianna. 2005. *The War Complex: World War II in Our Time*. Chicago: University of Chicago Press.

Trager, George L. 1943. "The Kinship and Status Terms of the Tiwa Languages." *American Anthropologist* 45, no. 4: 557–71.

——. 1974. "David Bond Stout." *American Anthropologist* 76: 72–75.

Trencher, Susan. 2002. "Charles Wagley." Pp. 217–20 in *Celebrating a Century of the American Anthropological Association*, eds. Regna Darnell and Frederic Gleach. Lincoln: University of Nebraska Press.

Trento, Joseph J. 2001. *The Secret History of the CIA*. New York: Carroll and Graf.

Trumpbour, John. 1989. "Harvard, the Cold War, and the National Security State." Pp. 51–128 in *How Harvard Rules: Reason in the Service of Empire*, ed. John Trumpbour. Boston: South End Press.

Tsu, Yun Hui. 2003. "For Science, Co-Prosperity, and Love: The Re-imagination of Taiwanese Folklore and Japan's Greater East Asian War." Pp. 189–207 in *Wartime Japanese Anthropology in Asia and the Pacific*, Senri Ethnological Studies No. 65, eds. Akitoshi Shimizu and Jan van Bremen. Osaka: National Museum of Ethnology.

Turner, Victor. 1985. *On the Edge of the Bush: Anthropology as Experience*. Tucson: University of Arizona Press.

Useem, John. 1945. "Governing the Occupied Areas of the South Pacific: Wartime Lessons and Peacetime Proposals." *Applied Anthropology* 4, no. 3: 1–10.

Useem, John, Gordon Magregor, and Ruth Hill Useem. 1943. "Wartime Employment and Cultural Adjustments of the Rosebud Sioux." *Applied Anthropology* 2, no. 2: 1–9.

USSBS (United States Strategic Bombing Survey). 1946. *U.S. Strategic Bombing Survey Summary Report, Pacific War*. Washington, D.C.: Government Printing Office.

U.S. Senate. 1946. "Hearings before a Subcommittee of the Committee on Military Affairs, United States Senate" S. Res. 107 and S. Res. 146, October 29–Nov 1, 1945. Washington, D.C.: Government Printing Office.

——. 1976. "Final Report of the Select Committee to Study Governmental Operations with Respect to Intelligence Activities" (Church report). Senate Report, 94 Cong., 2d sess., no. 94–755. Washington, D.C.: Government Printing Office.

Usuki, Akira. 2004. "Jewish Studies in Wartime Japan: Focusing on Relations with Islamic Studies." Paper presented at the East Asian Anthropology and Japanese Colonialism Forum, Third Conference, Seoul National University, November 13.

USWDSSU (U.S. War Department Strategic Services Unit History Project). 1976. *The Overseas Targets: War Report of the OSS*, vol. 2. New York: Walker.

van Bremen, Jan. 2003. "Wartime Anthropology: A Global Perspective." Pp. 13–48 in *Wartime Japanese Anthropology in Asia and the Pacific, Senri Ethnological Studies No. 65, eds. Akitoshi Shimizu and Jan van Bremen. Osaka: National Museum of Ethnology.

van Bremen, Jan, and Akitoshi Shimizu, eds. 1999. *Anthropology and Colonialism in Asia and Oceania*. London: Cruzon.

van Willigen, John. 1996 "Comments for John Bennett's 'Applied and Action Anthropology.'" *Current Anthropology* 36 (supp.): s44.

Verrier, Anthony. 1990. *Assassination in Algiers: Churchill, Roosevelt, de Gaulle, and the Murder of Admiral Darlan*. New York: W. W. Norton.

Voegelin, Ermine W. 1943. "Shawnee Musical Instruments." *American Anthropologist* 44, no. 3: 463–75.

Wagley, Charles. 1964. "Introduction." Pp. 1–32 in *Social Science Research on Latin America*. ed. Charles Wagley. New York: Columbia University Press.

Wakin, Eric. 1992. *Anthropology Goes to War: Professional Ethics and Counterinsurgency in Thailand*. Madison: University of Wisconsin Press.

Walker, Charles R. 1945. "Anthropology as a War Weapon." *American Mercury*, vol. 61, July, 85–89.

Walker, Ernest P. 1943. *Alaska: America's Continental Frontier Outpost*. War Background Studies, no. 13. Washington, D.C.: Smithsonian Institution.

Wallerstein, Immanuel. 1979. "Fernand Braudel." Pp. 69–72 in *International Encyclopedia of the Social Sciences, Biographical Supplement*, vol. 18. New York: Free Press.

Walraven, Boudewijn. 1999. "The Natives Next-Door: Ethnology in Colonial Korea." Pp. 219–44 in *Anthropology and Colonialism in Asia and Oceania*, eds. Jan van Bremen and Akitoshi Shimizu. Surrey: Curzon Press.

Warner, W. Lloyd. 1949. *Democracy in Jonesville*. New York: Harper.

Washburn S. L. 1968. "Franz Weidenreich." Pp. 502–503 in *International Encyclopedia of the Social Sciences*, vol. 16. New York: Free Press.

Watanabe, Kozo. 2004. "From Anthropological Knowledge to Technology of Colonial Domination." Paper presented at the East Asian Anthropology and Japanese Colonialism Forum, Third Conference, Seoul National University, November 13.

Watson, Goodwin, ed. 1942. *Civilian Morale*. Boston: Reynal and Hitchcock.

Wax, Murray. 1997. "My Life as a Commie–Trotskyite Menace, Blacklisted: A Personal Account." Undated manuscript in the author's possession.

——. 2002. "On Deconstructing Patriotism." Paper presented at the annual meeting of the American Anthropological Association, New Orleans, November 20, 2002.

——. 2003. "Rosalie H. Wax (née Rosalie Amelia Hankey), 1911–1998." *Anthropology Today* 19, no. 1: 25.

Wax, Rosalie H. 1971. *Doing Fieldwork: Warnings and Advice*. Chicago: University of Chicago Press.

Webb, G. Gregg. 2004. "The FBI and Foreign Intelligence: New Insights into J. Edgar Hoover's Role." *Studies in Intelligence* 48, no. 1: 45–58.

Webster, Donovan. 2003. *The Burma Road: The Epic Story of the China–Burma–India Theater in World War II*. New York: Farrar, Straus and Giroux.

Weckler Jr., J. E. 1943. *Polynesians Explorers of the Pacific*. War Background Studies, no. 6. Washington, D.C.: Smithsonian Institution.

Weglyn, Michi. 1976. *Years of Infamy: The Untold Story of America's Concentration Camps*. New York: William Morrow.

Weltfish, Gene. 1945. "American Racism: Japan's Secret Weapon." *Far Eastern Survey* 14, no. 7: 233–37.

Wenley, Archibald Gibson, and John A. Pope. 1944. *China*. War Background Studies, no. 20. Washington, D.C.: Smithsonian Institution.

West, Robert C. 1982. *Andean Reflections: Letters from Carl O. Sauer while on a South American Trip from the Rockefeller Foundation, 1942*. Dellplain Latin American Studies, no. 11. Boulder, Colo.: Westview Press.

White, Geoffrey M., and Lamont Lindstrom. 1989. *The Pacific Theater: Island Representations of World War II*. Pacific Islands Monograph Series, no. 8. Honolulu: University of Hawaii Press.

Willey, Gordon R. 1976. "Samuel Kirkland Lothrop." *National Academy of Sciences Biographical Memoirs* 48: 252–72.

Winkler, Allan M. 1978. *The Politics of Propaganda: The Office of War Information 1942–1945*. New Haven, Conn.: Yale University Press.

Winks, Robin W. 1987. *Cloak and Gown: Scholars in the Secret War, 1939–1961*. New York: William Morrow.

Wise, Tigger. 1985. *The Self-Made Anthropologist: A Life of A. P. Elkin*. Sydney: George Allen and Unwin.

Wolf, Eric R., and Joseph G. Jorgensen. 1970. "Anthropology on the Warpath in Thailand." *New York Review of Books* 15, no. 9, November 19, 27–35.

Woodbury, Nathalie F. S. 1993. "For God, Country and our Foreign Policy: (Mis)uses of Anthropological Fieldwork." *Anthropology Newsletter*, October, 31–32.

Woolley, Leonard. 1962. *As I Seem to Remember*. London: George Allen and Unwin.

Worsley, Peter. 1968. *The Trumpet Shall Sound: A Study of Cargo Cults in Melanesia*. New York: Schocken Books.

WRA (War Relocation Authority). 1943. *Relocation of Japanese Americans*. Washington, D.C.: War Relocation Authority.

Yans-McLaughlin, Virginia. 1986a. "Mead, Bateson and 'Hitler's Peculiar Makeup'—Applying Anthropology in the Era of Appeasement." *History of Anthropology Newsletter* 13, no 1: 3–8.

——. 1986b. "Science, Democracy and Ethics: Mobilizing Culture and Personality for World War II." Pp. 187–217 in *Malinowski, Rivers, Benedict and Others: Essays on Culture and Personality, Volume 4: History of Anthropology Series*, ed George W. Stocking. Madison: University of Wisconsin Press.

Yasuda, Muneo. 2004. "Military Education and War Storytelling." Paper presented at the East Asian Anthropology and Japanese Colonialism Forum, Third Conference, Seoul National University. November 13.

Yin, Se. 2004. "Ethnology Acted on the Ethnic Policies of Manzhou Puppet Regime." Paper

presented at the East Asian Anthropology and Japanese Colonialism Forum, Third
Conference, Seoul National University, November 13.

Young, John. 1966. *The Research Activities of the South Manchurian Railway Company, 1907–
1945: A History and a Bibliography*. New York: East Asian Institute, Columbia University.

Young, Michael, W. 2004. *Malinowski: Odyssey of an Anthropologist, 1884–1920*. New Haven,
Conn.: Yale University Press.

Young, Virginia Heyer. 2005. *Ruth Benedict: Beyond Relativity, beyond Pattern*. Lincoln:
University of Nebraska Press.

Yu, Maochun. 1996. *OSS in China: Prelude to Cold War*. New Haven, Conn.: Yale University
Press.

Zacharias, Ellis M. 1945. "Eighteen Words That Bagged Japan." *Saturday Evening Post*,
November 17, 1945, 17.

——. 1946. *Secret Missions: The Story of an Intelligence Officer*. New York: Paperback Library.

Žižek, Slavoj. 1992. *Everything You Always Wanted to Know about Lacan but Were Afraid to
Ask Hitchcock*. London: Verso.

Zuckerman, Solly. 1966. *Scientists and War*. New York: Harper and Row.

——. 1978. *From Apes to Warlords: The Autobiography of Solly Zuckerman*. London: Hamish
Hamilton.

DAVID H. PRICE is an associate professor of sociology and anthropology at St. Martin's University. He is the author of *Threatening Anthropology: McCarthyism and the FBI's Surveillance of Activist Anthropologists.*

Library of Congress Cataloging-in-Publication Data
Price, David H.
Anthropological intelligence : the deployment and neglect of
American anthropology in the Second World War / David H. Price.
    p. cm.
Includes bibliographical references and index.
ISBN-13: 978-0-8223-4219-9 (cloth : alk. paper)
ISBN-13: 978-0-8223-4237-3 (pbk. : alk. paper)
1. Anthropology—United States—History—20th century. 2. Anthro-
pologists—United States—History—20th century. 3. Military intelli-
gence—United States—History—20th century. 4. Science and state—
United States—History—20th century. 5. World War, 1939–1945—
Participation, American. 6. United States—History—1933–1945.
I. Title.
GN17.3.U6P75 2008
306.0973'0904—dc22   2007043856